Narrative Visions and Visual Narratives in Indian Buddhism

Narrative Visions and Visual Narratives in Indian Buddhism

Edited by Naomi Appleton

equinox

SHEFFIELD UK BRISTOL CT

Published by Equinox Publishing Ltd.

UK: Office 415, The Workstation, 15 Paternoster Row, Sheffield,
South Yorkshire S1 2BX

USA: ISD, 70 Enterprise Drive, Bristol, CT 06010

www.equinoxpub.com

First published 2022

British Library Cataloguing-in-Publication Data

A catalogue record for this book is available from the British Library.

ISBN-13	978 1 80050 130 0	(hardback)
	978 1 80050 131 7	(paperback)
	978 1 80050 132 4	(ePDF)
	978 1 80050 179 9	(ePub)

Library of Congress Cataloging-in-Publication Data

Names: Appleton, Naomi, 1982- editor.
Title: Narrative visions and visual narratives in Indian Buddhism / edited by Naomi Appleton.
Description: Bristol : Equinox Publishing Ltd, 2022. | Includes bibliographical references and index. | Summary: "This volume explores the interaction between text and image in Indian Buddhist contexts, including not only the complex relationship between verbal stories and visual representations at Indian sites, but also the ways in which visual imagery is used within textual narratives"-- Provided by publisher.
Identifiers: LCCN 2021052618 (print) | LCCN 2021052619 (ebook) | ISBN 9781800501300 (hardback) | ISBN 9781800501317 (paperback) | ISBN 9781800501324 (pdf) | ISBN 9781800501799 (epub)
Subjects: LCSH: Buddhism and art--India. | Narrative art, Indic. | Buddhist stories. | Illustration of books--India.
Classification: LCC BQ4570.A7 N37 2022 (print) | LCC BQ4570.A7 (ebook) | DDC 294.3/82325--dc23/eng/20220129
LC record available at https://lccn.loc.gov/2021052618
LC ebook record available at https://lccn.loc.gov/2021052619

Typeset by Sparks – www.sparkspublishing.com

Contents

PART III: NARRATIVE VISIONS

Abbreviations

cat.	catalogue number
ch.	chapter
Chin.	Chinese
ed.	edition/editor
Eng.	English
fig.	figure
Fr.	French
Ger.	German
identif.	identification
illus.	illustration(s)
inscr.	inscription
n.	note
P.	Pāli
p.	page
pl.	plate
Skt	Sanskrit
T	Taisho number
Tib.	Tibetan
trans.	translation/translator
v.	verse

Preface

This volume results from a symposium held at the University of Edinburgh in September 2019, which was itself convened as part of a research project into visual and verbal *jātaka* stories funded by a 2017 Philip Leverhulme Prize. I am deeply grateful to the Leverhulme Trust for making the symposium and this publication possible, as well as for funding the creation of an online database of *jātaka* stories in Indian texts and art, accessible here:

https://jatakastories.div.ed.ac.uk/

All except two of the papers in this volume were presented at the symposium, and then revised as a result of the conversations at that event. The chapter by myself and Dr Chris Clark, on Chaddanta in texts and art, was instead presented at a lecture at SOAS, University of London, in May 2019, and then reworked as our ideas about visual and verbal narrative networks continued to develop. Flavia Zaghet presented a very short snapshot of her research at the symposium, as part of an impromptu postgraduate panel, and her ideas were so pertinent to the discussions she kindly agreed to develop them further for a chapter here.

This volume has been a real delight to curate and edit, thanks to the outstanding contributors, encouraging (yet helpfully critical) peer reviewers, and the friendly efficiency of Equinox publishing. I only hope that readers gain as much enjoyment and stimulation from it as I have.

Naomi Appleton
Senior Lecturer in Asian Religions at the University of Edinburgh

LEVERHULME
TRUST

1

Setting the Scene

Verbal and Visual Narrative in Indian Buddhism

Naomi Appleton

Take a look at the central image of Figure 1.1, a stone relief from the early Buddhist site of Bharhut in Madhya Pradesh, dating to perhaps the first century BCE. What do you see? A scene of dramatic events. A person being hung upside down by the ankles. Another on a horse about to take flight, with someone else hanging onto the tail. Others around, watching, and a tree and a rocky landscape behind. If you have had prior experience of early Indian narrative art, you might realise that the image is not of lots of different characters, but fewer key ones repeated several times, indicating that multiple events are depicted. Even if you do not recognise the story, you know that it *is* a story, that something is going on here that involves characters and their actions and experiences over the course of time.

If you do not already know what the story is, from your prior reading (or hearing) of Buddhist narratives, you might hope that the inscriptional label will help. It reads, 'Vitura-Punakiyajatakaṃ' or 'the jataka of Vitura and Punaka' (Lüders 1963, 146–8). So, this is the story of a past life of the Buddha, when he was the wise man Vid(h)ura. In a rich and dramatic narrative extant in the *Vidhurapaṇḍita-jātaka* (*Jātakatthavaṇṇanā* 545), he is won at a gambling match by a *yakṣa* (P. *yakkha*) named Puṇṇaka, who is sent on a mission by a *nāga* princess whose mother wishes to hear Vidhura teach. Key scenes include Vidhura's flight through the air hanging on to the tail of his abductor's magical horse, or being hung upside down on a rocky mountain. Other scenes, albeit less dramatic, are depicted on further reliefs above and below, such that we might say that the pillar depicts the whole narrative. And this pillar is part of a larger decorative scheme adorning the Bharhut *stūpa* or reliquary mound.

This image is a good historical and historiographical starting point for this volume. Bharhut provides our earliest evidence for Buddhist narrative art, with its depictions of well over 30 *jātaka* stories, often accompanied by inscriptional labels, some of which are close to titles or even verse phrases still preserved

Figure 1.1. The *Vidhurapaṇḍita-jātaka* at Bharhut. Cunningham 1879, plate XVIII

in the Pāli *Jātaka* collection.[1] In part because of these labels, scholars have been quick to reach for textual versions of stories, usually from the great Pāli *Jātakatthavaṇṇanā*, to explain what is going on in the images. The presence of the reliefs and their labels can help us to date the emergence of a *jātaka* genre, and has even been used to make a case for the early origins of the Pāli collection, despite the clear mismatch between a text of over 500 stories and a site depicting less than ten percent of that number. The labels have also prompted discussions of how stories might have functioned at such sites: they have often been assumed to be mnemonic prompts for monastic storytellers, who could recall a story then use it to edify and entertain the illiterate lay visitors.

Figure 1.1 is just one of many examples we could find of an Indian Buddhist visual narrative, and it speaks to several key questions and issues at stake in the chapters that follow. Here is a narrative image, but what makes it a narrative image? Is it meant to be read as a narrative, or to prompt a person to recall a narrative? Or is there another purpose at play? What is the relationship between this visual narrative and the extant textual narratives that might help us to understand it, but – in the process – risk taking priority over it? What is the relationship between this visual narrative and the other images at the site?

1 See https://jatakastories.div.ed.ac.uk/artistic-sites/bharhut/ for the full list of stories identified so far, with images where available, and links to related visual and verbal narratives.

How does the different context of a material site and a textual collection affect the way we respond to – and study – stories? How can studying visual narratives enrich our understanding of verbal narratives (including lost oral and textual traditions), and vice versa? Does a mental image formed in response to a verbal narrative function in the same way as a visual image depicted in stone?

Indian Buddhism is overflowing with narrative. The Buddha himself is understood to be the Buddha because of his story, which extends beyond his pursuit of awakening in his final life to the many past lifetimes that are captured in *jātaka* tales.[2] Devotees become a part of the story of the Buddha and of Buddhist institutions by making their offerings or pilgrimages, by hearing or seeing stories about their revered teacher. This volume places narrative at the centre of explorations of Indian Buddhism, and seeks to bring together studies of visual and verbal narratives in pursuit of a more complete picture (pun fully intended) of early Buddhist practice and thought. The coming together is around the theme of the visual, both in the sense of visual narratives in art, but also in the sense of the visions we so often find in verbal narratives – from elaborate descriptions, to the creation of new realities through imaginative practices.

The papers in the volume fall into three sections: those in 'Part I: Visual Narratives' (Zaghet, Reddy, Zin) explore visual depictions of stories in their own right; those in 'Part II: Narrative Networks' (Mace, Appleton & Clark, Strong) seek to understand the relationship between specific visual and verbal narratives; and those in 'Part III: Narrative Visions' (Gummer, Fiordalis, Walters) primarily investigate how visual imagery and visualisation work in textual narratives. There are also threads that cross between the sections, however, and themes and concerns that echo throughout the chapters. In this opening chapter I seek to tease out some of these threads in a way that not only introduces the chapters that follow, but also explores the broader questions addressed by the volume as a whole.

I will begin by setting out some key definitions, of narrative and visual narrative, and justify why we might want to study verbal (by which I mean oral or textual, albeit primarily preserved in texts) and visual narratives as comparable units of analysis. I will then pick up three key themes that run through the volume: Firstly, what is the relationship between visual and verbal narratives, and between visual and textual evidence? Secondly, what is the role of vision in the narratives studied herein? Thirdly, what do the chapters in this volume contribute to our understanding of what narrative *does* and what makes it so powerful and prevalent?

---

2 As Gummer has argued, and notes in this volume (p.244), 'the *bodhisattva* path is in an important sense *always* a narrative path, a path accomplished in and through stories'.

What is a narrative?

An idea that is taken for granted within this volume – but also supported by the chapters within it – is that there is something special about stories. The tendency to think and communicate through narratives may be what makes us human, what makes us capable of empathy and socialisation, what lies at the heart of our culture.[3] Stories emerge and take root in different places, then travel and transform, and the ways in which they are retold (in verbal and visual forms) tells us about shared human concerns as well as specific historical circumstances. Narratives allow us to comprehend time and causal relationships between events,[4] including, in an Indian context, issues of karma. They have the ability to sooth, explore, subvert, construct, make present, communicate, and much more. They make us laugh or cry or wonder or despair, and can inspire faith and devotion in the process. As chapters in this volume demonstrate, they can even create or transform reality. In short, they have a power over us, and their central place in religious art and literature is testament to that power.

But what exactly *is* a narrative? Many books have been written exploring what narrative is and how it works, and I will not seek to replicate or compete with their analyses here. For the purposes of this volume, there are two distinctions that are worth keeping in mind. First of all, while in general conversation we might use the words 'story' and 'narrative' interchangeably, for narrative theorists the two have different meanings: A 'narrative' is the representation of a 'story' (broadly: events) through a form of 'narrative discourse'.[5] Narrative discourse is *how* a story is told, and can include characterisation, imagery, creative approaches to the presentation of time, and more. It is useful to hold this distinction in mind, as it allows for an appreciation of the aspects of narrative at play that go beyond a simple sequence of events.

While this is a helpful distinction, it has some potential dangers that are worth exposing at the outset. One of the implications of separating story from narrative in this way is that there can be many narratives told (or depicted) of a single story or series of events. This can be a helpful idea: for example, the lifestory of the Buddha is generally well-known, but various narratives come down to us

---

[3] As per the arguments of the likes of Carrithers 1992 and Gottschall 2012.

[4] For H. Porter Abbott this is their primary evolutionary benefit – see in particular Abbott 2008, 3ff. The role of narrative in enabling us to make sense of actions in the wider context of their significance is also key to the understanding of David Herman (for example Herman 2002, 14).

[5] This distinction goes back to Todorov's work in the 1960s and is the English rendering of his 'histoire' and 'discours'; it also maps on to the Russian formalist distinction between 'fabula' and 'sjuzhet'. For further explanation see, for example, Abbott 2008, 19ff, or Herman, Jahn and Ryan (eds) 2005, 566–568.

that tell his story in different ways. However, there is also a pitfall inherent in this distinction, namely the implication that the story may be stable (or 'true') even as it is represented in a range of narratives. In the context of the lifestory of the Buddha this leads us into the dangerous and ultimately futile world of trying to excavate the narratives to find the story, in other words the real events in the life of the Buddha. Narrative theorists are usually quick to point out that a story cannot exist prior to – or outside of – a narrative, though the question of how to deal with what look like different accounts of the same events becomes a thorny one (and is discussed by Appleton & Clark later in this volume).

Even in narrative traditions less riddled with historiographical urges than the Buddha's final-life story, it is important not to assume that there is a single original story that underpins all of its narratives. The story of Vidhura's abduction to the realm of the *nāga*s, for example, is only extant in a single Indian textual narrative (as far as I am aware[6]) but is depicted as a visual narrative at various sites in rather different ways. There are two reasons why it is assumed that broadly the same story underpins these different narratives: recognisably key events and characters are depicted, and inscriptional labels help us. At Kanaganahalli, for example, some key visual elements are missing – there is no flying horse, or swinging upside down – but the inscription, as at Bharhut, clearly identifies the story as the *jātaka* of 'Vidurapuṇaka'.[7] We can therefore be reasonably sure that these different narratives (visual and verbal) are underpinned by a similar story. Yet the story only exists because of the narratives that recount it, and if we assume a single story then we risk reading elements from one narrative into another; in particular scholars have a tendency to read details from a textual narrative into a visual one. Perhaps, in fact, the story narrated visually at Kanaganahalli is actually different to that depicted at Bharhut or Ajanta, and all are different to that narrated in the *Jātakatthavaṇṇanā*, which itself is a textual attempt to record what must have once been a dynamic oral tradition.[8]

---

6 The story is also alluded to in the Khotanese *Jātakastava* – see below.

7 For a discussion of the image and line drawings see Zin 2018, 35–40; she also reproduces the inscriptions from Nakanishi and von Hinüber 2014. See also https://jatakastories.div.ed.ac.uk/stories-in-art/vidurapunnaka-jataka-at-kanaganahalli/

8 On the history of the *Jātakatthavaṇṇanā* see Appleton 2010 especially Chapter 3. The distinction between verse ('canonical' and perhaps a fixed core for a more flexible storytelling endeavour) and the commentarial prose in this text is important but sometimes overstated. The verses can never have made sense without some prose. Some of the prose in the text likely preserves early oral narratives, while other parts are garbled and suggest a misunderstanding of verses or wider narrative tropes; yet others are later literary compositions or embellishments. The two aspects of the text – verse and prose – can sometimes provide insight into earlier and later narrative developments, but not reliably.

The situation is complicated further by the presence of Vidura, wise minister to the Kurus, in the Hindu epic *Mahābhārata*, where, however, he is not abducted by a *yakṣa* nor subjected to a precarious journey holding onto a magical horse's tail. His story is not the same, yet is *he* the same? After all, he is wise, a teacher of the *dharma* (indeed he is the god Dharma incarnate), and adviser and steward (*kattar*) to a Kuru king who is overly fond of gambling. The Pali text even contains a little resonance with a famous dilemma at the heart of the *Mahābhārata* when Queen Draupadī challenges the idea that she has been lost by her husband at dice, for there is a scene where Puṇṇaka asks Vidhura whether or not he is owned by the king. If he is, then he has been legitimately won and must leave his home and family and go wherever his new master desires. If he is not, then he may stay. Despite the obvious temptations, Vidhura reasons that there is no refuge in this world better than the truth, and so admits to being owned by the king.[9] The vast intertextuality of Indian narrative reminds us that, while we might posit the *events* that make up stories (or indeed *characters* therein) as worthy of study beyond the narratives that contain them, ultimately we only have the narratives to turn to for evidence.

The second distinction worth keeping in mind in thinking about definitions of narrative is that between *narrative* and *narrativity*. Gerald Prince, in his entry on the subject for the *Routledge Encyclopedia of Narrative Theory*, tells us that narrativity designates both 'the set of properties characterising narratives and distinguishing them from non-narratives' and 'the set of optional features that make narratives more prototypically narrative-like, more immediately identified, processed, and interpreted as narratives' (Herman, Jahn and Ryan 2005, 387). Under the second part of the definition, narrativity is understood to be on a spectrum. For example, a story with well-developed characters, a coherent narrative voice, and a plot that develops over time and space, will have a high degree of narrativity. A story in which little happens, or one that is hard to follow or incoherent, will have a lower degree of narrativity. As we are about to discover, narrativity is useful as applied not only to verbal narratives, but also to visual narratives.

What is a visual narrative?

I consider verbal (oral or textual) and visual narratives to be comparable units of analysis, and indeed it is a basic principle of this volume – and of the symposium from which it arose – that it is helpful to do so. However, while both

[9] For some further reflections on the comparison see the introduction to my translation in Appleton and Shaw 2015, 455–458, and also Moacanin 2009.

images and words can surely relate (or relate to) a narrative, the ways in which they do so differ. The distinction between story and narrative remains important here: the underlying events of a story can be presented through a range of narrative discourses, or – to use a phrase made famous by Vidya Dehejia – a range of 'modes of visual narration' (Dehejia 1990; see also 1997). Dehejia lamented the absence (at the time of her writing) of scholarship on the ways in which stories were depicted, and claimed that the attention of art historians was too often exclusively on identifying the underlying events of the story (Dehejia 1990, 375–6). There were in fact already some exceptions to this assessment (most notably the work of Dieter Schlingloff, made available in English in 1987) and many more have followed, greatly enriching our understanding of Indian Buddhist visual narrative.

Dehejia's own system mapped six or seven modes, or distinct ways in which a story is presented, sometimes with several modes used within a single site. In some of her modes, visual narratives use space to communicate the unfolding of events over time, with characters and plot clearly identifiable. In others, a key event alone may be depicted (her 'monoscenic' mode), or several scenes together ('synoptic' or 'conflated' depending on whether or not the figure of the protagonist is repeated) or a story represented according to an organisational principle unrelated to the progress of time (what she calls 'narrative networks'). Schlingloff's work offers a less systematic typology, but a rich assessment of how different modes might work. For example, he has demonstrated that many of the complex Ajanta 'narrative networks' are actually based on a principle of geography, with events arranged according to *where* they took place, rather than *when*.[10] Such approaches can help to enrich our understanding of visual narratives; and, as both Zin and Zaghet show in this volume, any typology of narrative modes continues to be supplemented and refined as research progresses.

As should now be clear, some modes of visual narration seem to undermine – or perhaps play with – notions of time. For example, the central Bharhut Vidhura image (Fig. 1.1) is a 'synoptic' narrative, as it expresses several scenes in one frame, with the key characters repeated. Taken together with the rest of the pillar, it is also a 'narrative network' as the upper relief depicts events in the *nāga* realm from both the early and later portions of the story, while the lower relief contains scenes of the human Kuru kingdom. In viewing the Vidhura visual narrative it would therefore be hard to extract the chronological series of events constituting the story without guidance. This is an important distinction

[10] As Zin puts it in a careful comparison of the approaches of these two scholars, 'while Dehejia analyses pictures, Schlingloff analyses stories' (2019, 141), hence his approach tends to pay more attention to principles of narrative, as well as being rooted in deep study of the literary sources.

between visual narrative discourse and verbal narrative discourse: you cannot see (or experience) a verbal story all at once, but you can see a visual story all at once. In a verbal narrative, there are two senses of time: the time it takes to read (or hear) the narrative, and the time in which the events recounted in the narrative play out. The creator of a verbal narrative can ensure the audience experiences both sorts of time under some degree of control. A visual narrative experience is very different, and can range from a momentary view of an entire image, to getting lost amongst different scenes and events and characters.

Different 'modes of visual narration' might therefore be seen as offering different degrees of 'narrativity'. Although this concept has not often been applied to visual imagery, some modern scholarship has started to address its applicability, most notably that by Werner Wolf.[11] In a 2003 article, Wolf first establishes that narrativity depends on the presence of key 'narratemes' such as an experience of time, representation of a storyworld, characters, action and setting, and meaningfulness and tellability. He then argues that images are capable of fulfilling some but not all of these narratemes; for example, it is harder to communicate time or internal states or intentions in a visual narrative. As such, he concludes that images can have a 'narrative dimension' but cannot be as 'convincingly narrative' as a verbal story: images 'refer to a story' or 'present moments that the viewer is then required to narrativize' (Wolf 2003, 191). In other words, visual narratives can vary in their narrativity, but always require some degree of outside reference or prior knowledge.

This notion that visual narratives are somehow deficient or inferior to verbal narratives in their ability to communicate a story is a recurring one in scholarship, and another issue addressed in this volume. There are a few problems with this idea. The first problem is that it prompts scholars to reach immediately for the supposedly superior form of narrative: a text. In particular when encountering a monoscenic or conflated narrative, the general solution is to reach for a textual narrative to help explain it at least by offering a set of events (a story) that seem likely to be depicted or referred to. A visual narrative has often been deemed 'explained' once a satisfyingly related text has been found, and textual priority (whether chronological or conceptual) is assumed.

The priority that tends to be given to textual narratives is evident even within this chapter, in my use of the name Vidhura for the protagonist of what I would also usually refer to as the *Vidhurapaṇḍita-jātaka* or '*jātaka* of the wise man Vidhura'. As noted above, a wise minister to the Kurus named Vidura (without the aspirated *dh*) is also present in the *Mahābhārata*, while the inscriptional titles at Bharhut and Kanaganahalli both give equal weight to

---

11 See also Wolf's entry on 'Pictorial Narrativity' in Herman, Jahn and Ryan (eds) 2005, 431–5. The recent volume edited by Alexandra Green (2013) offers some interesting new perspectives on visual narrativity in Asian art.

the character of Puṇṇaka (who, we might note, is not even important enough to the *Jātakatthavaṇṇanā* to merit a rebirth identification). Meanwhile, two other stories of the *Jātakatthavaṇṇanā* (441. *Catuposathika-jātaka* and 469. *Mahākaṇha-jātaka*) refer to a *Puṇṇaka-jātaka*, as their way of referring to what is elsewhere titled *Vidhurapaṇḍita-jātaka*. Might the title in the Pāli collection be an erroneous reproduction of *Vidurapuṇṇaka*? The vagaries of titling in both texts and art should not overly concern us here, but the point is that myself and other scholars routinely refer to visual narratives by the titles given to what we identify as the same story in a text. And this notion of textual priority in studying narratives is at least partly due to the perceived insufficiency of visual narrative modes, and the assumption that narrative images are therefore always dependent upon verbal narrative for their explanation.

The second problem with viewing visual narratives as deficient in their ability to tell stories is that it assumes that the purpose of a visual narrative is to prompt a narrative response of some kind in the audience – a recollection of a narrative, perhaps aided by a guide, or perhaps internally. Yet where is the evidence that visual narratives are seeking to tell stories in the same way as we might think verbal narratives do? It is clear that many artists ignored the modes of visual narration that were most conducive to communicating a linear narrative, in favour of modes where time and even plot events are difficult to determine. The Vidhura story at Bharhut, for example, could have been depicted as a series of bounded scenes moving through time, and doubtless this would have been more successful in allowing a viewer to 'read' the story, yet the artists chose a different approach. Rather than seeing this as a deficiency, we might better think about it as a conscious choice, and consider visual narratives on their own terms.

Another important piece of evidence against the narrative intent of visual narratives was explored by Robert Brown in an article on *jātaka* images in 1997. As he noted, many visual narratives at early Buddhist sites are inaccessible: high overhead, or covered over, or in darkened spaces. As such, they are impossible for a viewer to 'read' in any detail. Thus, he argued, we need to think a bit differently about the way *jātaka* images work. Brown's emphasis was on the ability of *jātaka* images to manifest the Buddha's presence, regardless of any narrative response in the audience. In contrast, Andy Rotman (2009, 180) suggests that such images might well have made the Buddha present precisely through a process of narrativisation, perhaps reliant upon site guides, another reminder of the intertwined nature of word and image. We could of course also add other layers of possible function to invisible or indecipherable images, such as the merit-making of donors and visitors, which could happen regardless of whether or not a visitor knows what is depicted, though presumably the artist (and donor) had some knowledge of a verbal story.

Kevin Carr offers another helpful perspective on this debate in his work on medieval Japanese scrolls illustrating the life of Prince Shotoku. These, he argues, are clearly narratives but, when made available to audiences, are better described as 'enshrined' rather than 'displayed' (Carr 2011, 39), as visibility or comprehensibility of the narrative is not deemed important. He proposes the term 'iconarrative' for 'an object that is narrative in form but which functions largely as an icon' (Carr 2011, 41). This is quite a rich idea, yet notice that Carr still maintains the idea of an image being 'narrative in form' in order to qualify. This is an interesting move, since one could go quite far in pursuing the idea of an iconarrative: an image of the Buddha touching the earth, for example, evokes a narrative, but it is not (we can *probably* all agree) narrative in form, and hence does not fit Carr's notion of an iconarrative. Likewise, the monoscenic *jātaka*s identified by Dehejia, or indeed the 'spotlight narratives' discussed by Zaghet in this volume, might struggle to meet the definition of 'narrative in form' yet might be helpfully considered under Carr's framework. I would suggest that his notion of the 'iconarrative' should be extended to visual narratives regardless of whether or not they are depicted in a form with high levels of narrativity.

But does an image still count as a narrative if its form does not exhibit much narrativity, and it is not intended to elicit a narrative response in the audience? I would argue that here we need to bring back into the discussion that distinction between narrative and story: it is helpful to consider a visual narrative as a narrative, even if it has little narrativity, as long as it seems to point to a story. In other words, I would like to suggest that there are three places we must look when exploring the narrative dimension to an image: the content or subject matter (the 'story'), the form or mode of depiction ('narrative discourse'), and the intended function or audience response.[12]

By including the separate dimension of content or subject matter, we can get around the question of whether or not an image is 'narrative' when it isn't depicted in a narrative mode, with character, time and plot explored visually. In other words, it gives us a way to include images – such as monoscenic *jātaka* images – that allude to a story that would have been familiar from other visual or verbal forms, but contain little narrativity in their form. And, crucially, that an image seeks to allude to a story does *not* necessarily mean that its intended function is to remind a viewer of a story or accompany a storytelling endeavour; it just means that the content or subject matter is narrative. Regardless of the mode of depiction, a narrative image can function in a variety of ways, including but not limited to evoking or prompting narration of a verbal story.

[12] Greg Thomas, in his 'Concluding Remarks' to Green, ed. 2013, also identifies three dimensions of narrativity in art, though he talks of 'modes of viewing' rather than purpose or audience response (2013, 246). For his analysis, the success of an image depends on communicating to an audience (2013, 248).

Indeed, an image might bypass this sort of function altogether to communicate or evoke emotions or values directly, or to take its place as an invisible yet powerful 'iconarrative' in a *stūpa* complex. An image may even have multiple functions at once, only some of which may have been anticipated by whoever decided on the subject matter and mode of depiction.

Bringing image and text together

Having reached this level of understanding of what a visual narrative might constitute, it is worth looking briefly at how this might change our understanding of verbal narrative sources too. The idea that there are benefits to looking at visual and verbal narrative together underpins this volume, which draws together scholarship by art historians and textual scholars around the theme of the visual. Before examining their contributions, I would like to lay out some of the reasons behind this interdisciplinary approach.

A few benefits of bringing verbal and visual narratives together have already come to light. Firstly, using ideas from narrative theory that are usually applied only to verbal narratives can help us to understand visual narrative better. So, being aware of the idea that a narrative is made up of both a story (events) and forms of narrative discourse (Dehejia's 'modes of visual narration'), with varying degrees of narrativity, ensures we pay attention to more than just identifying an image as a particular story. Secondly, some of the pitfalls of scholarship on visual narrative are exposed when compared with studies of textual narrative. To say that a textual narrative is 'explained' once the story has been identified is so clearly ridiculous that it means we are forced to also reject the – much more prevalent – idea that a visual narrative is 'explained' by such an identification. Thirdly, visual narratives raise striking and challenging questions about the intended audience response to a narrative, and thereby encourage us to ask questions about verbal narratives too.[13] Are verbal narratives intended simply to enable an audience to recall or learn a story? Other audience responses, such as devotion, and other purposes that go beyond any audience response, such as making *buddha*s present, may be just as relevant to verbal as to visual narratives. Identifying or communicating a story in and of itself is rarely the end point, but rather the starting point, and the visual and verbal may not be so far apart, once we look beyond the form and explore the function.

[13] For some of my own earlier reflections on how *jātaka* images can inform scholarship on the function of *jātaka* texts, see Appleton 2010, Chapter 7. See also the important comments in Zin 2017.

Another key benefit of thinking about visual and verbal narratives as parallel units of analysis is that we can also see artistic sites and textual collections as parallel units of analysis. For example, just as we might ask why a particular 34 stories were chosen for inclusion in Āryaśūra's *Jātakamālā*, and how his framing of the stories affects their impact, we might ask why the creators of the Bharhut visual scheme chose the particular images they did, and how their arrangement and framing affect their impact.[14] Perhaps we might even follow Leela Aditi Wood, who, in her 2005 doctoral thesis, refers to the Bharhut scheme and others like it as 'visual *jātakamālā*s' and claims they are 'similar to literary *jātakamālā*s in that they can be characterised as jātaka cycles in which the devotee encounters the deeds and bodies of the Buddha in his past lives' (Wood 2005, 1–2). At some sites (such as parts of Ajanta[15]) there may be a conscious attempt to illustrate a set of textual narratives, but often we can perceive no such agenda, and they need to be studied as independent narrative collections. As such, scholars should take into account the effect of encountering a curated and framed set of narratives, in addition to exploring specific individual stories, visual or textual.

Seeking to understand the effects of a visual collection of brief narrative images might even help us understand how brief textual allusions to narratives work. For example, the Khotanese *Jātakastava* contains accounts of 50 previous births of the Buddha, in the form of brief, second-person verses of praise. In such a setting, the story of Vidhura becomes (in the translation of Dresden 1955, 431–2):

> 71. You entered the ocean, into the house of the *nāga*s, O you gracious one, as the minister *Vidurā*, a servant to the king. The *nāga*s were evil with mouths blazing in anger; with smoke lightnings issued from their fearful mouths.
> 72. You remained there with them. On the fourth day you spoke to them the profound noble Law, the *Brahma* stages, resembling the nectarial elixir. They undertook the good course of action of the sages.
> 73. You made all the *nāga*s in turn wise, intelligent, to keep the moral laws, tamed in mind. Like the ocean you were in knowledge, O gracious one.

[14] Amanda Guyton attempts just such an analysis in a 2003 doctoral dissertation, though the challenges of working with a disassembled (and partly lost) monument hinder such efforts.

[15] The extensive work of Schlingloff (culminating in his 1999–2000 volumes) has made clear the literary links for many of the caves' visual schemes, in particular the *Mūlasarvāstivāda Vinaya*, as well as the *Jātakamālā*s of Āryaśūra and Haribhaṭṭa. As Zin cautions (2017, 289), even where such strong links are demonstrated, we must also consider the possibility that 'it is not that Ajanta illustrates stories known from the (*Mūla-*) *Sarvāstivādavinaya*, but rather that the scriptures of the (Mūla-) Sarvāstivādins preserved narratives from Deccan.'

These verses indicate quite a different story from that found in the *Jātakatthavaṇṇanā*, our only full extant Indian textual narrative, for there the *nāga*s are rather civilised, and the focus is more on the adventure of Vidhura's abduction. The focus on the subduing and preaching in the *nāga* realm is, we might note, more conducive with the Ajanta visual narrative (as discussed in Reddy's chapter in this volume). But setting these particular correspondences aside, what happens when we consider the textual context? The verse renditions in the *Jātakastava* are not full narratives, but rather references to past-life adventures. In other words, the content is narrative (allusions to known *jātaka* stories), but the form has little narrativity. And what of the function? Are we to read this list of allusions to stories and pause at each one to tell ourselves the full story, or ask a more learned companion or teacher to do so? That is certainly possible, though it is not encouraged by the text itself, and seems rather unlikely. More likely, I would suggest, and supported by the text's colophon, is that the mention of life after life after life of extraordinary demonstration of the perfections of the Bodhisattva, expresses awe at the deeds of the Buddha, and also highlights the seriousness of the *bodhisattva* path.

In other words, the experience of hearing or reading these allusions to *jātaka*s in the Khotanese *Jātakastava*, or indeed in several other texts that take a similar approach (such as the *Rāṣṭrapālaparipṛcchā-sūtra*), might not actually be that different to the experience of seeing monoscenic or other *jātaka*s decorating a *stūpa* site. These allusions give a fleeting impression of a story – might we even say a vision? A response such as feelings of devotion, awe and faith, take us beyond – and potentially bypass the necessity of – a simple narrative response. Indeed, it is not only a narrative response that might be by-passed: the presence of these allusions might well have potency even without any sort of audience interaction at all, simply by being created, or by being present, as acts of merit-making or ways of localising powerful forces.

It is worth noting, also, that it is not only these abridged textual narratives that are insufficient when it comes to communicating a full story. Indian verbal narratives, like visual narratives, very often require or expect some sort of broader awareness of characters or implications, due to their high levels of intertextuality; the wider resonances of Vidhura and his gambling royal patron serve as a good example of that. Both texts and images can therefore expect prior knowledge, or require explanation by a teacher or guide. Yet another benefit of looking at visual and verbal narratives together is the acknowledgement that intertextuality can occur across different media.[16] Not only do images

---

16 Some have begun to refer to 'intervisuality' as a parallel phenomenon to 'intertextuality', where 'text' is taken in the narrower sense of a verbal source; others consider 'intertextuality' to include images as considered within a broader definition of a 'text'. We might also talk of 'intermediality', a term coined in the 1980s to aid

draw on other images, and texts on other texts, but images can affect the telling of tales in words, as well as vice versa. Images are also in themselves key to verbal narratives, and these often rely upon visual experiences (recollected or imagined) for their impact. As Mieke Bal argues, 'the study of visuality in narrative constitutes the counterpart to the study of the discursive, specifically narrative aspects … of images in visual art' (Herman, Jahn and Ryan (eds) 2005, 629–30). This volume is founded upon this understanding that the visual in narrative encompasses both visualisation in verbal narrative and visual narrative images in stone or paint.

These are some of the reasons why studying images and texts side by side can be helpful when exploring Indian narrative traditions, and hence why this volume came into being. Having outlined my understanding of what narratives – verbal and visual – are, and justified the consideration of visual and verbal narratives alongside one another, including explorations of the visual in texts, let us briefly examine the contributions of the volume's nine remaining chapters to questions of how the visual and verbal relate, how vision works in narratives, and what narratives do.

Visual and verbal narratives

This volume explores visual and verbal narratives side by side, as two forms of narrative that are potentially influenced by similar concerns and constraints, but that also differ in important ways. I have argued that the simplistic view of their relationship – seeking textual 'explanations' for visual narratives – is unhelpful, and suggested that more fruitful investigations might explore how textual and visual 'narrative discourse' might work, as well as how visual and verbal narratives might seek to affect their audiences. However, the relationships between visual and verbal narratives remain important, as long as we move beyond the notion of textual priority. Texts and images – or literature and art – are not just parallel domains, but also interact and shed light on one another. The chapters in Part I and Part II of this volume offer a rich reframing of the relationship between these two domains.

Part I of the volume presents three chapters by art historians who all seek to understand narrative art on its own terms, yet all also draw on textual evidence in different ways. In Chapter 2, Zaghet explores the art of Sanchi Stūpa 2, a lesser-known companion site to the great narrative-covered Stūpa 1. The Stūpa 2 reliefs are particularly difficult to interpret because they offer very little

discussions of the relationship between visual and verbal sources (see Herman, Jahn and Ryan (eds) 2005, 252–6). However, there comes a point where terminological excess begins to obscure the real purpose of the discussion.

in the way of narrativity. Zaghet first rejects flawed attempts to date the site using textual narrative evidence, and then proposes a new understanding of the iconographic choices made at the site. Using several examples, she argues that the reliefs might function as a variant of Dehejia's 'monoscenic' mode that she calls the 'spotlight' mode, in which 'the subject takes up center stage, and its presence in the composition shifts the focus towards the identification of the main subject, rather than the series of events making up the narrative' (p.38). While she primarily compares images with other images, and emphasises the importance of understanding iconographic and stylistic choices, Zaghet also acknowledges the necessity of textual sources. She ends with a discussion of an image that must be a story, and that has parallels in the art of other sites, yet remains unidentified, because there is no verbal story with which to link it. As such, Zaghet's chapter demonstrates both the value of studying visual narratives on their own terms, and the challenges of working without some accompanying verbal materials.

Reddy (Chapter 3) also seeks to study visual narrative as a source in its own right, but links it to both textual narrative and to the oral/aural domain that she views as crucial to linking extant sources together. As she argues, 'To be explained and understood in its finer detail, [an image] may need to be compared or correlated with the text in a process that may best be seen as an interactive discourse' (p.56). She finds textual support for the power of a visual encounter to provoke faith, most famously in the *Divyāvadāna*, and uses this to help make the case for seeing certain Ajanta paintings of Buddha and Bodhisattva not as illustrations of narrative accounts, but as objects of devotion. She demonstrates that particular artistic techniques are used to highlight what she calls the 'divinity' of the Buddha and Bodhisattva, and present them as images that inspire faith in the viewer. In one example, we even witness a *dharma*-teaching from the Bodhisattva-as-Vidhura, and discover that the Ajanta portrayal of this story seems to emphasise not the drama of the central events, but the power of Vidhura's sermons. The visual, textual and oral/aural combine, to mould what she calls 'the images of the mind' (p.58) and to prompt a powerful transformation in the audience.

The power of a *dharma*-teaching is the main focus of Zin's study of the pictorial genre of the 'sermon scene' in the Kucha caves, in Chapter 4. Scenes of the Buddha teaching included depictions of his telling of stories, suggesting another dynamic relationship between visual and verbal narratives. Zin also offers a careful review of the different modes of visual narration at the site, from some highly reduced *jātaka* images to overpopulated sermon scenes. As she shows, the addition of more detail can sometimes make a scene harder, rather than easier, to identify. In any case, she argues that identifying stories may not be the most important thing, at least for Buddhist audiences, for '[m]aybe it was not the narrative content of the individual pictures that was important, but rather their general presence – and their number' (p.100). Sermon scenes are often particularly complex because they can conflate time and place inasmuch as the story told by the Buddha can include karmic backstories in a prior lifetime involving supplementary characters. This Central Asian artistic innovation is interesting in its own right, but also speaks to how complex the relationship between words and image can be. While Zin suggests ways in which we might fruitfully read their 'pictorial language' (p.113), she – like Zaghet – ends with an unidentified image, and the hope that future research will continue to advance our understanding of the highly complex world of visual narratives.

As such, these three chapters together demonstrate different ways in which textual sources can help in the interpretation of visual narratives, whether as literary parallels that illuminate details of the image, or as accounts of visual encounters. However, they also highlight the importance of exploring other aspects of the image, such as the mode of depiction, and how this compares with other visual narrative compositions at the same and other sites. They offer analyses of how visual narratives 'work' at three specific sites – Sanchi, Ajanta, Kucha – that go far beyond identifying the stories.

More explicit investigations of the relationships between visual and verbal narratives follow in Part II. In Chapter 5, Mace draws on textual narrative to better understand the portrayal of the nun Utpalavarṇā honouring the Buddha at Kaushambi. She notes the variation between stories as to who first meets the Buddha on his descent from his spell teaching in heaven, and uses this detail to explore the networks of stories expressed in both textual and visual narratives. She finds the closest verbal narrative tradition to the Kaushambi relief – in the *Mūlasarvāstivāda-vinaya* – but also explores the insufficiencies of using textual narratives in a world where so many other stories would have circulated that may not still exist for us today. Like Reddy, Mace avoids talking about texts as sources of explanation, preferring to seek 'a text that could be relevant for explaining the meaning or reception of the scene' (p.132) and, like Zaghet, she emphasises the importance of comparing with other visual narratives as well. Mace also emphasises other pieces of evidence that can help us understand her Kaushambi relief, notably the context of the monument. By looking at the image alongside the other visual narratives at the site, and by reflecting on the likelihood of a monastic audience for this particular railing, Mace is able to draw out the possible reasons for Utpalavarṇā's inclusion in the depiction. And by exploring a range of visual and verbal evidence, Mace offers a new perspective on the person and significance of this prominent nun.

Appleton and Clark (Chapter 6) also explore a complex narrative network: the popular story of the six-tusked elephant Bodhisattva, which is found in numerous visual and verbal narratives. They use this example to advance an argument about how we should study what appears to be the same or similar story in visual and verbal forms. While emphasising the value of studying texts and art alongside one another, they advocate a move away from seeing visual narratives as expressions of verbal narratives, or verbal narratives as 'versions' of one another or of a purported original story. Instead, they advocate a more flexible approach that acknowledges intertextuality and intervisuality, and that allows every narrative expression to be appreciated on its own terms. They draw on A. K. Ramanujan's notion of a narrative 'pool of signifiers' and propose the complementary notion of 'story cluster' as a way to group together related narrative 'crystallisations' that emerge from the pool across visual and verbal domains. Such an approach, they argue, opens up new avenues for research into the role of stories across different Buddhist contexts.

The final chapter in Part II, by Strong, explores three textual accounts of interpretations of images of the Buddha's lifestory, from three very different historical contexts. In the first example, a Buddhist monastic text recounts how the Buddhist King Ajātaśatru was eased towards a realisation that the Buddha had passed away through a visual biography. In the second, two seventeenth-century Portuguese Jesuits offer their own glosses upon a traditional Chinese pictorial life of the Buddha. In the third example, seventeenth- and eighteenth-century visitors to the Sri Lankan Buddhist site of Mulgirigala offer interpretations of the visual scheme that are 'rather spectacular' (p.200), drawing as they do on the story of Adam and Eve. As such, key questions for Strong include: What happens when you look at an image without a copy of the (right) text or with the expectation of the (wrong) narrative? What qualifies as a misinterpretation when it comes to viewing art? Is it the donor, artist, viewer, devotee, art historian or textual scholar who has the authority to determine what a visual narrative is really showing or doing? As Strong argues, 'Misinterpretation is not always just an uninformed reaction to a work of art waiting to be set right; it is also a transformative action on a work of art, which may have various motivations, political, cultural and religious' (p.205). And, as Strong shows, when an image is interpreted in relation to the wrong textual narrative, the misinterpretation itself can make for a fascinating study; and such a study is then only made possible through textual sources.

The chapters in Part II therefore supplement Part I by offering different models for how to understand the relationship between textual and visual sources. They highlight the importance of comparing images with other images as well as with texts, and of doing so in such a way that does not privilege the verbal over the visual. They also emphasise the role of both visual and verbal narrative in exposing the rich history of Buddhism, and Buddhist approaches to particular stories and key figures. Texts remain important to the study of narrative images, not only as preservers of verbal narrative traditions, but also as sources that often themselves explore the nature of the visual and the role of images. Part III goes on to explore textual accounts of the visual in greater detail.

Vision and narrative

The theme of this volume – vision – is not only designed to include visual arts, but also to bring together the study of the visual arts with visual imagery and visualisation practices in narrative texts. The three chapters in Part III, by textual scholars, explore the various ways in which vision plays an important role in verbal narratives. These explorations, though taking textual evidence as their starting point, resonate with important themes from Part I and II, and develop these in new directions.

In Chapter 8, Fiordalis explores the power of visual metaphor in narratives about the Buddha, and argues that a process of 'narrative figuration' is able to 'actualize the Buddha as a "spiritual sovereign"' (p.214). Fiordalis begins with the story of King Kapphiṇa, who is converted by the Buddha after the latter takes on the image of a *cakravartin* or universal sovereign, an appearance that is elaborately described. As Fiordalis argues, 'far from merely asserting it as proposition, the story seeks to establish the Buddha's special status through visual imagination and metaphor' (p.221). In particular, he argues, the image of the Buddha and the image of the *cakravartin* can be held simultaneously in the minds of the audience of the narrative, such that they can appreciate both the identity and difference between these two ideal figures (p.221). Likewise, in his second narrative example, the Buddha's display of the bodily marks of a *cakravartin* enables a vision that blurs 'the boundary between the literal and the metaphorical in regard to the relationship between the Buddha and the sovereign' (p.228).

Like Fiordalis, Gummer (Chapter 9) emphasises the importance of narrative visualisations, and like Zin and Reddy she focuses on the interface between the visual and the aural/oral *dharma*. Taking the *Vimalakīrtinirdeśa-sūtra* as her source, Gummer argues that 'Vimalakīrti makes *buddha*s present not through uttering their words, but by enabling audiences to "see" their non-material bodies and fields' (p.241). This happens, she argues, through 'what we might call a ritual of narration' (p.241). Furthermore, the powerful *dharma*-speech of Vimalakīrti has the power to transform audiences through the resulting visual encounter – or *darśan(a)* – with *buddha*s. As Gummer argues, other Mahāyāna *sūtra*s have related means of transforming their audiences, and image consecration can be a useful model for this: '*buddha*-speech is a ritual power substance, and narratives that encompass the listener – self-referential narratives – enable the experience of that substance as a ritual infusion' (pp.244–5) thereby consecrating the audience as future *buddha*s. Hence, narrative visualisations – which can also involve other senses, especially auditory experiences – have the power to make *buddha*s through 'imaginative *real-ization*' (p.253).

In the closing chapter of the volume, Walters broadens our focus from vision alone to the six senses, by demonstrating their role in the karmic stories of the *Apadāna*. Having demonstrated that an important early strand of Buddhist thought derided the senses and portrayed the ideal as a rejection of them, Walters shows that these *Apadāna* tales offer a very different perspective: 'In *Apadāna*, the sensual can be, and ideally is, not an obstacle but an opportunity. Engaging the sensual world to make it better – prettier, more sonorous, tastier, more fragrant, more comfortable and above all pleasanter – both shapes the performance of karma seeds and constitutes their results' (p.277). He explores a number of quite formulaic poems recounting the sensual deeds and results of apparently invented monks and nuns, and argues that through such stories the authors 'were able to experiment with sensorial narrative' (p.271) by linking, for example, visual gifts with visual benefits, epithets, and experiences. As Reddy and Fiordalis also emphasise in their chapters, bodies are the result of virtue (and vice), and so advanced beings such as *buddha*s and *arhat*s have better bodies; this means not only more beautiful or impressive bodies, but also – as Walters highlights – better senses and sense-experiences. In addition to the stories of these monks, Walters explores the *Buddhāpadāna*'s account of the Buddha-to-be's imaginary performance of a multi-sensory act of worship in an imaginary Buddha-palace. The elaborate description of the place and deed – filled with the best possible fragrances, images, couches and so on – glorifies the senses but also makes clear that a visualisation can have powerful karmic results. Echoing the two previous chapters, Walters too highlights the power of the narrative in creating images that have the power to transform their audience.

Together these three chapters demonstrate how the study of textual narrative exposes similar themes and concerns to the study of visual narrative, especially when one focuses on the visual experience. As Fiordalis notes, 'textual narratives have the capacity, perhaps inherently, of gesturing toward the visual domain' (p.232) and, when they do so, the resulting visual encounter can be as powerful – in communicating an idea or in transforming an audience – as an encounter with a visual image in stone or painted in a cave. Indeed, the visual and verbal domains are inherently intertwined, not least through the equivalence so often drawn between a vision of the Buddha and hearing his *dharma*. As Gummer reflects in her preamble: 'Mahāyāna *sūtra* narratives conjure with *buddha*-speech visions of past, present, and future *buddha*s and their fields (*kṣetra*); the *sūtra* murals at Dunhuang conjure with visual media the oral/aural experience of entering the presence of a *buddha* and listening to *buddha*-speech directly from his mouth' (p.239). And as Walters notes towards the end of his chapter, sensorial narrative – including that which celebrates the power of the visual – likely reflects the highly sensorial experiences of visiting and worshipping at the *stūpa* sites of Indian Buddhist devotion that are so richly decorated with narrative art.

Why narrative?

Although this volume is structured as these three parts with their different focal points, there are also many themes that cut across the different chapters, and these address some deeper (and broader) questions about the role of narrative in Indian Buddhism, or indeed in human societies. There is much we can never know about the function of Indian Buddhist narrative, not least because of the inadequate evidence we have of oral narrative practice in earlier historical periods. But both the great early monuments and the great works of Indian Buddhist literature take for granted a world full of narratives, about the Buddha, his key followers and adversaries, and his and other people's past lives. Whether verbal or visual, evidence in this volume suggests that such narratives were not meant to be mere descriptions of events: instead they establish authority and identity, explore ideas of karma and rebirth, change an audience's ideas, elicit emotional responses, lead to new behaviours, and prompt devotional and donative practice. So, what is it about narrative that enables it to do all of this?

As noted by several contributors, metaphor is an important method that narrative can use to transform its audience. Fiordalis argues that the two narratives that he examines 'argue for simultaneous identity and difference even as they blur the line between the metaphorical and the literal' (p.229) such that the Buddha both *is* and *is not* identified as a *cakravartin*: both positions can be held simultaneously thanks to the narrative form of the texts. Similarly, Gummer's study explores a 'highly performative metaphor' (p.249) that relies on playing with the dichotomy between *dharma* and *āmiṣa*: '*dharma* is the real food and true body of the Buddha and advanced *bodhisattva*s, not *āmiṣa* – yet the apparently stark contrast between *āmiṣa* and *dharma* depends upon the substitutability of one for the other' (p.255). While words might have a particularly strong performative ability, metaphorical endeavours are not limited to verbal narrative: as Reddy points out, juxtaposition of contrasting states (for example craving and dispassion, p.76) and visual metaphors (such as the procession of the Bodhisattva as if a divine image, p.68) are powerful tools in visual narrative too.

Both visual and verbal narratives also have the potential for self-referentiality, and this is a key means by which an audience can be drawn in and transformed. This can operate on a very straightforward level, as audiences are encouraged to imagine themselves into the storyworld. For example, Mace observes that an audience is able to view a narrative image of the nun Utpalavarṇā's overzealous devotion, and reflect on their own behaviour as part of the same monastic community, while narratives of karmic seeds of devotion examined by Walters help an audience imagine doing – and benefitting from – the same deeds themselves. As Reddy notes in relation to certain images at Ajanta, witnesses to the amazing acts of the Bodhisattva within the image draw the viewer in, through 'an ingenious double frame' (p.63), ensuring that the viewer 'participates alongside the witnesses – both visually and emotionally' (p.65). Another form of self-referentiality is evident in scenes at Kucha, examined by Zin, in which the Buddha is shown teaching an audience using a particular story: both audience and story-contents are depicted.[17] In textual examples examined by Gummer, self-referential speech acts effect the very results they describe, such that the audience are 'cooked' into future *buddha*s simply by witnessing the text's visualisations; Vimalakīrti's speech 'does what it says' (p.253).

This self-referentiality reaches intriguing heights when combined with the power of the imaginary. As Gummer and Walters explore, performing an imaginary (or imaginative) *pūjā* or *darśana* has real-life effects. The audience of the *Vimalakīrtinirdeśa* can see *buddha*s and their *buddha*-fields through the powerful speech of Vimalakīrti, and as a result of this vision they are transformed. Even the Buddha in his own past life, recounted in the *Apadāna*, performed a *pūjā* in his mind, with impressive karmic consequences. While some people might be inclined to dismiss the imaginary as less than real, research into various Indian understandings of the imaginary show it to often be, as

[17] Catherine Becker (2015, 106–37) makes a similar observation about the Andhran scenes that show a monk subduing an angry king using the story of the man in the well. Indeed her 2015 study discusses many themes that are also addressed in the present volume, including the self-referentiality evident in what she calls 'meta-stūpas', that is to say images of *stūpa* worship that are themselves used to adorn *stūpa*s, a relatively common occurrence at Andhran sites such as Amaravati. Such images sometimes reproduce the narrative imagery on the *stūpa*s too, raising interesting questions about how narrative imagery was understood to function. Such self-referentiality about the power of narrative reaches impressive heights in the fourteenth-century murals in the Tibetan temple of Shalu, which explore and expand a relatively abridged text in a format reminiscent of a book. As Sarah Richardson concludes (2016, 255): 'These paintings did not merely express the important content of books, but rather showed how books worked and how book knowledge was organised.' Self-referentiality therefore crosses between visual and verbal narrative sources.

Shulman entitled his 2012 monograph on the subject, more than real. Even in the modern west we might easily appreciate that imaginary encounters, such as in novels, films or (day-)dreams, can result in genuine emotional (and hence physiological) results, and that these experiences – like all experiences – have the power to change us.[18] In an Indian Buddhist context, we find competing accounts of the real. On the one hand mentation is considered one of the six senses (alongside vision, hearing, smelling, tasting, and touching), so mental activities are just as real as other sensory experiences. On the other hand, certain strands of Buddhist thought painted all experiences as ultimately illusory anyway. Against such a backdrop we can see that manipulating one's visual imagination (or, indeed, one's multisensory imagination) to enable an encounter with a *buddha* can compensate for the apparent absence of a *buddha* in the world. Visualisation becomes real-isation.

One of the ways in which a visual narrative encounter – whether 'real' or 'imaginary' – can have a powerful (and physical) effect on an audience is through an emotional response. These emotional responses are embodied responses, and often involve other senses as well as vision (as noted by Walters and Gummer amongst others), adding to evidence that rejection of the body and senses is just one of many strands of Buddhist thought. Sensory engagement with narrative is, in some quarters, encouraged and even lauded as a virtue: as Walters argues of the *Apadāna*, 'multi-sensorial narrative emerges as a method, a new approach to both worship and narrative in which the senses are the means, rather than the primary obstacle to religious progress' (p.284). As noted by several contributors including Reddy and Fiordalis, the body is the physical manifestation of virtue or vice, and so it makes sense for one's appearance to matter. The Buddha must look like a *buddha*, and because he does, a vision of him can overpower and transform an audience.

A powerful emotional response in turn has the power to prompt actions, especially devotional ones such as making an offering to the Buddhist monastic community, or even sponsoring one's own decorative scheme at a *stūpa* site. Such a process echoes descriptions in textual narratives – famously, thanks

[18] My own bias may well be inherent in this volume's theme, as I am a very visual person with an active imagination. To my surprise, 2015 saw the identification of a condition called *aphantasia*, or an inability to see things in one's mind (Zeman, Dewar and Della Sala 2015). While the condition was already documented as the result of brain injury, some scientists now think that congenital aphantasia could affect up to one in 50 people. Since this became the subject of popular discussion, I have been shocked to discover that several friends are indeed completely unable to see anything in their 'mind's eye' and would, of course, struggle with the imaginative and visualisation practices described here. We should therefore keep in mind that such practices, though clearly important within some Buddhist traditions, are not of universal appeal.

to Rotman's thought-provoking work (2009), in the *Divyāvadāna*, but also in other texts – that tell of a person encountering the vision that is the Buddha (or his *stūpa*), experiencing *prasāda* (faith) and making an offering. It seems likely, as discussed in particular by Reddy, that visual narratives sometimes also seek to prompt *prasāda* and the consequent acts of generosity that are the cornerstone of practice at these sites. In doing so they are part of the same endeavour as many textual narrative visual encounters too; after all, verbal narratives can both extol the benefits of such devotion and create the very same effects themselves (Gummer, Walters). And as Walters has argued previously (1997) the rise of *stūpa* worship is likely linked to the rise of *jātaka* and *avadāna* literature, as all are part of a discourse around how devotees were able to imagine themselves into a devotional relationship with the Buddha, through karmically potent acts of donation.

However, while embodied sensory and emotional responses are an important part of the story here, other chapters in the volume explore how narratives can also be the source of intellectual reflection or change in views. Fiordalis builds on Bruner's framework of 'narrative' and 'paradigmatic' modes of thought to demonstrate that narratives can also make arguments, albeit in a different way to paradigmatic or propositional modes of discourse; as he shows, narrative arguments are a key piece of evidence for Buddhist views about kingship and the state. Meanwhile Reddy, while seeing an embodied emotional response as key, argues that this is precisely what enables an image to communicate key Buddhist ideas – abstract and complex ideas that she refers to as the 'intangibles', made tangible and comprehensible through art. In contrast, the Kaushambi relief examined by Mace is likely, she argues, to 'have been intended to spur thought' (p.153), operating on a more intellectual and reflective level. It is perhaps wisest not to separate out these two domains of response. Emotions and multi-sensory experiences can change you, and so can arguments, which often in themselves make use of emotional responses. This change can be to one's views and understanding (both potentially, and revealingly, called 'vision') as well as to one's behaviour. And all these methods seem to be an important part of the ways in which narrative, in the form of art or literature, manages to affect an audience.

Yet, as other chapters have explored, sometimes narrative would appear to have little to do with audience response at all. At Kucha, for example, as examined by Zin, the innumerable (and largely unrecognisable) narrative images must serve a purpose through their very presence, while the purpose of Zaghet's spotlight narratives at Sanchi remains as obscure as some of the images themselves. Trying to understand the intentions behind narrative images is, of course, far harder than with textual sources, which often tell us why they are telling us a story (as noted by Appleton & Clark). And sometimes an image can be wilfully misrepresented, or completely misunderstood, as in two of the examples examined by Strong. One clear lesson of this volume, therefore, is that we must be attentive to context, and examine each narrative on its own terms, with an open mind as to its role in Buddhist practice or ideas.

More than any other, perhaps, Strong's chapter reminds us of the importance of historical context, of seeking the interpretive help of accompanying guides (textual or living), and also of studying the guidance that has been given to audiences of the past. As the *Divyāvadāna* story with which he opens his chapter suggests, it has long been accepted practice to appoint a 'competent' guide to explain imagery properly. Yet, as I hope is now well established, explaining a narrative image is about more than explaining what story it depicts. As Carr (2011, 31) notes, citing Kamanishi's work on the Japanese practice of etoki, '"pictorial exegesis" does not necessarily mean "elucidation *of* a picture" but rather "elucidation *by means of* a picture."' So, if there were monastic guides at – for example – Bharhut, perhaps they were more than storytellers seeking to explain the events depicted in the images. Perhaps they were instead using the images – or what they knew about the images – as a prompt for other sorts of elucidation. They may have drawn out morals, or sung the praises of the amazing virtues of the Buddha even in his past lives. Perhaps they would have drawn visitors' attention to the specific virtue of giving, so necessary to the maintenance of *stūpa* sites and monastic institutions. Perhaps they would have emphasised the ability of visitors to become a part of the web of devotional interactions with Śākyamuni Buddha, and with other *buddha*s. Or perhaps, as Rotman suggests, '[t]hrough their words, these monks would help bring these images to life' (2009, 184) in order to make the Buddha present for his devotees.

It is worth noting that similar sorts of exegesis would be likely if the starting point was a verbal narrative: the story is not the end point, but instead is a way into ideas and experiences. As I hope has become clear during this introductory chapter, while some aspects of how narrative works rely specifically on the media – words or pictures – most resonate between visual and verbal forms of narrative, especially when the latter make use of visual imagery and visualisation. Bringing together images and texts – and art-historians and textual scholars – therefore has clear benefits for our understanding of Indian Buddhism. We can together aspire to be a series of 'competent explainers' who, as a first step, seek to correctly identify a story, but then go beyond that to ask the more difficult questions about what narrative is doing and why.

Look again at Figure 1.1. What do we see now? A story that reaches out across visual and verbal domains, within and beyond diverse Buddhist contexts. A story that, even in this visual form, conjures up a strong aural/oral experience, that of hearing a *dharma* teaching from Vid(h)ura, the Bodhisattva, in the absence of a *buddha*. An image that therefore has the power to prompt an emotional response: awe at the Buddha's multi-life virtues; longing for the *dharma*. A visual narrative that forms part of the multi-sensory experience of visiting a great site of Buddhist devotion, a devotion that involves visitors in the multi-life karmic networks of future *buddha*s. A narrative that enables us to explore different aspects of the history of Buddhist ideas and practices, including artistic modes, and a reminder of the power of the visual in Indian Buddhist narrative.

Bibliography

Abbott, H. Porter 2008. *The Cambridge Introduction to Narrative* (2nd edn). Cambridge: Cambridge University Press.

Appleton, Naomi 2010. *Jātaka Stories in Theravāda Buddhism: Narrating the Bodhisatta Path*. Farnham: Ashgate.

Appleton, Naomi and Sarah Shaw, trans. 2015. *The Ten Great Birth Stories of the Bodhisatta*. Chiang Mai: Silkworm Press.

Becker, Catherine 2015. *Shifting Stones, Shaping the Past: Sculpture from the Buddhist Stūpas of Andhra Pradesh*. Oxford and New York: Oxford University Press.

Brown, Robert L. 1997. 'Narrative as Icon: The *Jātaka* Stories in Ancient Indian and Southeast Asian Architecture'. In Schober, J., ed. *Sacred Biography in the Buddhist Traditions of South and Southeast Asia* 64–109. Honolulu: University of Hawai'i Press.

Carr, Kevin Gray 2011. 'The Material Facts of Ritual: Revisioning Medieval Viewing through Material Analysis, Ethnographic Analogy, and Architectural History'. In Brown, R.M. and Hutton, S.H. (eds) *A Companion to Asian Art and Architecture* 23–47. Chichester: Wiley Blackwell.

Carrithers, Michael 1992. *Why Humans Have Cultures: Explaining Anthropology and Social Diversity*. Oxford and New York: Oxford University Press.

Cunningham, Alexander 1879. *The Stûpa of Bharhut: A Buddhist Monument Ornamented With Numerous Sculptures Illustrative of Buddhist Legend and History in the Third Century B.C.* London: W.H. Allen and Co.

Dehejia, Vidya 1990. 'On Modes of Visual Narration in Early Buddhist Art.' *The Art Bulletin* 72/3: 374–92. https://doi.org/10.2307/3045747

Dehejia, Vidya 1997. *Discourse in Early Buddhist Art: Visual Narratives of India*. New Delhi: Munshiram Manoharlal.

Dresden, Mark J., ed. and trans. 1955. 'The Jātakastava or "Praise of the Buddha's Former Births": Indo-Scythian (Khotanese) Text, English Translation, Grammatical Notes, and Glossaries'. *Transactions of the American Philosophical Society* 45/5: 397–508. https://doi.org/10.2307/1005767

Green, Alexandra, ed. 2013. *Rethinking Visual Narratives from Asia: Intercultural and Comparative Perspectives*. Hong Kong: Hong Kong University Press.

Gottschall, Jonathan 2012. *The Storytelling Animal: How Stories Make Us Human*. Boston and New York: Mariner Books and Houghton Mifflin Harcourt.

Guyton, Amanda Corinne 2003. *Bharhut: Narrative and Pilgrimage in Ancient India*. University of Virginia doctoral dissertation.

Herman, David 2002. *Story Logic: Problems and Possibilities of Narrative*. Lincoln and London: University of Nebraska Press.

Herman, David, Manfred Jahn, and Marie-Laure Ryan, eds. 2005. *The Routledge Encyclopedia of Narrative Theory*. London and New York: Routledge.

Lüders, H., revised by E. Waldschmidt and M. A. Mehendale, eds. 1963. *Corpus Inscriptionum Indicarum, Vol. II, Part II: Brāhmī Inscriptions From Bhārhut*. Ootacamund, India: Government Epigraphist for India.

Moacanin, Klara Gönc 2009. 'Epic vs. Buddhist Literature: the case of *Vidhurapaṇḍitajātaka*.' In Koskikallio, P., ed. *Parallels and Comparisons: Proceedings of the Fourth Dubrovnik International Conference on the Sanskrit Epics and Purāṇas*, 373–98. Zagreb: Croatian Academy of Sciences and Arts.

Nakanishi, Maiko and Oskar von Hinüber 2014. 'Kanaganahalli Inscripions.' *Annual Report of the International Research Institute for Advanced Buddhology and Soka University* 17 (supplement).

Richardson, Sarah 2016. *Painted Books for Plaster Walls: Visual Words in the Fourteenth-Century Tibetan Murals at the Buddhist Temple of Shalu*. University of Toronto doctoral dissertation.

Rotman, Andy 2009. *Thus Have I Seen: Visualising Faith in Early Indian Buddhism*. Oxford and New York: Oxford University Press.

Schlingloff, Dieter 1987. *Studies in the Ajanta Paintings: Identifications and Interpretations*. New Delhi: Ajanta Publications.

Schlingloff, Dieter 1999–2000. *Guide to the Ajanta Paintings I: Narrative Wall Paintings*. Delhi: Munshiram Manoharlal.

Shulman, David 2012. *More Than Real: A History of the Imagination in South India*. Cambridge MA: Harvard University Press.

Walters, Jonathan S. 1997. '*Stūpa*, Story, and Empire: Constructions of the Buddha Biography in Early Post-Aśokan India'. In Schober, J., ed. *Sacred Biography in the Buddhist Traditions of South and Southeast Asia* 160–92. Honolulu: University of Hawai'i Press.

Wolf, Werner 2003. 'Narrative and Narrativity: A narratological reconceptualization and its applicability to the visual arts.' *Word and Image* 19: 180–97. https://doi.org/10.1080/02666286.2003.10406232

Wood, Leela Aditi 2005. *The Buddha and the Shape of Belief: Indic Visual Jātakamālās*. University of Michigan doctoral thesis.

Zeman, Adam, Michaela Dewar and Sergio Della Sala, 2015. 'Lives without imagery: Congenital aphantasia.' *Cortex: A Journal Devoted to the Study of the Nervous System and Behavior* 73, 378–380. https://doi.org/10.1016/j.cortex.2015.05.019

Zin, Monika 2017. 'Narrated with Chisel and Paintbrush: On the Importance of Research into Art History for Understanding Buddhism – Some Examples.' *Rocznik Orientalistyczny* 70/2: 274–306.

Zin, Monika 2018. *The Kanaganahalli Stūpa: An Analysis of the 60 Massive Slabs Covering the Dome*. New Delhi: Aryan Books.

Zin, Monika 2019. 'The Techniques of the Narrative Representations in Old India.' In Wagner-Durand, E., Fath, B. and Heinemann A. (eds) *Image – Narration – Context: Visual Narration in Cultures and Societies of the Old World* 137–56. Heidelberg: Propylaeum.

Author biography

Naomi Appleton is Senior Lecturer in Asian Religions at the University of Edinburgh, where she researches and teaches in the areas of Buddhist and early Indian studies. Her research interest is the narrative literature of early India, with a particular focus on *jātaka* stories, as well as on ways in which the narratives of different religious groups relate to one another. She is the author of, amongst other things, *Jātaka Stories in Theravāda Buddhism* (Ashgate 2010), *Narrating Karma and Rebirth* (CUP 2014), *Shared Characters in Hindu, Jain and Buddhist Narrative* (Routledge 2017) and *Many Buddhas, One Buddha: A Study and Translation of Avadānaśataka 1–40* (Equinox 2020).

PART I: VISUAL NARRATIVES

2

Rethinking Chronology and Narrative Modes

The Case of Sanchi Stūpa 2

Flavia Zaghet

As already discussed in Chapter 1, different modes of visual narration were employed in early Buddhist art, including some modes that offer very low degrees of narrativity. As a result, visualizations of the same narrative are often both profoundly different and difficult to interpret (or even identify) in the absence of inscriptions or securely identified comparisons. The aim of this chapter is to illustrate the benefits of a reconsideration on the one hand of established chronologies (which have considerably influenced the history of iconographic studies) and on the other of visual narrative modes in order to deepen our knowledge of the visual expressions of narrative in early Buddhist art. The case of Sanchi Stūpa 2 provides a prime example, where a chronological reassessment and the identification of a variant of the monoscenic mode of visual narration (the *spotlight* mode) lead to the identification of a narrative vein including (as yet) unknown narratives. The same kind of approach could be fruitfully applied to well-studied reliefs as well as more obscure ones, hopefully paving the way for the development of studies in the future.

Stūpa 2 dating issues – The "Śunga" era

The majority of studies on early Buddhist art are based on a chronology that separates "Śunga" post-Mauryan monuments (belonging to the last two centuries BCE – i.e. the *stūpa*s of Bharhut, Bodhgaya and Sanchi 2) from the subsequent Sātavāhana/Kṣatrapa era (1st to 3rd century CE), represented by Sanchi *stūpa*s 1 and 3, early Mathura art and the rock-cut caves of the Deccan. This distinction is partially reflected in stylistic discrepancies between the two groups of monuments, with the former employing a cruder, more naïf character in both figure rendering and narrative composition. Perhaps contrastingly to these considerations, in iconographic studies Sanchi Stūpa 2 is at the same time treated as an *unicum* because of the preponderantly non-narrative character of its reliefs as opposed to the appearance of episodes from the life of the Buddha and *jātaka*s in Bharhut and Bodhgaya's reliefs. Studies on the iconography of this monument reached extremes in which the carved decoration was not only dismissed as lacking an iconographic program, but was even thought to have no Buddhist content (Bénisti 1986; Coomaraswamy 1927, 35; Dehejia 1992, 39; Marshall & Foucher 1940, 101–4; Mitra 1957, 64; Rowland 1953, 57–8; Taddei 1996). Quite surprisingly for approaches aiming to date the reliefs based on their style, none of these studies of iconography even considered epigraphic evidence, with the sole exception being Vidya Dehejia's "Collective and Popular Bases of Early Buddhist Patronage: Sacred Monuments, 100 BC – AD 250", where for the first time it was proposed to consider the reliefs of Sanchi *stūpa*s 1 and 2 as virtually contemporaneous, based on the recurrence of donors' names on both monuments (Dehejia 1992, 39).

In a recent work, Frederick Asher recapitulated the history of studies on the chronology of early Buddhist art (Coomaraswamy 1927a, b; Fergusson & Burgess 1865, 1876, 1884; Marshall & Foucher 1922; Smith 1911) to further demonstrate how the traditional periodization is mostly based on an excessive reliance on literary tradition, finding little or no actual evidence in archaeology (Asher 2006). In fact, the Śunga dating is mainly based on accounts of the semi-mythical Brahmanical texts *Matsya-, Vāyu-, Brahmāṇḍa-* and *Bhaviṣya Purāṇa*s (Bhandare 2006, 70), which consistently report a list of 10 Śunga kings who reigned following the killing of the last Maurya emperor, Bṛhadratha, by one of his commanders, Puṣyamitra Śunga. The report is borne out by the Buddhist tradition (specifically the *Vibhāṣā*, a second-century Kashmiri work of the Sarvāstivādin-Vaibhāṣika school, and the *Aśokāvadāna*, a narration of the life and deeds of emperor Aśoka; Lamotte 1985, 387), which, in addition, depicts Puṣyamitra as a ruthless persecutor of Buddhism.

In support of these textual accounts, several pieces of epigraphical evidence have been presented, the most solid of which is the so-called Dhanabhūti inscription of Bharhut, which reads:

1. Suganam raje râjno Gâgî-putasa VISA-DEVASA
2. pauteṇa, Gotiputasa AGA-RAJASA puteṇa
3. Vâchhi-putena DHANA-BHUTINA kâritam toranam
4. Sila kaṁmata cha upaṅna.

In the kingdom of Sugana (Srughna) this *Toran*, with its ornamented stonework and plinth, was caused to be made by king *Dhana-bhûti*, son of Vâchhi and Aga Baja son of Goti, and grandson of Visa Deva son of Gâgî. (Cunningham 1879, 128)

After this very first report and its translation by Alexander Cunningham, Georg Buhler (1883) and all subsequent scholars interpreted and reiterated the words *suganam raje* as *Śuṅganam raje*, and its meaning was changed to "during the reign of the Śungas". This is questionable on several levels, as pointed out by Asher. Firstly, no titles preface the expression *suganam raje*; secondly, king Dhanabhūti's father, the Gotiputa Agaraju named in the same inscription, struck coins in his own name – so he could hardly have been someone else's feudatory; thirdly, epigraphs of this kind usually bear chronological references naming a single royal figure, not an entire dynasty (Asher 2006, 58). Nevertheless, during the past century, the Bharhut Dhanabhūti inscription has been held as evidence for a dating of the Bharhut *stūpa* – as well as all the other stylistically related monuments (mainly the Sanchi Stūpa 2 and the Bodhgaya balustrades) – to a period considered to be that of the Śunga dynasty, supposedly following the Mauryan epoch, and preceding the *toraṇa*s of Sanchi Stūpa 1, which are dated to the Satāvahāna era by the Śātakarṇī inscription.[1]

In addition to Asher's, more recent studies have reconsidered the subject highlighting a generalized tendency in nineteenth-century authors to rely on textual accounts, producing works in which "textuality overrides actuality" (Schopen 1991, 7). Shailendra Bhandare (2006) re-examined the whole set of epigraphical evidence traditionally brought in support for the dating of the Śunga age (Indrāgnimitra inscription at Bodhgaya, Dhanabhūti inscription at Bharhut, Dāmamitra inscriptions at Erich and Musnagar, Āṣādhamitra inscription at Erich, Dhanadeva inscription at Ayodhya and Bhāgabadra inscription on the Heliodorus pillar at Besnagar), showing that none of these inscriptions can be considered a scientifically reliable landmark for the dating of monuments, nor sufficient to postulate the existence of a Śunga empire in the first place. Bhandare furthermore carried out a systematic analysis of region-specific coinage from the Gangetic plain, convincingly demonstrating that:

> The historical picture that coins offer is entirely contrary to the accepted notion of a Śunga empire. In a stark contrast with the puranic accounts reflecting a linear succession to an "imperial" throne, what we see is a spurt in urban centres, supporting localized money economics [...] A comparison between

1 The inscription on the upper architrave of the southern gateway of Stūpa 1 mentioning king Sātakarnī (Marshall & Foucher 1940, 349, inscr. 389) is the second fundamental chronological landmark found at the site (the first being Aśoka's edicts); although debate on the dates of Sātakarnī's reign is still ongoing (Shimada 2013, 54–8), the beginning of the first century CE is a plausible period for the building of the *toraṇa*s.

> texts on one hand and coins and inscriptions on the other for the list of ten "Śunga" kings would illustrate the point. First, the coins convincingly indicate that such a dynasty, if ever was called Śunga, existed in South Daśāṃa and not in Magadha. Second, only four of ten "Śunga" rulers are corroborated from coins. [...]"Śungas", if they ever existed, were probably as localized as the rest of the groups we know from coins in terms of their political prowess. Coins offer an entirely different picture of the post-Mauryan fragmentation, which links two singularly important phenomena of ancient Indian history – the fall of an empire and a concomitant spurt in urbanization with an increase in localized money economy. They also hint a probable non-sequitur – the fall of historical jargon that makes random use of terms like "Śunga supremacy" and "Śunga art". (Bhandare 2006, 97)

On a parallel plane, Ajit Kumar (2014) moves from the confutation of the Dhanabhūti inscription to link the style of the purported "Śunga" monuments (once again Bharhut, Sanchi Stūpa 2 and Bodhgaya balustrade) with the earliest phase of Mathura art, datable with a great degree of certainty to the beginning of the first century CE.[2] He points to potential epigraphical evidence in support of this hypothesis, assuming[3] that the Bharhut Dhanabhūti and the Dhanabhūti from a now lost Mathura inscription[4] are one and the same person. Kumar consequently assigns the Bharhut sculpture to the beginning of the common era. Sonia R. Quintanilla does support the same identification of Dhanabhūti (leaving, however, the question open; Quintanilla 2007, 12) but draws opposite conclusions, eventually dating the Mathura inscription within the canonical "Śunga" Bharhut timeframe (Quintanilla 2007, 10–13). Since the latter hypothesis is no longer acceptable in the light of the reconsidered date

---

2 The Amohini āyavati is a chronological benchmark for the Śoḍāsa era sculpture, being inscribed in 72 Vikram era i.e. 15 CE (Quintanilla 2007, 119–26, 168–217).

3 The author brings no evidence for this identification. Quintanilla (2007, 10–12) remains open to the possibility that the two could be the same person.

4 "Alexander Cunningham first published this inscription and asserted that it was from Mathura and housed in the Aligarh Institute; Heinrich Lüders proffered the same information. Unfortunately, however, according to Klaus Janert, the rail pillar with this inscription has been lost; no one has since been able to locate it. Therefore, we must rely on the descriptions and facsimile of Cunningham, who described the pillar as follows: «This inscription was originally cut on a corner pillar of an enclosure with sockets for rails on two adjacent faces, and sculptures on the other two faces. Afterwards another railing was attached, and fresh holes of a much larger size were then cut in the face bearing the inscription. Some of the letters in the last line are doubtful; but the general drift of the record is to announce some gift of Dhana-bhùti, the son of * * bhùti, in honour of all the Buddhas.»" (Quintanilla 2007, 11).

(or, better, the absence of a date) for the Bharhut balustrade, we must instead turn to palaeographic analysis. In the Mathura Dhanabhūti inscription, palaeography, and particularly the adoption of the word "*parisahi*" – epigraphically unrecorded before the Kuṣāṇa period and indicative of Sanskrit influence – would place the inscription towards the beginning of the common era. Nevertheless, given the mysterious nature of the Mathura inscription as well as the impossibility of carrying out a first-hand analysis of it, it would be more careful not to assume a link between the two Dhanabhūti-s.

A shift towards the end of the first century BCE for Bharhut, Sanchi Stūpa 2 and the Bodhgaya reliefs was already theorized on epigraphic grounds by Vidya Dehejia (1992, 39) and recently received additional support from research by Matthew M. Milligan (2016). His is an extensive study of the totality of donative inscriptions at Sanchi 1, 2 and 3. Through a detailed analysis of palaeography, donative formulas and identification of serial donors, Milligan proposes an internal chronology for the *stūpa*s and their balustrades and gateways. Most important to our ends is the identification of the same donors[5] on the Sanchi Stūpa 2 railing and the Great Stūpa's *toraṇa*s, berm *vedikā* and ground *vedikā* (Milligan 2016, 144–59): This series of identifications places the Sanchi Stūpa 2 *vedikā*, the Sanchi Stūpa 1 berm and ground *vedikā*s and its *toraṇa*s in the same timeframe (i.e. the life-span of a single person), a *terminus ante quem* for which should be around the mid-first century CE (Śrī Śātakarṇī's reign). Milligan subsequently establishes an internal division into two different generations of donors, leading to a (slight) antecedence of Stūpa 2 (and other phase 2 *stūpa*s) over Stūpa 1 (Milligan 2016, 152–56). His suggestions are confirmed by archaeological evidence from the Stūpa 2 balustrade: pillar 27 shows unquestionable signs of reworking in the same style as the *toraṇa*s of Stūpa 1. Therefore, although in such a limited timeframe as the life-span of a single person, we must position the Stūpa 2 balustrade decoration sometime before the *toraṇa*s of Stūpa 1.

To sum up, based on the current state of the art about the chronology of Sanchi Stūpa 2 and the related monuments, we must acknowledge three fundamental issues: (1) There is no archaeological evidence supporting a dating of the Bharhut Stūpa in the Śunga era; (2) There is no archaeological evidence to assume that Sanchi Stūpa 2 and Bharhut Stūpa are coeval. (3) There is archaeological evidence supporting an approximate contemporaneity (i e. the life-span of a single person) between the reliefs of Sanchi Stūpa 1 and Stūpa

[5] Or close relation between the donors, i. e. father–son, master–pupil, which limits the time distance between the two monuments to a lifespan at most.

2, with a dating between the end of the first century BCE and the mid first century CE, and with Stūpa 2 roughly preceding Stūpa 1.

These facts actually lead to a relevant conclusion, which needs to be carefully considered, namely: in an assessment of "Śunga" monuments, stylistic analysis is not indicative of chronology and can be profoundly misleading. Looking for a linear evolution in style can only be fruitful within a "coherent political and cultural identity" (Asher 2006, 61), whose existence is not testified in central India from the post-Mauryan to the Gupta era. On the contrary, in a world that has been demonstrated to have lacked a centralized power, regionalism was possibly the most influential factor in matters of stylistic evolution. Asher's regional cataloguing of the post-Mauryan reliefs, which postulates on the one hand a Magadha group (Bodhgaya), on the other a Madhyadeśa group, comprising Sanchi and Bharhut, and lastly a southeast group comprising Jaggayyapeṭa and Amaravati (Asher 2006, 63–4), seems extremely fruitful with an aim to produce a reasoned trans-regional iconographic analysis of post-Mauryan reliefs. The relevant stylistic differences between Sanchi Stūpa 2 and the reliefs on other monuments have to be investigated beyond regional distance, and will require further study. But, puzzling as they may look, they cannot be considered in and of themselves as evidence for a particular dating, as is shown by the Dhanabhūti inscription at Bharhut and the Śātakarṇī inscription at Sanchi.

Stūpa 2 narrative vein: The "spotlight" mode of visual narration

Moving from these considerations, I have carried out an iconographic analysis of Sanchi Stūpa 2, taking into account potential comparisons from early Buddhist figurative art, without the customary restrictions based on chronology. The aim of the research was to examine and, ideally, explain the specific character of these reliefs. As is well known, there are substantial differences between the form and content of the repertoire and those of all other coeval Buddhist monuments. Since it is no longer acceptable to justify these discrepancies solely on a chronological basis, the decoration of the Stūpa 2 *vedikā* can only be explained as the expression of a very specific conception of Buddhism and narrative – one that was not previously taken into account by scholars. Rejecting the utterly unreasonable possibility that a Buddhist monument in which the relics of eminent Buddhist saints were enshrined was decorated (in its entirety or for the most part) with non-Buddhist subjects and motifs, comparative analysis with examples from the early Buddhist art panorama revealed an iconographic program which includes both Buddhist decorative motifs and Buddhist narrative subjects.

The subjects of the narratives in the reliefs of Sanchi Stūpa 2 happen to be particularly obscure, on the one hand because of our imperfect knowledge of the narrative repertoire current at the time, and on the other because of the extremely cryptic character of the visual mode of representation adopted in this particular monument. Through the analysis and the identification of the themes represented in 74b (the Great Renunciation), 86b (the *Padakusalamāṇava-jātaka*) and 86a (the story of the elephant Nālāgiri), it will be demonstrated how the narrative mode adopted on this monument cannot be properly defined as either monoscenic or conflated, even if it partakes of both conceptions. In monoscenic depictions, the subject of a medallion is a single frame from the story, the final outcome of a series of events, which it suffices to recall; in conflated depictions, several happenings from a story surround the main character, being conflated in a single visual rendering. Both these modes of representation are meant to focus predominantly on the sanctity of the figure represented rather than on any particular actions; as pointed out by Vidya Dehejia concerning the monoscenic mode of visual narration:

> A static mode of monoscenic narration is frequently used by artists to present the viewer with scenes from the Buddha's life when the supremacy of the Buddha is the prime concern. In this mode, artists generally present the single, culminating episode of a story and focus thematically on the wisdom and presence of the Buddha. In such depictions, the narrative content is sharply reduced, and the reliefs represent scenes in which the action has already taken place. The artist presents us with the result of a narrative episode, or with the situation that immediately follows that narrative episode. In this context, "being in state," as contrasted with "being in action," seems suitable. [...] Meyer Schapiro, who discusses differences between "being in state," and "being in action," establishes that static depictions were regularly used where theological concerns were predominant. It appears that the artist [...] was interested in emphasizing the supremacy and power of the Buddha at the expense of the fascinating series of events leading up to the [...] miracle. (Dehejia 1997, 12–13)

Consistent with this tendency, the distinctive variant of the monoscenic visual mode found in Sanchi Stūpa 2 nevertheless differs from the typical monoscenic mode in that it is completely focused on the "being in state". It does not even represent the moment in which an action takes place, but only the main figure through which the underlying narrative can be apprehended. The elements presented to identify the figure are not scenes revolving around it, but proper attributes of the character central to the narrative.

In this variant of the monoscenic mode the subject takes up the center stage, and its presence in the composition shifts the focus towards the identification of the main subject, rather than the series of events making up the narrative. For practical reasons we will refer to it as "spotlight" mode: aware of the anachronistic shade such a contemporary term could imply, it is reminiscent of a series of elements such as theatrical act and movement on the one hand and illumination and gleam on the other which are extremely powerful images for early Buddhist visual art tradition as a whole and this specific expression of it.

If in some cases the difference with the monoscenic mode is virtually undetectable (for example in the central medallion of pillar 86a, where the representation could equally well be the moment of the story in which the elephant is brought out of the stable), in others the narrative aim itself would be unidentifiable without a series of comparisons (pillar 75b). The acknowledgement of the specific characteristics of the mode of visual narrative seen in Stūpa 2 opens up the possibility for future identification of several other narratives on this *vedikā*.[6]

Pillar 74b: The Great Renunciation

An example is the central medallion of pillar 74b (Figure 2.1), depicting a riderless horse, preceded by a male figure carrying a *chattra* with garlands and *caurī*. Above the animal's back (apparently perched on it, but most probably just occupying the available space within the medallion) is a *kiṃnara* holding garlands in its hands, with more garlands dangling from its bird-tail. At the horse's feet is a lustral vessel.

I agree with Marshall and Dehejia that these elements, combined together, are reminiscent of the Buddha's Great Renunciation, in which the groom Chandaka helped the Holy One to escape on horseback from the palace at Kapilavastu (Marshall & Foucher 1940, 187; Dehejia 1997, 77). After resolving to renounce courtly life to become a wandering mendicant, the Buddha decided to run away at night so that nobody could try and stop him from his purpose. The faithful servant Chandaka prepared Kaṇṭhaka, his master's mount, and *deva*s carried the horse in order to prevent its hooves from producing any sound and ensure a successful flight.

---

[6] Namely 1b, 11a, 14a, 14b, 27a, 27b, 40b, 52b, 63b, 70a, 76a, 80b, 82b, 82a, 84b.

Figure 2.1. Sanchi Stūpa 2, ground balustrade, pillar 74b, central medallion. Photograph by the author.

There are two main comparisons for this narrative in early Buddhist art: the central architrave of the east *toraṇa* of Sanchi Stūpa 1 and a Bharhut pillar.[7] Both are depicted in the continuous mode of visual narration, with different moments and places from the narrative represented through a repetition of the horse (with umbrella and accompanying groom), without any visual devices to separate the individual scenes. Although the right side of the Bharhut pillar is lost, a single footprint with *cakra* visible in the top right corner mirrors the

[7] For the former see Dehejia 1996b, 40–41 and for the latter Coomaraswamy 1956, pl. XXV, fig. 28. One more representation of the Great Departure is reported by Cunningham (1879, 16 – after Quintanilla 2007, 11n. 15) as being once carved on a now-lost railing pillar from Mathura. There are no surviving pictures of it, and Cunningham's description is not detailed enough to provide a useful comparison.

expedient used in Sanchi Stūpa 1 to visualize the moment in which Siddhārtha actually leaves the royal mansion, before the groom brings back the stallion Kaṇṭhaka without its master. Both occurrences feature an element representing the palace (two distraught women behind pillars in the upper portion of the Bharhut version). The main difference between the two reliefs is that on Sanchi 1 the *deva*s are actually waving scarves and *caurī*s above the horse and lifting up its hooves, while in Bharhut they are only depicted witnessing the sacred event and playing celestial instruments. In addition, in the relief of Sanchi 1, Chandaka invariably carries a spouted pot in his hand, every time he is shown in the narrative.[8] Even if this element is not hinted at in literary traditions on this event, it is often found in Gandharan visual depictions with the function of sealing a deal, as in the *Viśvaṃtara jātaka* (Zwalf 1996: 143 cat. 137), or to express astonishment and underline the supernatural and sacred nature of an event (the birth of the Buddha, the prediction of the Bodhisattva's destiny by the *ṛṣī* Asita, the taming of the elephant Nālāgiri and the Great Renunciation itself [Zwalf 1996, 149 n.13; 155–6 cat. 158; 158 cat. 162; 164n.15]).

Such a play of alternation and recurrence of the same structural elements in different representations confirms the hypothesis that the central medallion of pillar 74b depicts the Great Renunciation. In light of this analysis the flying *kiṃnara* no longer appears in contrast with the record of *deva*s carrying the horse, nor is the presence of the lustral vessel at the animal's feet incongruous. In addition to these considerations, it must be pointed out that in every single occurrence of a horse or elephant ride across the Sanchi Stūpa 2 balustrade, the animal is represented in profile with one of its front legs bent to convey a sense of movement.[9] The fact that only in this one example all of the horse's four legs are stiff should therefore be read as an allusion to the magically silenced galloping of the beast, whose movement is nonetheless expressed through Chandaka's bent leg. This receives confirmation from the Bharhut pillar, where both features appear in turn.

Pillar 86b: The Padakusalamāṇava-jātaka

Marshall & Foucher (1940, 181) linked the presence of an Aśvamukhī (horse-headed) *yakṣiṇī* on the central medallion of pillar face 86b (Figure 2.2) to the

---

8 Since the right portion of the pillar is now lost, it is not possible to tell if the groom was carrying a water pot in that instance as well.

9 On pillar faces 1b, 7b, 11a, 40b, 41b, 75b, 76a, 80b, 81b, 82a, 84b, 86a. In 2 out of 21 depictions of the elephant-with-lotus motif, the elephant's legs are still, but we cannot tell if the motif is meant to represent walking elephants in each of its variations.

Figure 2.2. Sanchi Stūpa 2, ground balustrade, pillar 86a, central medallion. Photograph by the author.

Padakusalamāṇava-jātaka, which illustrates the story of a meat-eating monstress who abducts young brahmans in order to eat them.[10] As mentioned, one day she falls in love with one of the men and they start living happily together: she goes on eating unfortunate travellers, while he survives on the food they carried with them. Eventually she bears him a son (the Bodhisattva), who, growing up, becomes aware of his condition and runs away together with his father, leaving the *yakṣiṇī* to die of a broken heart.

Several appearances of an Aśvamukhī *yakṣiṇī* in early Buddhist art are known, but not all of them can be connected with certainty to the

[10] However, Marshall interprets the male figure as the young Bodhisattva. For an English translation of the story (*Jātakatthavaṇṇanā* 432) see Cowell 1895–1907, vol.3, 298–300.

Padakusalamāṇava-jātaka;[11] the narratives underlying the representations on the veranda of Bhaja *vihāra* 19 (Huntington 1985, figs 5.27, 5.28, 5.29), the Sanchi Stūpa 3 *toraṇa* (Dehejia 1996b, fig. 12) and a Chandraketugarh terracotta (Sengupta 2007, 216) are in fact, to date, obscure, and present several unfamiliar elements, not found in the textual versions of this *jātaka*. A "borderline" instance is found in an upper half-medallion from the Bodhgaya balustrade, where the man-*yakṣiṇī* couple is shown playing a board game (Policardi 2018, fig. 5b): although probably representing a daily-life scene from the *Padakusalamāṇava-jātaka*, there are not enough elements to demonstrate this hypothesis. Most importantly, the relief does not share the same structural elements and characteristics as the following examples, which instead form a homogeneous group and must therefore be analyzed together.

These include medallions found on railing pillars from Patna (Coomaraswamy 2001 [1971], 1, pl. 12) and Gurgaon (Biswas 1987, fig. 30), another upper half-medallion from the railing at Bodhgaya (Coomaraswamy 1935, pl. IX) and a wall painting from the ceiling of Ajanta cave XVII (Behl 1998, 177). In all the cited occurrences the *yakṣiṇī* is accompanied by (or is dragging away) the young man; in the first medallion their son is also present, carried in her lap, while in the other three she or the man are carrying mango branches, as in the Sanchi 2 medallion.[12] From these instances, it may be inferred that the structural elements for the visual narration of the story were (1) the brahman, being abducted or living with the *yakṣiṇī*, and (2) the mango fruits, representing the dietary contrast between the dreadful meat-eating *kimnarī* and the righteous brahman.

Once again, the combination of these elements in the Sanchi 2 medallion would seem to represent not so much a frame, a single scene from the narrative, as the main character with his distinctive attributes.

Pillar 86a: The story of the elephant Nālāgiri

Pillar 86a (Figure 2.3) shows an elephant coming out of a stable, mounted by a mahout holding an *ankuśa*. The depiction in itself would not be particularly explanatory of the narrative, if it did not have an exact match in Ajanta cave 17 (Figure 2.4). There, it constitutes part of the continuous visual depiction of the Buddha's taming of the mad elephant Nālāgiri (or Dhanapāla), following the account found in the *Mūlasarvāstivāda-Vinaya*, in which the evil Devadatta

[11] This analysis follows a study of the Aśvamukhī *yakṣiṇī* between *jātaka*s and art by Chiara Policardi (2018).

[12] In the Gurgaon medallion the male figure holds a roughly round object in his hand, which could well be a flask (*kamaṇḍalu*) like that shown in the Ajanta fresco: an attribute pointing to the man's brahman status.

Figure 2.3. Sanchi Stūpa 2, ground balustrade, pillar 86a, central medallion. Photograph by the author.

(an apostate monk and a cousin of the Buddha) planned to release the beast and kill the Buddha by letting it loose in the city, but the Blessed One managed to stop its rampage with the power of his compassion, and the animal fell on its knees before him.[13]

This narrative has no counterparts in early Buddhist aniconic art, but can be analyzed alongside the aforementioned wall painting from Ajanta and two reliefs from Amaravati, a frieze and a medallion.[14] The latter two depictions are structurally identical, showing the frenzied animal running out of a city gate and into a a terrified crowd, grabbing a man and flinging him through the air before finally stopping at the sight of the Buddha, and bending its knees before him.

[13] Schlingloff et al. (2003, 41) note that the story is preserved in a Sanskrit manuscript, and found in Gnoli, R. ed. 1978. *The Gilgit Manuscript of Saṅgabhedavastu*, vols. I–II, Rome, pp. 186–190.

[14] The medallion is held in Chennai Government Museum. A photo by the American Institute of Indian Studies, Varanasi can be accessed at https://dsal.uchicago.edu/images/aiis/aiis_search.html. The frieze, held in the British Museum in London, can be found in Barret (1954): pl. XIV (a).

Figure 2.4. Ajanta cave 17 veranda, detail. Photograph by the author.

The Ajanta example presents the addition (in the left part of the composition, the narrative developing from left to right) of the moment in which the animal is being driven out of the stable by a mahout. This portion of the depiction is virtually identical to medallion 86a in the balustrade at Sanchi 2, allowing us to hypothesize that only this particular moment in the narrative was selected for depiction in the iconic narrative mode. Even though the medallion could equally well be read as monoscenic (it is actually one of the scenes in Ajanta's continuous depiction), it is equally possible that the architectural structure (the only element common to all three depictions, hence the key structural element for an interpretation of the iconography) is an attribute of the elephant in this case. It might have been intended as a feature to distinguish this narrative from similar ones, by setting the story in an urban environment and therefore referring to the Nālāgiri rampage episode.

Pillar 75b: The rescue of two girls from a flood

In the central medallion of pillar 75b (Figure 2.5) a couple is riding an elephant against a full-blown lotus background. The male figure, holding an *ankuśa*, is not a mahout but a man of higher standing; the woman riding behind him holds on to the man's arm and to a rope from the elephant's harness. The key structural elements for an identification of the episode are: the elephant, the male-female royal couple of riders, and the *abhayamudrā* gesture of the man (implying his reassuring role). These elements, combined together, suggest a resemblance with the lowest panel of pillar 27a from the same monument (Figure 2.6). Here the same royal couple (riding an elephant, with the man in *abhayamudrā*) is represented in a more articulate monoscenic narrative, intent on rescuing two girls from a flood by allowing them to climb onto the elephant, which walks unperturbed on the turbulent waters. Despite being unrelated to any known literary source, this is far from an isolated motif: it is found on a column capital in Nāsik cave 4 (Figure 2.7), carved twice on the

Figure 2.5. Sanchi, Stūpa 2, ground balustrade, pillar 75b, central medallion. Photograph by the author.

Figure 2.6. Sanchi, Stūpa 2, ground balustrade, pillar 27a, lower panel. Photograph by the author.

Figure 2.7. Nasik, cave 4, pillar capital. Photograph by the author.

Figure 2.8. Sanchi, Stūpa 3, toraṇa lower architrave (back), left end. Photograph by the author.

Figure 2.9. Sanchi, Stūpa 3, toraṇa lower architrave, (back) right end. Photograph by the author.

toraṇa of Sanchi Stūpa 3 (Figures 2.8 and 2.9), on the central architrave of the south *toraṇa* in Sanchi Stūpa 1 (Figure 2.10), and on the east pillar of its north *toraṇa* (Figure 2.11).

The identity of the royal couple (possibly fictional, due to the absence of epigraphic references) was possibly well known in the Sanchi area at the beginning of our era, considering it is the most frequently depicted narrative subject in the reliefs. Even though the specific narrative which inspired the reliefs is as yet unidentified, the flood and rescue motif is reasonably interpreted as a

Figure 2.10. Sanchi, Stūpa 1, south toraṇa central architrave (front), left end. Photograph by the author.

visual metaphor of salvation as a relief from pain, specifically related to water management.

In later Indian dynastic art (from the Gupta era) we find several expressions of this theme, notably in Viṣṇu's *Gajendra Mokṣa,* Viṣṇu as Varāha saving Pṛthvī, or Śiva as *Gangādhara.* As Heinrich von Stietencron remarks, "a myth and its visual representation can gain political actuality and be used to glorify a king or a dynasty" (Stietencron 1986, 18), using the metaphorical character of figurative expression to identify the ruler with the deity in his heroic deeds. The precise choice of myths that exemplify the ambivalent destructive and salvific power of water for life and humankind is explicative of how the ruling class conceived water management and these depictions to magnify their sovereignty. Similarly, the theme might have been utilized by the monastic community to reinforce its prestige in the region, creating parallels between the narratives and the introduction of techniques of water storage, which resulted in moral and physical relief from pain for the population.

It was previously demonstrated how the settlement and spread of Buddhism in the Sanchi area was directly linked with innovation in techniques of water management.[15] The spatial and temporal patterns of habitational settlements in the Vidiśā archaeological landscape – more specifically, monasteries and dams

[15] The building of irrigation embankments (16 in the area) and related reservoirs allowed a shift towards wet-rice cultivation and met the increased food-production demand due to urban growth and the development of the monastic settlement (Shaw 2007, 251).

Figure 2.11. Sanchi, Stūpa 1, north toraṇa east pillar (front), bottom panel. Photograph by the author

– testify to the existence of "exchange networks" between the two communities, with the *saṃgha* motivating the locals to extend their economic support to the monasteries through "practical" models of religious change (Shaw 2007, 252). Although we do not know who was in charge of the choice of the narrative repertoire of Sanchi's monuments (the artists, the donors, or the monks), the fact that the striking majority of donor inscriptions across the whole site mention nuns or monks (Dehejia 1992, 36–7) suggest the outstanding predilection for this motif was due to its role as a practical model of religious change. The metaphorical language of the narrative aimed to focus on the *saṃgha*'s control over water management as both a factual response to increased demand for food, and a spiritual response to the alleviation of *dukkha* (suffering).

Conclusions

This preliminary study, limited to the presentation and tentative interpretation of four narrative reliefs amongst the multitude found on the balustrade of Sanchi Stūpa 2, aims to illustrate the necessity of a drastic shift in our methodological approach towards the chronology and, most importantly, the iconography of the monument. A radical reconsideration of the dating of this *stūpa* as well as of some iconographic and stylistic choices leads to the acknowledgment of a narrative intent in the decorative program as well as a specific visual mode of narration, the *spotlight* mode. As this case shows, and as Strong further demonstrates later in this volume, textual explanations of the content or dating of images are not always correct. Textual evidence should therefore not be privileged over careful studies of iconography and visual modes of narration, such as I have hereby attempted.

A complete reassessment of the "Śunga era" appears necessary, with the detachment of stylistic analysis from the traditional chronology, enabling the advancement of studies on early Buddhist figurative art: a rich, yet potentially untapped, source. Further studies on early Buddhist iconography, taking into account the matter in this fresh perspective, are advisable in order to fully unveil the narrative potential of the panorama of early Buddhist art.

Bibliography

Asher, Frederick M. 2006. "Early Indian Art Reconsidered." In Olivelle, P., ed. *Between The Empires: Society in India 300 BCE to 400 CE* 51–66. New York: Oxford University Press.

Aubayer, Jeannine 1965. *Introduction à l'Étude de l'Art de l'Inde.* Rome: ISMEO.

Barret, Douglas 1954. *Sculptures from Amaravati in the British Museum.* London: The Trustees of the British Museum.

Behl, Benoy K. 1998. *The Ajantā Caves. Ancient Paintings of Buddhist India.* London: Thames-Hudson.

Bénisti Mireille, M. 1986. "Observations concernant le stūpa no.2 de Sānchī." *Bulletin d'études Indiennes* 4: 165–70.

Bhandare, Shailendra 2006 "Numismatic and History: the Maurya-Gupta Interlude in the Gangetic Plan." In Olivelle, P., ed. *Between The Empires: Society in India 300 BCE to 400 CE* 51–66. New York: Oxford University Press.

Biswas, Taran Kumar 1987. *Horse in Early Indian Art.* New Delhi: Munshiram Manoharlal.

Biswas, Sachindrasekhar 1981. *Terracotta Art of Bengal.* Delhi: Agam Kala Prakashan.

Brown, Percy 1942. *Indian Architecture (Buddhist and Hindu Periods).* Bombay: D. P. Taporevala.

Bühler, Georg 1994 [1883]. "Naneghat inscriptions and Kanheri Inscriptions." *Archaeological Survey of Western India vol.V, Report on Elura cave Temples.* Delhi: Burgess.

Chanda, Ramaprasad 1919. "Dates of the Votive Inscriptions on the Stupas at Sanchi." *Memoirs of the Archaeological Survey of India* 1: 7.

Coomaraswamy, Ananda Kentish 1927a. *History of Indian and Indonesian Art.* London: Goldston; Leipzig: Hiersemann; New York: Weyhe.

Coomaraswamy, Ananda Kentish 1927b. "The Origins of the Buddha Image." *The Art Bulletin* 9/4: 287–329.

Coomaraswamy, Ananda Kentish 1935. *La sculpture de Bodhgayā.* Paris: Vanoest Editions d'Art et D'Histoire.

Coomaraswamy, Ananda Kentish 1956. *La sculpture de Bharhut.* Paris: Vanoest Editions d'Art et D'Histoire.

Coomaraswamy, Ananda Kentish 2001 [1971]. *Yaksas.* Munshiram Manoharlal, Delhi 2001 [originally vol.1 1928, vol.2 1931].

Cowell, Edward Byles, ed., various translators 1895–1907. *The Jātaka or Stories of the Buddha's Former Births.* 6 vols. Cambridge: Cambridge University Press.

Cunningham, Alexander 1854. *The Bhilsa Topes, or, Buddhist Monuments in Central India: comprising a brief historical sketch of the rise, progress, and decline of Buddhism; with an account of the opening and examination of the various groups of topes around Bhilsa.* London: Smith, Elder & Co.

Cunningham, Alexander 1879. *The Stûpa of Bharhut: A Buddhist Monument Ornamented with Numerous Sculptures Illustrative of Buddhist Legend and History in Third Century B.C.* London: W.H. Allen and Company.

Dehejia, Vidya 1972. *Early Buddhist Rock Temples.* London: Thames & Hudson.

Dehejia, Vidya 1992. "Collective and Popular Bases of Early Buddhist Patronage: Sacred Monuments, 100 BC – AD 250." In Miller, B.S., ed. *The Power of Art – Patronage in Indian Culture* 35–45. Delhi: Oxford University Press.

Dehejia, Vidya 1991. "Aniconism and the Multivalence of Emblems." *Ars Orientalis* 21: 45–66.

Dehejia, Vidya 1996a. *Unseen Presence: The Buddha and Sāñcī*. Mumbai: Marg Publications.

Dehejia, Vidya 1996b. "Introduction: Sāñcī and the Art of Buddhism." In Dehejia, ed. 1996a: xvi–xxxi.

Dehejia, Vidya 1997. *Discourse in early Buddhist art: visual narratives of India*. Delhi: Munshiram Manoharlal Publishers Pvt. Ltd.

Fergusson, James and James Burgess 1865. *A History of Architecture in all Countries: from the Earliest Times to the Present Day.* London: J. Murray.

Fergusson, James and James Burgess 1876. *History of Indian and Eastern Architecture*. London: J. Murray.

Fergusson, James and James Burgess 1880. *Cave Temples of India.* London: W. H. Allen.

Fergusson, James and James Burgess 1884. *Archaeology in India, with Especial Reference to the Work of Babu Rajendralala Mitra.* London: Lübner.

Gosh, Arabinda 1978. *Remains of the Bharhut Stupa in the Indian Museum*. Calcutta: Indian Museum.

Hallade, Madeleine 1968. *Inde, un Millénaire d'Art Bouddhique: Rencontre de l'Orient et de l'Occident*. Paris: Biblioteque des Arts.

Huntington, Susan L. 1985. *The Art of Ancient India: Buddhist, Hindu, Jain.* Boston: Weather Hill.

Kail, Owen C. 1975. *Buddhist Cave Temples of India*. Bombay: Taraporevala Sons & Co. Private Ltd.

Knox, Robert 1992. *Amaravati – Buddhist Sculpture from the Great Stūpa*. London: British Museum Press.

Kumar, Ajit 2013. *Sculptural Art in Early Buddhist (Hinayana) Caves of Western Maharashtra: A Stylo-chrono Study*. Delhi: New Bharatiya Book Corporation.

Kumar, Ajit 2014. "Bharhut Sculptures and Their Untenable Sunga Association." *Heritage: Journal of multidisciplinary Studies in Archaeology* 2: 223–41.

Lamotte, Étienne 1958. *Histoire du bouddhisme indien: des origines à l'ère Śaka*. Louvain: Publications universitaires, Institut orientaliste.

Maisey, Frederick Charles 1892. *Sanchi and its Remains: a Full Description of the Ancient Buildings, Sculptures and Inscritptions at Sanchi, near Bhilsa, in Central India with Remarks on the Evidence They Supply as to the Comparatively Modern Date of the Buddhism of Gotama, Or Sákya Muni*. London: K. Paul, Trench, Trübner & Co. Limited.

Marshall, John H. 1922. "The Monuments of Ancient India." In Rapson, J.P., ed. *The Cambridge History of India 1* 612–49. Cambridge: Cambridge University Press.

Marshall, John and Alfred Foucher 1940. *The Monuments of Sāñcī.* Calcutta: The Government of India Press.

Milligan, Matthew D. 2014. "Five Unnoticed Donative Inscriptions and the Relative Chronology of Sanchi Stūpa II for the Evaluation of Buddhist Historical Traditions." *Annual Report of The International Research Institute for Advanced Buddhology at Soka University* 18: 11–22.

Milligan, Matthew D. 2016. *Of Rags and Riches: Indian Buddhist Patronage Networks in the Early Historic Period*. Unpublished PhD Thesis: University of Texas at Austin.

Mitra, Debala 1957. *Sanchi*. New Delhi: Archaeological Survey of India.

Mitra, Debala 1960. *Udayagiri and Khandagiri*, New Delhi: Director General of Archaeology in India.

Mitra, Debala 1971. *Buddhist Monuments*, Calcutta: Sahitya Samsad.

Mohapatra, Ramesh Prasad 1981. *Udayagiri and Khandagiri Caves*. Delhi: D.K. Publications.

Nagar, Shantilal L. 1993. *Jātakas in Indian Art*. Delhi: Parimal Publications.

Nagaraju, S. 1981. *Buddhist Architecture of Western India (c. 250 B.C. – c. A.D. 300)*. Delhi: Agam Kala Prakashan.

Niharranjan, Ray 1975. *Maurya and Post-Maurya Art*. New Delhi: Indian Council of Historical Research.

Olivelle, Patrick, ed. 2006. *Between the Empires: Society in India 300 BCE to 400 CE*. New York: Oxford University Press.

Policardi, Chiara 2018. "The case of the *yakṣiṇī* Aśvamukhī: remarks between jātaka and art." *Rivista degli Studi Orientali* XCI: 137–60.

Quintanilla, Sonia Rye 2007. *History of early stone sculpture at Mathura, ca. 150 BCE – 100 CE*. Leiden: Brill

Ray, Niharranjan 1945. *Maurya and Śuṇga Art.* Calcutta: University of Calcutta.

Rowland, Benjamin 1953. *The Art and Architecture of India: Hindu, Buddhist, Jain.* London: Penguin Books.

Sharma, Ramesh Chandra 1994. *Bharhut Sculptures.* Delhi: Abhinav Publications.

Schlingloff, Dieter, Monika Zin, M. Helmdach, M. Higgins and J. Wedow 2003. *A Guide to Ajanta Paintings*. 2 vols. Delhi: Munshiram Manoharlal Publishers.

Schopen, George 1991. "Archaeology and Protestant Presuppositions in the Study of Indian Buddhism." *History of Religions* 31/1: 1–23. https://doi.org/10.1086/463253

Sengupta, Gautam 2007. *Eloquent Earth: Early Terracottas in the State Archaeological Museum of West Bengal*. Kolkata: Directorate of Archaeology and Museum, Government of West Bengal.

Shaw, Julia 2007. *Buddhist Landscapes in Central India: Sāncī Hill and Archaeologies of Religious and Social Change, c. 3rd century BC to 5th century CE*. London: The British Academy.

Shimada, Akira 2013. *Early Buddhist Architecture in context – The Great Stūpa at Amarāvatī (ca. 300 BCE – 300 CE)*. Leiden: Brill.

Sivaravamurti, Calambur 1942. *Amaravati Sculptures in the Madras Government Museum*. Madras: Thompson & Company Pvt. Ltd.

Smith, Vincent Arthur 1911. *A History of Fine Art in India and Ceylon*. Oxford: Clarendon Press.

Srivastava, A. L. 1983. *Life in Sanchi Sculpture*. New Delhi: Hans Raj Gupta & Sons.

Stietencron, Heinrich von. 1986. "Political aspects of Indian Religious Art." *Visible Religion – Annual for Religious Iconography*, IV–V (1985–1986): 16–36.

Taddei, Maurizio 1996. "The First Beginning: Sculptures on Stūpa 2." In Dehejia, ed. 1996a: 74–91.

Author biography

Dr. Flavia Zaghet obtained her PhD in February 2020 in Sapienza University of Rome under the supervisor of Prof Ciro Lo Muzio with a dissertation titled *Sanchi Stūpa 2: A Reassessment of its Context, Dating and Iconographic Repertoire*. Her interests focus on early Indian art and archeology, Buddhist narratives and Buddhist studies in particular. She has also carried out research in India during two fieldwork trips at the archeological sites of early Buddhism such as Sanchi in Madhya Pradesh, Kanheri, Bhaja, Bedsa, Karle, Pithalkora and Nasik in Maharashtra, Udayagiri and Kandagiri in Orissa.

3

The Power of Image and Imagery

Visualizing the Divine and the Human in the Painted Narratives of Ajanta

Madhulika Reddy *

Introduction

> He was like the dharma embodied
> like a sacrificial fire that had been fed with oblations,
> like a lamp placed in a golden vessel,
> like a mountain of gold that moved,
> and like a golden object variegated with many jewels.
> That is to say, they saw the Lord Buddha,
> whose great intellect is expansive and quick,
> spotless and stainless.
> (*Prātihārya-sūtra, Divyāvadāna*, trans. Rotman 2008, 274–5)[1]

And having seen the Buddha, the five hundred sages approached him, paid their respects and expressed their desire to renounce, become monks and live the religious life ordained by the Blessed One.

---

* I would like to thank David Cooper, Susanne Mrozik, Reiko Ohnuma, Andy Rotman, John Strong and Monika Zin for their informed reading of an earlier draft of this chapter, and for their insightful comments. For access to the Ajanta Archive of the Sächsische Akademie der Wissenschaften zu Leipzig, University of Leipzig, I am indebted to Monika Zin. Peter Skilling responded with patience and kindness to a veritable avalanche of requests; I thank him. This chapter is based on a paper I had presented at the symposium "Indian Buddhist Narrative: Text and Image," held in Edinburgh in September 2019. I would like to thank Naomi Appleton for inviting me to participate at the symposium, and for her generous hospitality during my stay in Edinburgh.

[1] For the Sanskrit original, see Cowell and Neil, ed., 1886, 158.

Buddhist art and Buddhist texts are replete with images and imagery conceived to communicate the divine nature of the Buddha and the message of the *dharma*. Using three strands integral to early Buddhist narratives – the oral, the visual and the textual – this chapter will attempt to explore in its multiple dimensions the concept of *avagamanaśakti* – literally, "the capacity to lead [the audience] to comprehension."[2] Each strand is distinct, yet interacts symbiotically with the other. In this chapter I shall attempt to weave them together to demonstrate the power of communicating narratives through a variety of media. My aim is not only to emphasize the value of studying visual, textual and oral narrative together, but also to show how forms of aesthetic contrast achieve strikingly edifying visualizations of the Buddha and his *dharma*. I achieve this through a careful exploration of five visual narratives painted in the caves of Ajanta.

With a pervading presence that incorporates images in the text and images of the mind, conjured up by the visual and the aural, the image – specifically the visual image – enjoys primacy in this study as a source in itself.[3] As Skilling (forthcoming, Foreword, 3) reminds us: the "oldest records of 'early Buddhism'" are the Buddhist monuments themselves. And yet, the image does not stand alone. To be explained and understood in its finer detail, it may need to be compared or correlated with the text in a process that may best be seen as an interactive discourse. Visual narratives of great complexity become entirely "readable" if correlated with a text bearing the same version of the story. Such correlations may indicate a flow of narrative between the two, based on a strong, unbroken oral tradition.

---

[2] The concept of *avagamanaśakti* is debated and preserved in Abhinavagupta's *Abhinavabhāratī*, a commentary on Bharata's *Nāṭyaśāstra*. See Ramakrishnakavi 1926–1964, especially Abhinavagupta's commentary on *Nāṭyaśāstra* VI, prose after v. 33. On the significance of the *Abhinavabhāratī* for understanding the Indian aesthetic tradition, see Gnoli 1956, xiiiff. Abhinava's relevance to the art of Ajanta, which precedes him by several centuries, is underlined by "the universality of the aesthetic experience" elaborated in the *Abhinavabhāratī*, whereby both time and space are eliminated (Gnoli 1956, XXI). Abhinava's *rasa* concepts are particularly relevant for probing the impact of the divine image since they explore the relationship between the aesthetic and the religious experience. This study uses individual *rasa* concepts of Abhinava for their emotive essence and cognitive reach "to lead to comprehension" the recipient of this study.

[3] On the independent nature of the visual image, see for instance Schlingloff (1988, 221–4), Malandra (1993, 181–2), and H. P. Ray (1994–95, 349–55). The painted scenes "can and should be understood *without reading the text*" (Schlingloff 1988, 263; italics added). In fact, the painted narratives may themselves be "read" as artistic texts (Dehejia 1997, 55).

And, indeed, the oral resonates through several early texts.[4] The earliest surviving art to explicitly portray the life of the Buddha alongside the *jātaka* stories is that of Bharhut, whose sculptural representations bear the strong impress of local cults and folk oral traditions that evolved independently of canonical literature.[5] Interestingly, the Chinese pilgrim Faxian was known to have found it difficult to source written texts in the fifth century CE.[6]

In the realm of Buddhist monastic art with which this study is concerned, the oral appears to have been assigned a specific role and function. An episode from the *Divyāvadāna,* a collection of thirty-six *āvadāna*s or stories[7] that constitutes one of the most important sources of visual culture in early Buddhism, illustrates this point: In the *Sahasodgata-avadāna*, the Buddha himself issues instructions that "a competent monk" (*pratibalo bhikṣu*) be appointed to explain to "the Brahmans and householders who would come" the significance of the *saṃsāracakra* represented in the entrance hall of the monastery.[8] If indeed the Buddha's instructions were heeded and monks enlisted as guides, then we have the power of the visual coalescing with the resonance of the oral to provide the visitor an enhanced visual–aural experience. The monk-guide, in effect, would have "empowered" both image and text, enhancing their impact.[9]

---

4 The opening words to the Buddha's discourses "Thus have I heard" (Skt, *evaṃ mayā śrutam*; Pali, *evaṃ me sutam*), attributed to Ānanda, are strong reminders of the place of the oral/aural in early Buddhist literature. On the antiquity and abiding importance of oral transmission in the early Buddhist tradition, see Collins 1992 (especially 125 and 129 on the orality of the *jātaka*s) and Skilling 2011, especially 53, 63.

5 Brancaccio 2005, 47. On the role of folk traditions in the transmission of Buddhist stories and the "entirely new dimension" they lend to early Buddhist art, see Ray (1994–95, 351).

6 Legge 1971, 98.

7 Compiled in the Sanskrit edition by Cowell and Neil (1886), on which the recent translations by Rotman (2008, 2017) are based. More than half the stories in the *Divyāvadāna* have been traced back to the *Mūlasarvāstivāda-vinaya*, whose narrative versions, according to Schlingloff (2013, especially 301–2, 375–6, 449–50), correlate with a number of the fifth-century narrative paintings at Ajanta. Accordingly, this study sees the early visual culture of the *Divyāvadāna* as being of particular relevance to Ajanta.

8 For an insightful discussion of this episode, see Rotman 2009, 54–5, 227–8, n. 57.

9 Dehejia (1997, 210) raises the possibility of painted labels in a cell at the left end of Cave II's verandah in Ajanta having served as cues for monk-guides, while verses from Ārya-Śūra's *Jātakamāla* (Yazdani 1930–55, vol II, *Appendix*, 60–61), together with the images they complemented, provided an aural-visual experience to visitors and resident monks.

The combined efficacy of the textual, the pictorial and the aural represents a synthesis in the power of communicating the word of the Buddha: What we have here is the image that can be "read," the text that can be visualized and the aural that straddles the two to mould – with an enduring resonance – the images of the mind. This paper shall attempt to explore – in the context of Ajanta – the image in the text, the image as text, and the aural in both image and text. The visual image shall form the centrepiece, with a special focus on what I call the "intangibles" – Buddhist ideals, concepts and virtues visualized through images, metaphors and analogies. The importance of virtues in Buddhist narratives is underlined by the Buddha having spent aeons practicing and perfecting the *pāramitā*s (P. *pāramī*s) or perfections, thereby enhancing the significance of "embodied virtue" (Mrozik 2002, 1–33) in the divine image.

Probing the "intangibles" also means probing the possible impact of the visual, the textual and the oral on the viewer, reader or listener. The viewer is a complex entity: her aesthetic judgment is subjective, contingent on the person, her prior knowledge and sensitivity, and engagement with the philosophy of the art she perceives. To reveal the many layers of experience – both cognitive and emotional – that the painted scenes analyzed here could provide, it was necessary to devise a deliberate construct: the initiated, empathetic viewer whose powers of receptivity make her capable of transcending the individual self to reach the highest point in the "religio-aesthetic" experience.[10]

The viewer's communion with the image commences with the process of *darśana* – an intense visual engagement with the image that encompasses both perception and reception. Alongside *darśana,* this study will explore the viewer's *rasa* (taste, flavour, aesthetic experience) as a prime category in probing the efficacy of the image. If *darśana* is the starting point of the mechanism that could arouse emotion and instill *śraddhā* (faith) and *prasāda* (faith, joy etc.), emotion and faith in turn are suffused with *rasa*. Arguably the single most important concept in Indian aesthetics, the theory of *rasa* is inextricably linked with the theory of *dhvani* (the power of suggestion).

Rasa, as applied to this study, is not a set progression of emotional states but, rather, an exploration of possibilities in the many layers of viewer reception and response. Given the highly subjective "intangible" that emotional response involves, it is not the intention of this study to categorize the viewer's emotional experience. Rather, the reconstruction of viewer response is hypothetical, guided by the intent to explore the power of communication vested in the image.

---

[10] Using such a construct to explore subtleties in aesthetic experience is by no means an attempt to project all viewers of these paintings as being highly receptive.

As the title suggests, this study of select narrative images will be based on contrast – contrast in the visualization of the divine and the human,[11] with the physical form (*rūpakāya*) and the dharmic form (*dharmakāya*), primarily of the Buddha but also of the Bodhisattva, embodying the divine against which the human is juxtaposed. With a clear focus on the divine, this paper will see the human assuming form and shape as a counterpoint to the divine. To probe the human–divine contrast, I shall use two concepts that will be woven into the fabric of this study: *laukika-alaukika* (this-worldly/other-worldly, both in terms of tangible physicality and intangible morality, rendered visible through a state of mind or a divine act); and, secondly, *anvaya-vyatireka*, a concept used primarily in logic, rhetoric and poetry (*anvaya* denoting presence or agreement in presence between two things: "where there is smoke, there is fire," and *vyatireka* denoting absence or agreement in absence between two things: "where there is no smoke, there is no fire").[12] The concept of *anvaya-vyatireka* has been applied to Ajanta's narrative paintings[13] not only to highlight contrasting states of mind grounded in contrasting levels of evolution of the human and the divine, but also to bring home the edifying message in the images under study.[14]

Before we examine the images, let me explain why I have chosen Ajanta's paintings over its sculpture for this study. The caves of the monastic complex of Ajanta have whole expanses of painted narratives still preserved – a unique documentation of the art in Ancient India. Painting, as ancient texts such as the *Citrasūtra* and the *Atthasālinī* emphasize, is a highly nuanced and versatile medium offering artistic possibilities that sculpture in the round and relief do not.[15] To illustrate this point, I shall introduce some of the techniques dis-

---

[11] For the purpose of this study, the term "divine" as distinct from "human" shall be defined by the conceptualization of the Buddha and the Bodhisattva – as figures of central importance, bearing the physical and mental attributes of highly evolved beings, or demonstrating acts of perfected virtue that inspire awe and devotion. The term "divine" as used here is set within the context of *darśana*.

[12] The composite term *anvaya-vyatireka* is used when both presence and absence occur side by side, and has been defined by Monier-Williams (1960, 46) as "agreement and contrariety; a positive and negative proposition; ...logical connection and disconnection."

[13] The images examined below are all from the second phase of cave decoration in Ajanta (fifth century CE). Due to space constraints, it was possible to examine only a very small sample of the paintings here.

[14] The concept is also meant to serve as a frame to demonstrate the logical connection between the physical form and the mental state. It seeks to provide a contrasting view beyond the physical.

[15] On the versatile nature of painting, see the *Atthasālinī*, ed. Müller 1897, 64; trans. in Coomaraswamy 1931, 218.

tinctive to painting elaborated in the *Citrasūtra.*[16] They have been used ingeniously in Ajanta, particularly to portray the *alaukika* in the divine.

Visualizing the divine and the human

Manifest in images of the Buddha and the Bodhisattva is a distinct aesthetic, which this paper shall attempt to probe through the category of the divine. The distinct character of such images, often representations of perfected virtue, may reveal itself through characterizations that underline the virtue embodied in them.[17] The question of whether Buddhist art expresses forms of beauty centred on distinct virtues, whether it articulates a distinct perception of the good, needs to be pondered.[18]

Virtues are to be seen in relation to bodies, rather than as qualities *exclusively* cognitive and affective (Mrozik 2002, 3). Bodies, consequently, are the outcome of virtues and vices, the "material effects" of deeds done both in the past and in the present (Mrozik 2002, 5–8). Merit-making activities such as *dāna* (giving, generosity) would thus be key to "create material conditions for future moral agency" (Mrozik 2002, 13) – an aspect of great significance both for the *saṅgha* and the laity.

The figure of the Bodhisattva, protagonist of the *jātaka*s, embodies an ideal of both physical and moral perfection.[19] Like the Buddha, images of *bodhisattva*s demonstrating extraordinary acts of virtue are powerful because they are embodiments of the *dharma*. The images examined below represent such embodiments.

Śibi-jātaka

Narrated in three main episodes on the left wall of the front aisle of Cave I, the climactic scene of the *Śibi-jātaka* (Figure 3.1) serves as a powerful example of the Bodhisattva depicted as an "icon".[20] Another depiction of this ver-

16 Ed. and trans. Sivaramamurti 1978.

17 Kidd (2017a, 2017b), for instance, speaks of the "aesthetics of religious [or spiritual] exemplarity," religious exemplars being those whose perfected virtues have rendered them beautiful.

18 Consider, for instance, the perception of inner beauty in Bodhi (2001, 13).

19 On the principles of ideal proportion or *pramāṇa*, see Sivaramamurti 1978, 167–8, 171–2.

20 The term "icon" is used here in the broad sense of a divine figure conceived for *darśana*. The phenomenon that is *darśana* would be enhanced by the visualization of the Bodhisattva's virtue.

Figure 3.1. *Śibi-jātaka*: the Bodhisattva's bodily gift. Cave I, fifth century CE. Photo: Andreas Stellmacher. Courtesy of the Sächsische Akademie der Wissenschaften zu Leipzig (Saxon Academy of Sciences and Humanities), Ajanta Archive. University of Leipzig.

sion of the *Śibi-jātaka* may be found in Cave II,[21] on the right wall of the front corridor.

The *Śibi-jātaka* is the story of King Śibi's boundless capacity for *dāna*. Known across the worlds for his compassion and generosity, King Śibi is challenged by Indra and the *deva*s. Indra appears before Śibi as a hawk chasing a dove which seeks refuge with Śibi, pleading with him to save it from the hawk. But the hawk too demands justice and its pound of flesh. Śibi, who cannot bring himself to sacrifice any other living being to satiate the hawk's demand, offers the latter as much of his own flesh as equals the weight of the dove. But when the dove outweighs every piece of flesh offered by the Bodhisattva, the latter is faced with the ultimate test of sacrifice involving his very life. What we see here (Figure 3.1) is the dramatic scene that marks the climax of the story, as depicted in Cave I.

---

21 Both the Cave I and Cave II depictions partly correspond with the version in the *Kalpanāmaṇḍitikā* (Schlingloff 2013, 228 and 230).

The Bodhisattva Śibi is portrayed in strikingly large proportions – a technique often used for Bodhisattva figures to emphasize their *lokottara* (supramundane) character, and to draw the viewer's attention to the significance of the divine act. He is on the verge of mounting the pan of a pair of scales, in a demonstrative gesture of sacrificing himself to save the dove. In this palpably dramatic scene – dramatic not merely on account of the nature of the act but, more so, because Śibi's virtue is put to the ultimate test – the Bodhisattva faces anguished members of the court, witnesses to the great act,[22] in a stance that is both frontal and supreme.

Śibi's posture (*sthāna*) is fearless, erect, his look distant and unflinching, indicating perhaps non-attachment towards everything that is worldly. With one leg firmly planted on the ground and the other placed purposefully on the pan of the scales, Śibi has an air of tremendous resolve and detachment. His conspicuously individual placement, the figure towering over those in front of it, appears to send out the message that virtue stands above material wealth, even above life, as expounded in Dhammapāla's commentary on the *Cariyāpiṭaka*, a work dedicated to the Theravāda *pāramī*s or perfections (Bodhi, trans. 1996, 16). The arresting *sthāna* is demonstrative of the act that Śibi is performing, rendered all the more striking through the use of *kṣayavṛddhi* (foreshortening),[23] the right shoulder thrust slightly forward due to the torsion of the body. The figure has a visual power that communicates – most dramatically – the momentousness of the act performed.

The story of Śibi generally has *dāna* associated with it, his tremendous act of bodily *dāna* (*dehadāna* or *adhyātmikadāna*)[24] rendering him *alaukika*. The first of the *pāramitā*s, *dāna* is the only virtue to be invoked by Śākyamuni on the eve of Enlightenment. As a virtue of overriding importance, it was to be pursued by Bodhisattva and layman alike, though at varying levels. The *dāna* in Śibi's case is unique to the Bodhisattva: it is an act involving the gifting of a part of the body – a supreme form of the perfection (*paramārthapāramitā*).[25]

Yet, at the same time, virtues such as *karuṇā* (compassion) and *adhiṣṭhāna* (P. *adhiṭṭhāna*; resoluteness, the eighth of the Theravāda perfections) are also deeply embedded in the Bodhisattva's *dāna*. In Ārya-Śūra's *Jātakamālā,* Śakra is filled with admiration for Śibi's unshakeable resolve, while supernatural beings hail the Bodhisattva's compassion (Khoroche 1989, 15–16). The visual

[22] The courtiers are more than witnesses here: they are actually participants, with a level of involvement more immediate than that of the viewer of the painting.

[23] A technique used to achieve perspective through projection and recession. See Sivaramamurti, 1978, 5–6 and *Citrasūtra* chap. 39, 39–43, trans. in Sivaramamurti 1978, 178–9.

[24] On the layered dimensions of *adhyātmikadāna* and what distinguishes it from *bāhira* (external) *dāna,* see Ohnuma 2007, 173–4.

[25] On the varying levels of practice of the perfections, see Bodhi, trans., 1996, 44.

imprint of *adhiṣṭhāna* in our scene (Figure 3.1) is particularly striking: in his resoluteness, the Bodhisattva holds his body very erect, his gaze firm and unwavering. Śibi's resolve is unshakeable, like a "...mountain, a rock" – an analogy used in the *Jātakanidāna.*[26]

Buddhist texts speak of the power of the religious image and its impact on the viewer. The visualization of "religious exemplars" (Kidd 2017a) in forms conspicuously beautiful appears to have a specific intent: to draw the viewer towards the divine form, inspire reverence and pursuit of the Buddhist path, paving the way for the fulfillment of the soteriological promise held out by such visualizations. "Religious exemplars" are accordingly visualized as sources of attraction and emulation,[27] who lead disciples on to the spiritual path, rendering the aesthetics of religious figures into the "aesthetics of religious exemplarity" (Kidd 2017a, 172–3). Such visual encounters with religious exemplars[28] are thus crucial to moral and spiritual advancement.

Śibi's great act of *dehadāna* (Figure 3.1) has human witnesses displaying a range of reactions to the Bodhisattva's act. The reactions are steeped in *rasa.* The divine attains the stature of the divine through the gaze of the viewer and the *rasa* she experiences; the divine is an object known and therefore felt, for *rasa* is both perception and knowing.[29] The power of the image is therefore best judged through the response of the viewer, in our case, through the original witnesses to the divine act.

The scene shows the Bodhisattva in a posture ideal for *darśana*, the foreshortening used bringing the figure closer to the viewer's gaze and touch. Given the extraordinary nature of the Bodhisattva's act (the determinant or *vibhāva*), the *rasa* experience here transcends the ordinary: it is *alaukika* (other-worldly). The viewer participates in the *alaukika*, which in turn is set in a *laukika* (this-worldly) frame. What we have here is an ingenious double frame: the viewer is witness to the dramatic act through the painted scene; participating and reacting to the same scene are the original witnesses to the act, perceived by our viewer. The *anubhāva*s or emotional responses of the witnesses may serve as cues for the rise of *rasa* in the viewer.[30] For the viewer, the Bodhisattva's self-sacrifice is primarily an emotive experience, one of *saṁvega*

---

[26] *Jātakanidāna*, v. 163: Shaw, trans., 2006, 4.

[27] On the convergence of attraction and emulation, see the Sudhana-Sāradhvaja episode in the *Śikṣāsamuccaya* (36.8–13, cited in Mrozik 2007, 33, 139, n. 59).

[28] "Artistic and material cultures...enable imaginative encounters with Buddhist exemplars." Kidd 2017b, 341.

[29] *Rasa* according to Abhinavagupta is a "special type of knowing." *Locana* 2.4, cited in Dehejia 1996, 63, n. 29.

[30] On the factors leading to the birth of *rasa*, see *Nāṭyaśāstra* VI, prose after v. 33. Trans. in Gnoli 1956, 29.

Figure 3.2. *Śibi-jātaka*: women and *Brahmalokadeva*s witnessing the Bodhisattva's act, detail. Cave I, fifth century CE.
Photo: Andreas Stellmacher. Courtesy of the Sächsische Akademie der Wissenschaften zu Leipzig, Ajanta Archive. University of Leipzig.

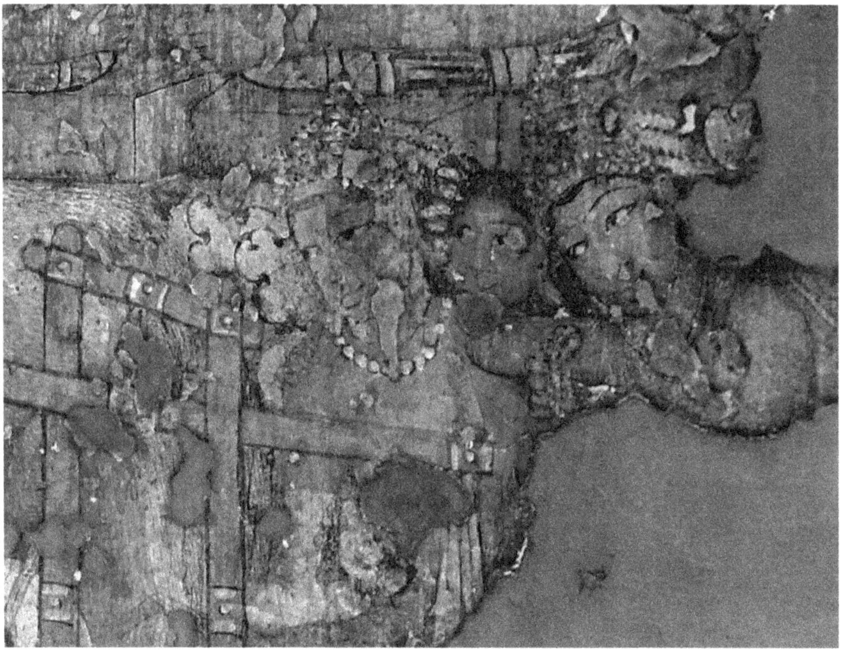

Figure 3.3. *Śibi-jātaka*: *Indralokadevas* witnessing the Bodhisattva's act, detail. Cave I, fifth century CE.
Photo: Andreas Stellmacher. Courtesy of the Sächsische Akademie der Wissenschaften zu Leipzig, Ajanta Archive. University of Leipzig.

– shock at the extreme nature of the act; awe and wonder at the extent of the Bodhisattva's selflessness and the perfected state of his virtue.[31]

The figures witnessing Śibi's dramatic act serve as points of contact between the Bodhisattva and the viewer of the painted scene. In the left foreground are three women in gestures of shock, anguish and lamentation – *anubhāva*s to the Bodhisattva's sacrificial act (Figure 3.2). The reactions (raising of an arm or beating of the breast in shock or grief) are examples of *upacaya* – an intensification of emotion (see Gnoli 1956, 33, n.3). As visual stimulants, the painted witnesses may draw the viewer more deeply into the scene. The viewer then participates alongside the witnesses – both visually and emotionally. The Bodhisattva is thus gazed upon by two sets of viewers: one within the painting and the other without.

The scene has other onlookers too: the *Brahmalokadeva*s immediately above the agitated women, looking down at the Bodhisattva with watchful curiosity and quiet reverence (Figure 3.2); the *deva*s of *Indraloka* at the other end watching intently while Śibi is being put to the ultimate test (Figure 3.3).

[31] On the phenomenon of *saṁvega*, see Coomaraswamy 1946, 200–204.

The use of contrast in the portrayal of the onlookers is conspicuous: the anguished women on the one hand and the serene *devas* on the other.

The scene is a vivid example of the impact that the aesthetic tool of contrast can have: the serene figure of the Bodhisattva, *alaukika* in virtue and act, provides a stark contrast to the agitated members of his royal court (*laukika*). The juxtaposition seems to have a philosophical message to convey: unrest, agitation and anguish are expressions of *duḥkha*. As a divine being, the Bodhisattva has understood the nature of *duḥkha* and transcended it.

Viśvantara-jātaka

In Cave XVII's main hall, extending almost across the entire sweep of the left wall, is a large, detailed composition depicting the *Viśvantara-jātaka.*[32] The most prominent narrations of the *Viśvantara-jātaka* are in the Pali *Jātaka* and Ārya-Śūra's *Jātakamālā.*[33] In Ajanta, the place and prominence given to the *Viśvantara-jātaka* is indicated by its being depicted twice: once in Cave XVI, in the far-right corner of the front aisle and, more elaborately, on the left wall of Cave XVII's main hall, which will be the focus of this study.

The *Viśvantara-jātaka* is the story of Prince Viśvantara, known far and wide for his generosity (*dāna*).[34] But when he incurs the wrath of the people after gifting away a wish-fulfilling state elephant, the Bodhisattva is banished from his father's kingdom. On his way to his forest-exile, accompanied by his wife Madrī and his two children, he demonstrates his generosity once again by first giving away the horses drawing his carriage to a brahmin.

In the scene in Cave XVII that depicts this act (Figure 3.4), the Bodhisattva and his consort Madrī are seen flanked by the object of *dāna*, the horses, with the brahmin facing them. What is interesting here is the pronounced forward lean of the two figures and the skilful use of *kṣayavṛddhi* (foreshortening), making them project outward towards the viewer. Both appear to "tilt into the act," leaning eagerly forward towards the recipient. Would their conspicuous posture be meant to evoke the spirit of *dāna*, which lies in giving freely and

[32] Schlingloff (2013, 202) has identified 25 scenes in all.

[33] For the story in the Pali *Jātaka,* see Cowell, trans., 1895–1907, vol. 6: 246–305; Cone and Gombrich, trans., 1977; Appleton and Shaw, trans., 2015, 534–639. For the *Viśvantara-jātaka* in Ārya-Śūra's *Jātakamālā*, see Khoroche, trans., 1989, 58–73.

[34] *Dāna* is the thread running through the entire story. All the major acts of Viśvantara's *dāna* in Cave XVII have been identified by Foucher (1921: ser 2. pt. 17, cited in Francoeur 1998, 130). Schlingloff (1999, 49–50) has identified six *dāna* scenes.

Figure 3.4. *Viśvantara-jātaka*: gift of the horses. Cave XVII, fifth century CE. Photo: Andreas Stellmacher. Courtesy of the Sächsische Akademie der Wissenschaften zu Leipzig, Ajanta Archive. University of Leipzig.

unrestrainedly?[35] Interestingly, the *Jātakanidāna* uses the following analogy for unrestrained *dāna*: that of a brimming water jar that topples and allows its entire content to flow out freely, with nothing remaining within.[36] The brahmin, in a similar posture, seems to match Viśvantara's inclination towards *dāna* with a corresponding eagerness to accept. However, his eagerness is wholly material, an expression of *upādāna* (clinging, attachment), and therefore in direct contrast to Viśvantara's detachment from all things worldly. The aesthetic contrast between the two sets of figures is an expression of the contrasting philosophical motifs they embody; it is a visualization of *anvaya-vyatireka*.

A scene from the *Viśvantara-jātaka* in Cave XVII is a striking example of the phenomenon that is *darśana*, and the *śraddhā* and *prasāda* it evokes in the witnesses to the scene.[37] On the left wall of Cave XVII's central hall, be-

[35] On the possible linkage between virtues and body postures, see Mrozik 2002, 2.

[36] *Jātakanidāna*, vv. 128–9, trans. Shaw 2006, 2.

[37] *Śraddhā* and *prasāda* (both commonly rendered as "faith" or "belief") are requisites for spiritual advancement and fundamental to studying viewer impact. For a detailed discussion see Rotman 2009, part I and part II.

Figure 3.5. *Viśvantara-jātaka*: the Bodhisattva's chariot procession. Cave XVII, fifth century CE.
Photo: Griffiths, I.O., vol. 73, no. 6083 [3775]. Courtesy of the Sächsische Akademie der Wissenschaften zu Leipzig, Ajanta Archive. University of Leipzig.

tween the second and third cell door, Prince Viśvantara and his consort Madrī are seen driving through the city's main thoroughfare in a horse-drawn chariot (Figure 3.5).[38] The Bodhisattva is being paraded through the city in the manner of a temple deity, his placement atop the chariot most conducive to adoration. His figure is riveting because of the power of the *pāramitā* he embodies: we know from Ārya-Śūra's *Jātakamālā* that the Bodhisattva, generous and compassionate, fought the distress of his people "with a shower of arrows in the form of gifts from his broad bow of compassion."[39]

The Bodhisattva is a *prāsādika* object, one who arouses *prasāda*, both in the witness to the procession and in the viewer of the painting.[40] The *darśana*

[38] The placement of this scene at eye level has maximum impact from the ambulatory passage, an indication perhaps of the significance attached to this scene.

[39] Khoroche 1989, 59.

[40] In the *Divyāvadāna, prasāda* generally arises through a visual medium which is *prāsādika* or "worthy of being seen" (*prāsādikaṃpradarśanīyam*), most importantly objects that embody and represent the *dharma.* See Rotman 2009, 67 and 232, n. 20.

of the Bodhisattva triggers in the onlookers visible *anubhāvas*: one of them, standing on the street just in front of the chariot, is looking up in awe and raising his arm in salutation, while immediately above him, the figure in the pavilion on the extreme left is acknowledging the Bodhisattva's appearance by raising his arms above his head in a gesture of deep adoration reserved for divine figures.[41] The gestures of obeisance and the devout gaze are evocative of the devotee's experience of the divine, and of the mental state of *prasāda.* The veneration brings to mind the description of the Bodhisattva in Ārya-Śūra's *Jātakamālā* 10: "...he appeared like the embodied Dharma" (Speyer, trans. 1895, 94). Like the dramatic scene of Śibi's *dāna*, this scene too has a "double-framed" perspective: the first set of onlookers, the immediate witnesses to the scene, express emotions that may well trigger similar responses in the second set of onlookers, viewing the painted scene. A monastic cult described in the *Mūlasarvāstivāda-vinaya* provides an evocative parallel: there, the image of the Bodhisattva Siddhārtha is taken out in procession through whole towns (Schopen 2005, 299–300). Would the painted scene of Viśvantara and Madrī driving through the city have triggered in the lay viewer images of the Siddhārtha-cult procession?

The oral/aural in image and text

In the introduction to this chapter, I spoke of the oral or aural as having a distinct place in both text and image. The confluence of the visual and the aural represents a mode of communication at once distinct and powerful. A single image from the *Vidhurapaṇḍita-jātaka* (Figure 3.6) is presented here as a particularly striking example of the power of the oral/aural, enhanced by the power of the visual.

Depicted in Cave II across a large expanse of the right wall, the *Vidhurapaṇḍita-jātaka* has been conceived as a monumental narrative in fourteen scenes, extending from floor to ceiling (Schlingloff 2013, 165–8). *Prajñā* (P. *paññā*; wisdom), a perfection both in the Theravāda and Mahāyāna traditions, has an abiding presence throughout the story, infusing the narrative with a distinctive quality. The Bodhisattva Vidhura, minister of the Kuru kings, was much sought after for his wisdom. The *nāga* queen Vimalā yearns to hear him speak, whereupon the *nāga* king has Vidhura brought to his kingdom after winning him in a game of dice. There, Vidhura delivers a sermon on the

[41] The celebrated artist Gulam Muhammed Sheikh (1983, 14) observes: "The figures speak as much (or more) with their bodies as with their heads."

dharma to the royal *nāga* couple and members of their family, demonstrating his perfected state of wisdom.[42]

It is with this wisdom that Vidhura cuts through all doubts "like an ivory worker cuts the tooth of an elephant with a saw," says the Pali *Jātaka* (Appleton and Shaw, trans. 2015, 463). With his sweet sermons, he holds in thrall the one hundred kings of Jambudīpa, just like "rutting elephants that have been seduced by the sound of the elephant-pleasing lute" (Appleton and Shaw 2015, 459). Vidhura's listeners long to hear his words much before they actually hear him speak: It is the *nāga* queen Vimalā's longing for Vidhura's discourse on the *dharma* that sets the entire narrative in motion.

The sermon is a sensory experience that is both aural and visual; the longing to hear the Bodhisattva preach goes with the longing to see his physical form. Thus the vast assembly gathered to hear Vidhura discourse was "filled with joy, beholding the seer after he had come" (Cowell 1895–1907, vol. 6, 155). Similarly, when Vidhura was brought to her, the *nāga* queen Vimalā, on seeing him, addressed him "with her whole soul full of delight" (Cowell 1895–1907, vol. 6, 152).

Visual and aural imagery in the *jātaka*s anticipate the longing for the sermon: The Buddha once gives a sermon on the *dharma* while staying at Jetavana, his body effulgent, his face, gazed upon by the assembled lay-disciples, as resplendent as the full moon (*puṇṇacandasassirīkaṃmukhaṃ*). And when he opens his lotus of a mouth, it is like the opening of a jewelled casket filled with fragrances of all kinds (*nānāgandhapūritaṃratanakaraṇḍakaṃ*).[43] His voice is like the roar of a young lion or a thundering monsoon cloud, his sermon pleasing, like a garland of knotted jewels.[44]

The image from the *Vidhurapaṇḍita-jātaka* (Figure 3.6) shows the Bodhisattva Vidhura instructing the *nāga* king Varuṇa, his consort Vimalā and daughter Irandatī in the *dharma*. Seated to the (viewer's) left of Vidhura is the *yakṣa* Puṇṇaka. The *nāga*s, their gaze directed at the Bodhisattva, are immersed in *śruta* (the act of listening), the very foundation for acquiring *prajñā*, while Puṇṇaka, who had benefitted from an earlier *dharma*-sermon by Vidhura, has turned his gaze upward, perhaps in a state of reflection (*cintāmayī*)?[45]

---

[42] *Vidhurapaṇḍita-jātaka*, trans. Appleton and Shaw 2015, 455–505.

[43] *Apaṇṇaka-jātaka,* Fausbøll, ed., 1877–1896, vol. 1, 96. Trans. Shaw 2006, 12.

[44] *Apaṇṇaka-jātaka*. Trans. Shaw 2006, 11–12.

[45] The *Mahāyāna-sūtrālaṅkāra* (XVIII, 43–4, cited in Meadows 1986, 148; see also 252–3, vv.47–50) speaks of three kinds of *prajñā*: *śrutamayīprajñā* – wisdom or knowledge gained by listening to a discourse; *cintāmayīprajñā* – wisdom gained through reflection; and *cintanabhāvanā* – wisdom gained through cultivation and realization.

Figure 3.6. *Vidhurapaṇḍita-jātaka*: the sermon scene. Cave II, fifth century CE. Photo: Andreas Stellmacher. Courtesy of the Sächsische Akademie der Wissenschaften zu Leipzig, Ajanta Archive. University of Leipzig.

The Bodhisattva and his listeners are seated in a pillared pavilion, the intimacy of the enclosed space binding the group into a close-knit circle.The sermon scene represents a symbiotic relationship between preacher and listener: it involves the imparting of *prajñā* by the Bodhisattva, and the imbibing of *prajñā* by the *śrāvakas* or "*dharma*-hearers."[46] Vidhura imparts the truth, and the *nāga*s receive it.

As the preacher of the *dharma*, Vidhura forms the focal point of the sermon scene and the object of *darśana*. His central position, with his audience turned reverentially towards him, is further accentuated by the prominent *dharmacakramudrā* which appears to be extended outward towards his audience. The Bodhisattva's *mudrā* serves as a cue to help the viewer "read" the scene. It is a symbol of *dharma*, of *dharma-dāna*. Vidhura's frame is angled to partially face the viewer – a skilful use of *kṣayavṛddhi* not only to draw

46 The term *śrāvaka* is used here in a broad sense to denote all those who accept the Buddha as their teacher – both *bhikṣus*/*bhikṣunis* and *upāsakas*/*upāsikās*. As a preacher of the *dharma*, the Bodhisattva represents the Buddha as teacher. See Bodhi's introduction to Nyanaponika and Hecker 2003, 3.

him closer to the viewer, but also direct the latter's gaze instantly to the divine preacher. The *ujjotana* (highlights) on his face suggests *prajñā*, while the subtle play of *aujjvalya* (light) and *chhāyā* (shadow) produces an inner radiance that marks him out as a divine being.[47] The figure has the volume and plasticity of a sculpture.

The preaching Bodhisattva is a *prāsādika* object; his *nāga-śrāvaka*s derive *prasāda* both from *śruta* as well as *darśana*: they not only *hear* the wisdom dispensed by the Bodhisattva but also *see* his physical form directly in front of them. Grouped together, the three *nāga*s exude an air of devout submission, even supplication, towards the wise Vidhura; their grouping magnifies the impact threefold. The foreshortening used accentuates the forward lean of their torsos, expressing not only extreme attentiveness – an important prerequisite for *śrutamayīprajñā* (see Meadows 1986, 252–3, v. 47) – but also a sense of "spiritual urgency," *saṁvega*, an eagerness to imbibe which is an integral part of the quest for *prajñā*.[48]

The Vidhura sermon scene is a brilliant visualization of both *prasāda* and *bhakti*,[49] states of mind aroused by the divine, enabling the listener to develop trust and conviction in the word of the Buddha (*abhisaṃpratyaya*).[50] What we see here is a visualization of the experience of *rasa*, in this case, a spiritual experience that involves listening to and contemplating the *dharma*: it is *dharmarasa* (P. *dhammarasa*).[51] The *śrāvaka* experiences spiritual delight by transcending the personal (*laukika*) to enter the universal (*alaukika*).[52] In our sermon scene, the *nāga-śrāvaka*s appear to identify wholeheartedly with what they see and hear. Their *rasa* is grounded in *hṛdayasaṃvāda* ("sympathetic response")[53] – testimony to the power and resonance of the Bodhisattva's sermon.

The aesthetic tools used to portray the *nāga*s are similar to those employed for the Bodhisattva. The use of *ujjotana* is conspicuous, for the function of

---

47 On *aujjvalya* and *chhāyā*, see *Citrasūtra*, trans. Sivaramamurti 1978, 47, 57–8, 125–6. On *ujjotana*, a term used in the *Atthasālinī*, see Coomaraswamy 1931, 218.

48 On this connotation of *saṁvega*, see Bodhi 1996, 6.

49 *Bhakti* as used here denotes an emotional state of devotion and not the state of total surrender to the divine.

50 On *abhisaṃpratyaya*, see Rotman 2009, 146.

51 See for instance the *Majjhima-nikāya* (trans. Horner 1954–59, 35ff), where *dhammarasa* denotes the taste and flavor of the *dhamma*.

52 For Abhinavagupta, this process (called *sādhāraṇīkaraṇa* or "generalisation") is a requisite for aesthetic experience (Gnoli 1956, 50–51). See also Thampi 1965, 78 and 80, n.11.

53 On the repeated occurrence of *hṛdayasaṃvāda* in the *Abhinavabhāratī* and its rendering as "sympathetic response," see Masson and Patwardhan, 1969, 49.

wisdom is to penetrate[54] and illuminate. As seekers of *prajñā*, the *nāga*s are fully engrossed in *śruta*; this is strikingly visible on the *nāga* king's face.[55]

The *Vidhurapaṇḍita-jātaka* sermon scene is a graphic visualization of the power of *śruta*, honed to receive that greatest of all gifts: *dharma-dāna*.[56] But it is not only the image that visualizes the power of the aural. Early Buddhist texts, as we know, reverberate with passages composed for *śruta*. The *gāthā*s of the *jātaka*s resonate with the power of the aural embedded in the text.[57] With their compelling rhythm and intensity, these *gāthā*s served as a powerful medium to communicate the word of the Buddha.

Divine images and images of the mind: The Buddha and his dharma in image and text

On the left wall of the main hall of Cave XVI is a sequence of twelve painted scenes illustrating the story of the conversion of Nanda. Schlingloff (2013, 415ff) has identified the version in Aśvaghoṣa's *Saundarananda* as largely corresponding with the Cave XVI depiction.[58]

The best known, and certainly most poignant, of the scenes is that of Sundarī swooning in shock and grief at the sight of her husband Nanda's crown, produced as proof of Nanda having been initiated into monkhood by the Buddha (Figure 3.7). Strewn across ten scenes painted along the wall to its right are a series of serene Buddha figures, their rhythmic recurrence carrying the *dhvani* of the *dharma* across the expanse of the narrative (Figure 3.8).[59] Asceticism, the physical attribute of the perfection of renunciation (P. *nekkhamma*; Skt *naiṣkramya*), the third perfection on the Theravāda list, marks the Buddha's divine frame. Each of his ascetic attributes is a symbol of his virtue. The white-robed figures of detached bearing – at least six images of the Buddha from different episodes in the narrative are identifiable[60] – provide a vivid

54 "...like the penetration of an arrow." See Bodhi 1996, 6.

55 On the virtue of imbibing to the fullest extent, see the *Pāramitāsamāsa* (6.50; Meadows 1986, 252–3), a later text consulted here for the deep insights it offers into the *pāramitā*s.

56 *Dhammapada* v. 354: Thanissaro, trans. 1998, 116.

57 A particularly resonant example would be verses 25–119 of the *Mahājanaka-jātaka*. Trans. Appleton and Shaw 2015, 101–107. The *Mahājanaka-jātaka* has been depicted on the left wall of Cave I at Ajanta.

58 This correspondence rests largely on visual and literary portrayals of the grieving Sundarī.

59 "Only the Right Law is precious." *Buddhacarita* XII.33: Willemen, trans. 2009, 160.

60 Schlingloff 2013, 417–19.

Figure 3.7. Sundarī. Conversion of Nanda. Cave XVI, fifth century CE. Photo: Andreas Stellmacher. Courtesy of the Sächsische Akademie der Wissenschaften zu Leipzig, Ajanta Archive. University of Leipzig.

counterpoint to Sundarī's state of anguish: the *alaukika* in the Buddha figures is approached and understood through the *laukika* in Sundarī and Nanda (whose anguish we will witness below).

The grieving Sundarī is depicted in a royal pavilion in which she is being ministered to by her attendants (Figure 3.7). In her moment of sorrow at losing her beloved Nanda, she slumps forward as though on the verge of losing consciousness. Canto 6 (*bhāryāvilāpaḥ*, The Wife's Lament) of Aśvaghoṣa's *Saundarananda* describes in vivid detail the depth of Sundarī's grief: it burned like a fire in the depths of her heart and she seemed to be losing her mind (*Saundarananda* 6:33). She cried aloud, wilted, screamed, fainted... (6:24, 6:25, 6:32, 6:34). In a poetic description that comes close to the painted scene, Sundarī enters a realm of intense darkness to then sink deep, as if into a mire (6:32). Delicate imagery traces her state of anguish: Shorn of her ornaments, she drooped, like a creeper whose blossoms had scattered (6:28); her face was like a pale moon in an early-winter sky (6:9); she was like a lotus-garland left to wither in the sun (6:26).[61]

[61] Canto 6, *Saundarananda*, ed. Johnston 1928, 37–40.

Figure 3.8. Standing Buddha figures. Conversion of Nanda. Cave XVI, fifth century CE.
Photo: Andreas Stellmacher. Courtesy of the Sächsische Akademie der Wissenschaften zu Leipzig, Ajanta Archive. University of Leipzig.

In a compositional programme of erect figures, either seated or standing (like the Buddha images in Figure 3.8), this depiction of a reclining female figure is arresting. Soft and vulnerable, Sundarī's figure displays no angularity whatsoever; its contours are free-flowing like the outpouring of her grief. Sundarī's portrayal throws into stark relief an all-too-human emotion immediately recognizable as a manifestation of *duḥkha.*[62] Her *duḥkha* is born of *upādāna* (clinging), which in turn arises from her craving or desire (*tṛṣṇā*).[63] Her debilitating state is a powerful visual reminder of the necessity of freeing oneself from *tṛṣṇā* to achieve *duḥkha-nirodha* (cessation of suffering). An

[62] For definitions of sorrow that correspond with Sundarī's state, see the *Majjhima-nikāya* (*sutta* 141, sections 14 and 17; trans. Ñāṇamoli and Bodhi 1995, 1098–1100). I wish to draw a distinction here between sorrow visualized as an emotion (to which the viewer of the painting is immediately receptive) and the overarching condition of *duḥkha* as conceptualized in Buddhism. I thank David Cooper for drawing my attention to this subtle distinction.

[63] On the need to overcome *tṛṣṇā* (P. *taṇhā*) as the root cause of suffering, see the *Saṃyutta-nikāya* (1.63: Ireland, trans.1981, 3) and the *Majjhima-nikāya* (*sutta* 141, sections 20–21, trans. in Ñāṇamoli and Bodhi 1995, 1099).

interesting corollary to Sundarī's intense grief, born of her craving, is Nanda's craving for the wife he was forced to abandon. When in his yearning for Sundarī Nanda draws her picture on a rock, the Buddha censures the act as folly, forbidding his *bhikṣus* from making pictures.[64] The case is revealing: it indicates the early *saṅgha*'s awareness of the power of the visual over the senses and the mind – reason enough for the Buddha to initially ban all paintings of human figures in monasteries.[65]

Indeed, the impact of the slumped, grieving Sundarī is powerful; it suffuses the viewer with *karuṇārasa.*[66] In feeling *karuṇā*, the viewer may take her cue from Sundarī's attendants, who are seen attending on her with deep concern, their *anubhāvas* triggered by Sundarī's grief.

But it is in the contrast provided by the erect, serene Buddha figures (Figure 3.8), in the scenes to the right of Sundarī, that the latter "comes into her own" and has the greatest impact. The juxtaposition is a striking example of *anvaya-vyatireka*. In the context of the Nanda-Sundarī narrative, the states of "agreement in presence" (*anvaya*) and "agreement in absence" (*vyatireka*) may be illustrated using the following equation: where there is *tṛṣṇā*, there is *duḥkha* (*anvaya* – as in the case of both Sundarī and Nanda) and where there is no *tṛṣṇā*, there is no *duḥkha* (*vyatireka* – as in the case of the multiple Buddha figures). To Sundarī's *duḥkha,* the Buddha responds with his *duḥkha-nirodha*; to the fetters of *tṛṣṇā* that bind her to her sorrowful state,[67] the Buddha responds with his flawless *vairagya* (detachment, dispassion); to her abject submission to *saṃsāra* and the *duḥkha* it entails, the Buddha responds with his *samyag-dṛṣṭi* (P. *sammā-diṭṭhi*; 'right view').[68] In perceiving the *laukika* first and then resting her gaze and mind on the *alaukika*, the viewer may undergo *parāvṛtti* (transformation).[69] The experience is deeply edifying.

The contrast between *duḥkha* and *duḥkha-nirodha*, among the most powerful messages of the *dharma*, is strikingly visualized in a scene where Nanda is being tonsured prior to his initiation into monkhood (Figure 3.9). The serene-faced, nimbus-bearing *bhikṣu* facing Nanda[70] is evocative of the ideal monk

---

64 T 1451, *Mūlasarvāstivāda-vinaya*, cited in Soper 1950, 148, n. 9.

65 *Cullavagga* 6.3.2: Horner, trans. 1963, 213.

66 This universal capacity to feel compassion echoes the *karuṇā* of the *buddhas* and the *bodhisattvas*, though at the *laukika* level.

67 "Thicket of desire" is the imagery used in the *Mahājanaka-jātaka*, v. 23; trans. Appleton and Shaw 2015, 100.

68 On *sammā-diṭṭhi* being knowledge of *dukkha* and the Four Noble Truths, see the *Majjhima-nikāya* (141, section 24, trans. Ñāṇamoli and Bodhi 1995, 1100).

69 On the phenomenon of *parāvṛtti* in Asaṅga's *Mahāyāna Sūtrālaṅkāra*, see Coomaraswamy 1933, 232.

70 Zin (2003, 109) suggests that the *bhikṣu* bearing *lakṣaṇas* generally reserved for the Buddha may be Ānanda.

Figure 3.9. Nanda's initiation. Cave XVI, fifth century CE.
Photo: Andreas Stellmacher. Courtesy of the Sächsische Akademie der Wissenschaften zu Leipzig, Ajanta Archive. University of Leipzig.

whose attributes are described in the *Majjhima-nikāya* as: one who strives to develop a serene mind and is detached from the worldly.[71] A trope used in the *Divyāvadāna* describes monks freshly ordained by the Buddha as acquiring "tranquility of the senses."[72] Above all, an ideal *bhikṣu* must free his mind of all taints by not clinging – thus spoke the Buddha.[73]

The state of *duḥkha* as opposed to *duḥkha-nirodha* is carried forward to the scene to the right of the serene-faced *bhikṣu*, where an anguished Nanda sits holding his face in his palm (Figure 3.9, extreme right). The visualization of the folly of staying fettered to worldly existence is powerful; even more so is the wisdom in the words of the Buddha:

> I am a victim of suffering, a prey of suffering.
> Surely an ending of this whole mass of suffering can be known?[74]

---

71 *Majjhima-nikāya, sutta* 32, sections 4–7, trans. Ñaṇamoli and Bodhi 1995, 308–9.
72 See, for instance, the *Pūrṇāvadāna*: Rotman, trans. 2008,106.
73 *Majjhima-nikāya* 32, section 17, trans. Ñaṇamoli and Bodhi 1995, 312.
74 *Majjhima-nikāya* 68, section 5, trans. Ñāṇamoli and Bodhi 1995, 567.

This end to all suffering, the point of culmination on the Eightfold Path, reaches a dramatic climax in the episode of Māravijaya – perhaps the most defining event in the life of Gautama Buddha. Poised on the threshold of Enlightenment, the Bodhisattva faces his ultimate test when he is challenged by Māra, King of the Sensual World (*kāmadhātu-rāja*), Tempter (*pramattabandhu*), the Evil One (*pāpiyān*).

The painted scene reproduced here (Figure 3.10) is from the antechamber of Cave I at Ajanta. Seated calm and unperturbed under the *bodhi* tree, surrounded by Māra's wild hosts "like a lion king ... among the herd of animals" (*Buddhacarita* XIII.38: Willemen, trans. 2009, 96), the Bodhisattva is the focal point of the many-figured scene. As the repository of the *dharma*, the Bodhisattva is likened to "the great tree of wisdom," whose fruit is "the unsurpassed Law" (*Buddhacarita* XIII.60: Willemen, trans. 2009, 97) – imagery whose sanctity is underlined by the centrality of the Bodhisattva figure, for he is the Buddha-to-be.

The Bodhisattva of the Māravijaya scene is *alaukika* in nature and looms over the lesser beings around: flanking him is Māra, with his seductive daughters immediately beneath the Buddha-to-be, while to their left, beneath the Bodhisattva's hand in *bhūmisparśamudrā*, is the figure of the Earth-goddess testifying to his virtue. The Bodhisattva is visibly in *dhyāna*, which is intimately woven into the state of concentration, *samādhi.* His fearlessness at the ferocious assault, his state of dispassionate equilibrium (*upekṣā*) appears to be echoed in the perfect balance of his seated figure.[75] In his preparedness for Buddhahood, the Bodhisattva is divine.

His divine nature makes him a solitary figure, the rigours of the solitude he has embraced reflected in the resolute manner he bears and the quietude he has established himself in.[76] His is "the quietude of the *muni*..."[77] The *Majjhima-nikāya* talks of his embracing solitude after conquering desire, acquiring a peaceful mind, and establishing himself in mindfulness (P. *sati*; Skt *smṛti*).[78] Even in his moment of victory over Māra, the Bodhisattva's face is devoid of all emotion. Impervious to the assault mounted on him, he is still, tranquil,[79] his attention turned entirely inward. His inward gaze is steady like the "eyes

---

75 On the Buddha abiding in *upekkhā* (Skt *upekṣā*), never allowing any hatred to rise in him, see *Majjhima-nikāya,* 12, section 51, trans. Ñaṇamoli and Bodhi 1995, 175.

76 *Buddhacarita* XIII.38: Willemen, trans. 2009, 96. Compare the Bodhisattva Sumedha's retreat into solitude to reflect on the virtues he has resolved to perfect to attain Buddhahood (*Buddhavaṃsa* and *Cariyāpiṭaka*, trans. Horner 1975, 19–23, vv. 116–66).

77 *Buddhacarita,* XIII.10: Willemen, trans. 2009, 94.

78 *Bhayabherava-sutta* (*Majjhima-nikāya* 4): Ñaṇamoli and Bodhi, trans. 1995,103–4.

79 *Buddhacarita* XIII.66, XIV.1: Willemen, trans. 2009, 98–9.

Figure 3.10. Māravijaya. Cave I, fifth century CE.
Photo: Andreas Stellmacher. Courtesy of the Sächsische Akademie der Wissenschaften zu Leipzig, Ajanta Archive. University of Leipzig.

of an ox king,"[80] fixed, unwinking and turned on a point beyond the realm of the *laukika* – for he is *lokottara*. "He was like an ocean but calm, like a cloud but full of water...like a mighty elephant..."[81]

With his supremely controlled mind, the Buddha-to-be is a striking contrast to the agitated beings around: an explicit case of *anvaya-vyatireka*. Still and passionless, he sits alone – an edifying counterpoint to the frenzied aggression of Māra's hosts and the seductive wiles of his daughters. In his divine state, he is free of anger towards his attackers, and free of desire for his seducers.[82] If Māra is the wielder of poisoned arrows,[83] the Buddha-to-be is the bestower of peace. Subtly visible on his face are two contrasting qualities: he is at once

80 *Buddhacarita* XIV.77: Willemen, trans. 2009, 105.

81 *Prātihārya-sūtra*, *Divyāvadāna*: Rotman, trans. 2008, 261.

82 *Buddhacarita*, XIII.36: Willemen, trans. 2009, 96. In the *Buddhacarita* (XXII.21; Willemen, trans.2009, 159), the Buddha warns his *bhikṣus* against being ensnared by women. "Even painted images [of women] reveal their seductive appearance." *Buddhacarita* XXII.19: Willemen, trans. 2009, 158).

83 *Buddhacarita*, XIII. 15–20: Willemen, trans. 2009, 94.

dispassionate and compassionate towards all beings. A veil of sadness, soft and diffused, marks the countenance of the Buddha-to-be.[84]

But the quality that defines the figure of the Bodhisattva and imprints itself on the viewer's mind is *śāntarasa* – the *rasa* of Enlightenment, a state of tranquility achieved in the pursuit of Buddhahood. *Śānta* is the stillest of *rasas*, its stillness powerfully evoked in the figure of the serene Buddha-to-be. For Abhinavagupta, the great tenth/eleventh-century aesthetician (*ālaṃkārika*), the god of *śānta is* the Buddha.[85]

And therein lies the power of the Buddha image.[86] The Buddha-to-be in *śānta* embodies a state of mind intrinsic to the Buddha, its visual power moulding that which is fundamental to aesthetic experience: *mānasapratyakṣa* or the perception of the mind.[87]

Conclusions

In exploring image and imagery in narratives centred on the divine, this study of select painted narratives from Ajanta has attempted to reveal the complex interplay of narrative media and the possible interlinkages between them. The role of the oral narrative and its probable flow – as an enduring medium – into both the textual and the visual needs to be pondered; in drawing a distinction between the oral and the written, I take a different approach to that of Appleton in Chapter 1, whose conflation of these under the single category of "verbal" narrative, potentially obscures the symbiotic relationship between oral, textual and visual forms. Imagery in Buddhist texts may find pictorial echoes in visual representations; visual representations may find metaphorical echoes in texts, both mutually enriching each other while presumably drawing from an older oral tradition.

---

[84] The sadness may be born of the realization that suffering is intrinsic to the cycle of life and death. *Buddhacarita*, XIV.32: Willemen, trans. 2009, 101.

[85] *Abhinavabhāratī* VI.44, vol. 1, quoted in Masson and Patwardhan 1969, 139, n.2. The timeless relevance of Abhinava's aesthetics, and its significance for understanding Buddhist aesthetics, is visually reinforced by this fifth-century image of the Buddha-to-be in *śānta*.

[86] On the power of the Buddha to move, see for instance the use of the term *anubhāva* in the *Divyāvadāna* (*Pūrṇāvadāna*). Rotman (2008, 412–13, n. 347) renders the term as the "effects of power," "innate power" or just "power." On the "morally persuasive power" of the bodies of monastics, *arhat*s, and *buddha*s, see Mrozik 2002, 23. Cf. also Strong 1995, 50.

[87] On aesthetic experience being a form of *mānasapratyakṣa,* see Gnoli 1956, 38, n. 2.

The primacy of the visual as a sensory experience has been underlined in this chapter. Early Buddhist texts provide ample evidence of monastic recognition of the power of the visual and its impact on the mind, particularly illustrative examples being the episodes of the Elder (*thera*) Cittagutta (*Visuddhimagga, Sīlaniddeso* 105),[88] the nun Kala (*Sarvāstivāda-vinaya*)[89] and the unwilling convert Nanda (*Mūlasarvāstivāda-vinaya*).[90] Was the visual image perceived as an imperative to engender and reinforce faith, bringing potency to the encounter with the divine?[91]

This study maintains a clear focus on the viewer of the paintings – as the recipient of the art and perhaps the most crucial variable in the monastics' scheme of things. The viewer's encounter with the religious exemplar and the possible emotional impact of the *darśana* of the divine constitute significant aspects of this study. Of particular relevance to the viewer of the divine image, conceived to inspire faith, is the soteriological promise held out by the cultivation of faith through *darśana*.[92] To fulfil this promise, the divine in his *alaukika* form had to be clearly defined – in the case of Ajanta's narrative paintings, this is achieved through the ingenious use of aesthetic tools of visualization, conceived for the painted image and elaborated in the *Citrasūtra*. The study also uses the approach of contrast in juxtaposition to examine the distinct physical and moral character of divine bodies vis-à-vis their human counterparts. The emotional responses of human witnesses to divine acts of virtue, visualized in the painted image and explored in this paper through the aesthetic frame of *rasa*, appear to have been conceived to trigger similar responses in the viewer of the paintings, thereby planting the roots of virtue (*kuśalamūla*) for that transformative state that is *prasāda*[93]– a state of mind that engenders acts of merit, most crucially *dāna* to the *saṅgha* (Mrozik 2002, 16; Schopen 2004, 19–37).

Bodies are not "morally neutral" in Buddhist texts (or for that matter in Buddhist art). Rather, they are the outcome of virtues and vices of past lives

---

[88] Cited in Dutt 1988, 199, n.1.

[89] T 1435; cited in Soper 1950, 147, n. 1.

[90] T 1451; cited in Soper 1950, 148, n. 9.

[91] Consider the yearning of the monks Vakkali (*Vakkalisutta* 87, *Saṃyutta-nikāya*, trans. Bodhi 2000, 938–41), Koṭikarṇa (*Divyāvadāna*; trans. Rotman 2008, 62ff) and Upagupta (*Aśoka-avadāna*, trans. Strong 1989, 185–98; discussed in Rotman 2009, 168–75) to see the physical form of the Buddha, and the faith engendered in them on seeing the Buddha's image. The *Aśokavarṇa-avadāna* (*Divyāvadāna*, trans. Rotman 2008, 244–5) is another powerful narrative of faith instantly aroused by the *darśana* of the Buddha.

[92] See, for instance, the *Stutibrāhmaṇa-avadāna* (*Divyāvadāna* no. 5; trans. Rotman 2008, 144).

[93] See Rotman 2009, 87 and 241, n. 100.

(Mrozik 2002, 5). Images and imagery conceived for the divine illustrate how bodies of the Buddha and the Bodhisattva were perceived as repositories of "embodied virtue" (Mrozik 2002, 2007), a theme also taken up by Fiordalis and Walters in later chapters of this volume. Probing the moral dimensions of the Buddhist divine image is therefore crucial to understanding Buddhist aesthetics, leaving us to ponder the question: How did the "aesthetics of spiritual exemplarity" (Kidd 2017a) in early Buddhist images impact the viewer and mould what I call the "images of the mind,"[94] evoked to visualize and venerate the physical form of the Buddha (*rūpakāya*) and the moral message it embodies (*dharmakāya*)?

Bibliography

Appleton, Naomi and Sarah Shaw, trans. 2015. *The Ten Great Birth Stories of the Buddha: The Mahānipāta of the Jātakatthavaṇṇanā*. 2 vols. Chiang Mai: Silkworm Books.

Banerji, Sures Chandra 1989. *A Companion to Sanskrit Literature*. Delhi: Motilal Banarsidass.

Bendall, Cecil and W. H. D. Rouse, trans. 1971 [1922]. *Śikṣāsamuccaya: A Compendium of Buddhist Doctrine. Compiled by Śāntideva Chiefly from Earlier Mahāyāna Sūtras*. Delhi: Motilal Banarsidass.

Bodhi, Bhikkhu, trans. 1996. *A Treatise on the Pāramīs: From the Commentary to the Cariyāpiṭaka by Ācariya Dhammapāla*. Kandy: Buddhist Publication Society. Wheel Publication 409/411.

Bodhi, Bhikkhu. 1999 [1984]. *The Noble Eightfold Path: The Way to the End of Suffering*. Access to Insight: https://www.accesstoinsight.org/lib/authors/bodhi/waytoend.html

Bodhi, Bhikkhu, trans. 2000. *The Connected Discourses of the Buddha. A New Translation of the Saṃyutta Nikāya*. 2 vols. Boston: Wisdom Publications.

Bodhi, Bhikkhu 2001. *The Good, the Beautiful, and the True*. Kandy: Buddhist Publication Society.

Brancaccio, Pia 2005. "The Making of a Life: Re-reading Bhārhut Sculpture." *South Asian Studies* 21: 47–52.

---

94 The symbiotic relationship between the visual image and the image of the mind is best revealed in the Upagupta episode: When the monk Upagupta sees the image of the Buddha assumed by Māra, he uses this image to dwell on the Buddha's virtues and perform *buddhānusmṛti,* the practice of bringing to mind the Buddha (*Aśokāvadāna* 15–28: Strong, trans. 1989, 185–98). For an analysis of the episode as a phenomenon of seeing, visualizing and venerating the Buddha, see Rotman 2009, 168–74. On the concept of *buddhānusmṛti*, see Rotman 2009, especially 171–4.

Collins, Steven 1992. "Notes on Some Oral Aspects of Pali Literature." *Indo-Iranian Journal* 35, no. 2/3:121–35.

Cone, Margaret and Richard Gombrich 1977. *The Perfect Generosity of Prince Vessantara: A Buddhist Epic translated from the Pāli and illustrated by unpublished paintings from Sinhalese temples*. Oxford: Clarendon Press.

Coomaraswamy, Ananda K. 1931. "An Early Passage on Indian Painting." *Eastern Art* 3: 218–19.

Coomaraswamy, Ananda K. 1933. "*Parāvṛtti* = Transformation, Regeneration, Anagogy." In Stein, Otto and Wilhelm Gampert (eds.) *Festschrift Moriz Winternitz*, 232–6. Leipzig: Otto Harrassowitz.

Coomaraswamy, Ananda K. 1946. *Figures of Speech or Figures of Thought*. London: Luzac & Co.

Coomaraswamy, Ananda K. 1956. "The Theory of Art in Asia." In *The Transformation of Nature in Art*, 1–57. New York: Dover Publications.

Cooper, David E. 2017. "Buddhism, Beauty and Virtue." In Higgins, K.M., Shakti Maira, and Sonia Sikka (eds.) *Artistic Visions and the Promise of Beauty: Cross-Cultural Perspectives*, 123–38. Dordrecht: Springer.

Cowell, E. B. ed., Robert Chalmers, W. H. D. Rouse, H. T. Francis, R. A. Neil and E. B. Cowell, trans. 1895–1907. *The Jātaka or Stories of the Buddha's Former Births*. 6 vols. Cambridge: Cambridge University Press.

Cowell, Edward B. and Robert A. Neil, eds. 1886. *The Divyāvadāna. A Collection of Early Buddhist Legends.* Cambridge: The University Press.

Dehejia, Harsha V. 1996. *The Advaita of Art*. Delhi: Motilal Banarsidass.

Dehejia, Vidya 1997. *Discourse in Early Buddhist Art*. Delhi: Munshiram Manoharlal Publishers.

Dutt, Sukumar 1988. *Buddhist Monks and Monasteries of India*. Delhi: Motilal Banarsidass.

Fausbøll, V. ed. 1877–96. *The Jātaka Together With its Commentary Being Tales of the Anterior Births of Gotama Buddha*. 6 vols. London: Trübner and Co.

Francoeur, Susanne. 1998."Style and Workshop in the Ajaṇṭā Paintings." PhD diss., Columbia University.

Ghosh Manomohan, ed. and trans. 1967. *The Nāṭyaśāstra: A Treatise on Ancient Dramaturgy and Histrionics Ascribed to Bharata-Muni.* 2 vols text and 2 vols translation. Revised 2nd edn. Calcutta: Granthalaya.

Gnoli, Raniero 1956. *The Aesthetic Experience According to Abhinavagupta.* Serie Orientale Roma, XI. Rome: Istituto Italiano per il Medio ed Estremo Oriente.

Gnoli, Raniero, ed. 1978. *The Gilgit Manuscript of the Saṅghabhedavastu, Being the 17th and Last Section of the Vinaya of the Mūlasarvāstivādin*. 2 vols. Rome: Istituto Italiano per il Medio ed Estremo Oriente.

Hahn, Michael, ed. 2011. *Poetical Vision of the Buddha's Former Lives: Seventeen Legends from Haribhaṭṭa's Jātakamāla*. New Delhi: Aditya Prakashan.

Harvey, Peter 2000. *An Introduction to Buddhist Ethics*. Cambridge: Cambridge University Press.

Horner, I. B., trans. 1954–59. *The Collection of Middle Length Sayings: (Majjhima-nikāya)*. London: Pāli Text Society by Luzac & Co.

Horner, I. B., trans. 1963. *The Book of the Discipline* (*Vinaya-piṭaka*), *Volume V: Cullavagga*. London: Luzac & Co.

Horner, I. B., trans. 1975. *The Minor Anthologies of the Pali Canon, Part 3: Buddhavaṃsa and Cariyāpiṭaka*. Sacred Books of the Buddhists, vol. 31. London: Pāli Text Society.

Ireland, John D., trans. 1981. *Saṃyutta-nikāya. An Anthology, Part I*. Kandy: Buddhist Publication Society/Wheel Publication No. 107.

Johnston, E. H. ed. 1928. *The Saundarananda of Aśvaghoṣa*. Panjab University Oriental Series. London: Humphrey Milford.

Kern, Hendrik trans. 1884. *Saddharma-Pundarīka or The Lotus of the True Law*. Sacred Books of the East, vol. XXI. Oxford: Clarendon Press.

Khoroche, Peter, trans. 1989. *Once the Buddha was a Monkey: Ārya Śūra's Jātakamālā*. Chicago: University of Chicago Press.

Kidd, Ian James 2017a. "Beauty, Virtue, and Religious Exemplars." *Religious Studies* 53: 171–81.

Kidd, Ian James 2017b. "Beautiful Bodhisattvas: The Aesthetics of Spiritual Exemplarity." *Contemporary Buddhism* 18/2: 331–45.

Kramrisch, Stella, trans. 1928. *The Vishṇudharmottara (Part III): A Treatise on Indian Painting and Image-Making*. 2nd revised and enlarged edn. Calcutta: Calcutta University Press.

Lalou, Marcelle 1928. "Notes sur la décoration des monasteries bouddhiques." *Revue des arts asiatique* 5: 183–5.

Legge, James, trans. 1971 [1886]. *The Travels of Fa-Hien. Fâ-Hien's Record of Buddhistic Kingdoms*. Delhi: Oriental Publishers.

Malandra, Geri H. 1993. *Unfolding a Maṇḍala: The Buddhist Cave Temples at Ellora*. Albany: State University of New York Press.

Masson, Jeffrey Moussaieff and M.V. Patwardhan 1969. *Śantarasa and Abhinavagupta's Philosophy of Aesthetics*. Poona: Bhandarkar Oriental Research Institute.

Meadows, Carol, trans. 1986. *Ārya-Śūra's Compendium of the Perfections: Text, Translation and Analysis of the Pāramitāsamāsa*. Bonn: Indica et Tibetica Verlag.

Monier-Williams, Monier 1960 [1899]. *A Sanskrit–English Dictionary*. New and enlarged edn. Oxford: Oxford University Press.

Mrozik, Susanne 2002. "The Value of Human Differences: South Asian Buddhist Contributions Toward an Embodied Virtue Theory." *Journal of Buddhist Ethics* 9: 1–33.

Mrozik, Susanne 2007. *Virtuous Bodies: The Physical Dimensions of Morality in Buddhist Ethics*. New York: Oxford University Press.

Müller, Edward, ed. 1897. *The Atthasālinī: Buddhaghosa's Commentary on the Dhammasanganī*. London: PāliText Society.

Ñāṇamoli, Bhikkhu and Bhikkhu Bodhi, trans. 1995. *The Middle Length Discourses of the Buddha: A New Translation of the Majjhima Nikāya*. Original translation from the Pāli by Bhikkhu Ñaṇamoli. Edited and revised by Bhikkhu Bodhi. Kandy: Buddhist Publication Society.

Ñāṇamoli, Bhikkhu and Bhikkhu Bodhi 2006. "Dukkha According to the Theravāda." In *The Three Basic Facts of Existence II: Suffering (Dukkha), Collected Essays*, 40–48. Kandy: Buddhist Publication Society, Wheel Publication no. 191–3. BPS online edition.

Nyanaponika, Thera and Hellmuth Hecker 2003. *Great Disciples of the Buddha. Their Lives, their Works, their Legacy*. Edited and with an Introduction by Bhikkhu Bodhi. Boston: Wisdom Publications in collaboration with the Buddhist Publication Society of Kandy.

Nyanatiloka, Thera 1968. *The Word of the Buddha*. Kandy: Buddhist Publication Society.

Ohnuma, Reiko 2007. *Head, Eyes, Flesh and Blood: Giving Away the Body in Indian Buddhist Literature*. New York: Columbia University Press.

Radhakrishnan, S., ed. and trans. 2011 [1950]. *The Dhammapada. With introductory essays, Pali text, English translations and notes*. 13th edn. New Delhi: Oxford University Press.

Ramakrishnakavi, Manavalli, ed. 1926–64. *Bharata's Nāṭyaśāstra. With the Abhinavabhāratī Commentary of Abhinavagupta*. Gaekwad's Oriental Series vols. 36, 68, 124 and 145. Baroda: Oriental Institute.

Ray, Himanshu, Prabha 1994–95. "The Parallel Tradition: Early Buddhist Narrative Sculpture." *Bulletin of the Deccan College Research Institute* 54/55: 349–55. Sir William Jones Volume Commemorating the Bicentenary.

Rhys Davids, T. W., trans., revised by C.A.F. Rhys Davids 1878. *Buddhist Birth-Stories (Jātaka Tales): The Commentarial Introduction Entitled Nidāna Kathā, The Story of the Lineage*. London: Routledge & Sons.

Rotman, Andy, trans. 2008. *Divine Stories: Divyāvadāna, Part I*. Boston: Wisdom Publications.

Rotman, Andy 2009. *Thus Have I Seen: Visualizing Faith in Early Indian Buddhism*. New York: Oxford University Press.

Rotman, Andy, trans. 2017. *Divine Stories: Divyāvadāna, Part II*. Boston: Wisdom Publications.

Schlingloff, Dieter 1987/1988. *Studies in the Ajanta Paintings: Identifications and Interpretations*. Delhi: Ajanta Publications.

Schlingloff, Dieter 1999. *Guide to the Ajanta Paintings. Vol. 1: Narrative Wall Paintings*. New Delhi: Munshiram Manoharlal Publishers.

Schlingloff, Dieter 2013. *Ajanta: Handbook of the Paintings 1. Narrative Wall-Paintings*. 3 volumes. New Delhi: IGNCA.

Schopen, Gregory 2004. "Art, Beauty and the Business of Running a Buddhist Monastery in Early Northwest India." In *Buddhist Monks and Business Matters: Still More Papers on Monastic Buddhism in India*, 19–44. Honolulu: University of Hawai'i Press.

Schopen, Gregory 2005. "Taking the Bodhisattva into Town: More Texts on the Image of 'the Bodhisattva' and Image Processions in the Mūlasarvāstivādavinaya." *East and West* 55/1–4: 299–311.

Shaw, Sarah, trans. 2006. *The Jātakas: Birth Stories of the Bodhisatta*. New Delhi: Penguin Books.

Sheikh, Gulam Mohammed 1983. "Viewer's View: Looking at Pictures." *Journal of Arts and Ideas* 3: 5–20.

Sivaramamurti, C. ed. and trans. 1978. *Chitrasūtra of the Vishnudharmottara*. New Delhi: Kanak Publications.

Skilling, Peter 2011. "Redaction, Recitation, and Writing: Transmission of the Buddha's Teaching in India in the Early Period." In Berkwitz, S.C., Juliane Schober, and Claudia Brown (eds.) *Buddhist Manuscript Cultures: Knowledge, Ritual, and Art*, 53–75. London and New York: Routledge.

Skilling, Peter, Forthcoming. "Foreword." In Ganvir, S., ed. *Buddhist Caves of the Deccan: Issues and Interpretations*. New Delhi: Kaveri Books.

Soper, Alexander 1950. "Early Buddhist Attitudes Toward the Art of Painting." *The Art Bulletin* 32/2: 147–51.

Speyer, Jacob Samuel, trans. 1895. *The Gātakamālā or Garland of Birth Stories by Ārya Sūra*. Sacred Books of the Buddhists Vol. 1. London: Oxford University Press.

Strong, John, trans. 1989. *The Legend of King Aśoka* (*Aśokāvadāna*). Princeton, NJ: Princeton University Press.

Strong, John S. 1995. *The Experience of Buddhism: Sources and Interpretations*. Belmont, CA: Wadsworth.

Thampi, Mohan G. B. 1965. "'Rasa' as Aesthetic Experience." *The Journal of Aesthetic and Art Criticism* 24/1: 75–80.

Thanissaro, Bhikkhu, trans. 1998. *Dhammapada. A Translation*. Barre, Massachusetts: Dhamma Dana Publications.

Vaidya, P. L. ed. *Jātakamālā*. Darbhanga: Mithila Institute, 1959.

Willemen, Charles, trans. 2009. *Buddhacarita: In Praise of the Buddha's Acts. Translated from the Chinese. Taishō vol. 4, no. 192*. Berkeley: Numata Center for Buddhist Translations and Research.

Yazdani, Ghulam 1930–55. *Ajanta: The Colour and Monochrome Reproductions of the Ajanta Frescoes Based on Photography*. 4 vols. London: Oxford University Press.

Zin, Monika 2003. "The *uṣṇīṣa* as a Physical Characteristic of the Buddha's Relatives and Successors." *Journal of the Institute of Silk Road Studies* 9: 107–27.

Author biography

Madhulika Reddy holds a PhD from the University of Mumbai. Her dissertation probes the narrative paintings of Ajanta for their aesthetic visualization of Buddhist values and concepts. Her research interests focus on the aesthetics of early Buddhist art in India and the visual culture that informs it; the interface between aesthetics and ethics in the conceptualization of the early image; and the complex relationship between the early *saṅgha* and the lay community as reflected in the art of the early Buddhist sites of India. She is currently revising her PhD dissertation for publication.

4

Visualizing a Teaching

Sermon Scenes in Kucha

Monika Zin

Introduction

In this chapter I present an overview of the latest research into the narrative paintings found in the Kucha caves, in order to offer a different perspective on the relationship between visual and verbal narrative. In Kucha we find a very large number of narrative paintings, often linked closely to literary sources, sometimes to Sanskrit tradition imported from India, sometimes to local variants familiar from sources in vernacular languages Tocharian, Uyghur or Khotanese, yet many paintings remain unidentified. In particular I look at a Kucha innovation: "sermon scenes", or images of the Buddha preaching a particular sermon, including sermons that contain narratives of past and future lifetimes. These scenes offer a rich insight into the relationship between visual encounters with the Buddha and the oral/aural/verbal experience of the *dharma*, a theme also discussed elsewhere in this volume (Reddy, Gummer), by showing the Buddha-as-teacher, his audience and the content of his sermons in one image. I show that these images sometimes use an extremely simplified form of representation that I refer to as a "telegraphic" style to display the contents of a *dharma* teaching but sometimes a sophisticated and complicated pictorial language. As part of the broader visual scheme of the site, sermon scenes raise questions about the ways in which narrative images may have been intended to function, as well as about their relationship with Buddhist literature.

From one to 100: the swelling number of narratives in Kucha

The paintings illustrating narratives were certainly of crucial importance for the donors and visitors of the caves in the area of Kucha on the Northern

Silk Road (Xinjiang Uyghur Autonomous Region of the People's Republic of China) since they form by far the largest part of the murals. In the caves, an interesting process can be observed: the number of the narratives depicted in an interior grew over time so that its development correlates with the caves' dating.[1] A brief description of some paintings in relation to interiors will help to introduce the narratives and styles present in Kucha, and show how sermon scenes fit into the overall visual agenda as it shifts from the First to the Second Indo-Iranian Style.

The caves painted in the First Indo-Iranian Style (possibly belonging still to the fifth century) can contain only a few narratives, in some cases even only one. For example, in Cave 118 in Kizil (Hippokampenhöhle)[2] both lunettes and the rear wall, in other words all those surfaces used for depictions of narrative character in the cave, illustrate the story of Māndhātar[3] with a scene playing on Sumeru in one lunette and the sick Māndhātar after his fall to earth in the other. Big pictures covering entire walls that were surrounded by opulent ornamental frames dominate the interiors in Subashi[4] (the narratives have not been identified yet).[5] Some caves in the First Indo-Iranian Style depict narratives in horizontally arranged, consecutive scenes reminiscent of Gandharan relief friezes. All walls of Cave 149A (Zebuwagenhöhle)[6] depict the narrative of Pūrṇa in

---

1 The exact dating of the paintings in Kucha is not possible by the present state of knowledge. This chapter follows the chronological order of the First and the Second Indo-Iranian Styles given by Waldschmidt (in Le Coq and Waldschmidt 1933, 24–31) – and it turns out to support this order in full extent – and approximately also Waldschmidt's dating, considering the First Style as beginning around 500 CE (quite possibly *circa* one generation earlier) and the Second Style around the middle of the sixth century. The strongly China-influenced Third Style begins after the Tang invasion in 647. The overlappings of the styles are of course very much possible. This is true also concerning the much later so-called Uyghur Style (ninth century and later) being a continuation of the Second Indo-Iranian Style.

2 Left lunette: Museum für Asiatische Kunst, Staatliche Museen zu Berlin, no. III 8412, right lunette: no. IB 8411, lost in the second world war, see Dreyer, Sander, and Weis 2002, 142 (with references to earlier publications), mural on the rear wall *in situ*; illus. Grünwedel 1912, fig. 228 (drawing); *Mural Paintings in Xinjiang of China* 2009, vol. 1, 5–7, pls. 1–2; Yaldiz et al. 2000, no. 293 (with references to earlier publications); Ding 2015, 74–5; both lunettes illus. in Le Coq 1924a, pls. 1–2.

3 Identif. Hiyama 2012; for literary sources and other representations see Zin 2001; for the narrative see Rotman, trans. 2008, 337–71 (*Divyāvadāna* 17).

4 Illus. Hallade and Goulier 1982, pls. 55–60, and drawings ("dessin") 1–3.

5 The paintings in the cave are being scrutinized by Vignato and Hiyama 2022, 104–10, 198–202.

6 Historical photographs in Museum für Indische Kunst, nos. B 821, 822, 1517; original water-coloured drawings by Grünwedel nos. TA 6510, 6528, 6534, 6535; illus. in Grünwedel 1912, figs. 279–84; Schlingloff 1991 (drawings, references to earlier publications).

this way,[7] while the walls of Cave 81 are filled with the *Viśvantarajātaka*.[8] Only two narratives, each consisting of several consecutive scenes were represented in Cave 212 (Seefahrerhöhle): Śroṇakoṭikarṇa[9] on the right wall[10] and Maitrakanyaka[11] on the left;[12] Cave 76 (Pfauenhöhle) was devoted to the life story of the Buddha.[13] The antechamber displayed two big scenes on the side walls, the enlightenment on the left and the first sermon on the right, while the main chamber contained many, more or less square, scenes in three registers showing Buddha's *vita* in a chronological sequence.[14] As recently opined by Vignato and Hiyama, these paintings were probably not meant to be looked at by the visitors since the passageways between the walls and the massive pedestal for the Buddha statue in the middle of the chamber were quite narrow.[15]

In the lunette above the entrance door in Cave 92 (Höhle mit der Äffin) Indra in his heaven is represented (Figure 4.1). The facing lunette, above the rear wall (Figure 4.2),[16] shows Indra and his *vīṇā*-playing musician, Pañcaśikha, paying a visit to the Buddha meditating in the cave (this is the same narrative that in later caves will often be represented at the rear wall on both sides of the sculpture of the Buddha in the niche; Indra in the lunette above the entrance will be replaced in the Second Style by Maitreya). Similar to the representation of Māndhātar in Kizil 118, in Cave 92 we can presume, too, that both opposing lunettes illustrated a single narrative, that of Indra's visit.[17] Unlike in

---

7 Identif. Schlingloff 1991; for literary sources and representation in Ajanta see Schlingloff 2000/2013, no. 79: for the narrative see Tatelman 2000; Rotman, trans. 2008, 71–117 (*Divyāvadāna* 2).

8 See Nakagawara 2011; for literary sources and representations in art see Schlingloff 2000/2013, no. 42.

9 Identif. Grünwedel 1920, II 33–41; for the ascertainment of the literary source of the painting (the *vinaya* of the Sarvāstivādins) see Waldschmidt 1952; for the narrative see Rotman, trans. 2008, 39–70 (*Divyāvadāna* 1).

10 Berlin, Museum für Asiatische Kunst, no. III 8401, illus. Yaldiz et al. 2000, no. 288 (with references to earlier publications); Ding 2015, 160–61.

11 Identif. Grünwedel 1920, II 41–50; for the literary sources see Klaus 1983.

12 Berlin, no. IB 8400; see Dreyer, Sander, and Weis 2002, 142 (with references to earlier publications).

13 See Grünwedel's descriptions: 1912, 87–91 and 1920, II 3–17.

14 The well preserved scenes were taken to Berlin, but were destroyed during the war: Berlin, no. IB 8648; see Dreyer, Sander, and Weis 2002, 160 (with references to earlier publications); illus. Grünwedel 1912, figs. 196–204 and Grünwedel 1920, pls. 1–4, 9–10 and figs. 15–17 (drawings); *Mural Paintings in Xinjiang of China* 2009, vol. 1, 148–51, pls. 131–4 (= plates from Grünwedel 1920).

15 See Vignato and Hiyama 2022, 24–6, 237–8, chapter 5; Vignato and Hiyama call the chamber *gandhakuṭī*.

16 Illus. Tan and An 1981, vol. 1, pl. 185; *Mural Paintings in Xinjiang of China* 2009, vol. 1, 16, pl. 9.

17 For the literary sources and representations in art, see Rhi 2009; for the narrative see Soper 1949–50.

Figure 4.1. Kizil, Cave 92 (Höhle mit der Äffin), main chamber, front wall, lunette above the door, *in situ*; drawing by the author © Monika Zin CC BY-NC-SA

Figure 4.2. Kizil, Cave 92 (Höhle mit der Äffin), main chamber, lunette above the rear wall, *in situ*; drawing by the author © Monika Zin CC BY-NC-SA

Kizil 118 (see notes 2–3), however, here the walls were covered with several narrative scenes each centred around the Buddha. Grünwedel called these depictions "Buddhapredigten" (Buddha's sermons) or "Predigtbilder" (sermon pictures); today they are usually called "sermon scenes" or "preaching scenes". Chinese researchers prefer to call them "scenes from the life of the Buddha". This is correct in a way, since the scenes indeed show the Buddha; but, as we will see below, the particular composition of these scenes actually indicates that they form a specific genre quite different from the common depictions of the Buddha's *vita*, as in Kizil 76 (see n. 13) or in Kizil 110 (see n. 35).

In Kizil 92, sermon scenes were arranged in two registers, four scenes in every row.[18] Unfortunately most of the murals on the walls are destroyed and only the uppermost row is partly preserved. One of the scenes still preserved[19] shows Devadatta throwing the rock at the Buddha and the *yakṣa* Kumbhīra catching it (Figure 4.3).[20] There is another scene with male figures gesticulating dramatically, and still another one[21] showing listening monks, deities and Vajrapāṇi. These scenes are not divided and only the arrangement of the figures around the Buddha defines the pictorial unit.

That the scenes on the walls in Kizil 77 (Statuenhöhle) are divided by vertical patterns is not the reason why they are here assigned to a later date – scenes without any dividers can also appear in much later paintings – however, as will be discussed in more detail below, there is a considerable change in the way the narratives in Kizil 77 were illustrated and this possibly allows us to consider them as more developed. The scenes with the Buddha were depicted here in one register (?) on the side walls of the main chamber and in two registers (?) on the inner walls of the corridors leading to the rear chamber; the paintings were severely destroyed already in Grünwedel's time.[22] One of the scenes is the famous depiction of the Buddha preaching to the monks in the presence of the herdsman Nanda who, while listening to the sermon, unintentionally stabbed and killed a frog with his staff[23] (Figure 4.4).[24]

The number of depicted narratives increases in some of the latest caves of the First Indo-Iranian Style: while Cave 83 (Schatzhöhle C) displayed only one narrative on the rear wall, the story of King Udrāyaṇa (Rudrāyaṇa),[25]

---

18 See Grünwedel's descriptions: 1912, 100–102.

19 Illus. Tan and An 1981, vol. 1, pl. 184; *Kizil Grottoes* 1983–85/1989–97, vol. 2, pl. 76; *Mural Paintings in Xinjiang of China* 2009, vol. 1, 15, pl. 8.

20 Identif. Zin 2006a, 329–37; for the literary sources and representations in Gandhara and Kucha also see ibid.; for the narrative see Rockhill 1884, 92–3 (*Mūlasavāstivādavinaya, Saṅghabhedavastu*).

21 Illus. *Kizil Grottoes* 1983–85/1989–97, vol. 2, pl. 75; *Mural Paintings in Xinjiang of China* 2009, vol. 1, 15, pl. 8.

22 Description in Grünwedel 1912, 91–3.

23 An identification – Schlingloff (1997–98, 180) – was only possible after the fragments of the scene were put together (for an earlier picture see, for example, Le Coq and Waldschmidt 1928, pl. 3). For the literary sources see Salomon 2018, 138–44; see also ibid., 153–6 for translation of the Gāndhārī version and of the additional narrative of the frog as given in the *Bhaiṣajyavastu* of the *Mūlasarvāstivādavinaya*.

24 Berlin, Museum für Asiatische Kunst, nos. III 8838 and III 8840, illus. Yaldiz et al. 2000, no. 284 (with references to earlier publications); Ding 2015, 158.

25 Identif. Waldschmidt 1925, 63–4; for sources and representation in Ajanta see Schlingloff 2000/2013, no. 75; for the narrative see Rotman, trans. 2017, 287–344 (*Divyāvadāna* 37).

Figure 4.3. Kizil, Cave 92 (Höhle mit der Äffin), main chamber, rear wall, *in situ*; drawing by the author incorporated drawing by Grünwedel, from Grünwedel 1912, fig. 225

Figure 4.4. Kizil, Cave 77 (Statuenhöhle), exact position in the cave unknown, taken to Berlin; nos. III 8838 and III 8840

surrounded by the wide ornamental frame,[26] the neighbouring cave, Kizil 84 (Schatzhöhle B), presented merging narrative scenes with sitting or standing *buddhas* arranged in no less than four registers (the lowest one being narrower) (Figure 4.5).[27]

Of crucial importance is Cave 207 (Malerhöhle), datable to ca. 510–530 CE (Hiyama 2016, 219). This is the only cave painted in the First Indo-Iranian Style that displays an architectural form and pictorial programme that will become characteristic for the Second Style: the so called "central pillar cave" (see Figure 4.7). Most of the paintings have been destroyed and are known only from Grünwedel's drawings and descriptions[28] – yet it is clear that the cave contained the earliest representation of the *parinirvāṇa* cycle in Kucha, located on all six walls in the corridors at the rear.[29] On the side walls of the main chamber 18 scenes were represented, nine scenes in three registers on each wall (Figure 4.6)[30] (see also Figure 4.17 below).

The model of Kizil 207 with the *parinirvāṇa* cycle in the rear corridors and sermon scenes on the side walls of the main chamber is then repeated in most of the "central pillar caves" (Figure 4.7) of the Second Indo-Iranian Style, and is even continued into the late phase referred to as the "Uyghur Style" (for example Simsim 44).

The number of sermon scenes in caves of the Second Indo-Iranian Style can change depending on the size of the individual cave, and the quality of execution of the paintings varies considerably. There are caves with large sermon scenes covering the entire height of the walls (like in Kizil 8 or 38); more prevalent is the model with scenes in two registers (like in Kizil 14, 17, 63, 114, 171, 175, 179, 189, 193, 205, 206, 219, 224, Kumtura 23 or Simsim 42),

---

26 Berlin, Museum für Asiatische Kunst, nos. III 8443 and 8444, illus. Grünwedel 1920, pls. 40–41; fig. 72 (drawing); Le Coq 1924a, pl. 3; Waldschmidt 1925, pl. 54; Yaldiz 1987, pl. 40; *Mural Paintings in Xinjiang of China* 2009, vol. 1, 173–4, pls. 83–4; Ding 2015: 48–9.

27 The painting has been brought to Berlin and is today in the Museum für Asiatische Kunst, no. III 8444, a, b, c, illus. Grünwedel 1920, pls. 32–5; *Mural Paintings in Xinjiang of China* 2009, vol. 1, 175–83, pls. 155–61; Ding 2015, 50–55; drawing by Grünwedel in the archives of the Museum für Asiatische Kunst, no. TA 6608 and TA 6501 (= Grünwedel 1920, fig. 73)

28 See Grünwedel 1912, 152–6, figs. 339–54 and 1920, II 19–25, figs. 23–5; for the comprehensive analysis of the sermon scenes in this cave see Hiyama 2016, 104–95.

29 Grünwedel 1912, 156–7, figs. 355–7 (drawings); 1920, II 109–13, figs. 88–9 (drawings), Hiyama 2016, 196–210; Zin 2020, 227–32.

30 Original drawings of separate scenes are kept today in the Museum für Asiatische Kunst in Berlin (nos. and TA 6634, TA 6337, TA 6639, TA 6749, TA 6560, the latter painting is preserved and today in Berlin, no. III 9148a) and in the Museum der Fünf Kontinente in Munich (nos. 11.710, 11.711, 11.712, 11.713, 11.714).

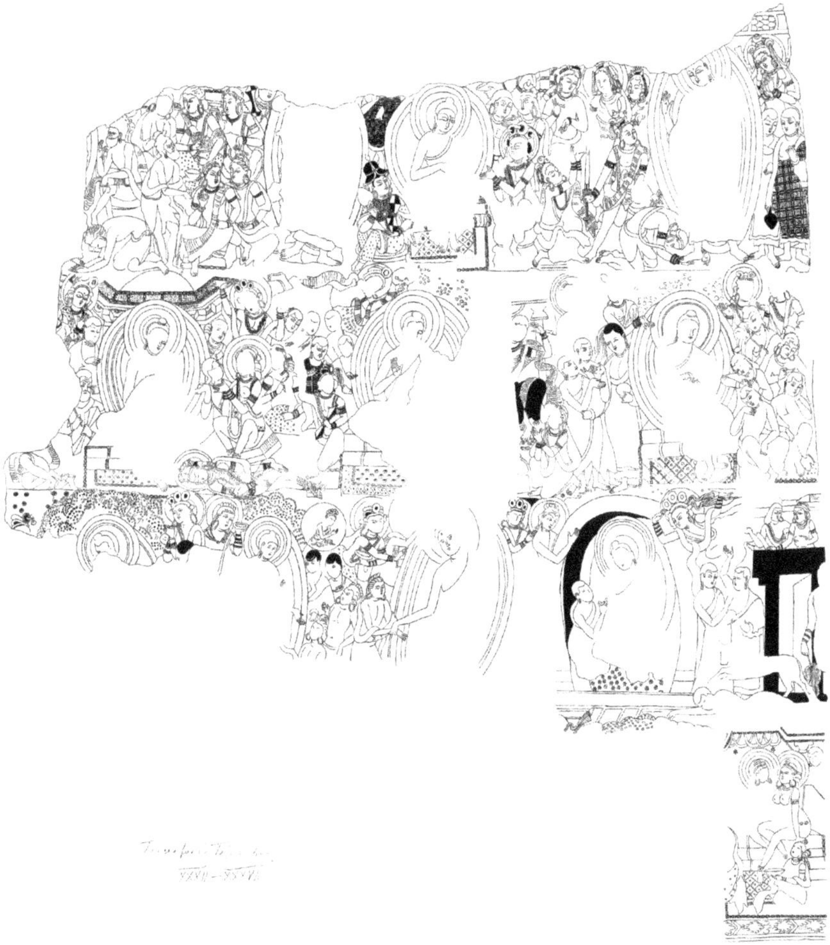

Figure 4.5. Kizil, Cave 84 (Schatzhöhle B), main chamber, rear wall, taken to Berlin; no. III 8444, drawing by Grünwedel, no. TA 6608 © Museum für Asiatische Kunst – Staatliche Museen zu Berlin, CC BY-NC-SA

but three (like in Kizil 100 or 161), five (Kumtura 34)[31] or even seven registers (Kizil 227)[32] can be found occasionally. The growing number of scenes culminates in Kumtura 50[33] with 15 registers of tiny scenes. As the inscriptions labelling the pictures prove, each scene depicts a situation in which a person provides an object or a service to a *buddha* thus marking his or her own way towards attaining buddhahood in a future birth (the inscriptions correspond

[31] Illus. *Mural Paintings in Xinjiang of China* 2009, vol. 4, 153–71, pls. 150–67.

[32] Illus. *Mural Paintings in Xinjiang of China* 2009, vol. 3, 257–62, pls. 233–8.

[33] Illus. *Kumtula Grottoes* 1985, pls. 125–33; *Mural Paintings in Xinjiang of China* 2009, vol. 4, 117–35, pls. 114–38.

Figure 4.6. Kizil, Cave 207 (Malerhöhle), main chamber, right side wall, two upper registers of scenes, today lost; drawings by Grünwedel; after Grünwedel 1920, II 18, fig. 23

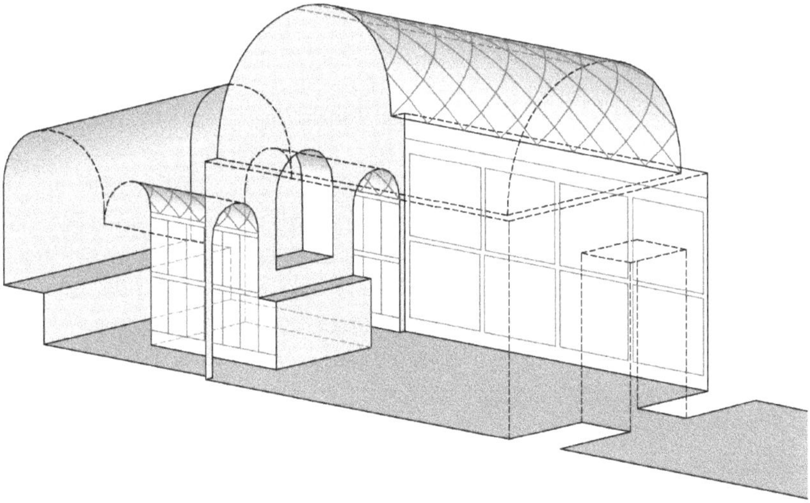

Figure 4.7. Axonometric projection of a "central pillar cave"; drawing by Dominik Oczkowski

with the list of *buddhas*' names listed in the *Bhadrakalpikasūtra*; see Ogihara 2015). The scenes display different figures who often are shown with their attributes or with architectural devices so that we still have to understand them as depictions of narrative character.

In several caves supplementary figurative depictions were added below the sermon scenes: these are sequences of *jātakas*.[34] Since the lowest parts of the wall are often lost, it may be presumed that the *jātakas* were depicted in this location quite often. A frieze with *jātakas* is still visible in Kizil 110, below the Buddha's life-story, in 60 chronologically arranged square scenes.[35]

The representations of one narrative in frieze-like, consecutive scenes, similar to those familiar from the First Indo-Iranian Style in Kizil 149A or 212 (see notes 6–12), are very rare in the Second Indo-Iranian Style. Among the

[34] Like the friezes removed to Berlin from Kizil 186 (Mittlere Höhle der zweiten Schlucht); Museum für Asiatische Kunst, no. III 8851, illus. Le Coq and Waldschmidt 1928, pl. A; *Kizil Grottoes* 1983–85/1989–97, vol. 3, pls. 209–10.

[35] Historical photographs published in Le Coq 1924b, pls. 6–10, und Yaldiz 1987, pls. 45–50; illus. Tan and An 1981, vol. 2, pls. 1–8; *Kizil Grottoes* 1983–85/1989–97, vol. 2, pls. 106–16; *Mural Paintings in Xinjiang of China* 2009, vol. 2, 7, 12–16, pls. 5, 9–13; for the parts which were taken to Berlin, Museum für Asiatische Kunst, no. III 8376, illus. *Kizil Grottoes* 1983–85/1989–97, vol. 3, pl. 194; for the parts destroyed during the war, no. IB 8376; see Dreyer, Sander, and Weis 2002, 135 (with references to earlier publications).

few examples are the *Viśvantarajātaka* in Kizil 198[36] or the *Sudhanajātaka*[37] in Kizil 199.[38] Already this observation shows that the creators of the image programmes in the Second Style wanted to include more different narratives, but no longer cared about the elaborate depiction of one narrative in a large sequence of scenes.

The vaults of the earlier caves (like Kizil 77, 92 or 118)[39] represented conventional mountains populated by animals, birds, deities, meditating monks and *ṛṣi*s, but narratives were not depicted on these surfaces. In the Second Style, on the contrary, every lozenge-shape "mountain" on the barrel vault is filled with a narrative (Figure 4.8).[40] In some caves (for example Kizil 171) more than 80 narratives are to be found in the barrel vault;[41] the big vault of the later cave Simsim 44 must have once encompassed more than 100.[42]

The typical "central pillar cave" of the Second Indo-Iranian Style thus contained an enormous number of different narratives: larger representations in the lunettes, on the main wall around the niche and on the walls in the corridors of the rear part of the cave, and many smaller scenes on the side walls and on the barrel vaults. It is extremely rare (possibly by mistake only) that one and the same narrative is depicted in a cave twice. We may venture to state that nowhere in the Buddhist world has a similar number of narratives ever been represented in one architectural unit. This may even be true if we include non-Buddhist establishments as well.

---

36 Tan and An 1981, vol. 2, pls. 151–2; *Kizil Grottoes* 1983–85/1989–97, vol. 3, pls. 104–6; *Mural Paintings in Xinjiang of China* 2009, vol. 3, 225, pl. 202.

37 Identif. Charpentier 1925, 817–19; for the narrative, see *Mahāvastu*: Jones, trans. 1949–56, vol. 2, 91–111.

38 Berlin, Museum für Asiatische Kunst, no. III 8431; illus. Le Coq 1924a, pl. 9c; *Kizil Grottoes* 1983–85/1989–97, vol. 3, pl. 13; *Mural Paintings in Xinjiang of China* 2009, vol. 3, 237, pl. 213; for descriptions and drawings of the parts which are destroyed or were taken by the Russian expedition to St. Petersburg see Grünwedel 1912, 134–5; original drawings are being kept in Berlin, nos. TA 6435 and 6436.

39 Illus. for example, in *Mural Paintings in Xinjiang of China* 2009, vol. 1, 9–14, 17–29, pls. 3–7, 10–22.

40 For an inventory of caves with *jātaka*s and the so-called *avadāna*s (scenes with the Buddha) see Zhu 2012; for an overview of frequently depicted stories see Waldschmidt in Le Coq and Waldschmidt 1928, 40–62; for an overview of the representations of scenes with the Buddha see Lesbre 2001.

41 Illus. for example, in *Kizil Grottoes* 1983–85/1989–97, vol. 3, pls. 5, 8; *Mural Paintings in Xinjiang of China* 2009, vol. 1, 250–75, pls. 224–46.

42 Illus. for example, in *Mural Paintings in Xinjiang of China* 2009, vol. 5, 108–13, pls. 99–106.

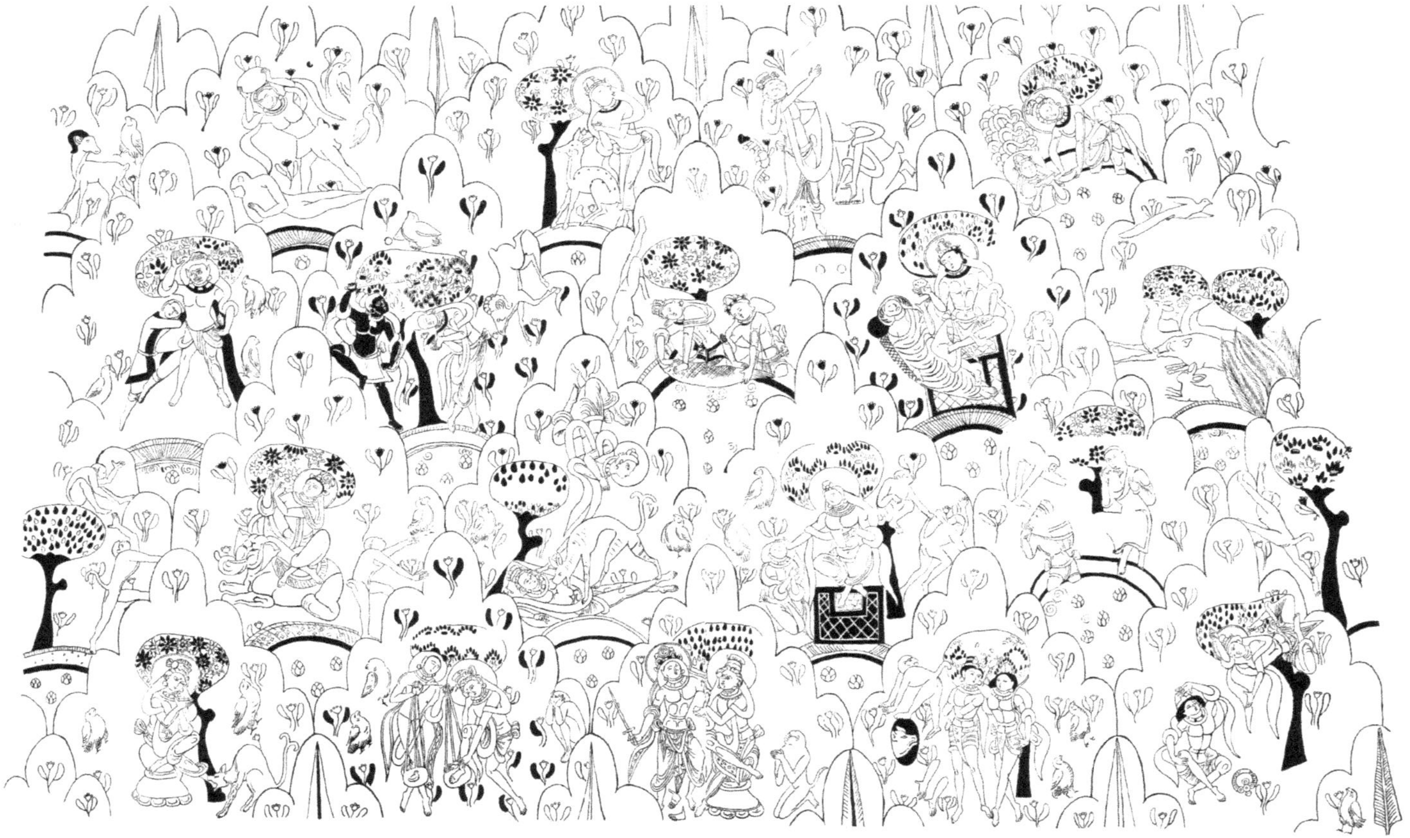

Figure 4.8. Kizil, Cave 178 (Schluchthöhle), main chamber, barrel vault, right side, taken to Berlin; no. III 8450; drawing by Grünwedel, Museum für Asiatische Kunst, no. TA 6604, after Grünwedel 1920, II 83, fig. 45

To reduce or to densify: how to cast an entire tale into a single picture

In order to fit the content of a narrative into each "mountain" on the vault, the invention of what may be called a "telegraphic style" was necessary: this reduced a narrative to the bare minimum. The picture now only indicated to the viewer which story is meant. In the vaults both *jātaka*s and scenes centering around the Buddha – that is to say, abridged sermon scenes – can be presented. The depictions are arranged in a rather procedural manner, for example registers of lozenges with *jātaka*s and scenes with the Buddha are alternating. As argued elsewhere (Zin 2015) the representations are often reduced so rigorously to only a few elements – recognizable to us today only thanks to comparative material and good light – that they could not have been recognizable for visitors to the caves. Maybe it was not the narrative content of the individual pictures that was important but rather their general presence – and their number.

However, the comparative study of the *jātaka*s in barrel vaults proves (Chang 2020) that individual stories were depicted in the caves of Kucha following different literary sources; this indicates that the depictions were not created as mindless repetitions of a once established composition but were consciously executed. The pictures (see Waldschmidt in: Le Coq and Waldschmidt 1928: 9–25) reduce an entire narrative to one, the most characteristic, scene (such as *śaśa* in the fire in front of the ascetic); in some cases two courses of action appear in one lozenge (for example, 1. a prince/ascetic falling down, and 2. being eaten by tigress and her cubs). Only rarely was more than one iconography created for one narrative (1. king Prabhāsa on the galloping elephant; 2. elephant in front of the glowing iron balls). Despite – or perhaps rather because of – their reduced compositions, most of the pictures on the barrel vaults, especially the *jātaka*s, are well scrutinized and most of them are identified.

The identification of the content of the sermon scenes on the side walls is more complicated; the small number of identifications provided by Grünwedel and Waldschmidt bears witness to their difficulties in dealing with these scenes. The representations are the opposite of "reductions", they are rather overloaded with persons and objects. Additional difficulties are caused by the fact that the murals on the walls are usually poorly preserved. Those preserved well enough were taken to Berlin, where unfortunately entire series of sermon scenes from Kizil 175 (Versuchungshöhle)[43] and Kizil 179 (Japanerhöhle)[44]

[43] Berlin, nos. IB 9174 and 9175; see Dreyer, Sander, and Weis 2002, 198 (with references to earlier publications).

[44] Berlin, nos. IB 9172; see Dreyer, Sander, and Weis 2002, 198 (the catalogue gives Kizil 176 as providence of the painting); Ding 2015, 104–7.

were destroyed in the Second World War; only black and white photographs of them survived (see Figure 4.20 below). More sermon scenes from the same Kizil 179[45] as well as those from Kizil 178 (Schluchthöhle)[46] are still kept in Berlin today. The side walls in several caves – among others Kizil 114 (Gebetmühlenhöhle), Kizil 219 (Ajātaśatruhöhle), or Kizil 205 and 224 (Māyāhöhlen) – have been severely destroyed by cutting off small fragments, mostly faces; the removed fragments were sent to collections around the globe. To safely determine to which scene a cut off fragment originally belonged is a difficult task. There are many scenes shown on the walls in Kucha about which we can say that they recur in several caves while we have not (yet) succeeded in explaining their content. Some scenes are unspecific therefore their meaning may remain unclear for ever. Other scenes are very specific, like the one showing a couple in an embrace, an old and a young Brahmin (Figure 4.9, Figure 4.10).[47] For these an explanation by means of literary sources appears very much possible. In recent times, since comparative material is available, several narratives in the sermon scenes have been convincingly identified,[48] so the hope for more identifications is well-founded.

However, even well-preserved scenes are difficult to read. But why is it such an enormous challenge to find proper explanations? The chapter in hand attempts to provide an answer to this question by giving a brief introduction into how to read these scenes and into the current state of work for the interpretation of one of these scenes. It cannot be made clear enough that what follows is just a snap shot of work in progress; research into this topic may easily take many more years.

---

[45] Berlin, Museum für Asiatische Kunst no. III 8660.

[46] Berlin, Museum für Asiatische Kunst no. III 8725; illus. Grünwedel 1920, pls. 24–7; Härtel and Yaldiz 1982, no. 24; *Kizil Grottoes* 1983–85/1989–97, vol. 3, pl. 205; Ding 2015, 98–103.

[47] Only the middle part, the remains of the Buddha, is today *in situ*, the rest of the painting was removed and taken to Berlin; the right side of the scene is today kept in Museum für Asiatische Kunst, no. III 9189 (illus. in Ding 2015, 173); the left side and the part below the Buddha are in Smithsonian American Art Museum, nos. LTS 1985-1-325-15 and LTS 1985-1-325-16, respectively. The same narrative is depicted also in Kizil 99 (left wall, unpublished) and in Kizil 205, illus. Grünwedel 1912, fig. 374.

[48] Arlt and Hiyama 2013 (Prasenajit's visit; Muktikā); Hamada 2003 (Ajātaśatru in Jīvaka's park); Hiyama 2016 (143–6: Gautama meeting Bimbisāra on Pāṇḍava mountain; 139–46: conversion of Kāśyapa brothers; 112–18: conversion of the Jaina Śātyaki; 135–8: *Aggaññasutta*); Inoue 2014 (Jetavana); Inoue 2017 (Roruka); Konczak-Nagel 2021 (*Āṭānāṭikasūtra*); Zin 2005 (Mākandika); Zin 2006a (Devadatta); Zin 2006b, 13 (Ambāṣṭha); Zin 2007 (Bṛhaddyuti); Zin 2010a (The Promise of Four Kings, only tentative identification); Zin 2011a (Elapatra); Zin 2018 (Ciñcā Māṇavikā).

Figure 4.9. Kizil, Cave 224 (Māyā-Höhle der 3. Anlage) main chamber, left wall; middle part: *in situ*, left part: Washington DC, Smithsonian American Art Museum, no. LTS 1985-1-325-15; lower part: Washington DC, Smithsonian American Art Museum, no. LTS 1985-1-325-16; right part: Berlin, Museum für Asiatische Kunst, no, III 9189; reconstructive drawing by the author © Monika Zin CC BY-NC-SA

Figure 4.10. Kizil, Cave 99, main chamber, left wall, lower register, *in situ*; drawing by the author © Monika Zin CC BY-NC-SA

How to read a sermon scene and what makes it so special?

The composition of the sermon scene is closely connected to the transmission of its narrative content. It is based on a conflated mode of representation[49] commonly used in India for the main scenes of Buddha's life story, like the *Māravijaya*. In these scenes, surrounding the Buddha appear consecutive episodes: Māra's soldiers are attacking, his daughters are dancing, Māra himself is approaching and is leaving again after his defeat. In Gandhara, as well as in a few examples in Andhra, this kind of composition was also used for less important events to depict progress of action. The arrangement is suitable for the depictions of difficult conversions showing a malicious person, for example Āṭavika or Aṅgulimāla (Zin 2006b, chapters 1 and 6), on one side of the Buddha and the same, now reformed person, on the other. However, the conversions as well as the *Māravijaya* contain those persons necessary for the delineation of the story and both these events take place in one location and within a short period of time. As we will see, the Kuchean sermons scenes are more complicated (Hiyama forthcoming, chapter 3); they introduce supplementary persons without which the pictures would be more easily readable, and often ignore the unity of time and place completely.

The famous – and frequently depicted in Kucha – scene showing the monk Kāśyapa (a former ascetic from the Urubilva wood) performing miracles in front of King Bimbisāra[50] may serve as an example of a typical sermon scene in the Second Indo-Iranian Style (Figure 4.11).[51] The scene was recognized already in 1930 by Waldschmidt (and again, independently, in 2001 by Mori). The significant iconographical element of the story is the monk shown once flying in the air, emitting fire and water currents (his four heads might perhaps denote that he appeared in every cardinal direction as described in the text or that he multiplied himself), and for a second time kneeling in front of the Buddha. The monk is clad in a patchwork robe (*pāṃśukūla*); this particular garment is actually of significance in the narrative of another Kāśyapa, the monk Mahākāśyapa from the *parinirvāṇa* cycle. In Kucha Urubilva-Kāśyapa, too, wears the *pāṃśukūla*, perhaps due to a misunderstanding, or rather out of a

---

49 The German term "komplettierende Darstellungsart" (completing mode of representation) holds better; for the analysis of Indian modes of representations and for comparison between the research on the subject by Dehejia (1997) and Schlingloff (1981), see Zin 2019.

50 For the literary sources see Waldschmidt 1951, 113–18; for the narrative Kloppenborg 1973, 83–4.

51 Kizil 178 (Schluchthöhle), illus. Grünwedel 1920, pl. 24–5, fig. 1; Härtel and Yaldiz 1982, no. 35; Yaldiz 1987, pl. XI.

wish to create an easily readable iconography indicating: "this is Kāśyapa". All elements of this depiction send pieces of information concerning the narrative: deities and persons of higher social status are shown nimbate, while Brahmins and monks, even the enlightened *arhat*s, are not. If in a rare case a monk appears equipped with a nimbus, this certainly is of significance. It obviously is therefore of utmost importance to distinguish the elements relevant to the plot.

The comparison of sermon scenes allows us to recognize a number of almost invariably recurring elements like the gods in the uppermost row – Indra with the third eye, Brahma with ascetic hair and musicians with different instruments – Vajrapāṇi or monks; such elements of the composition certainly are not part of the recognizable iconography of one particular scene. This, however, is only partially true since for instance the presence of the monks clearly indicates a certain point of time in the life story of the Buddha, that is to say after the first sermon. (Monks are not shown, for example, in the scene with Trapuṣa and Bhallika offering to the Buddha his first meal after the enlightenment; see Figure 4.21 below.) The monks are therefore indicators for a particular time period, just as the moon, burning torches or lamps were shown to indicate night time, such as in depictions of Ajātaśatru's visit to the Buddha in Jīvaka's grove; this narrative was recognized by Hamada (2003).[52]

The significance of the diverting appearance of Vajrapāṇi – shown like a demonic *yakṣa* or a general clad in knight's armour, sometimes wearing a princely crown, sometimes a very particular hat, or Hercules' lion skin – has not yet been fully understood. It might also carry a meaning which was recognizable to the ancient viewer. Certainly of importance was the setting of the scene – tree, palace, monastery or cave – represented in a tiny stripe above the nimbus of the Buddha.

An identification of sermon scenes is only possible if those elements that do not belong to the generic visual repertoire of this particular genre are specific enough; comparisons are crucial. The challenge is created by the multitude of figures and objects surrounding the Buddha, since their role in the visualization of the narrative is difficult to recognize. In our Figure 4.11 for instance, behind the interlocutor of the Buddha, King Bimbisāra seated on a throne beside his consort, three persons appear. Only for an experienced observer is it possible to ascertain that in this case these persons are only of minor importance; they carry regalia (umbrella, sword and crown, marked in the drawing) and their only purpose is to show that the person below is a great king (compare left side of Figure 4.14). The small figures below also belong to the royal retinue; the one near the Buddha is a jester characterized by the cap with many pompoms

---

[52] The small man seated beside the king who is stretched out on the ground must be the youth Boxian (帛賢) from the *Śrāmaṇyaphalasūtra*, preserved in Chinese (T 22, ed. vol. 1: 270c28–276b7); see Arlt and Hiyama 2015; for the narrative see *Dīghanikāya* 2 (*Sāmaññaphalasutta*) and Rockhill 1884, 95–106.

Figure 4.11. Kizil, Cave 178 (Schluchthöhle), main chamber, left wall, taken to Berlin; Museum für Asiatische Kunst, no. III 8725a; drawing by the author © Monika Zin CC BY-NC-SA

Figure 4.12. Simsim, Cave 44 (Höhle mit den kranztragenden Tauben), main chamber, barrel vault, right side, *in situ*; drawing by the author © Monika Zin CC BY-NC-SA

(Arlt and Hiyama 2015 & Hiyama and Arlt 2016). These elements, unnecessary for the transmission of the plot, do not appear in the Kāśyapa narrative in "telegraphic style" on the barrel vault where, except for the Buddha, only Bimbisāra and Kāśyapa (flying in the air and bowing down) are depicted (Figure 4.12).[53] The presence of additional persons in the scenes on the walls makes it more difficult to understand these scenes; the important elements actually seem to be downright hidden among the multitude of adoring gods and minor characters like the bearers of regalia. Even if it may not have been explicitly intended, at least the risk was evidently taken of actually obscuring these meaningful elements by cluttering the composition with additional details.

The scene with Kāśyapa (like our Figure 4.11) can also contain depictions of Brahmanical ascetics;[54] these must be Kāśyapa and his brothers before their conversion in the Urubilva wood (Figure 4.13). But the sermon scenes can also contain visual elements referring to far more distant places. The representations of a king (probably Bimbisāra) paying a visit to the Buddha, like for example in Kizil 175 (see n. 43) (Figure 4.14), display in the corners tiny persons being buried under showers of sand in the city of Roruka. The king of Roruka, Udrāyaṇa, a pen friend of Bimbisāra, became a monk and the city was later punished for bad deeds that occurred under the reign of his wrongful son.[55] The measuring of the ground for the Jetavana monastery (Figure 4.15)[56] shows in its upper corner a pavilion for Anāthapiṇḍada which appeared in Tuṣita Heaven at the same time as the construction of the monastery was taken up.[57] In these cases, the unity of space is ignored.

The same is true for the unity of time. The sermon scenes can represent events from different time periods in one picture and the hiatus between the depicted episodes can be large. The illustration of the narrative of Elapatra (Figure 4.16)[58] – a *nāgarāja* with an *ela* tree growing on his head causing terrible pain[59] – often (but not always) includes a depiction of the bad deed that

---

[53] Simsim, Cave 44, illus. *Mural Paintings in Xinjiang of China* 2009, vol. 5, 106, pl. 100.

[54] Kizil, Cave 179, Berlin, Museum für Asiatische Kunst, no. III 8660; unpublished.

[55] Identif. Inoue 2017; for the narrative see n. 25.

[56] Kumtura 23, illus. *Mural Paintings in Xinjiang of China* 2009, vol. 4, 53, pl. 51; the drawing was made from the historical photograph taken by the French expedition, archives of the Musée Guimet, no. AP 7024.

[57] Identif. Inoue 2014; the narrative of the donation of the Jetavana is well known from many sources and was already depicted in Indian art (see Zin 2010b); the particular version with the pavilion for Anāthapiṇḍada appearing in heaven is known only from the *vinaya* of the Sarvāstivādins (T 1450, ed. vol. 24: 141b12–23) and the *Sūtra of the Wise and the Foolish* (T 202, ed. vol. 4: 420c25–421a6).

[58] Kizil, Cave 98, not published.

[59] Identif. Zin 2011a; for literary sources see Zin 2000 and Zin 2011a; for the narrative (Ger. trans. from Tibetan) see Schiefner 1875, 11–14 (*Mūlasarvāstivādavinaya*), short summary in Rockhill 1884, 46.

Figure 4.13. Kizil, Cave 179 (Japanerhöhle), main chamber, ? wall, taken to Berlin, Museum für Asiatische Kunst, no. III 8660; drawing by the author © Monika Zin CC BY-NC-SA

Figure 4.14. Kizil, Cave 175 (Versuchungshöhle), main chamber, left wall; taken to Berlin, no. 9175, lost due to war; drawing by the author © Monika Zin CC BY-NC-SA

Figure 4.15. Kumtura, Cave 23 (Höhle 19), main chamber, left wall, *in situ*; drawing by the author © Monika Zin CC BY-NC-SA

Figure 4.16. Kizil, Cave 98, main chamber, left wall, *in situ*; drawing by the author © Monika Zin CC BY-NC-SA

was the reason for this ordeal. Represented is a monk, the former birth of the *nāgarāja* during the life time of the Buddha Kāśyapa, who destroys the leaves of an *ela* tree. There, unity of time is ignored; it is substituted by the Buddha who in his sermon explains to the *nāgarāja* why the tree is growing on his head. In fact, the picture illustrates the "present" as well as the "previous" stories (like the stories of the "present" time of the Buddha and of his past lifetime in a *jātaka*). The depicted monk, who lived thousands of years earlier, actually belongs to the content of the Buddha's sermon. The Elapatra narrative has been represented in Ajanta as well (Zin 2000: 1172–83) but of course without the monk; it is only the pictorial genre of the "sermon scene" which makes such representations possible.

The depictions of the content of the sermons within these scenes is an invention of Kucha,[60] and it appears that we can even trace its development during the First Indo-Iranian Style. The First Style "sermon scenes" in Kizil 92 (see notes 16–20), at least the preserved ones, show the Buddha in the centre while around him the events are represented in a conflated manner (this is the same type of scene as the *Māravijaya* or the Gandharan conversion scenes). In Kizil 77 (Figure 4.4), the piece of wood in the water illustrates the Buddha's teaching. It refers to the *Dāruskandasūtra* that contains the simile of the log (see notes 23–24). By means of the simile the Buddha explains to the monks that they can reach *nirvāṇa* if they do not meet obstacles like the log that can reach the ocean unless it falls into a whirlpool, and so on. Two fragments in Berlin belonging to the same cave, Kizil 77, one showing two birds in front of the Buddha's throne,[61] and the other three swimming persons,[62] certainly do not illustrate episodes from Buddha's life but the content of his preaching, although the scenes have not yet been identified.[63]

The sermon scenes in the late First Style cave Kizil 207 (Malerhöhle) are quite well documented thanks to Grünwedel's drawings (see Figure 4.6). Compared with sermon scenes of the Second Indo-Iranian Style the compositions in this cave are far less complex; elements not related to the transmission of the narrative are few and they are not yet standardized, therefore figures like the deities with musical instruments or the bearers of regalia do not appear. According to Hiyama (2016, ch. 4), the scenes make an anthology of stories

60 To the best of my knowledge, in Indian art only the parable "Man in the well" (reliefs from Andhra from the second and third century) is represented besides the monk preaching it (Zin 2011b). None of the depictions reveals the model used in Kucha with the sermonizer located in the centre.

61 Berlin, Museum für Asiatische Kunst, no. III 8839; illus. Yaldiz et al. 2000, no. 286 (with references to earlier publications); Ding 2015, 158.

62 Berlin, Museum für Asiatische Kunst, no. III 8398; illus. Yaldiz et al. 2000, no. 292 (with references to earlier publications); Ding 2015, 163.

63 Schlingloff (1997–98, 180, fn. 18) presumes that other scenes in the cave also illustrated sermons from the *Bhaiṣajyavastu* of the *Mūlasarvāstivādavinaya*.

compiled in the *āgama*s of the (Mūla-)Sarvāstivāda schools (some of the narratives have not been taken into the *vinaya*s).

The scenes include the first sermon, our episode with Kāśyapa performing miracles and several conversions, like the conversion of the Jaina Sātyaki[64] on whom Vajrapāṇi casts fire from his *vajra* (see Figure 4.6, lower left).[65] At least two sermon scenes in Kizil 207 provide evidence that the representation of the content of the Buddha's sermon must have been self-explanatory at the time: Grünwedel already recognized their topics, of the one as dealing with the destruction of the world and of another with the appearing of the new world (see Figure 4.6, lower middle).[66] The destruction, comes at the end of a *kalpa* when seven suns burn down the earth.[67] The painting illustrates the occurrence as Mount Sumeru with seven discs above it. The appearance of the new world is shown in a very similar scene also showing Sumeru but without the seven suns above (Figure 4.17),[68] Hiyama recognized god Brahma, responsible for the creation of the world in the Brahmanical worldview, hiding himself behind Sumeru.[69] Interestingly both scenes with Sumeru were placed facing each other in the cave.

In paintings belonging to the Second Indo-Iranian Style the Buddha's teaching can be represented within the scene, too. Hiyama (2016: 138) recognized the depiction of Sumeru in the lower part of a sermon scene in Kizil 161 painted in the Second Style. An easily recognized scene is the simile of the turtle.[70] The simile describes a one-eyed or blind turtle rising to the surface of the ocean only once in 100 years. That he puts his head through the yoke floating on the surface in the moment he raises his head out of the water illustrates how rare the chances are to be reborn as a human being or to be reborn during the lifetime of the Buddha. The simile was often represented in Kucha, always

64 Identif. Hiyama 2016, 112–18; Saccaka Nigaṇṭhaputta, *Majjhimanikāya* 35 and T 99, vol. 2: 35a17–37b37; see Hiyama for analysis and further literary sources.

65 Kizil, Cave 207, main chamber, right side wall; original drawing by Grünwedel kept in the archives of the Museum für Asiatische Kunst, no. TA 6639 (= Grünwedel 1912, fig. 344) and in the Museum Fünf Kontinente in Munich, no. 11.710.

66 Kizil, Cave 207, original drawing by Grünwedel kept in the archives of the Museum Fünf Kontinente in Munich, no. 11.714; Grünwedel 1912, fig. 343; Grünwedel 1920, fig. 23; identif. Grünwedel 1920, II 22.

67 For the analysis and literary sources, among others the *Saptasūryodayasūtra*, in Hiyama 2016, 122–6.

68 Kizil, Cave 207, original drawing by Grünwedel kept in the archives of the Museum für Asiatische Kunst, no. TA 6638 (= Grünwedel 1912, fig. 352); Munich, Museum Fünf Kontinente, no. 11.709.

69 For references to the literary sources, among others the *Aggaññasutta*, see Hiyama 2016, 135–8.

70 For literary sources see Allon 2007 and Ogihara 2010, the latter also for an edition of the Tocharian version; for the parable in other Central Asian languages see Wilkens 2015, 256–8.

Figure 4.17. Kizil, Cave 207 (Malerhöhle), main chamber, left wall, today lost; drawing by Grünwedel, no. TA 6638 © Museum für Asiatische Kunst - Staatliche Museen zu Berlin, CC BY-NC-SA

besides the Buddha (teaching it): it was depicted in a simplified manner in the barrel vaults (Figure 4.18)[71] and in a more complex way. A beautiful, now destroyed, representation from Kizil, Cave 219 (Ajātaśatruhöhle), is preserved in a historical photograph only (Figure 4.19) on the walls. Interestingly the depictions in Kucha show not a yoke but a plank; the Tocharian B version of the simile (manuscript THT 407) uses the world *pyorye* which – as was recently shown by Pinault (2015: 392–3) – refers to a log or plank.[72]

To summarize: sermon scenes of the Second Indo-Iranian Style can contain the content of the Buddha's sermon, episodes from the previous lives of the acting personages, elements characterizing a person, allusions to locations and time periods, even very distant ones. At the same time they contain adoring

[71] Kizil, Cave 163, illus. *Kizil Grottoes* 1983–85/1989–97, vol. 2, pls. 173, 178 (right side); Tan and An 1981, vol. 2, pl. 64 (right side); very good photograph in Ma and Fan 2007, 214–15.

[72] I would like to thank Prof. Georges-Jean Pinault for detailed information, references and his translation of the simile from Tocharian (private communication 28.07.2019).

Figure 4.18. Kizil, Cave 163, main chamber, barrel vault, left side, *in situ*; drawing by the author © Monika Zin CC BY-NC-SA

Figure 4.19. Kizil, Cave 219 (Ajātaśatruhöhle), main chamber, left wall, today destroyed; documented in historical photograph in Museum für Asiatische Kunst, no. B 1539; drawing by the author © Monika Zin CC BY-NC-SA

deities who add nothing to the plot but only serve to demonstrate the glory of the Buddha. The sermon scenes are certainly a continuation of Indian conflated depictions which recall a story to the memory of the viewer rather than illustrate it, but they go much further: they "translate" complex narratives, including multiple (life-)times and places, and the content of Buddha's teaching into a pictorial language.

Can we read all sermon scenes?

The previously stated optimistic opinion that the scenes having distinctive iconographical signs will be explained one day by means of literary sources has to be put into perspective: the scenes will only be explained if we can understand these iconographical signs.

I would like to show here a scene which – for the time being – appears to belong to the unexplainable ones. The scene is a unique specimen among the preserved murals. "Preserved" is not the proper word; the mural was removed from Kizil 179 (Japanerhöhle) and taken to Berlin in 1914 where it was destroyed by the end of the Second World War. Only a single black and white photograph showing three scenes and a part of the third exists (Figure 4.20).[73] The photograph was taken in Berlin after the parts of the mural were joined together. Two parts of the upper left scene do not match. The right side makes a perfect unit with a part of a sermon scene which is being kept today in the Museum für Asiatische Kunst and shows the donation of food by the first lay-followers, Trapuṣa and Bhallika, and bowls by the Four Great Kings[74] (Figure 4.21). The fragment which was erroneously joined to the left part of the donation of food and bowls most probably belonged to the left part of IB 9172 (Figure 4.22).[75] The fragment is poorly preserved; still visible are a monk, above him Vajrapāṇi, and the partly preserved head of a male person with a white earring next to the Buddha. Because of the earring we can be sure that this was not another monk. The head is not surrounded by a nimbus; this indicates he is a person of low rank. Nothing else can be said about the man except that the Buddha is talking to him, apparently about what is depicted below and on the other side of the sermon scene.

---

[73] Berlin, no. IB 9172, destroyed during the war; historical photograph in Museum für Asiatische Kunst, no. C 9; illus. in Dreyer, Sander, and Weis 2002, 198; for other mural fragments from the cave see n. 44.

[74] For the literary tradition see Waldschmidt 1951, 88–90; for the narrative see Kloppenborg, trans. 1973, 7–10.

[75] The left side of the drawing: historical photograph in Museum für Asiatische Kunst, no. C 9; right side: fragment of the painting from Kizil 179 (Japanerhöhle) in Museum für Asiatische Kunst, no. III 8660.

Figure 4.20. Kizil, Cave 179 (Japanerhöhle), main chamber, ? wall, taken to Berlin, IB 9172, today destroyed; historical photograph no. C 9 © Museum für Asiatische Kunst - Staatliche Museen zu Berlin, CC BY-NC-SA

The rest of the depiction is most remarkable (Figure 4.23). As we have seen before, the representation of the content of Buddha's teaching is usually shown below, in front of the Buddha's throne. Our picture shows in this location a water reservoir – the ocean – in which a man and a skeleton are swimming. The representation may perhaps refer to a characteristic of the ocean which is believed not to cohabit with corpses (it washes them ashore), a feature compared to the *saṅgha* refusing to keep immoral monks.[76] Based on this

[76] For references to this often repeated simile see Lamotte 1944–80, vol. 3, 1400 n.1448.

Figure 4.21. Kizil, Cave 179 (Japanerhöhle), computer-generated photograph; left side: fragment of no. III 8660 © Museum für Asiatische Kunst – Staatliche Museen zu Berlin / Jürgen Liepe, CC BY-NC-SA; right side: part of historical photograph no. C 9 (Figure 4.20)

Figure 4.22. Kizil, Cave 179 (Japanerhöhle), computer-generated photograph; left side: part of historical photograph no. C 9 (Figure 4.20); right side: fragment of no. III 8660 © Museum für Asiatische Kunst – Staatliche Museen zu Berlin / Jürgen Liepe, CC BY-NC-SA

imagery stories exist about drowning people who reached the shore clinging to dead bodies or even about a sacrifice of the Bodhisatva who killed himself at sea thus enabling his companions to survive.[77] The depiction does not, however, really match these descriptions since the man in the ocean is swimming by himself and not holding on to the skeleton (which might perhaps illustrate the corpse). Furthermore, the scene apparently continues to the left. In the left lower corner sits a male person whose appearance is that of a young Brahmin (Brahma and Brahmins are shown with hair piled high and decorated with a lotus flower); he wears a rich necklace. The gesture of his hands with both palms turned up is unusual. The round object below is incomprehensible. It resembles a head surrounded by a nimbus but there is no space for the rest of the body in this picture. Above the round object a male person is standing, or rather emerging from the water reservoir. This person in much bigger but looks similar to the swimmer; both are young Brahmins with heads surrounded by nimbi. The man emerging from the water holds an object in his right hand (a dark coloured flower?), while the left hand and his eyes are directed towards the sitting male in the upper left corner, again a young Brahmin wearing a rich necklace. Both sitting persons (young Brahmins wearing a rich necklace) might be one and the same individual. It is most remarkable that the upper person is shown in a mandorla (it might be true of the lower too). In Kucha, only the *buddha*s, and among them only the *saṃyaksaṃbuddha*s, but not the *pratyekabuddha*s (Konczak-Nagel 2020, 51–4), and the "great *bodhisatva*s" (Maitreya in the lunettes or standing *bodhisatva*s, for example in some domes)[78] are shown with mandorlas. As a matter of fact, only Siddhārtha and Maitreya are recognized in a mandorla in Kuchean paintings of the First and Second Indo-Iranian Style.

To my knowledge, no other person with a mandorla is depicted in any other sermon scene. The context of our scene, with a Bodhisatva being approached by a person rising from the water, is suggestive of Avalokiteśvara, the saviour from perils, as described in chapter 24 of the *Saddharmapuṇḍarīkasūtra*,[79] or as depicted in the so-called "Aṣṭamahābhaya Avalokiteśvaras", or the "litanies of Avalokiteśvara" in Maharashtra. From Kucha, however, we do not have – by the present state of knowledge – any evidence that Avalokiteśvara was worshipped there. It rather seems that the paintings intentionally avoid his representation; triads with the Buddha, Vajrapāṇi and Padmapāṇi (Avalokiteśvara) do not appear. To representations of the "pensive Bodhisatva" (characteristic representations of Avalokiteśvara for Gandhara or Mathura), the Kuchean

[77] For references see Lamotte 1944–80, vol. 1, 284 n. 489.

[78] As, for example, in Kumtura GK 20; illus. *Mural Paintings in Xinjiang of China* 2009, vol. 4, 3–10, pls. 1–8.

[79] Kern and Nanjio, ed. 1908, 438–41, 448–51.

Figure 4.23. Kizil, Cave 179 (Japanerhöhle), drawing of fig. 4.22; drawing by the author © Monika Zin CC BY-NC-SA

Figure 4.24. Kizil, Cave 123 (Höhle mit den ringtragenden Tauben), main chamber, lunette above the rear wall, taken to Berlin, no. III 9063; drawing by the author © Monika Zin CC BY-NC-SA

painters added a bird with a snake in its beak or a ploughing man[80] to define the scenes as depictions of the first meditation of Siddhārtha (Figure 4.24).[81]

Can the Bodhisatva in our scene be Maitreya? There is evidence that Maitreya, too, was understood to be a saviour from perils. Leese (1988), who sought to explain the Bodhisatva in Maharashtra's "litanies" as Maitreya, refers to a tale from the life-story of Xuanzang by Huili: Xuanzang was saved from the hands of the pirates due to the torrential rainfall sent by Maitreya.[82]

The scene in Figure 4.22 remains unexplained. As previous research has shown, the paintings in Kucha illustrate narratives well known from literary sources. Most probably this is also the case in this and in several other representations as yet unexplained. The depictions are apparently too sophisticated to be easily understood. For the time being we do not possess sufficient knowledge to convincingly explain a scene in which Maitreya or another great *bodhisatva* plays a role. The issue may be more essential than it appears and concern not just the identification of one or another painting but may have an impact on our understanding of Buddhism as a whole in Kucha. The Mahāyāna pantheon or illustrations of the topics familiar from Mahāyāna literature do not appear in the First and the Second Indo-Iranian Style but the general message of the cave decorations with their increasing numbers of the self-sacrifices of a *bodhisatva* or the announcements of the future buddhahood convey a quite "mahāyānistic" atmosphere in which perhaps even the adoption of Mahāyāna's helping saints was possible.

The sermon scenes of Kucha show how interconnected images are with both literary sources and oral teaching activities. Whether or not these images were meant to be recognized, they show us a Buddha actively engaged in communicating the *dharma* to his followers, using similes, past-life stories and other devices. The resulting scenes – including complex components both relevant to and unrelated to the narrative itself – can be very difficult to identify. However, as our understanding of the iconography improves, we will learn more about how this site and its visual programme expressed Buddhist ideas about the Buddha and his teaching.

80 Kizil, Cave 38, *Kizil Grottoes* 1983–85/1989–97, vol. 1, pl. 88; Kizil, Cave 229; illus. *Kizil Grottoes* 1983–85/1989–97, vol. 3, pl. 165.

81 Kizil, Cave 123, the drawing was made from the historical photograph taken by the French expedition, archives of the Musée Guimet, no. AP 7508.

82 T 2053, ed. vol. 50: 233c25–234b10; trans. Beal 1911, 87–8.

Bibliography

Allon, M. 2007. "A Gāndhārī Version of the Simile of the Turtle and the Hole in the Yoke." *Journal of the Pali Text Society*: 229–62.

Arlt, R. and S. Hiyama 2013. "Fruits of Research on the History of Central Asian Art in Berlin: The Identification of Two Sermon Scenes from Kizil Cave 206 (Fußwaschungshöhle)." *Indo-Asiatische Zeitschrift* 17: 16–26.

Arlt, R. and S. Hiyama 2015. "Theatrical Figures in the Mural Paintings of Kucha." *Journal of the International Association of Buddhist Studies* 38: 313–48.

Beal, S. 1911. *The Life of Hiuen-Tsiang by Shaman Hwui Li with an Introduction Containing an Account of the Works of I-Tsing, with a preface by L. Cranmer-Byng*, London: Trübner.

Chang, Wen-ling 2020. *Feststellung der literarischen Vorlagen der jātaka Darstellungen in Höhle 17 in Kizil* [Assessment of the literary sources of the jātaka representations in the Cave 17 at Kizil]. Dissertation 2017, Freie Universität, Berlin.

Charpentier, J. 1925. "Ergebnisse der Kgl. Preussischen Turfan-Expeditionen. Die Buddhistische Spätantike in Mittelasien. Dritter Teil: Die Wandmalereien. Vierter Teil: Atlas zu den Wandmalereien by A. von Le Coq". *Bulletin of the School of Oriental and African Studies* 3: 814–20.

Dehejia, V. 1997. *Discourse in Early Buddhist Art. Visual Narratives of India*, Delhi: Munshiram Manoharlal.

Ding, H. 2015. *Dezang Xinjiang bihua* [Wall paintings of Xinjiang housed in Germany]. Shanghai: Shanghai Press Publishing Bureau.

Dreyer, C., L. Sander, and F. Weis 2002. *Staatliche Museen zu Berlin, Dokumentation der Verluste, Band III: Museum für Indische Kunst (Verzeichnis seit 1945 vermisster Bestände der ehemaligen Indischen Abteilung des Museums für Völkerkunde, des heutigen Museums für Indische Kunst)*. Berlin: Museum für Indische Kunst, SMB.

Grünwedel, A. 1912. *Altbuddhistische Kultstätten in Chinesisch-Turkistan: Königlich Preussische Turfan Expeditionen*. Berlin: Reimer.

Grünwedel, A. 1920. *Alt-Kutscha, archäologische und religionsgeschichtliche Forschungen an Tempera-Gemälden aus Buddhistischen Höhlen der ersten acht Jahrhunderte nach Christi Geburt, Veröffentlichungen der Preussischen Turfan-Expeditionen*, Berlin: Elsner.

Hallade, M. and S. Goulier, with the participation of L. Courtois 1982. *Douldour-Âquour et Soubachi, Mission Paul Pelliot IV*, Centre de Recherche sur l'Asie Centrale et la Haute-Asie Instituts d'Asie Collège de France, Paris: Éditions Recherché sur les civilisations.

Hamada, T. 2003. "Kijiru chūshinchū kutsu no butsu seppozu ni tsuite" [A study on Buddha's preaching scenes on the Kizil paintings]. *Fūdo to Bunka* 4: 21–34.

Härtel, H. and M. Yaldiz. 1982). *Along the Ancient Silk Routes: Central Asian Art from the West Berlin State Museums. An exhibition lent by the Museum of Indische Kunst, Staatliche Museen Preussischer Kulturbesitz, Berlin, Federal Republic of Germany, held at The Metropolitan Museum of Art, New York, April 3 – June 20, 1982*, New York: The Metropolitan Museum of Art.

Hiyama, S. 2012. "New identification of murals in Kizil Cave 118 as the story of King Māndhātar." *Journal of Inner Asian Art and Archaeology* 5: 145–70.

Hiyama, S. 2016. *The Wall Paintings of "The Painters' Cave" (Kizil Cave 207)*, PhD Dissertation, Freie Universität Berlin, 2014 (microfiche publication, Ketsch: Mikroform).

Hiyama, Satomi, Forthcoming. *Reading the Murals: Buddhist Art of Kucha along the Silk Road in the 5-7th Centuries (Connecting Art Histories in the Museum)*. Dortmund: Kettler.

Hiyama, S. and R. Arlt 2016. "Kucha no hekiga ni mirareru kyūtei dōke shi Vidūshaka no zuzō" [Iconography of the courtly jester Vidusaka in the mural paintings of Kucha]. *Bukkyō geijutsu / Ars Buddhica* 349: 76–100.

Inoue, M. 2014. "Kijiru sekkutsu butsudenzu hekiga Gion shōja no konryū no sisōteki haikei" [An Attempt to Identify the Scene about Jetavana Anathapindadasya-arama in Qizil Paintings and its Religious Background]. *Herenizumu-isrāmu kōkokaku kenkyū / Japan Society for Hellenistic-Islam Archaeological Studies* 21: 27–39.

Inoue, M. 2017. "Kijiru sekkutsu hekiga ni okeru butsuden zu no gadai hitei – Bukkyō setuwazu 'Zen-on-jo no monogatari' to sono igi" [Identification of painted subject of the Buddha's life scenes in the mural paintings of Kizil grottoes – the Buddhist tale "Story of Roruka" and its significance]. *Kashima Bijutsu Kenkyu* 34: 381–9.

Jones, J. J., trans. 1949–56. *The Mahāvastu*. 3 vols. London: Luzac and co.

Kern, H. and B. Nanjio, eds. 1908. *Saddharmapuṇḍarīkasūtra*. Bibliotheca Buddhica 10, St. Petersburg.

Kizil Grottoes 1983–85. Shinkyō Uiguru jichiku bunbutsu kanri i inkai / Baiki ken Kijiru senbutsudō bubutsu hokanjo, ed. 1983–85. *Chūgoku sekkutsu: Kijiru sekkutsu* [The Grotto Art of China: The Kizil Grottoes]. 3 vols. Tokyo: Heibonsha.

Kizil Grottoes 1989–97. Xinjiang weiwu'er zizhiqu wenwu guanli weiyuanhui / Baicheng xian Kezi'er qianfodong wenwu baoguansuo, ed. 1989–1997. *Zhongguo shiku: Kezi'er shiku* [The Grotto Art of China: The Kizil Grottoes]. 3 vols. Beijing: Wenwu chubanshe.

Klaus, K. 1983. *Das Maitrakanyakāvadāna, Sanskrittext und deutsche Übersetzung*, Bonn: Indica et Tibetica 2.

Kloppenborg, R., trans. 1973. *The Sūtra on the Foundation of the Buddhist Order (Catuṣpariṣatsūtra)*. Leiden: Brill.

Konczak-Nagel, I. 2020. “Representations of Architecture and Architectural Elements in the Mural Paintings of Kucha.” In E. Franco and M. Zin (eds.) *Essays and Studies in the Art of Kucha*. Saxon Academy of Sciences and Humanities, Leipzig Kucha Studies 1, Delhi: Dev Publishers, 11–106, 185–225.

Konczak-Nagel, I. 2021. “Dämonendarstellungen in Kizil: Überlegungen zu ihren regionalen Eigenheiten und bildlichen Vorlagen am Beispiel eines Wandgemäldes aus der Höhle 178 (Schluchthöhle) am Museum für Asiatische Kunst (III 8725a)”. *Indo-Asiatische Zeitschrift* 25, 4–13.

Kumtula Grottoes 1985. Shinkyō Uiguru jichiku bunbutsu kanri i inkai / Kucha ken bunbutsu hokanjo, ed. 1985. *Chūgoku sekkutsu: Kumutora sekkutsu* [The Grotto Art of China: The Kumtula Grottoes]. Tokyo: Heibonsha.

Lamotte, É. 1944–80. *Le traité de la grande vertu de sagesse de Nāgārjuna: Mahāprajñāpāramitāśāstra*, 5 vols.. Louvain: Institute Orientaliste, Publication de l’Institut Orientaliste de Louvain.

Le Coq, A. von 1924a. *Die buddhistische Spätantike in Mittelasien. Ergebnisse der Kgl.-Preussischen Turfan-Expeditionen IV, Atlas zu den Wandmalereien.* Berlin: Reimer und Vohsen.

Le Coq, A. von 1924b. *Die buddhistische Spätantike in Mittelasien. Ergebnisse der Kgl.-Preussischen Turfan-Expeditionen III, Die Wandmalereien.* Berlin: Reimer und Vohsen.

Le Coq, A. von and E. Waldschmidt 1928. *Die buddhistische Spätantike in Mittelasien = Ergebnisse der Kgl. Preussischen Turfan Expeditionen VI, Neue Bildwerke 2.* Berlin: Reimer und Vohsen.

Le Coq, A. von and E. Waldschmidt. 1933. *Die buddhistische Spätantike in Mittelasien = Ergebnisse der Kgl.-Preussischen Turfan-Expeditionen VII, Neue Bildwerke 3*. Berlin: Reimer und Vohsen.

Leese, M.E. 1988. “Ellora and the Development of the Litany Scene in Western India.” In R. Parimoo et al. (eds.) *Ellora Caves: Sculptures and Architecture*, 164–79. New Delhi: Books & Books.

Lesbre, E. 2001. “An Attempt to Identify and Classify Scenes with a Central Buddha Depicted on Ceilings of the Kizil Caves (Former Kingdom of Kutcha, Central Asia).” *Artibus Asiae* 61/2: 305–52.

Ma, Q. and S. Fan 2007. *Qiuci: Zaoxiang* [Figural images in Kucha]. Beijing: Wenwu chubanshe.

Mori, M. 2001. “Kucha no Seppozu ni kansuru ichi Kosatsu” [Study on the sermon scenes of Kucha], *Waseda Daigaku Daigakuin Bungaku Kenkyuka Kiyo* III 47, Tokyo: Waseda University: 149–164.

Mural Paintings in Xinjiang of China 2009. Zhongguo Xinjiang bihua yishu bianji weiyuanhui, ed. 2009. *Zhongguo Xinjiang bihua yishu* [Mural Paintings in Xinjiang of China]. 6 vols. Urumqi: Xinjiang meishu sheying chubanshe.

Nakagawara, I. 2011 "Kizil dai 81 kutsu no Sudana Taishi honjo hekiga ni tsuite [A brief study on the wall paintings of prince Sudana-Jataka in Kizil Cave 81]." *Nagoya daigaku bungakubu kenkyū ronshu shigaku* 57: 109–29.

Ogihara, H. 2010. "Qiuci yu 'Manggui zhi fumukong' biyu [The parable of the blind turtle and the hole in the wood]." *Proceedings of the 1st International Colloquium on Ancient Manuscripts and Literatures of the Minorities in China*, Beijing: Minzu chubanshe: 325–38.

Ogihara, H. 2015. "Shilun Kumutula di 50 ku zhushi zhengbi fokan qianfo tuxiang de chengxu 50 [Arrangement of the Paintings of Thousand Buddhas in the Niche on the Main Wall of the Main Chamber of Cave No. 50 in the Kumtura Grottoes]." *Xiyu yanjiu / The Western Regions Studies*: 36–42.

Pinault, G.-J. 2015. "Résumé des conférences de l'année 2013–2014." *Annuaire de l'Ecole Pratiques des Hautes Etudes, Section des sciences historiques et philologiques* 146: 391–3. https://doi.org/10.4000/ashp.1765

Rhi, J. 이주형. 2009. "Indo pulgyo munhŏn kwa misul e poinŭn Chesŏkkul sammae sŏlbŏp 인도 불교 문헌과 미술에 보이는 <제석굴 삼매/설법 > / [The "Visit of Indra" in Textual and Visual Traditions of Early Indian Buddhism]" *Chungang Asia yŏn'gu* 중앙아시아연구 / *Central Asian Studies* 14: 109–40. https://doi.org/10.29174/cas.2009.14..005

Rockhill, W.W. 1884. *The Life of the Buddha and the Early History of His Order Derived from Tibetan Works in the Bkah-hgyur and Bstan-hgyur*. London: Trübner.

Rotman, A., trans. 2008. *The Divine Stories. Divyāvadāna Part I*. Boston: Wisdom Publications.

Rotman, A., trans. 2017. *The Divine Stories, Divyāvadāna Part II*. Boston: Wisdom Publications.

Salomon, R. 2018. *The Buddhist Literature of Ancient Gandhāra: An Introduction with Selected Translations*. Somerville MA: Wisdom Publications.

Schiefner, A. 1875. *Mahākatjājana und König Tschaṇḍa-Pradjota, Mémoires de l'Académie Impériale des Sciences de St. Pétersbourg*, 7.22.7, St. Petersburg.

Schlingloff, D. 1981. "Erzählung und Bild. Die Darstellungsformen von Handlungsabläufen in der Europäischen und Indischen Kunst." *Beiträge zur Allgemeinen und Vergleichenden Archäologie* 3: 87–213 (Eng.: Narrative Art in Europe and India. In: Schlingloff, 1987: 227–80.

Schlingloff, D. 1987. *Studies in the Ajanta Paintings, Identifications and Interpretations*, New Delhi: Ajanta Books International.

Schlingloff, D. 1991. "Traditions of Indian Narrative Painting in Central Asia." In G. Bhattacharya, ed. *Akṣayanīvī: Essays Presented to Dr. Debala Mitra* 163–9. Delhi: Sri Satguru Publications; repr. in Shashibala, ed. 2016: 286–304.

Schlingloff, D. 1997–98. "Das *Mahāprātihārya* in der zentralasiatischen Hinayana-Kunst." *Indologica Taurinensia* 23–24: 175–94.

Schlingloff, D. 2000. *Ajanta – Handbuch der Malereien / Handbook of the Paintings 1. Erzählende Wandmalereien / Narrative Wall-paintings.* Wiesbaden: Harrassowitz.

Schlingloff, D. 2013. *Ajanta – Handbook of the Paintings 1. Narrative Wall-paintings.* New Delhi: IGNCA.

Shashibala, ed. 2016. *Sanskrit on the Silk Route*. Delhi: Bharatiya Vidya Bhavan.

Soper, A. C. 1949–50. "Aspects of Light Symbolism in Gandhāran Sculpture." *Artibus Asiae* 12: 252–83. https://doi.org/10.2307/3248387

Tan, S. and C. An 1981. *Murals for Xinjiang, The Thousand-Buddha Caves at Kizil, Shinkyō no hekiga: Kijiru senbutsudō*, vols. 1–2. Kyoto: Binobi.

Tatelman, J. 2000. *The Glorious Deeds of Pūrṇa*, Richmond, Surrey: Curzon.

Vignato, G. and S. Hiyama 2022. *Traces of the Sarvāstivādins in the Buddhist Monasteries of Kucha,* with appendices by P. Kieffer-Pülz and Y. Taniguchi. Delhi: Dev Publishers, Saxon Academy of Sciences and Humanities, Leipzig Kucha Studies 3.

Waldschmidt, E. 1925. *Gandhāra, Kutscha, Turfan, eine Einführung in die frühmittelalterliche Kunst Zentralasiens*, Leipzig: Klinkhardt & Biermann.

Waldschmidt, E. 1930. "Wundertätige Mönche in der osttürkischen Hīnayāna-Kunst." *Ostasiatische Zeitschrift*, N.F. 6: 3–9; repr. in Waldschmidt 1967: 27–33.

Waldschmidt, E. 1951. "Vergleichende Analyse des Catuṣpariṣatsūtra." *Beiträge zur indischen Philologie und Altertumskunde, FS Walter Schubring*, Hamburg: 84–122; repr. in Waldschmidt 1967: 164–202.

Waldschmidt, E. 1952. "Zur Śroṇkoṭikarṇa-Legende." *Nachrichten der Akademie der Wissenschaften in Göttingen, Philologisch-Historische Klasse* 1952, 6: 129–151; repr. in Waldschmidt 1967: 203–25.

Waldschmidt, E. 1967. *Von Ceylon bis Turfan, Schriften zur Geschichte, Literatur, Religion und Kunst des indischen Kulturraumes; Festgabe zum 70. Geburtstag am 15. Juli 1967*, Göttingen: Vandenhoeck & Ruprecht.

Wilkens J. 2015. "Die altuigurische *Daśakarmapathāvadānamālā* und die buddhistische Literatur Zentralasiens." *Journal of the International Association of Buddhist Studies* 38: 245–70.

Yaldiz, M. 1987. *Archäologie und Kunstgeschichte Chinesisch-Zentralasiens (Xinjiang) = Handbuch der Orientalistik*, 7.3,2. Leiden: Brill.

Yaldiz, M. et al. 2000. *Magische Götterwelten: Werke aus dem Museum für Indische Kunst Berlin*, Staatliche Museen zu Berlin – Preußischer Kulturbesitz, Museum für Indische Kunst. Potsdam: UNZE Verlgs- und Druckgesellschaft.

Zhu, T. 2012. "Reshaping the Jātaka Stories: from Jātakas to Avadānas and Praṇidhānas in Paintings at Kucha and Turfan." *Buddhist Studies Review* 29/1: 57–83.

Zin, M. 2000. "Two Nāga-Stories in the Oldest Paintings of Ajanta IX." In M. Taddei and G. de Marco (eds.) *South Asian Archaeology 1997, Proceedings of the 14th International Conference of the European Association of South Asian Archaeologists in Rome*, 1171–99. Rome: Istituto Italiano per l'Africa e l'Oriente.

Zin, M. 2001. "The Identification of the Bagh Painting." *East & West* 51: 299–322.

Zin, M. 2005. "The Identification of Kizil Paintings I (1. Yaśa, 2. Mākandika)." *Indo-Asiatische Zeitschrift* 9: 23–36; repr. in Shashibala, ed. 2016: 199–215.

Zin, M. 2006a. "About Two Rocks in the Buddha's Life Story." *East & West* 56: 329–58.

Zin, M. 2006b. *Mitleid und Wunderkraft. Schwierige Bekehrungen und ihre Ikonographie im indischen Buddhismus*. Wiesbaden: Harrassowitz.

Zin, M. 2007. "The Identification of Kizil Paintings II (3. Sudāya, 4. Bṛhaddyuti)." *Indo-Asiatische Zeitschrift* 11: 43–52; repr. in Shashibala, ed. 2016: 216–26.

Zin, M. 2010a. "The Identification of Kizil Paintings IV (7. Kapila, 8. The Promise of the Four Kings)." *Indo-Asiatische Zeitschrift* 14: 22–30; repr. in Shashibala, ed. 2016: 241–52.

Zin, M. 2010b. "The Purchase of Jetavana in an Amaravati-Relief." In P. Callieri and L. Colliva (eds.) *Proceedings of the 19th Meeting of the European Association of South Asian Archaeology in Ravenna, Italy, July 2007, II*, 369–73. Oxford: Archeopress, BAR.

Zin, M. 2011a. "The Identification of Kizil Paintings V (9. The painted dome from Simsim and its narrative programme, 10. Elapatra)." *Indo-Asiatische Zeitschrift* 15: 57–69; repr. in Shashibala, ed. 2016: 253–70.

Zin, M. 2011b. "The Parable of 'The Man in the Well'. Its Travels and its Pictorial Traditions from Amaravati to Today." In P. Balcerowicz and J. Malinowski (eds.) *Art, Myths and Visual Culture of South Asia*, 33–93. Delhi: Manohar.

Zin, M. 2015. "Reflections on the Purpose of the Kucha Paintings." *Journal of the International Association of Buddhist Studies* 38: 373–90.

Zin, M. 2018. "Ciñcā Māṇavikā, the Identification of Some Paintings in Kizil and a Gandhara Relief in the Asian Art Museum, Berlin." In O. von Criegern, G. Melzer, and J. Schneider (eds.) *Saddharmāmṛtaṃ, Festschrift für Jens-Uwe Hartmann zum 65 Geburtstag*, 541–59. Wien, Wiener Studien zur Tibetologie und Buddhismuskunde 93.

Zin, M. 2019. "The Techniques of the Narrative Representations in Old India (with an identification of one relief in Kanaganahalli)". In E. Wagner-Durand, B. Fath, and A. Heinemann (eds.) *Image . Narration . Context – Visual Narratives in the Cultures and Societies of the Old World, Proceedings of the Workshop held at the Freiburg Institute for Advanced Studies, Albert-Ludwigs-Universität Freiburg, 18-21.03.2015*, 137–56. Heidelberg: Propylaeum.

Zin, M. 2020. *Representations of the* Parinirvāṇa *Story Cycle in Kucha*. Saxon Academy of Sciences and Humanities, Leipzig Kucha Studies 2, Delhi: Dev Publishers.

Author biography

Monika Zin studied Art History, Indology and Dramatics in Krakow and Munich. Between 1994 and 2016 she taught Indian Art History in Munich at the Institute of Indology, Ludwig-Maximilians-Universität, in Berlin at the Freie Universität and at the Universität Leipzig. Since April 2016 Professor Zin is team leader of the Research Centre "Buddhist Murals of Kucha on the Northern Silk Road" at the Saxon Academy of Sciences and Humanities in Leipzig. Her scholarly contributions include numerous articles on the identification of narratives in early Indian Art and several monographs: *Ajanta – Handbuch der Malereien, 2: Devotionale und ornamentale Malereien* (2003), *Mitleid und Wunderkraft. Schwierige Bekehrungen und ihre Ikonographie im indischen Buddhismus* (2006), *Saṃsāracakra* (2007 and 2022, with Dieter Schlingloff), *The Kanaganahalli Stūpa* (2018) and *Representations of the Parinirvāṇa Story Cycle in Kucha* (2020).

PART II: NARRATIVE NETWORKS

5

Localizing Narrative Through Image

The Nun Utpalavarṇā in a Stone Relief from Kaushambi

Sonya Rhie Mace[*]

Introduction

A remarkable stone relief depicting the nun Utpalavarṇā worshipping the Buddha upon his descent from the Trāyastriṁśa at Saṃkāśya was carved on a small railing dating to the earliest phase of Indian Buddhist narrative sculpture, around the early first century BCE (Figure 5.1).[1] The monolithic railing, now in the collection of the Allahabad University Museum, was excavated from the site of Ghoṣitārāma Monastery at Kaushambi (Skt Kauśāmbī) near the city of Prayagraj, located at the auspicious and strategic confluence of the Ganges and Yamuna Rivers in Uttar Pradesh.[2] This narrative relief sculpture from

---

[*] The first iteration of this paper was presented at a conference organized by Phyllis Granoff and Koichi Shinohara in 2004 at McMaster University in Hamilton, Ontario. Its subsequent numerous incarnations have benefitted from their input as well as discussions and translations generously provided especially by Gregory Schopen, as well as Ju-hyung Rhi, Young H. Rhie, and Jonathan Silk. I am also grateful to Naomi Appleton, Osmund Bopearachchi, Robert L. Brown, and the late Pramod Chandra and Marylin Rhie for their many invaluable contributions to this work.

[1] This rather badly abraded sculpture has appeared in three previous publications with minimal analysis (Sharma et al. 1980, 30; Tripathi 2003, 65–8; and Koizumi 2005, 34). I am grateful to Young H. Rhie for translating from Japanese the substantial article on images and narratives of the Buddha's Descent from the Trāyaśtriṁśa Heaven by Koizumi Yoshihide.

[2] Sukumar Dutt identified Ghoṣitārāma Monastery as one of several *saṅghārāma*s mentioned by name in textual and epigraphical sources dating from the third to first century BCE and as one of only three that have been traced by archaeologists: Jīvakārāma at Rājgir, Jetavana near Śrāvastī, and Ghoṣitārāma at Kauśāmbī (Dutt

Kaushambi differs from other known examples of the same scene made during the second to first century BCE, because it features the figure of the nun. Since monks or nuns were rarely depicted in Buddhist art before the introduction of the human figural image of the Buddha,[3] the incorporation of the image of Utpalavarṇā on the Kaushambi railing is all the more noteworthy. In the depictions of the Buddha's descent at Saṃkāśya from the *stūpa*s at Bharhut, Kanaganahalli and Sanchi, the pageantry of the Buddha's miraculous descent with the gods is foregrounded, and there is no trace of Utpalavarṇā. Perhaps a different narrative that included Utpalavarṇā was current among the Buddhist community at Kaushambi, or possibly its makers chose to emphasize a different aspect of the story more pertinent to a residential community of monks, rather than lay or non-Buddhist visitors or would-be donors.

1962, 60–61.) Dutt defines an *ārāma* as an enclosed garden or park with dwellings donated by a lay person to the Buddhist monastic community in or near a town to be used as a monks' residence during the rain retreat. In time, *ārāma* came to mean a campus for a large monastery (Dutt 1962, 59). He provides a history of Ghoṣitārāma of Kaushambi as founded by a wealthy merchant named Ghoṣita, whom some consider to have been the treasurer of King Udayana of Vatsa, the name of the kingdom whose capital was at Kaushambi, and who was one of the royal disciples of the Buddha (Malalasekara 1960, 829). According to the archaeological excavations, Ghoṣitārāma Monastery at Kaushambi had a thousand-year habitation until the Hūṇa attacks of the sixth century (Dutt 1962, 65). By the time Xuanzang visited in 636 CE, it was already in ruins (Beal 1968 [1884], 236). Excavations at Kaushambi were led by G. R. Sharma and the Department of Ancient History, Culture and Archaeology of the Allahabad University between 1949 and 1964 (Sharma 1960, 1969; Sharma et al. 1980). A large *stūpa* on a square plinth measuring 81× 81 feet enlarged during the time of Aśoka, dwellings for monks, shrines for images, and other smaller *stūpa*s were all surrounded by a square enclosure wall (Sharma et al. 1980, 13–14). A monolithic sandstone pillar carved with the so-called schism edict of Aśoka was established at Kaushambi during the reign of Aśoka in the mid-third century BCE (Tripathi 2003, 13).

3 The absence of monks from the art of Bharhut and Sanchi has led scholars to contend that there must have been a prohibition against depicting monks in the earliest Buddhist art. Coincidentally, no image of the Buddha in human form has been identified at these sites, and hence scholars have linked the two phenomena to a common reason. Alfred Foucher was one of the first to articulate the problem: "… the old school of Bharhut and Sanchi never, to our knowledge showed a *bhikshu* any more than they showed the Buddha himself; and the two facts are evidently not without close connection" (Marshall, Foucher and Majumdar 1940, 198). Recent excavations of the *stūpa* at Kanaganahalli, however, have yielded three depictions of monks and at least one nun dating from 63 or 36 BCE, before the introduction of the human image of the Buddha (Poonacha 2011, CXXXIX.10 [p. 464, no. 102], pl. CIX, fig. 48b; CXXXIX.14 [p. 464, no.106], pl. LXIX; and CXLI.4 [p. 467, no. 138], pl. CII).

Figure 5.1. Utpalavarṇā Worships the Buddha at Saṃkāśya, c. 100–50 BCE. Ghoṣitārāma Monastery, Kaushambi, Uttar Pradesh, India. Allahabad University Museum (KS208). Photo: American Institute of Indian Studies.

Many texts contain accounts of the life of Utpalavarṇā and her role in the narrative of the Buddha's descent at Saṃkāśya, but they vary in details, gloss, and meaning. Scholars have referenced one or another text as the basis for their identifications of later images of Utpalavarṇā at the Buddha's Descent, which are fairly common in art of the first century CE and later,[4] though often without clear justification. Most of the known texts that place Utpalavarṇā at the scene, however, cannot be dated earlier than the first century CE either, so using a text to explain the appearance of the figure of Utpalavarṇā in the early relief sculpture at Kaushambi—or any early Indian site for that matter—is particularly problematic. This problem is compounded by the uncertainty as to whether any text as it exists today was known in a particular locale or used by a specific community. Inscriptions and the visual content of a stone sculpture made at a known time and place communicate the elements of the story that were significant to the makers of the image, and they can then guide the selection of a text that could be relevant for explaining the meaning or reception of the scene. An analysis of the Kaushambi relief suggests that, among the texts known to us today, the story of Utpalavarṇā found in the *Mūlasarvāstivāda-vinaya* contains elements that appear to have been significant to the makers of the sculpture. However, as also noted by other chapters in the volume (Zaghet, Reddy, Zin), visual evidence, including other images of the same story or at the same site, can be just as important as textual evidence when understanding a visual narrative.

The Kaushambi relief and the descent of the Buddha in early Indian art

The Kaushambi relief depicting the Buddha's descent from the Trāyastriṁśa Heaven at Saṃkāśya features a standing figure with shaven head wearing the loose robes of a Buddhist renunciant (Figure 5.1). In the space above the figure

---

4 Osmund Bopearachahi has made a thorough survey and analysis of the reliefs made in Gandhāra, including many examples from Mathura, depicting Utpalavarṇā worshipping the Buddha at Saṃkāśya (Bopearachchi 2011). Koizumi Yoshihide published an extensive list of texts in which the scene occurs in Buddhist literature along with a discussion of numerous examples from Indian art of the second century BCE through the fifth century CE (Koizumi 2005). Focusing on the painted versions of Ajanta of the fifth century CE, Dieter Schlingloff also referenced numerous textual sources and examples from the early Indian visual record (Schlingloff 2000, vol. 2, 95–9). Eva Allinger has also delved into the issues of the images and texts of this episode, focusing mainly on works from the fifth to the eleventh century (Allinger 1999 and 2010).

Figure 5.2. Worship of a *Dharmacakrastambha*, c. 50 BCE–50 CE. Stūpa 3, Sanchi, Madhya Pradesh, India. Sandstone. Photo: American Institute of Indian Studies 40204.

is a Brāhmī inscription: *u pa la va* on one line and then *ṇā* below on a second line; all together, the syllables read "Upalavaṇā." This simple label inscription is a name, that of a nun found in numerous Buddhist texts, and corresponds to Utpalavarṇā in Sanskrit. In this relief, Utpalavarṇā reverentially touches her forehead to a high altar with a tall base. The plain flat surface of the horizontal top slab of the altar is visible just above and to the right of Utpalavarṇā's head. She appears to be worshipping the Buddha, who is visually denoted as an altar, an indexical locus of sanctity, rather than a human figural image—a common practice in the art of India during this period. Her posture and gesture of veneration, in which she bends forward to touch her brow to the altar and reaches towards it with both hands, are similar to those of women worshipping a *dharmacakrastambha* in a relief at the Buddhist *stūpa* site of Sanchi (Figure 5.2). The women touch their foreheads to the top of the pillar at the juncture with the capital. Behind them, four men cup their hands together in *añjalī-mudrā*, confirming that the pillar is a sacred object of worship.[5]

The altar being venerated by Utpalavarṇā is located just below the bottom step of a diagonal staircase with two balustrades consisting of uprights, crossbars, and railings. Although the relief is broken at the top, we can conclude

5 The deer at the bottom of the panel locate this scene of the veneration at the Deer Park of Sārnāth, where the Buddha delivered his first teaching of the *dharma*.

that a figure once stood on the stairs, since a hand with heavy bracelets rests on the far rail, and legs with the long swath of a layperson's lower garment remain on the staircase itself. The staircase in combination with the figure of the nun reveals that this relief depicts Utpalavarṇā's worship of the Buddha upon his arrival at Saṃkāśya, where he descended a staircase from the Trāyastriṁśa Heaven. The bejeweled figure on the staircase may be Indra or another god who accompanied the Buddha in a scene often called the *devorohana*, or "Coming down from the realm of the gods."[6]

The unusual vertical elongation of the base of the altar can be understood as indicating the downward movement of the Buddha as he alights from the staircase to the ground. When the Buddha was shown non-figurally, artists found creative solutions to the problem of showing him in motion. An example from Sanchi shows how the unit of the altar has been extended across the composition to convey the horizontal motion of the Buddha while walking, surrounded by a crowd of worshippers (Figure 5.3).[7] The top slab of the altar appears as a long rectangular bar, while the base of the altar stretches along, inset beneath it. In the Kaushambi relief, the movement of the Buddha is downward, visually communicated by the extension of the base of the altar to the ground. The vertical elongation of the altar shows that Utpalavarṇā is worshipping the Buddha at the very moment when he is stepping from the staircase to the ground, implying that she is the first to greet him upon his return to earth. He has not yet had time to sit and address his followers.

The date of the narrative relief carving of Utpalavarṇā worshipping the Buddha at Saṃkāśya can be judged to fall within the first century BCE. In all five depictions of the Buddha on the Kaushambi *vedikā* an altar stands in for him, so the figural image has not yet been adopted to mark his presence. The use of a simple label inscription in Brāhmī within the compositional space of a narrative relief was standard throughout India at sites such as Bharhut, Kanaganahalli, and Amaravati around 150 to 100 BCE. Furthermore, the flattened and angular quality of the figural sculpture accords with carvings of this period. All in all, the Kaushambi relief can be confidently attributed to the earliest period of Buddhist narrative relief sculpture, before the introduction of the human image of the Buddha, and stylistically it may date to around the time of the early reliefs at Bodhgaya, namely a generation later than the carvings at Bharhut and earlier than those at Stūpa 1 at Sanchi, that is, the first quarter of the first century BCE. The significance of such an early date for this relief

[6] The term *devorohana* has been used since the time of the inscriptions on the drum slabs of the *stūpa* at Kanaganahalli (Figure 5.4) and in modern Thai reenactments of the Buddha's descent from Indra's heaven (Strong 2010, 973).

[7] Since many figures in the crowd are looking up, the Buddha appears to be performing a miracle of levitation in which he walks through the air.

Figure 5.3. Worship of the Walking Buddha, c. 50 BCE–50 CE. Stūpa 1, Sanchi, Madhya Pradesh, India. Sandstone. Photo: Huntington Archive 1302.

is that it stands as the sole surviving example of this narrative scene from the early period in which the figure of Utpalavarṇā is unequivocally present. This is an important addition to our knowledge of the visual history of this episode.[8] The Kaushambi relief shows that the nun was known by the first century BCE in the Gangetic plain, well before the earliest images from Gandhāra.

Utpalavarṇā is not included in the three other known narrative relief sculptures of the Buddha's descent at Saṃkāśya from the period preceding the

---

8 Otherwise it would appear that Utpalavarṇā was introduced in the art of Gandhāra and then spread south after the influence of Gandhāran art on the sculpture of Mathura. T. Koezuka has suggested that the Utpalavarṇā story was separate from the Buddha's descent from the Trāyastriṁśa Heaven and that the two became merged around the end of the first century CE when Gandhāran images became popular (Koezuka 1978, 31).

Figure 5.4. Descent at Saṃkāśya, c. 150–125 BCE. Bharhut, Madhya Pradesh, India. Sandstone. Indian Museum, Kolkata. Photo: ArtStor

introduction of the human image of the Buddha, namely at Bharhut (Figure 5.4) and Sanchi (Figure 5.5) in Madhya Pradesh and Kanaganahalli (Figure 5.6) in Karnataka. In those three examples, only gods and laypeople, all young and bejeweled, are portrayed in the scene, and the Buddha is shown non-figurally by means of footprints, an altar under a tree, or a throne with footprints under a tree. The emphasis is on the pageantry of the miraculous descent of the Buddha from heaven and how the gods worshipped and celebrated the momentous occasion. John Strong has called attention to the importance of this miracle as a moment when "gods can see humans and humans can see gods, and all can see the Buddha" (Strong 2010, 974), and Richard Cohen has noted that Saṃkāśya is the place where the human and divine *saṅgha*s meet (Cohen 2001, 195–6). Indeed the Brāhmī inscription under the Kanaganahalli relief

Figure 5.5. Descent at Saṃkāśya, c. 50 BCE–50 CE. Stūpa 1, Sanchi, Madhya Pradesh, India. Sandstone. Photo: AIISIG_10311745506.

(Figure 5.6) identifies the scene as *dev(o)har(o)ṇa*, or "Coming down from the realm of the gods."[9]

All three compositions at Bharhut, Sanchi, and Kanaganahalli are more extensive and complex than that of the relief from Kaushambi, and yet neither Utpalavarṇā nor any Buddhist monk is to be found in those three portrayals of the descent scene from the early period. In contrast, Utpalavarṇā is an important feature of the Kaushambi version of the narrative, such that she is the sole worshipper, and her name has been inscribed above her figure to confirm her identity. The very presence of any image of a monk or nun on a Buddhist relief of this early period is extremely rare, much less one identified by

[9] Although this inscription was probably added later, during the second century CE, it is nevertheless a valid identification of this scene, unlike others that were re-identified (Quintanilla 2017, 117–26).

Figure 5.6. Descent from the Realm of the Gods, 63 or 36 BCE. Kanaganahalli, Karnataka, India. Limestone. Photo: Author.

name. Such a singular instance of the image of Utpalavarṇā at Saṃkāśya that deviates from the norms of both omitting figures of monks and nuns as well as emphasizing the pageantry of the Buddha's descent from heaven suggests that her role in this narrative held special significance for the community at Goṣitārāma Monastery.

The difference in visual emphasis between the Kaushambi relief and those from Bharhut, Kanaganahalli, and Sanchi may be explained by a difference in intended audience. The Descent scenes from those three sites all were carved as part of the adornment of the main *stūpa* at each respective site, on a railing, gateway, or drum slab of monumental scale. The emphasis on auspicious imagery and notable lack of themes generally considered inauspicious—including shaven-headed renunciants[10]—suggests that the art on those monuments

[10] Numerous references to the inauspiciousness of seeing a shaven-headed ascetic wearing reddish (*kāṣāya*) robes, namely a Buddhist monk or nun, occur throughout early Indian literature, including the Brahmanical *Viṣṇu Smṛiti* (Jolly 1880, 202) and *Dharmaśāstra* (Kane 1962, 622), the Mahāyāna Buddhist *Mahāratnakūṭa-sūtra*

was intended to attract widespread public audiences[11] and portend the success of Buddhist devotions. On the other hand, the modest scale of the Kaushambi railing from Ghoṣitārāma indicates that its carvings may have been intended for an intimate monastic audience or a viewership of the already converted.

The Kaushambi depiction of the Buddha's descent at Saṃkāśya has been carved on a diminutive monolithic railing, the surviving section of which measures 53 cm in height and 124 cm in width (Figure 5.7). It consists of ten uprights and three crossbars; the coping stone has completely fallen away. It could have marked a kind of sacred space as part of a square *vedikā*, or it could have been a section of a railing along a venerated walkway (*caṅkrama*).[12] The railing has been carved only on one side; alternate uprights are filled with a narrative or devotional scene. In between, every other upright has a half lotus medallion at the bottom, and in the middle an animal of the type frequently found on early Indian monuments occupies a roundel: *makara*, peacock, bull, and winged lion. These animals all face to the right, which would be the opposite direction of circumambulation if the carvings faced outward, which may support the interpretation of this railing's having been the demarcation for a *caṅkrama*, rather than part of a square *vedikā*. Otherwise, the exterior would have been plain, and the carvings would have faced in, towards a circumambulatory path. Either way, the scale and orientation of the carvings suggest intimate, thoughtful viewing. As such, the Kaushambi relief differs from those at Bharhut, Kanaganahalli, and Sanchi in that it is less concerned with auspicious imagery as external adornment of a *stūpa*. Instead, its reliefs could have been more for communicating themes of concern to monastic practitioners during a time of close viewing or meditative retreat.

Among the five surviving vertical relief compositions that are carved on every other upright, three are identifiable as scenes from episodes in the life of the Buddha. Utpalavarṇā worshipping the Buddha at Saṃkāśya is on the central upright; the next composition to the viewer's left is Indra's visit to the Buddha in a cave (Figure 5.8). At the bottom of the vertical space is the

---

(Chang 1983, 75), in the context of the conversion of King Udayana of Kaushambi (Rockhill 1907,74), the drama *Mṛcchakaṭika* of King Śudraka (van Buitenen 1968, 133), and Jain *vinaya* text *Oghaniryukti* (Acharya 1958, verse 82, 212–13).

11 Gregory Schopen called attention to a passage from the Pāli *vinaya* implying that monasteries were meant to be beautiful, "something of a tourist attraction …": "The monastery of that Venerable was beautiful, something to see, and lovely … Many people came to see the Venerable Udāyin's monastery. A brahman and his wife approached the Venerable Udāyin and said they would like to see his monastery." (Schopen 1995, 475)

12 Inscriptions of the nun Buddhamitrā dating to the early second century CE on pedestals of Buddha images excavated at Kaushambi record that sculptures were set up at the *caṅkrama* (promenade) of the Buddha (Chandra 1970, 62; Tripathi 2003, 85–7).

Figure 5.7. *Vedikā*, c. 100–50 BCE. Ghoṣitārāma Monastery, Kaushambi, Uttar Pradesh, India. Allahabad University Museum (KS208). Photo: American Institute of Indian Studies.

Figure 5.8. Indraśailaguha. Detail of Figure 5.7. Photo: AIIS.

elephant Airāvata, the mount of Indra. Above the elephant on the platform with his back to the viewer is Indra himself, seated with legs drawn up on either side and his right hand raised with index and middle fingers extended, presumably in a gesture of address. The flat-topped crown distinctive to Indra is here rendered in an idiosyncratic form not noted at other sites. Indra faces the Buddha, whose presence is indicated by an altar in a cave, below which stylized rocks denote the natural mountainous setting. The carving depicts the so-called Indraśailaguha episode from the life of the Buddha, in which Indra interrupted the Buddha's meditations in a cave. Further details of the episode differ from one textual source to another, like those of the Descent episode.

The next narrative scene to the left is badly damaged; only approximately the lower third of the relief survives (Figure 5.9). It depicts the figure of

Figure 5.9. Monkey's Gift of Honey. Detail of Figure 5.7. Photo: Author.

Figure 5.10. Detail of Figure 5.7. Photo: AIIS.

a monkey standing with feet facing right, while his head faces left. His right hand is held up in a salute, and his left hand holds up a bowl, identifying the scene as the monkey's gift of honey to the Buddha at Vaiśālī. In this narrative, a monkey filled an alms bowl with honey and offered it to the Buddha, and the Buddha blessed him. The monkey died shortly thereafter in a way that varies among the known texts (Brown 2009).

To the right of the Utpalavarṇā scene a corpulent demonic figure raises his hands in *añjalī* to an altar with curved elongated base. The top of the upright is broken, so it is not possible to conclude more about the setting. The rightmost vertical upright depicts a *deva* or well-dressed layman offering a garland to the Buddha, whose presence is indicated by an altar in a structure with a garland hanging above (Figure 5.10). If these two reliefs portrayed narratives or an episode from the Buddha's life, they remain unidentified.[13]

In the context of the other reliefs on the Kaushambi railing, the Saṃkāśya scene is one in a series of devotional interactions with the Buddha that were

[13] Next to the right leg of the male figure are the remains of an undeciphered, incomplete Brāhmī inscription.

each somewhat problematic. Utpalavarṇā is grouped with a monkey whose demise was imminent, Indra causing disruption to the Buddha's meditation, and a demonic figure. This context provides a clue as to how the actions of the nun may have been viewed during this early period at a major monastery in the Gangetic plain and which textual sources may be most helpful in our understanding of the significance of the story at Kaushambi.

Textual accounts of Utpalavarṇā and the Buddha's descent at Saṃkāśya

Utpalavarṇā is a fairly prominent figure in literature throughout the Buddhist world, and her character is described in both laudatory and derogatory terms. When the range of textual narratives is considered, she is sometimes presented as a paragon among the Buddha's followers, and sometimes she is derided as a perpetrator of inappropriate behavior.[14]

In Pāli sources she is called Uppalavaṇṇā, and is cast in a largely positive light.[15] She is named in twenty-eight different *jātaka* stories in the *Jātakatthavaṇṇanā* (Commentary on the Birth Stories) dating between the third century BCE and sixth century CE.[16] In many of her previous births, she had a close relationship with the Buddha in one of his past lives; among them she was the daughter of Vessantara, the Buddha in his antepenultimate birth (*Jātakatthavaṇṇanā* 547). In the *Kaṇha-jātaka* (*Jātakatthavaṇṇanā* 29), which the Buddha recounted to an assembly after his descent from the Trāyastriṁśa Heaven at Saṃkāśya, he was born as a bull, and Uppalavaṇṇā in one of her past lives was the woman who cared for him as though he were her own son.[17] In the *Kurudhamma-jātaka* (*Jātakatthavaṇṇanā* 276), she was a courtesan in a past life, but one possessed of honour and virtue. The *Apadānapāli* (Legends of the Buddhists Saints), datable to the second century BCE, contains a lengthy poem written in the first person, ascribed to Uppalavaṇṇā herself, that

---

[14] The positive attitude cannot clearly be considered as chronologically earlier than the derisive, as Robert DeCaroli has indicated (DeCaroli 2015, 121–2 and 126–7).

[15] Alice Collett has summarized her life and past-life stories in Pāli sources, underscoring her popularity in the Pāli tradition (Collett 2016, 66–87).

[16] The twenty-eight *jātaka*s mentioning Utpalavarṇā can be accessed on the Jātaka Stories website of the University of Edinburgh: https://jatakastories.div.ed.ac.uk/characters/utpalavarna/

[17] Chris Clark kindly drew my attention to the close temporal proximity between the descent at Saṃkāśya and the Buddha's telling of the *Kaṇha-jātaka* that places Utpalavarṇā in a close relationship with the Buddha in a prior lifetime.

lists the experiences and virtuous acts she performed in past births that led to her current birth as an enlightened nun (Walters 2018, 1059–70).[18]

Among the texts providing an account of her last lifetime, when she became a Buddhist nun and follower of Śākymuni Buddha, two widely divergent origin stories emerge. In the Pāli texts she was a radiant beauty, born into a wealthy family in Śrāvastī. The *Apadānapāli*, which was apparently current by the time the Kaushambi relief was carved, though in what regions is not certain, states that she was desired by hundreds of millionaires' sons (Walters 2018, 1068). It goes on to say that after abandoning her home, she "went forth" (*Therī-apadāna* 19.69 [580] and 19.79 [590]) to become a nun and achieved the status of "best among those nuns who possess superpowers" (Walters 2018, 1070), and the Buddha encouraged her to show her superpowers, that is, perform feats of magic in order to eliminate doubts in the *saṅgha*. She became a master of magic, able to make varied transformations and to generate apparitions:

> "With superpowers creating
> a chariot with four horses,
> I will worship the feet of the
> Buddha, World's Lord, Resplendent One."
> (*Therī-apadāna* 19.70 [581]; Walters 2018, 1069)

According to the verses in the *Apadāna*, Uppalavaṇṇā reached arhatship, was able to recall her past lives, will not be born again into the world, and will attain *nirvāṇa*. Overall, the *Apadāna* presents a glowingly positive, laudatory image of Uppalavaṇṇā (Walters 2018, 1059 n. 324). Basically the same narrative appears in the Pāli commentaries of around the fifth century CE: the *Dhammapada-aṭṭhakathā* (Commentary on the Path of Wisdom), and the *Manoratha-pūraṇī* (The Wish Fulfiller);[19] it also persists in the Sinhalese *Saddharma Ratnāvali* (Precious Garland of the True Teaching) of the twelfth century.[20] Karen Muldoon-Hules has identified the trope of the wealthy, beautiful

18 The *Apadāna* is also available at http://apadanatranslation.org/text/chapter-4/poem-019.html. One of her acts in a past life as a "human, in a great clan" was to give an arhat a robe of costly saffron-colored silk (Walters 2018, 1066). In Japan, the Zen master Dōgen (1200–1253) related the story that in her past life she was a prostitute who put on a nun's robe as a joke, which led to her rebirth and ordination as a nun during the time of a Buddha of the past, Kāśyapa, followed by her eventual arhatship under Śākyamuni (Faure 1998, 158).

19 For the former see Muldoon-Hules 2017, 67; Burlingame 1921, 127; for the latter, which is a Sri Lankan commentary on the *Aṅguttara-nikāya*, see Bode 1893, 540, 551–2.

20 This text is a Sinhalese translation of the *Dhammapada-aṭṭakathā* (Bopearachchi 2011, 353 n. 4).

girl whose father's anxiety about an overwhelming number of suitors propels her into becoming a nun (Muldoon-Hules 2017, 66–7).

Another early Pāli text, the *Therīgāthā* (Verses of the Elder Nuns), which is probably just as early as the *Apadāna*, having been written by around the mid-first century BCE and possibly even as early as the fourth or third century BCE (Hallisey 2015, x), includes four disconnected verse compositions written in the first person. One recounts the story of a woman who was so horrified to learn that she had unwittingly been sharing a husband with her own daughter, that she renounced the life of the senses to become a mendicant (Rhys Davids 1909, 113; Hallisey 2015, 117). Mrs. Rhys Davids and Charles Hallisey both include a commentary explaining this verse as a story Uppalavaṇṇā was telling about someone else. However, in Dhammapāla's *Therīgāthā-aṭṭhakathā* (Commentary on the Verses of the Elder Nuns), that core content becomes Uppalavaṇṇa's story, which also resonates with the second version of her origin story found in Sanskrit sources of northern India, in which she suffered tragedies in her marriages, culminating in the discovery that she and her daughter were both married to her son. In anguish and disgust, she renounced worldly life to become a nun (Silk 2009, 137–38).

None of the Sanskrit versions of Utpalavarṇā's story can be dated earlier than the first century CE, but presumably much of the content existed before then. The most extensive Sanskrit version of her story, preserved most fully in a Tibetan translation, is in the *Vinaya-vibhaṅga* of the *Mūlasarvāstivāda-vinaya*, which may date to the first to fourth century CE and appears to have been redacted in northwestern India, around the region of Gandhara.[21] Jonathan Silk has translated the text, which states that she was born in Taxila and was known as the "Gandhāran woman." She was married twice, but both marriages ended in heartbreak—her first husband was sleeping with her mother, and her second husband had also married her daughter—and she was driven into a life as a courtesan and became a redoubtable seductress. When 500 men had bought her for one night of enjoyment in a park, the Buddha's disciple Mahāmaudgalyāyana appeared. Unable to seduce him in spite of her best efforts that had never before failed, she experienced an epiphany that propelled her into recognizing the meaninglessness of a life based on desire and sensuality, and she decided to renounce the world to become a follower of the Buddha (Silk 2009, 141–54).[22] Phyllis Granoff and Jonathan Silk have demonstrated that this too is a literary trope in Jain and Hindu literature, in which sudden

---

[21] Jonathan Silk cites the Tibetan version as Derge Kanjur 3, *'dul ba*, *nya* 216a3–226a3; sTog Kanjur 3, *'dul ba*, *ja* 475a2–489a6 and an abbreviated version in Chinese in T. 1442 (XXIII) 897a23–899a17 (*juan* 49). (Silk 2009, 275 n. 6).

[22] This story is also found in Schiefner 1906, 206–15.

recognition of incest or disgust with a life of sensuality leads to renunciation (Granoff 1994, 26; Silk 2009, 156–63).[23]

Is the Utpalavarṇā on the relief at Kaushambi the beautiful wealthy girl from Śrāvastī who joined a nunnery to spare her father from having to deal with too many suitors and then achieved an exalted status as a skilled adept and *arhat*, encouraged by the Buddha to perform magic? Or is she the unfortunate woman from Taxila who fled two repugnant domestic situations to become an unrepentant prostitute before having a sudden conversion experience? The former, from Pāli texts, was probably written by the time of the carving, but there is no evidence that Pāli sources were current in the Gangetic plain. The Sanskrit version from the *Mūlasarvāstivāda-vinaya* is considered to have been written and redacted somewhat later than the creation of the relief, but this monastic code may well have been extant at least in a similar form for centuries. An examination of the Pāli and Sanskrit accounts of the descent of the Buddha at Saṃkāśya points to the latter's being the most relevant to Kaushambi of the first century BCE.

No Pāli account states that Uppalavaṇṇā was the first to greet the Buddha after his return from three months in the Trāyastriṁśa Heaven. Instead, the monk Sāriputta (Skt Śāriputra) welcomed him, according to the *Dhammapada-aṭṭhakathā* (3:199–230; Burlingame 1921, vol. 3, 35–6), the *Sarabha-Miga-jātaka* (Cowell 1895–1907, vol. 4, 168), the 13th-century Sinhalese *Pujawaliya* (Young 2004, 193), and the modern *Mahābuddhavaṁsa* (Vicittasarabivamsa 1992, 357), which shows that the conservative tradition remained unchanged until the twentieth century. In the *Sutta-Nipāta-aṭṭhakathā* (Commentary on the Collection of Discourses) Sāriputta worshipped the Buddha first, followed by Uppalavaṇṇā (Smith 1917, 570). Since the Kaushambi relief unmistakably depicts Utpalavarṇā worshipping the Buddha at the moment of his descent, the version of the story as told in the Pāli sources seems not to have been relevant there at the time when the *vedikā* was carved.

The episode of the Buddha's descent from the Trāyastriṁśa Heaven at Saṃkāśya also occurs in different versions in Sanskrit texts from northern India that often are known to us only in Chinese or Tibetan translations, and none of them specifies Śāriputra as the monk who greets him, as do the Pāli sources. The *Buddhacarita* (Acts of the Buddha) of the early second century CE simply states that gods and humans saw the Buddha descend from the Trāyastriṁśa Heaven down a staircase of seven precious things, and

[23] The Jain story of Kuberadattā shares some similarities with the story of Utpalavarṇā. "A protagonist leads a seemingly normal life, convinced of his or her identity and then is suddenly brought to a catastrophic revelation that that entity is totally false. This dissolution of identity leads in turn to the emergence of a new identity as monk or nun" (Granoff 1994, 26).

rulers and people on Jambudvīpa held their palms together (xxi.1).[24] In the *Avadānaśataka* (One Hundred Stories) of the second to fifth century CE, an apparitional (*upapāduka*) monk welcomed the Buddha back to earth with a magical feast (Vaidya 1958, 216). The Chinese *Zabaozang-jing* (Storehouse of Sundry Valuables) based on a lost Indian source and dated 472 CE does not mention Utpalavarṇā or even the staircase at all after the Buddha's return from teaching the *dharma* to his mother in heaven as an exemplar of filial piety (Willemen, 1994, 19–20).

Most northern Indian Sanskrit Buddhist texts, however, place the nun Utpalavarṇā at Saṃkāśya on the occasion of the Buddha's descent. The *Aśokāvadāna* (Story of Ashoka) of the second century CE (Strong 1983, 262), the *Divyāvadāna* (Divine Stories) of the fifth century CE, and the *Samyuktāgama* of at least the fourth century CE (Koezuka 1978, 31) all mention incidentally that Utpalavarṇā transformed herself into a *cakravartin* (king with all the ideal trappings of a supreme monarch) in order to see the Buddha at Saṃkāśya, but they do not comment or pass judgment on her feat.[25]

---

[24] The *Buddhacarita* was composed by Aśvaghoṣa, a brahmin from Sāketa in central India who converted to Sarvāstivāda Buddhism. Ostensibly, this text should be relevant to the residents at Kaushambi, but the version of the descent at Saṃkāśya does not include Utpalavarṇā. It does not mention Indra, Brahma, or a triple ladder, so that aspect may relate to the single staircases seen in the reliefs of Sanchi and Kaushambi. Charles Willemen translated the Chinese version of the *Buddhacarita* (T.192):

> 54. In order to expound the Law to his mother, he immediately ascended to the Trāyastriṁśa Heaven. Three months he dwelled in his celestial palace and converted gods and humans all around. After he had saved his mother and shown his gratitude, he returned after the summer retreat had passed.
>
> 55. As all the attendants of the gods mounted a staircase of seven precious things, [the Buddha] descended to Jambudvīpa, to the place to which buddhas have always descended.
>
> 56. Countless gods and humans saw him off in their palaces. The rulers and their people in Jambudvīpa held their palms together and gazed up at [the Buddha]. (Willemen 2009, 150)

[25] A number of original Chinese sources also mention Utpalavarṇā at Saṃkāśya, and they are all neutral about her actions: Saṁghapāla's *Biography of Aśoka* (Li 1993, 44), Faxian's fourth century account of his visit (Legge 1886, 49–51), and Xuanzang's seventh century record (Beal 1968 [1884], 205). In Xuanzang's account, Utpalavarṇā is compared to Subhūti as the first to truly see him, but there is no explicit rebuke of the nun. A nineteenth-century Tibetan summary of the eleventh-century Kashmiri poet Kṣemendra's Sanskrit rendition of the episode from the *Bodhisattvāvadānakalpalatā* states that Utpalavarṇā was transformed into a *cakravartin* through the blessings of the Buddha. When Udāyin recognized her disguise, the Buddha defended her by stating that most demonstrations of magic

The most numerous and detailed versions of the episode are from Sanskrit sources that criticize Utpalavarṇā for using her powers to transform herself into a *cakravartin* in order to be the first to greet the Buddha on his return to earth at Saṃkāśya. The authors of the *Arthapada-sūtra* (Chapter of Eights) of the second century CE or earlier (Bapat 1951, 136–7),[26] the *Mahāprajñāpāramitā-śāstra* (Treatise on Highest Wisdom) dating to the second to third century CE (Lamotte 1944, 634–36), the *Ekottarāgama-sūtra* (Numbered Discourses) of the third to fourth century CE (Rhie 2002, 435–6), *Tathāgatapratibimba-pratiṣṭhānuśaṁsa-saṁvādana* (Agreement on the Benefit of Establishing Images of the Buddha) of the second century CE,[27] *Karmavibhaṅgopadeśa* (Discussion on the Great Classification of Actions) the dating of which seems uncertain but which predates or at least excludes Mahāyāna elements (Levi 1932, 174), and the *Kṣudrakavastu* of the *Mūlasarvāstivāda-vinaya* redacted between the first and fourth century CE all agree that Utpalavarṇā should not have transformed herself into a *cakravartin* and that her desire to be the first to see the Buddha upon his descent at Saṃkāśya was ultimately misguided. These texts also contrast her inappropriate actions to those of Subhūti, who was meditating some distance away and recognized the Buddha's corporeal body as impermanent and empty like all other created phenomena, and achieved an advanced state of awareness, called "Entering the Stream" (Bapat 1951, 136).

---

are made through pride, but that is not the case when it comes to Utpalavarṇā. The Buddha then recounted a different story of her past lives than those found in other Pāli or Sanskrit traditions that indicate her proclivity toward attachment, thereby casting oblique aspersion on her desire to see his body. (Padma-chos-'phel 1997, 73–9) Since this story derives from Kashmir more than one thousand years after the creation of the Kaushambi *vedikā*, it is unlikely to be relevant to our interpretation of the pictorial scene.

26 As Bapat translates:

> [8] At that time there was the Bhikṣuṇī, Utpalavarṇā, who by a miracle transformed herself into a golden-wheel-monarch, bedecked with seven kinds of jewels, leading in front and followed by an army of strong men. She hastened to the Buddha. This large assemblage of people, noblemen and kings, saw, from afar, the golden wheel-monarch coming down all the way, dared not go in front of Him, and made the road wide [to welcome Him]. The Bhikṣuṇī, Utpalavarṇā, went to the place where the Buddha was…
>
> [9] At that time, the Bhikṣuṇī Utpalavarṇā just came in front of the Buddha, and withdrew the miracle. The seven jewels and all disappeared and were [no longer] seen. She stood alone with her head shaved and with religious garments on. With her head and face, she touched the feet of the Buddha. The Buddha then came to the root of the Udumbara tree, sat down on the seat already prepared among the mass of people, and immediately preached in detail the doctrine. He talked about charity, conduct, heaven, the disadvantageous and painful nature of desires and their lowness. (Bapat 1951, 137)

27 T.694, cited in Lamotte 1944, 634–5, n. 1.

These texts that are critical of Utpalavarṇā's use of her powers of transformation, however, vary as to the reasons why her actions were inappropriate. Some simply make oblique implications, while others amount to public shaming.

In the *Arthapada-sūtra*, known in a Chinese translation of a Prakrit and Sanskrit source, the monk who can probably be identified as Subhūti considered the delight of the assemblage in seeing the miracle of the descent to have resulted from greed and craving, and the Buddha praised him as the one who alone has seen the truth, but he did not directly and publicly admonish Utpalavarṇā (Bapat 1951, 137).[28] Similarly, the *Ekottarāgama-sūtra*, also preserved in Chinese, describes the Buddha's descent down a triple staircase at Saṃkāśya in some detail in the context of his followers' anxiety over not seeing him while he was in the Trāyastriṁśa Heaven for three months, which led King Udayana of Kaushambi to make a sandalwood image of the Buddha, so he could worship him in his absence.[29] When the Buddha returned by way of the triple stairway, Utpalavarṇā transformed herself into a *cakravartin* complete with the seven treasures and was the first one to worship him. The Buddha then gently rebuked her by saying that, though she has good karma that resulted in her great accomplishments, true homage is achieved through seeing the *dharma* of no independent reality, which is what Subhūti did. The Buddha then went on to approve of King Udayana's sandalwood image by saying that making a Buddha image leads to an abundance of blessings and then gave a sermon about almsgiving and rebirth in heaven.[30] The main concern of this text seems to be the justification of image-making as an appropriate

---

[28] This text is considered to be a Sanskrit and Prakrit version of the *Arthavaggiya-sūtra* of the Pāli *Sutta-nipāta*, and the section is called the *Utpalavarṇā-bhikṣuṇī-sūtra* (T.198).

[29] When the Buddha finally descended to earth at Saṃkāśya by way of a triple path, Utpalavarṇā determined that she would go to greet him, but thought there would be many kings and ministers assembled there and that "it would not be appropriate for her to use her usual form. So she secretly transformed herself into the form of a cakravartin, complete with the 7 treasures" (Rhie 2002, 435). The crowd made way for her, and after the Buddha stepped on land, she transformed herself back into a nun and bowed to his feet. This text includes a component of resentment among the crowd: "The five kings saw this, and each one felt resentment and said among themselves, 'Today we greatly lost out. We are the ones who should first greet the Tathāgata, but this bhikṣunī greeted him first.' At this time the bhikṣunī went to the place of the World-Honored One, bowed her head and face to his feet, then said to the Buddha, 'Now I am paying respect to the most high Honored One. Today I first attained chin sheng (obtained visualizing the past). I, Utpala-flower-bhikṣunī, am the Tathāgata's disciple.'" (Rhie 2002, 436).

[30] This episode from *Juan* 28 of the *Ekotarāgama-sūtra* is also summarized in Koezuka 1978, 30. Stephen Teiser's terse summary of the scene states simply that the Buddha praised her after she regained her original form and does not mention that he then compared her to Subhūti (Teiser 1996, 139).

substitution for seeing the corporeal body of the Buddha, though understanding the *dharma* is still the best. This concern would not have been so relevant in Kaushambi before Buddha images were being made.

As for the *Mahāprajñāpāramitā-śāstra*, also known only from a Chinese translation,[31] Utpalavarṇā is described as having transformed herself into a *cakravartin* to be the first to see the Buddha, and he rebuked her more pointedly by saying to her directly that she was not the first one to greet him, that it was Subhūti, because Subhūti recognized emptiness and saw the *dharmakāya*. The Buddha then ordered Subhūti to preach the *Prajñāpāramitā* (Lamotte 1944, 634–6). Like the *Arthapada-sūtra* and the *Ekottarāgama-sūtra*, the *Prajñāpāramitā-śāstra* does not say what happened to Utpalavarṇā after that. The reference in the *Karmavibhaṅgopadeśa* gives a summary version of the same idea (Levi 1932, 174). All of these versions preserved in Chinese translations seem to have been modulated to speak to an audience that was concerned with propounding Mahāyāna philosophical ideas and filial piety, which were not the interests among monks in a mainstream Buddhist monastery of first century BCE India.[32]

The *Kṣudrakavastu* of the *Mūlasarvāstivāda*-vinaya, preserved in Tibetan, recounts an even more extensive version of the episode in which Utpalavarṇā worships the Buddha at Saṃkāśya. The following summary and translated excerpt are courtesy of Gregory Schopen.[33] To set the scene, the descent at Saṃkāśya took place at the end of the rainy season when Śākyamuni went to give *Abhidharma* teachings to his mother Māyā in the Trāyastriṃśa Heaven. After then giving teachings to the occupants in all the heavens, the Buddha was ready to return to earth, and Indra ordered Viśvakarma to construct a triple staircase, made of crystal, *vaidurya*,[34] and gold. As the Buddha descended, he performed several miracles. The first was to descend half by means of magic, in order to avoid the false accusations of non-believers who might otherwise say that he used up all his karmic merit enjoying himself in heaven and

31 According to Lamotte (Lamotte 1944, vii), the *Mahāprajñāpāramitā-śāstra* was written by Nāgārjuna in Sanskrit during the second century CE and translated into Chinese by the Central Asian master Kumārajīva of Kucha in Xian from 404 to 405; T.1509.

32 For a cogent analysis of the care that should be taken with applying textual sources known only from Chinese translations, see Schopen 2000, 1–25.

33 I am indebted to Gregory Schopen for guiding me through a translation of the Descent at Saṃkāśya and for providing me with his own unpublished translation of this section of the Dulva from the Tibetan Tripitaka, Peking Kanjur 'dul ba, Ne 85a1 to 90b8 (Suzuki 1958, vol. 44, 156-2-1 to 158-3-8). Heavily abridged summaries of this text have been published in Rockhill 1907, 81; Allinger 1999, 321–2; Thakur 2003/4, 36; and Koizumi 2005, 9–10.

34 Vaidurya is a kind of gemstone, such as beryl or cat's eye, that has the effect of moving in the light and casts a golden glow.

as a result was no longer able to perform magic. He also descended half on foot, so that the karmic merit of having built the staircase would still accrue to Viśvakarma. The second miracle was to transform the stench of humanity into fragrance of *gośīrṣa* sandal paste, so the gods would not be sickened as they descend to earth with him. The third was that he made the women see only goddesses, and the men see only gods, to protect them from being so overcome by the beauty of celestial beings of the opposite sex that they would vomit warm blood and die. As he was performing these thoughtful miraculous acts, his disciple, the monk Subhūti, who was sitting some distance away under a tree performing his daily meditations, saw the wondrous triple staircase from afar and thought that he should go pay his respects to the Teacher, but then entered into a mental concentration on the five appropriated aggregates as impermanent, miserable, empty and without self, entered the Stream of Wisdom, and then got down on one knee and offered reverence to the Buddha right there. Meanwhile, the nun Utpalavarṇā was approaching the crowd and thought:

> "How will I be able to be the first to worship the Blessed One when he descends from the Trāyastriṃśa Heaven to Jambudvīpa? If I go there as I am, someone will say, 'You are just a nun,' and I will not be permitted to pass within the area of the great assembly of gods and men surrounding the Blessed One." So, she transformed herself into a *cakravartin*, complete with all the trappings and retinue, and the crowd parted and let her through.
>
> At that time, Venerable Udāyin had come and was seated among those assembled. He then said, "Hey! This one is not a *cakravartin*; this one is the nun named Utpalavarṇā, come by means of magic in order see the Blessed One."
>
> All of them said, "Noble, how do you know that this is the nun Utpalavarṇā?"
>
> Then he said, "Oh, if indeed one smells the fragrance of the blue lotus, it is none other than Utpalavarṇā herself, who has come close to the Blessed One by means of magic."
>
> Then the nun Utpalavarṇā withdrew the apparition she had generated through magical powers and went to where the Blessed One was and bowed down to him, touching her head to the foot of the Blessed One, and sat down to one side.
>
> Then the Blessed One said this to the nun Utpalavarṇā: "Go! Do not sit in front of me! It is improper for a nun to perform feats of magic in the presence of her teacher."[35]

The account concludes with the creation of a rule prohibiting nuns from performing magic in front of an audience as the ultimate message of the episode. Further to that, the Buddha was obliged to undo the damage that seeing Utpalavarṇā's apparition of a *cakravartin* had on some members of the

[35] Translation by Gregory Schopen, unpublished.

assembly, who generated the desire to be reborn as human, rather than Enter the Stream. He had to give a sermon with the purpose of turning them away from desiring rebirth as men or gods. In this text of the Mūlasarvāstivāda monastic code, Utpalavarṇā is featured, publicly rebuked, sent away in shame, and held up to the *saṅgha* as one who has behaved improperly. Her strong desire to worship the Buddha first and her deceitful methods of fulfilling her desire are deemed transgressive.

From this survey of textual accounts of the life of Utpalavarṇā and the Buddha's descent at Saṃkāśya, the Pāli and Sanskrit traditions emerge as distinct from one another. The only crossovers between the Pāli and Sanskrit sources are that she was physically attractive, which attribute ultimately resulted in her renunciation of worldly life to become a nun and high-ranking follower of the Buddha, skilled in working magic, especially feats of transformation.[36] Indeed, none of the Pāli texts appear to have placed Utpalavarṇā as the first to greet the Buddha at the scene. That being the case, then the Pāli version of her life story is probably not what the viewers at Ghoṣitārāma Monastery would have had in mind when seeing her image on the *vedikā*. The Sanskrit *Mūlasarvāstivāda-vinaya*, on the other hand, features Utpalavarṇā as a central figure in the Descent and is also the source of the most lengthy and descriptive excursus of her life story. Returning to the Kaushambi *vedikā*, the importance afforded to her in the relief accords with her prominence in the *Mūlasarvāstivāda-vinaya*.

There are some inconsistencies between the *Mūlasarvāstivāda-vinaya* account and the Kaushambi relief. First, in the relief the staircase is single and not triple, as is specified by the story in the *Kṣudrakavastu*. Some early texts, the *Buddhacarita*, for example, do not specify a triple staircase for the Buddha's descent, and the reliefs at Kanaganahalli and Sanchi also have a single ladder or staircase. Even later depictions of the scene, as at Tabo, which was made during the eleventh century when the tradition of a triple ladder or staircase was thoroughly established, artists opted not to depict three sets of stairs

---

36 The references in the early Pāli *Apadāna* (Walters 2018, 1069) and *Therīgāthā* note her ability to conjure a chariot and four horses in order to worship the Buddha, which resonates with her autotransformation into a *cakravartin* at Saṃkāśya, but it does not specify a connection to that scene:

> With chariot and horses four I came,
> Made visible by supernormal power,
> And worshipped, wonder working, at his feet,
> The wondrous Buddha, Sovran of the world.
> (*Therīgāthā* v.229; Rhys Davids 1909, 113)

It is a generic statement that is not explicitly connected with any narrative, and the commentaries do not explain that verse as a description of her at the Buddha's descent at Saṃkāśya.

(Thakur 2003/4, fig. 3). Therefore, this discrepancy at Kaushambi can be explained as the artist's choice—the space of the narrow upright was not particularly conducive to the carving of a triple stairway. The image-maker may also have wished to downplay the stairway-from-heaven aspect of the narrative, focusing the viewer's attention instead on the action of the nun. Perhaps this too is why she has been rendered as standing, rather than kneeling—to emphasize her figure.[37]

A *vinaya*, or a monastic code of conduct, also would seem to be a fitting type of text to contain the version of a story relevant to understanding the significance of a small railing meant for intimate viewing by monks within the confines of an *ārāma*. As such, the scene, along with those of the Indraśailaguha and the Monkey's Gift of Honey carved on the same *vedikā*, could have been intended to spur thought, rather than serve a talismanic, apotropaic, or ornamental purpose. This draws attention to the importance of understanding the context of a visual narrative in order to understand its potential purposes, and how these might differ from other images at other sites, for example those explored by Zaghet, Reddy and Zin elsewhere in this volume.

The Buddhist sect active at Ghoṣitārāma Monastery at the time when the relief was carved is not known for certain, but by the second century CE, inscriptions indicate that the Sarvāstivādins were influential at Kaushambi (Tripathi 2003, 35). According to G. C. Pande, Kaushambi, Mathura, and Avanti (near Sanchi) were strongholds of Sthaviravādins (Tripathi 2003, 34), and Jonathan Silk explained that the Sthaviras gave rise to the Sarvāstivādin sect, which, in turn, gave rise to the Mūlasarvāstivāda (Silk 2009, 14). In sum, it seems acceptable to recognize the *Mūlasarvāstivāda-vinaya* as containing the story of Utpalavarṇā known to Buddhist audiences and artists at Ghoṣitārāma Monastery in Kaushambi during the first century BCE, though further research into her treatment in *vinaya*s of other sects of mainstream monastic Buddhism may provide further nuances.

Using the *Mūlasarvāstivada-vinaya* to understand the Kaushambi relief

With the content of the *Mūlasarvāstivāda-vinaya* as background, the narrative relief of Utpalavarṇā at Kaushambi possibly communicated a number of messages concerning issues relevant to monks. Her figure may well have

[37] All other later examples of Utpalavarṇā show her kneeling (Pal 1993, 53 and 63; Allinger 2010, fig. 7; Bopearachchi 2011, figs. 3–5, 7–12).

evoked the unforgettable, dramatic story of her pre-ordination life as contained in this *vinaya,* which underscores the abhorrence of remaining within the sensual world, as it is tantamount to committing incest and every other repugnant taboo relationship, so the celibate life of a renunciant should be appreciated. Further to this point, if Utpalavarṇā, the most accomplished seductress, came to realize that the life of sensuality is meaningless, then anyone else should arrive at a similar conclusion. Her figure on the relief would also have brought to mind the way she went to extreme lengths for the sake of worshipping the body of the Buddha but, in the relief, his body is not even there, since it has been replaced by a non-figural index of sanctity, the altar. Perhaps this visual admonition would have implied that the presence of the physical body of the Buddha is not needed for fruitful religious practice; they only need to understand the *dharma,* like Subhūti. Further, the resulting rule in the *Mūlasarvāstivāda-vinaya* that nuns should not perform magic or show off their exceptional skills in front of the Teacher, might have communicated to the monks of Ghoṣitārāma that they were justified in projecting a public image of superiority over nuns; this *vinaya,* written by monks for monks about the behavior of a nun may have served to bolster male dominance in the *saṅgha* (Muldoon-Hules 2017, 1–2). Furthermore, the Buddha's subsequent teachings about following Subhūti's example rather than that of Utpalavarṇā would communicate that people might get the wrong idea if they become more impressed with the accomplishments of a nun, and possibly even support nunneries more than the monastery. The concern with public reputation dominates the *Mūlasarvāstivāda-vinaya*'s account of the Buddha's descent down the celestial ladder: he did not want people to think he sapped his potency enjoying himself in heaven; he did not want the gods to be sickened by the stench of humans; and he did not want humans to vomit warm blood. The themes implicit in the *Mūlasarvāstivāda-vinaya* accounts of the life of Utpalavarṇā and the descent of the Buddha at Saṃkāśya are that it's good to be a monk, even though the Buddha is not physically there, and the nuns should not publicly upstage the monks. The makers of the Kaushambi relief may have intended to project these themes in the sculpted depiction of this scene. Further research into the Monkey's Gift of Honey and the Indraśāilaguha episodes in the *vinaya* promises to further explain the concerns of monks at the heart of mainstream monastic Buddhism in the Gangetic plain during the second and first century BCE—a time and place about which otherwise little is firmly understood.

The varied content and ranges of meanings of the textual stories of the Buddha's descent from the Trāyastriṁśa Heaven indicate that different authors used the episode to communicate about issues that were relevant to the time and cultural milieu for which they were intended, and they could still resonate with readers during particular times and places that are much later and far distant. The same stories could accrue new interpretations over time or among different groups. The standing figure of Utpalavarṇā in the Kaushambi relief may have signaled a different message than did the kneeling nun at the magnificent triple staircase in the two known reliefs carved after the introduction of the figural image of the Buddha that nevertheless exclude his human form at Swat and Mathura, even if they were all associated with the same text; there, the message may have been more related to the inherent emptiness of his birth body as understood by Subhūti.[38] The portrayals of the scene showing her as the glorious *cakravartin* in reliefs from Gandhara probably communicated yet another aspect more to do with conveying the literary details in a coherent narrative, as was customary in the art of the northwestern regions during the second and third centuries CE (Bopearachchi 2011, figs. 1, 5–6, 9–10; Koizumi 2005, 22). Her figure may have meant something else entirely on the Gupta and Pāla steles or the palm-leaf manuscripts that show her nimbate with the Buddha, Indra, and Brahma, where the staircase is omitted, and the only indication of his Descent is the Buddha's extended arm with fingers pointing down; no ladder was included at all.[39] The changes to her signification over time and place is a subject for another study. In the case of the Kaushambi relief, however, since no specific written text can be definitively identified as the basis or source of the image, the internal visual elements, emphasis on her name and form, along with what we know about the context of the carvings on the *vedikā* and the overall site from which it came, point to the story from the *Mūlasarvāstivada-vinaya* as the most relevant, leading us to more fully understand how the image of the nun Utpalavarṇā was understood by image makers and audiences in the heartland of early Indian monasticism.

---

[38] The image of the Descent from Butkara I in Swat, dating to the mid-first century CE, showing Utpalavarṇā kneeling and worshipping the Buddha who is not shown in human figural form, was found with other contemporaneous narrative scenes that do depict him in human form (Bopearachchi 2011, 361, fig. 8). The other example of this phenomenon is from Mathura and is datable to the early third century CE, well after the proliferation of the human image of the Buddha (Bopearachchi 2011, fig. 3).

[39] The Descent from the Trāyastriṁśa Heaven is one of the eight main events of the life of the Buddha as codified from the fifth century onward. This scene, often including the kneeling nun Utpalavarṇā, is found on stelae from Sārnāth dating to the fifth century, as well as on sculptures and manuscripts of eastern India from the eighth to twelfth century, where often she is given a halo, suggesting a more exalted status than she had in the stone relief at Kaushambi (Pal 1993, 53 and 63; Allinger 2010).

Bibliography

Acharya, Purva 1958. *Shrimati Oghaniryukti*. Surat: Bhawnagar Shri Mahodaya Mudranalaya.

Allinger, Eva 1999. "Observations on a Scene from the Life of the Buddha at Tabo Monastery." In C.A. Scherrer-Schaub and E. Steinkellner (eds.) *Tabo Studies II: Manuscripts, Texts, Inscriptions, and the Arts*, 321–35. Roma: Istituto Italiano per l'Africa e l'Oriente.

Allinger, Eva 2010. "The Descent of the Buddha from the Heaven of the Trayastriṁśa Gods—One of the Eight Great Events in the Life of the Buddha." In E. Franco and M. Zin (eds.) *From Turfan to Ajanta*, vol. 1. 3–13. Bhairahawa, Rupandehi, Nepal: Lumbini International Research Institute.

Bapat, Purushottam Vishvanath 1951. *The Arthapada Sutra.* Visva-Bharati Studies 13. Santinikatan: Visva-Bharati.

Beal, Samuel 1968 [1884]. *Si-yu-ki. Buddhist Records of the Western World Translated from the Chinese of Hiuen Tsiang*, vol. 1. London: Kegan Paul, Trench, Trübner & Co.; New York: Paragon.

Bode, Mabel 1893. "Women Leaders of the Buddhist Reformation," *The Journal of the Royal Asiatic Society of Great Britain and Ireland* (Jul. 1893): 517–566.

Bopearachchi, Osmund 2011. "In Search of Utpalavarṇā in Gandhāran Buddhist Art." In C. Lippolis and S. de Martino (eds.) *Un impaziente desiderio di scorrere il mondo*, 353–68. Monografie di Mesopotamia XIV. Firenze: Le Lettere.

Brown, Robert L. 2009. "Telling the Story in Art of the Monkey's Gift of Honey to the Buddha." *Bulletin of the Asia Institute*, New Series, 23: 43–52.

Buitenen, Johannes Adranus Bernardus van 1968. *Two Plays of Ancient India*. New York and London: Columbia University Press.

Burlingame, Eugene Watson, tr. 1921. *Buddhist Legends*. Cambridge, Massachusetts: Harvard University Press.

Chandra, Pramod 1970. *Stone Sculpture in the Allahabad Museum: A Descriptive Catalogue*. Poona: American Institute of Indian Studies.

Chang, Garma Chen-chi, ed. 1983. *Treasury of Mahāyāna Sutras: Selections from the Mahāratnakūta Sūtra*. University Park: Pennsylvania State University Press.

Cohen, Richard S. 2001. "Shakyamuni: Buddhism's Founder in Ten Acts." In David Noel Freedman and Michael J. McClymond (eds.) *The Rivers of Paradise*, 121–232, 663–71. Grand Rapids, MI: William B. Eerdmans Publishing Co.

Collett, Alice 2016. *Lives of Early Buddhist Nuns: Biographies as History*. Oxford: Oxford University Press.

Cowell, Edward B., ed., various translators 1895–1907. *The Jātaka or Stories of the Buddha's Former Births*. 6 vols. Cambridge: Cambridge University Press.

Cunningham, Alexander 1873. *The Stūpa of Bharhut*. Varanasi: Indological Book House, reprinted 1962.

DeCaroli, Robert 2015. *Image Problems*. Seattle: University of Washington Press.

Dutt, Sukumar 1962. *Buddhist Monks and Monasteries of India*. London: George Allen & Unwin Ltd.

Faure, Bernard 1998. *The Red Thread: Buddhist Approaches to Sexuality*. Princeton, NJ: Princeton University Press.

Granoff, Phyllis 1994. "Life as Ritual Process: Remembrance of Past Births in Jain Religious Narratives." In Phyllis Granoff and Koichi Shinohara (eds.) *Other Selves: Autobiography and Biography in Cross-Cultural Perspective*, 16–34. Oakville, Ontario and Buffalo, NY: Mosaic Press.

Hallisey, Charles 2015. *Therigatha: Poems of the First Buddhist Women*. Cambridge, Massachusetts: Harvard University Press.

Jolly, Julius 1880. *The Institutes of Vishnu*. Oxford: Clarendon; reprinted Varanasi: Motilal Banarsidass, 1965.

Kane, Pandurang Vaman 1962. *History of Dharmaśāstra: ancient and mediaeval religions and civil law in India*, vol. 5. Poona: Bhandarkar Oriental Research Inst.

Koezuka, Takashi 1978. "*Jū Sanjūsanten Kōka* (Pictorial Images of Descent from the Heaven of the Thirty-three Gods)." *Journal of the Osaka University Literary Association* 3: 29–48.

Koizumi, Yoshihide 2005. "*Kodai Indo no Jū Sanjūsan Ten Kō ka Zu: Pakisutan Zāruderī isseki shuttohin o chūshin ni* (Images of the Descent from Trāyastriṁśa Heaven from Ancient India: study on the relief from Zar Dheri, Pakistan)" *Museum* 598 (2005.10): 7–36.

Lamotte, Etienne 1944. *Le Traité de la Grande Vertu de Sagesse*. Louvain: Bureaux du Muséon.

Legge, James 1886. *A Record of Buddhistic Kingdoms: Being an Account by the Chinese Monk Fa-Hien of His Travels in India and Ceylon (AD 399–414) in Search of the Buddhist Books of Discipline*. Oxford: Clarendon Press.

Lévi, Sylvain 1932. *Mahākarmavibhaṅga, la grande classification des actes, et Karmavibhaṅgopadeśa, discussion sur le Mahā Karmavibhaṅga*. Paris: E. Leroux.

Li, Rongxi 1993. *The Biographical Scripture of King Aśoka: Translated from the Chinese of Saṃghapāla (Taishō, Volume 50, Number 2043)*. Berkeley CA: Numata Center for Buddhist Translation and Research.

Malalasekara, Gunapala 1960. *Dictionary of Pāli Proper Names*. London: Luzac & Co.

Marshall, John, Alfred Foucher and Nani Gopal Majumdar. 1940. *Monuments of Sāñci*, vol. 1. Calcutta: Government of India Press.

Muldoon-Hules, Karen 2017. *Brides of the Buddha: Nuns' Stories from the Avadānaśataka*. Lanham, Maryland: Lexington Books.

Nakanishi, Maiko, and Oskar von Hinüber 2014. *Kanaganahalli Inscriptions. Annual Report of the International Research Institute for Advanced Buddhology at Soka University for the Academic Year 2013, 17*. Tokyo: International Research Inst. for Advanced Buddhology.

Padma-chos-'phel, Deborah Black; Kṣemendra. *Leaves of the Heaven Tree: The Great Compassion of Buddha*. Berkeley, CA: Dharma Pub., 1997.

Pal, Pratapaditya 1993. *Indian painting*. Los Angeles CA: Los Angeles County Museum of Art.

Poonacha, K. P. 2011. *Excavations at Kanaganahalli (Sannati). Memoirs of the Archaeological Survey of India 106*. New Delhi: Archaeological Survey of India.

Quintanilla, Sonya 2017. "Transformations of Identity and the Buddha's Infancy Narratives at Kanaganahalli." *Archives of Asian Art* 67/1: 111–42. https://doi.org/10.1215/00666637-3788663

Rhie, Marylin Martin 2002. *Early Buddhist Art of China and Central Asia*, vol. 2: The Eastern Chin and Sixteen Kingdoms Period in China and Tumshuk, Kucha and Karashar in Central Asia. Handbook of Oriental Studies, Sect. 4 China, Vol. 12. Leiden: E. J. Brill.

Rhys Davids, Caroline A. F. 1909. *Psalms of the Early Buddhists I. Psalms of the Sisters*. London: Pali Text Society.

Rockhill, William Woodville 1907. *The Life of the Buddha and the Early History of His Order*. London: Kegan, Paul, Trench, Trübner & Co.

Schiefner, Franz Anton von 1906. *Tibetan Tales Derived from Indian Sources*. Translated into English by William Ralston Shedden Ralston. London: K. Paul, Trench, Trübner.

Schlingloff, Dieter 2000. *Ajanta—Handbuch der Malerein, vol. II: Supplement*. Wiesbaden: Harrassowitz.

Schopen, Gregory 1995. "Deaths, Funerals, and the Division of Property in a Monastic Code." In Donald S. Lopez, Jr., ed. *Buddhism in Practice*, 473–502. Princeton, New Jersey: Princeton University Press.

Schopen, Gregory 2000. "The Mahāyāna and the Middle Period in Indian Buddhism: Through a Chinese Looking-Glass." *The Eastern Buddhist* 32/2: 1–25.

Sharma, Govardhan Raj 1960. *The Excavations at Kauśāmbī (1957–59): The Defences and the Śyenaciti of the Puruṣamedha*. Allahabad: Dept. of Ancient History, Culture & Archaeology, University of Allahabad.

Sharma, Govardhan Raj 1969. *Excavations at Kauśāmbī, 1949–50*. Delhi: Manager of Publications.

Sharma, Govardhan Raj, D. Mandal, and G. K. Rai, eds. 1980. *History to Prehistory: Contribution of the Department to the Archaeology of the Ganga Valley and the Vindhyas*. Allahabad, India: University of Allahabad.

Silk, Jonathan 2009. *Riven by Lust: Incest and Schism in Indian Buddhist Legend and Historiography*, Honolulu: University of Hawai'i Press.

Smith, Helmer, ed. 1917. *Sutta-nipāta commentary, being Paramatthajotikā II*. London: Pali text Society.

Strong, John S. 1983. *The Legend of King Aśoka*. Princeton: Princeton University Press.

Strong, John S. 2010. "The Triple Ladder at Saṃkāśya: Traditions about the Buddha's Descent from Trāyastriṁśa Heaven." In Eli Franco and Monica Zin (eds.) *From Turfan to Ajanta : Festschrift for Dieter Schlingloff on the occasion of his eightieth birthday*, vol. 2, 967–78. Bhairahawa, Rupandehi, Nepal: Lumbini International Research Institute.

Suzuki, Daisetz Teitaro 1958. *The Tibetan Tripitaka, Peking edition, [Ab Vol. 5:] kept in the Library of the Otani University, Kyoto: [Auch m. jap. T.: Eiin-Hokukyō-ban Chibetto-Daizōkyō.] Repr. under the supervision of the Otani University, Kyoto. Ed. by Daisetz T[eitaro] Suzuki. 44. 44.* Tokyo, Kyoto: Tibetan Tripitaka Research Institute.

Teiser, Stephen Fredrick 1996. *The Ghost Festival in Medieval China*. Princeton, N.J.: Princeton University Press.

Thakur, Laxman Singh 2003/4. "Narrative Modes in Buddhist Art at Tabo: Some Rare Scenes from the Life of Buddha in the gTsug-lag-khang (Eastern Wall)." *Orientations* 49/3: 32–8.

Tripathi, Aruna 2003. *The Buddhist Art of Kauśāmbī: (from 300 BC to AD 550).* Emerging perceptions in Buddhist studies, 17. New Delhi: DK Printworld.

Vaidya, Parashuram Lakshman, ed. 1958. *Avādana-Śataka*. Darbhanga: Mithila Institute of Post-Graduate Studies and Research in Sanskrit Learning.

Vicittasarabhivamsa, U 1992. *The Great Chronicle of Buddhas*. Yangon, Myanmar: Ti=Ni Press.

Walters, Jonathan S. 2018. *Legends of the Buddhist Saints: Apadānapāli*. Walla Walla, WA: Whitman College. Also at http://apadanatranslation.org/

Willemen, Charles 1994. *The Storehouse of Sundry Valuables*. BDK English Tripitaka, 010-I. Berkeley, CA: Numata Center for Buddhist Translation and Research.

Willemen, Charles 2009. *Buddhacarita: In Praise of Buddha's Acts*. Moraga, CA: BDK America, Inc.

Young, Serenity 2004. *Courtesans and Tantric Consorts: Sexualities in Buddhist Narrative, Iconography, and Ritual*. New York and London: Routledge.

Author biography

Sonya Rhie Mace, Ph.D. is the George P. Bickford Curator of Indian and Southeast Asian Art at the Cleveland Museum of Art and Adjunct Professor of Art History at Case Western Reserve University. Her publications include *History of Early Stone Sculpture at Mathura, ca. 150 BCE to 100 CE* (Brill 2007), "Transformations of Identity and the Buddha's Infancy Narratives at Kanaganahalli" *Archives of Asian Art* 67:1 (2017), and "Clearing the Course: Folio 348 of the Nepalese *Gaṇḍavyūha-sūtra* in the Cleveland Museum of Art" *Religions* 11 (2020). Her most recent exhibition and accompanying publication feature the art and site of Phnom Da. *Revealing Krishna: Journey to Cambodia's Sacred Mountain* was on view at the Cleveland Museum of Art from November 2021 to January 2022 and the National Museum of Asian Art, Washington, D.C. from April to September 2022.

6

Beyond Textual and Visual "Versions"

The Story Cluster of the Six-Tusked Elephant Bodhisattva

*Naomi Appleton and Chris Clark**

Introduction

Buddhist narratives, in particular *jātaka*s (stories of the Buddha's past lives), are commonly found in Indian literature and art, and often we find what appears to be the same story in multiple textual forms as well as depicted visually at one or more of the early Buddhist *stūpa* or cave sites. Past scholarship on such stories exhibits two main tendencies: Firstly, scholars have often sought to trace the development of the story, positing earlier or original forms from which various "versions" or "variants" were created. Secondly, where visual evidence comes into play, a lot of attention has been paid to seeking a textual source for each visual depiction, or at least finding the textual "version" most closely allied to the image.

While such studies can offer valuable insights into the development and spread of both stories themselves and the ideas and values they contain, the notion that early Indian stories are best studied as "versions" or "variants" of one another is potentially problematic. As leading narratologist A. K. Ramanujan

* This chapter began life as a paper for the Buddhist Forum at SOAS, University of London, in May 2019. We are grateful to Christian Luczanits for the opportunity to present, and to both him and the wider audience at the lecture and seminar for their engagement with the story and issues. We are particularly grateful to Janine Nicol for helping us to navigate the Chinese sources, including by making the major findings of Chen 2007 available to us, and by providing English translations of the story in the *Liudu ji jing* and *Za piyu jing*. Gregory Richter was kind enough to let us use his unpublished study and English translation of the Tocharian story.

noted long ago, to talk of versions or variants can and often does imply an original invariant narrative (Ramanujan 1991, 24–5). Yet in most cases, such a narrative is impossible to find, since stories circulated orally as well as in textual and visual forms no longer extant. The evidence we have for each *jātaka* story rarely suggests a single point of composition followed by the variant versions of other authors and artists. Instead, we have different tellings in different texts of varying provenance, and visual depictions that are often earlier than any of the extant textual evidence and which sometimes differ from the textual narratives in important ways.

The chapters in this volume so far have amply demonstrated the importance of viewing narratives in their broad visual and verbal context, and of not privileging textual evidence in either identifying, dating or "explaining" visual narratives. In this chapter we focus on a specific aspect of this broader relationship between visual and verbal narratives, by offering a model for exploring and understanding the relationship between different instances of what appears to be the same or similar story. Our starting point is a series of basic questions: What do we mean when we call a story a "version" of another story, and is this a helpful way to think of the relationship between textual stories? To what extent is it helpful to think of visual *jātaka*s as "versions" of textual *jātaka*s? Might we gain more from viewing them on their own terms? How can we best understand the relationship between different depictions, and between visual and verbal narratives? Addressing these questions leads us to offer our own model for dealing with the complex relationships between visual and verbal *jātaka* stories: the notion of story clusters. In turn, this concept has the potential to open up new understandings of the uses of and attitudes towards *jātaka* stories in Indian Buddhism.

In order to make our argument we will focus on one particular story, that of the (usually six-tusked) elephant-king Bodhisattva[1] who gives away his tusks to a hunter. This makes a good case study in part because of the sheer number of narratives available in Indian textual and visual forms. The variations also prompt rich ways of thinking differently about how visual and verbal narratives inter-relate. After some investigations into the "versions" of this story – first textual, then visual – we offer our new model of story clusters and explore some of its implications for our understanding of Indian *jātaka* stories.

---

[1] In general, we use "Bodhisattva" throughout this chapter to refer to the Buddha (Śākyamuni or Gotama, the Buddha of our time) in a past life. We use the Pali form, Bodhisatta, only when discussing Pali texts.

The *jātaka* of the six-tusked elephant Bodhisattva

If you wander around the great *stūpa* of Sanchi in Madhya Pradesh, you will find several *jātaka* stories depicted on the elaborately carved gateways. On the southern pillar of the western gateway, for example, you will find a celebrated image of a *jātaka* story in which the Bodhisattva is a monkey king who makes his body into a bridge in order to save his troop from a human king, before giving a sermon to the latter. On the opposite pillar a similar-sized image depicts the *jātaka* of Sāma (P.) or Śyāma (Skt), in which the Bodhisattva looks after his blind ascetic parents, until he is shot by a king. The story of the Bodhisattva's birth as the extraordinarily generous prince Vessantara (P.) or Viśvantara (Skt), long acknowledged as one of the most important *jātaka*s of the Buddhist world, occupies both faces of the entire lower architrave on the northern gateway. And on three separate architraves on three separate gateways we find the *jataka* of Chaddanta (P.) or Ṣaḍdanta (Skt) – the six-tusked elephant who gives away his tusks to a hunter who (according to some stories at least) has been sent by a human reincarnation of the elephant's jealous former wife (Figure 6.1).[2]

The three depictions do not offer a narrative sequence; each is a separate depiction, and two of them appear to simply present a single scene: elephants, including at least one with six tusks, surround a central tree. The third depiction (on the southern gateway) has some discernable narrative content, moving left to right: the elephants frolic in the lotus pool, then the hunter, visible on the right with his bow and arrow, takes aim at the king of the elephants.

The presence of three separate images of this story at a site where only five *jātaka*s have been identified likely reflects the system of patronage and sponsorship that allowed the site to be constructed. There is, after all, no clear logic to the arrangement of images at Sanchi: various scenes from the Buddha's final and past lives are depicted, along with scenes of *stūpa*-worship, images representing past *buddha*s, and scenes of magical animals. It is possible that the space was divided up and sold off to merit-seekers, and each patron was able, relatively freely, to choose what would be depicted in their allotted space.

This system of patronage might explain why three separate depictions of a single story are found here, but it does not explain why this particular story was so popular that it appears to have been chosen by multiple patrons. And Sanchi is not the only evidence of the story's popularity, for it makes an impressive number of appearances in early Buddhist texts and art.

2 Additionally, on the railing surrounding *stūpa* one of Sanchi we find a medallion depicting a six-tusked elephant. Whether or not this image was intended to depict the *jātaka* of the six-tusked elephant is an open question.

Figure 6.1. *Jātaka* of the six-tusked elephant on three Sanchi gateways.

Top: Northern architrave, photograph courtesy of James Hegarty.
Middle: Southern architrave, photograph by Anandajoti Bhikkhu, CC-BY-2.0.
Bottom: Western architrave, photograph courtesy of Flavia Zaghet.

As early as 1895, Léon Feer noted – in an article for the *Journal Asiatique* – the presence of five distinct textual versions of the story, namely, the Pali *Chaddanta-jātaka*, a Pali tale in the commentary to *Dhammapada* verses 9–10, the Sanskrit (and Tibetan translation of the) *Ṣaḍdantāvadāna* of the *Kalpadrumāvadānamālā*, and two Chinese stories, in the *Zabaozang jing* (T203) and the *Liudu ji jing* (T152).

The starting point for Feer's analysis, and perhaps the best-known textual story of the six-tusked elephant Bodhisattva, is the *Chaddanta-jātaka*, number 514 of the great Pali *jātaka* collection called the *Jātakatthavaṇṇanā*. The opening narrative of this *jātaka* is set at the time of Gotama Buddha, with a young nun remembering a previous rebirth in which she was an elephant queen. After the Buddha sees her animated reaction to this memory, he smiles and begins to recount the rebirth to the *saṅgha*. In this story, the Bodhisatta is reborn as the king of a large herd of elephants living by Lake Chaddanta in the Himalayas. He is described as being white and either having six tusks or two tusks emitting rays of six colours – the Pali version is curiously ambivalent on this point.[3] One day while frolicking in the forest, he strikes a great Sāl tree in full bloom, causing flowers, green leaves and pollen to fall upon one of his two elephant queens, and dry twigs, dead leaves and red ants to fall upon his other elephant queen. The latter is thoroughly unimpressed by this event and begins to despise the elephant king. On another occasion, while bathing in Lake Chaddanta, the jealous elephant queen sees the elephant king presenting a lotus flower to the other elephant queen, which infuriates her. After giving alms and flowers to a group of *paccekabuddhas*, she makes a fervent aspiration to be able to take revenge on the elephant king. Following this, she starves herself to death and is reborn as a human in a royal family. After becoming a queen, she recalls her former life as an elephant and manages to convince the king to send a hunter to kill the elephant king and bring back his tusks. The hunter, we are later told, is none other than a previous rebirth of Devadatta, the infamous monk who attempted to murder the Buddha on several occasions. After a long journey the hunter finds the elephant king and, dressing up as an ascetic with an ochre robe, he shoots the elephant king with an arrow. Out of respect for the attire of the hunter, the Bodhisatta elephant king does not retaliate. After learning the reason for the hunter's attempt to kill him, he kneels down so that the hunter can reach his tusks to saw them off. Despite his best efforts, the hunter is unable to do so and the elephant king takes the saw in his trunk and cuts them off himself. Shortly afterwards he dies and, when the hunter returns to the human queen, she is so upset at the sight of the tusks that she dies of a broken heart.

Feer took the *Chaddanta-jātaka* as the benchmark for his comparison with other narratives, yet it is worth noting that even the small collection of related textual tales that he identified offers challenges around inclusion and relation. To begin with, the *Dhammapada* commentarial narrative bears far less resemblance to the others, with its focus almost exclusively on Devadatta's attempt to trick the Bodhisattva-elephant by wearing false robes. Without any gift of tusks or multi-life romantic entanglement, we might question whether this is really a "version" (or, to use the terminology explained in Chapter 1, "narrative") of the Chaddanta story at all. Meanwhile Feer also discussed, in the opening section of his article, several other stories that contain an elephant-hero, and/or which include the motif of false wearing of robes, but which he did not consider to be "versions" of the Chaddanta story. The entangled nature of these various narratives will be discussed further below.

---

3 While the verses describe him as having six tusks, the prose usually – but not always – describes him as having two tusks emitting rays of six colours. Differences between verses and prose in the *Jātakatthavaṇṇanā* are common, with the verses considered to be an older tradition (see Appleton 2010, especially chapter 3).

Alfred Foucher added three more textual versions to the comparison in a book chapter in 1911 (revised and translated into English in 1917), namely, in the *Kalpanāmaṇḍitikā*,[4] which is known from Kumārajīva's Chinese translation (T201), rendered into French by Huber (1908, 403–11), in the Chinese *Da zhidu lun* (T1509), and as a single verse summary in the *Lalitavistara*. Foucher also considered multiple visual depictions: at Bharhut, Sanchi, Amaravati, Gandhara, and twice at Ajanta, in an earlier and a later cave. A careful study of these different occurrences of the six-tusked elephant helped Foucher to advance a theory relating to the chronology of the different versions of the story.

Besides these eight narratives identified by Feer (1895) and Foucher (1911/1917), we are now able to add an additional 14 textual narratives. (For a list of the textual occurrences of the story with full details, see the Bibliography.) In the Pali *Jātakatthavaṇṇanā* there are two additional related stories, the *Kāsāva-jātaka* and *Sīlavanāga-jātaka*. Also in Pali, we find a short passage in the *Milindapañha* and a related story about a Bodhisatta who will become a future Buddha in the *Dasabodhisattuppattikathā*. In Sanskrit, we have the *Hasti-jātaka* in Haribhaṭṭa's *Jātakamālā*, a rather similar account in plot to the Pali *Chaddanta-jātaka*, though very different in style. Also in Sanskrit is the *Ṣaḍdantāvadāna* of the *Bodhisattvāvadānakalpalatā*, which is a shorter and slightly modified version of a story of the same name in the *Kalpadrumāvadānamālā*. In Chinese, there are versions in the *Mohe sengqi lu* (T1425) and the *Za piyu jing* (T205). The story appears in the *Mūlasarvāstivāda-vinaya*, extant in Tibetan and Chinese (T1448). There are also Tocharian and Uighur narratives, and brief references to the heroic elephant in celebrations of the Bodhisattva's deeds including the Khotanese *Jātakastava* and the Mahāyāna *Rāṣṭrapālaparipṛcchā-sūtra*. To the visual depictions we can add those at Goli and Kanaganahalli. In addition, the seventh century Chinese pilgrim Xuanzang mentions a *stūpa* site near Varanasi associated with the story:

> Not far from the pond is a stupa at the place where the Tathāgata, in the course of practicing the deeds of a Bodhisattva, was a six-tusked elephant king. A hunter who wished to obtain its tusks disguised himself in a monk's robe and drew his bow to catch the elephant. Out of respect for the robe, the elephant king extracted its tusks and gave them to the hunter. (Li Rongxi, trans. 1996, 198)

Because of all these occurrences, the story of the generous six-tusked elephant Bodhisattva provides an ideal case study for an exploration of the relationship between *jātaka* texts and images in Indian Buddhism. As such, we will

[4] Lüders (1926, 17–27) argued that this work was most likely initially called the *Kalpanāmaṇḍitikā* or *Kalpanālaṃkṛtikā*, yet the Chinese translator did not understand this title and changed it to the *Sūtrālaṃkāraśāstra*.

be using the story to frame this chapter, and to explore how we might study stories both within textual sources, and across the boundary between textual and visual *jātaka*s.

Textual "versions"

So far we have traced 22 textual versions of the story of the six-tusked elephant Bodhisattva. Each varies in its length, style, theme, pattern of narrative elements and plot architecture, and the ways in which the stories relate to one another also vary. For instance, the *Hasti-jātaka* found in Haribhaṭṭa's *Jātakamālā* has the same basic plot architecture as the *Chaddanta-jātaka*, with essentially the same storyline events in essentially the same sequence and involving essentially the same characters. Yet as soon as one reads these two narratives side-by-side, some major differences are immediately apparent. Firstly, this telling is considerably less gruesome and less tragic than the Pali version – the elephant king pulls his tusks out and they then regrow, and neither the elephant king nor the human queen dies. Secondly, the *Hasti-jātaka* is composed in ornate Sanskrit *kāvya* and is mainly in verse, while the *Chaddanta-jātaka* is composed in relatively unadorned Pali and is mainly in prose. Thirdly, the *Hasti-jātaka* begins and ends by praising the perfection of forbearance and is therefore quite literally framed by this concern, whereas the *Chaddanta-jātaka* is not explicitly linked with any particular perfection. Instead the *Chaddanta-jātaka* begins and ends by highlighting multi-life connections and providing several rebirth identifications. Indeed we are told that, through listening to the past-life story she is intimately connected with, the young nun who was once the jealous elephant queen achieves liberation. In contrast, the *Hasti-jātaka* gives only one rebirth identification, that of the Bodhisattva, and shows little concern for multi-life connections. These parallel versions therefore appear to serve different purposes. In the case of the *Hasti-jātaka*, a major purpose seems to have been to entertain a highly educated audience with a fine example of Sanskrit *kāvya*, complete with beautiful and lucid visual imagery, similes, alliteration, the employment of a wide variety of metres, etc. The narrative belongs to a consciously structured and unified work, with each story presented as an example of the Bodhisattva's practice of one of the six perfections in his path to buddhahood, in this case the perfection of forbearance, so this telling more explicitly emphasizes the Bodhisattva's practice of the perfections.

Different to either of these is the *Sīlavanāga-jātaka* of the Pali *Jātakatthavaṇṇanā*. This narrative begins by describing that once the Bodhisatta was reborn as a white elephant king living in the Himalayas. He sees a man lost in the forest, who we are later told is Devadatta in a previous rebirth.

Taking pity on him, the elephant king provides him with food and leads him out of the forest and back to the road. Later, learning that ivory is highly sought after in the city market, he travels back to the Himalayas and asks the elephant king for some ivory, to which he agrees and kneels down so that the hunter can saw off his tusks.[5] The man then sells this but, greedy for more, returns to the forest and successfully requests that the elephant king give more ivory, which he again sells. A third time he returns and saws off the stumps of the tusks, but, when leaving, is swallowed by the earth which is unable to bear such terrible behaviour. The plot architecture and theme of this story are somewhat different to the *Chaddanta-jātaka*. While the *Sīlavanāga-jātaka* is focused on Devadatta and his multi-life lack of gratitude and remorse, the *Chaddanta-jātaka* is focused on the jealous elephant queen and her subsequent regret. Indeed, it is a matter of debate as to whether we should categorize these as parallel versions; however, they are very clearly related and might be thought of as belonging to a family of stories.

A reconsideration of the most helpful methodological lens through which to view related stories such as these was prompted by our creation of an online database of *jātaka* stories in Indian texts and art (https://jatakastories.div.ed.ac.uk). This project was led by Naomi Appleton and funded by a 2017 Philip Leverhulme Prize, with Chris Clark taking the lead in creating and populating the resource during 2019. One of the main purposes of the database was to link similar narratives in different texts and images. The analysis of textual parallels, and perhaps to a lesser extent visual parallels, has long been a major methodical approach used in Buddhist studies and thus we originally intended to link similar narratives using a "parallel stories" feature. The process of judging whether or not a story is a parallel version of another story naturally raised the question: What exactly constitutes a parallel? A number of different types of parallels are apparent, including (1) parallels within a single text; (2) parallels between different texts ascribed to the same Buddhist school, often belonging to different genres; (3) parallels between texts ascribed to different Buddhist schools; (4) parallels between texts and images; (5) parallels between different images found at a single artistic site; and (6) parallels between images found at different artistic sites. By no means is this an exhaustive list, but it does indicate a number of possibilities open to us when we look for and analyze parallels. So, what do we mean by parallel versions? Different kinds of parallels often require different sets of criteria, but in the case of narrative stories in texts, we are primarily referring to a strong similarity in the plot architecture of two or more stories, that is, central storyline events in roughly the same sequence with roughly the same characters. Other elements seem less important in determining whether or not we can call two or more stories

5 It is not stated how many tusks the elephant king has in this story.

"parallel versions", for example, names of characters and places, length of story, literary style, language and even themes.

However, the more we worked on the question of what constitutes a parallel story, the more we realized that the concept would not produce particularly helpful data queries for our relational database. In the case of the six-tusked elephant Bodhisattva, about half of the total number of related textual narratives would fail to be classed as "parallels", since their plot architecture is simply too divergent. If we only think in terms of parallel stories, we miss an important aspect of narrative literature, namely, the tendency for groupings of stories that do not fit the relatively narrow definition of a parallel but are obviously related in some way. In addition, it was unclear how best to link visual and textual *jātaka* narratives, since a direct relationship is rarely apparent, and visual sources often provide different details or emphases to the texts so often pointed to as their "source". As the project progressed, we decided upon a different concept for linking the narratives, both within textual forms and across the divide between verbal and visual: the notion of "story clusters".

In order to better understand complex story families, we drew inspiration from Ramanujan's work on the many and varied tellings of the *Rāmāyaṇa*. He offers a wonderful metaphor to explain their formation, namely, a large pool of signifiers "that include plots, characters, names, geography, incidents, and relationships" which each author dips into "and brings out a unique crystallization, a new text with a unique texture and a fresh context" (Ramanujan 1991, 46). This approach challenges the potential implication that a parallel version is a variant of an invariant original exemplar and also allows us to consider more expansive definitions of related stories. It also fits quite nicely what we see in this family of stories about an elephant and his tusks, in that each of these tellings contains a unique and select group of signifiers from a larger pool.

Ramanujan's pool of signifiers helps us to think through all the possible characters or motifs that might be drawn upon.[6] We believe that a helpful extension of this idea is the notion of "story clusters", which groups existing "crystallisations" that have come out of the pool. The notion of a story cluster differs from that of a parallel in a number of ways. Firstly, it is a more inclusive concept that is able to group together related stories that may not necessarily qualify as parallel versions due to their divergent plot architectures. Secondly, story clusters are better able to map the overlapping intertextual complexities

---

[6] In some ways this approach resonates with the motif-index approach of Stith Thompson and other folklorists. However, motif-index analysis has a tendency to subdivide narratives into very small elements in a way that ignores specific cultural settings. Our own approach, building on Ramanujan, seeks to account for motifs and characters shared within a particular cultural setting, as well as the other forms of intertextuality (and intervisuality) that are so commonly found in our materials.

evident in large collections of stories, such as the *Jātakatthavaṇṇanā*. It is important to note that not all narratives are best viewed as original "crystallizations" taken directly from the fluid pool; some appear to be deliberate responses to existing known stories.[7] Story clusters can allow us to appreciate conscious intertextuality alongside other examples of narrative relationship, without implying any search for an "original" text.

The notion of clusters is deliberately flexible, with stories able to belong to more than one cluster, and larger clusters divided into smaller sub-clusters. For instance, within the overall cluster of stories we have identified concerning the six-tusked elephant Bodhisattva, we have two clear sub-clusters, namely, (1) stories describing the multi-life bonds of a jealous queen and (2) stories describing a self-motivated hunter in robes (not involving a jealous queen). Within this overall cluster of stories concerning the six-tusked elephant Bodhisattva, there are additional stories that are unaligned to either of these two sub-clusters. Beyond this, some of these stories also belong to a separate cluster in which a queen dreams of an unusually coloured animal whom a hunter is sent to kill. Some of these stories also belong to yet another cluster of stories in which a man or animal is convinced by his wife to obtain a part of the Bodhisattva's body, such as his tusks or heart. Meanwhile we might usefully consider another cluster to be stories of Devadatta's ingratitude, and this would include several stories which do not mention elephants at all (Table 6.1).

If we start to look at individual signifiers, yet another picture emerges. For instance, in the *Chaddanta-jātaka* the human queen states that she dreamed of a white six-tusked elephant, which echoes passages in which queen Mahāmāyā dreams of a white six-tusked elephant prior to the Bodhisattva's final birth (Lefmann 1902, 55; Gnoli 1977, 40). Similarly, in both the *Chaddanta-jātaka* and related *Sīlavanāga-jātaka* the elephant king states that the tusks of omniscience are much more valuable to him that his actual tusks, which echoes a statement in the *Sivi-jātaka* (499) in which the Bodhisatta states that the eye of omniscience is much more valuable to him than his actual eye. In the *Zabaozang jing* (T203), we find a passage in which the elephant king appears to refer to uprooting his tusks as a parallel process to uprooting the three poisons

---

[7] It is worth noting that Ramanujan's model could be criticized for failing to account for the frequently conscious and explicit intertextuality evident in vernacular *Rāmāyaṇa* stories, which often respond quite directly to Vālmīki's classic text or other authoritative tellings. Examples of this are discussed in the *Many Rāmāyaṇas* volume in which Ramanujan's chapter appears. Indeed, his model may well apply more easily to a genre such as the *jātaka*s, where there is far less evidence of authors responding to established or authoritative texts.

Table 6.1. Clusters of stories in texts

text	language	six tusks?	jealous queen?	hunter in robes?	hunter is Devadatta?	weapon(s)	elephant helps remove tusks?	major theme
Sub-cluster one: Jealous queen								
Chaddanta-jātaka	Pali	Y	Y	Y	Y	poisoned arrow and saw	Y, saws them off	multi-life bonds
Hasti-jātaka	Sanskrit	Y	Y	Y	N	poisoned arrow	Y, pulls them out	forbearance
Kalpanāmaṇḍitikā	Chinese	Y	Y	Y	N	poisoned arrow	Y, pulls them out	compassion and generosity
Liudu ji jing	Chinese	Y	Y	Y	Y	arrow	N	morality
Mūlasarvāstivāda-vinaya	Tibetan, Chinese	Y	Y	Y	?†	poisoned arrow	Y, pulls them out	compassion and generosity
Ṣaḍdantāvadāna (Bodhisattvāvadānakalpalatā)	Sanskrit	Y	Y	Y	Y	poisoned arrow	Y, levers them in a rock	multi-life bonds
Ṣaḍdantāvadāna (Kalpadrumāvadānamālā)	Sanskrit	Y	Y	Y	Y	poisoned arrow	Y, levers them in a rock	multi-life bonds
Tocharian version	Tocharian	Y	Y	Y	N	poisoned arrow	Y, pulls them out	multi-life bonds
Uighur version	Uighur	Y	Y	Y	N	poisoned arrow	Y, pulls them out	compassion and generosity
Zabaozang jing	Chinese	Y	Y	Y	N	poisoned arrow	Y, breaks them against a tree	multi-life bonds
Za piyu jing	Chinese	Y	Y	Y	N	poisoned arrow	Y, cuts them off	multi-life bonds

				Sub-cluster two: Self-motivated hunter in robes				
Dhammapada-aṭṭhakathā	Pali	N	N	Y	Y	spear	N	Devadatta wearing false robes
Kāsāva-jātaka	Pali	N	N	Y	Y	unspecified	N	Devadatta wearing false robes
Mohe sengqi lu	Chinese	Y	N	Y	N	poisoned arrow	N	hunter wearing false robes
Xuanzang's Da Tang Xiyu ji	Chinese	Y	N	Y	N	arrow	Y, pulls them out	hunter wearing false robes
				Unaligned stories				
Dasabodhisattuppattikathā	Pali	N	N	N	N	saw	Y	act of homage by a Bodhisatta
Da zhidu lun	Chinese	Y	N	N	N	poisoned arrow	Y, levers them in a rock	compassion and generosity
Jātakastava	Khotanese	Y	N	N	N	unstated	Y, pulls them out	generosity
Lalitavistara	Sanskrit, Chinese, Tibetan	N	N	N	N	arrow	N	compassion and generosity
Milindapañha	Pali	N	N	N	Y	unstated	N	Devadatta's rebirth status
Rāṣṭrapālaparipṛcchā	Sanskrit	N	N	N	N	poisoned arrow	N	forbearance
Sīlavanāga-jātaka	Pali	N	N	N	Y	saw	N, but he kneels down	Devadatta's ingratitude

† The summary by Panglung (1981, 44–5) does not mention Devadatta; however, we have not accessed the Tibetan or Chinese full text to confirm that he is not identified with the hunter.

or unwholesome roots, which might be seen as a related motif.[8] There are hundreds of other such passages that join together – at times disparate – parts of Buddhist literature to create complex networks of ideas in which any given passage is likely to resonate with several others, creating multiple layers of meaning.

Visual "versions"

The notion of clustering together stories on the basis of their shared "signifiers" is also helpful when exploring visual *jātaka*s. It offers us something rather different to the more traditional approach, which tends to emphasize chronology, to seek textual sources for images, and to use the more readily datable material evidence of artistic sites to shore up the dating of texts.

This more standard approach to studying texts and art as applied to the six-tusked elephant story is well exemplified by Foucher's 1911/1917 study, in which he matched certain images with certain textual versions. In particular, he highlighted a key movement in the story from those versions in which the hunter saws off the elephant's tusks (with or without the elephant's help) to those in which the elephant pulls his own tusks out, in which Foucher notes the elephant is usually shown with only two tusks, rather than six. The two depictions in the Ajanta caves help to illustrate this movement, for the earlier depiction, in cave ten, has a clearly six-tusked elephant and a hunter with a saw of some sort. In the later depiction, in cave 17, the hunter bows as the elephant pulls his two tusks out. As Foucher argues, this change reflects a textual shift, with the likely innovation traced to what he refers to as the *Sūtrālaṅkāra* (now identified as the *Kalpanāmaṇḍitikā*).[9] In a neat little argument, Foucher also demonstrates that this shift could explain the apparent disagreements between the earlier verses and later prose of the *Jātakatthavaṇṇanā* narrative of the story, not least with respect to how many tusks the elephant is said to have.

---

8 The passage is translated by Chavannes (1934, 102) as, "Par ce don de mes défenses, je souhaite à l'avenir de sauver tous les êtres vivants des défenses (qui sont les armes) des trois poisons". Janine Nicol has suggested (in personal communication) that this is an attempt to mirror a somewhat different pun in the Chinese, in which the words for "sprouts" (of the three poisons or unwholesome roots) and "teeth/tusks" are homophones, but it is a reference to the "sprouts of the three poisons" within the written text. Either way, this story appears to use the image of uprooting to connect the removal of tusks and the removal of the obstacles to *nirvāṇa*.

9 More recently scholars agree that the cave 17 depiction of the story relies upon Haribhaṭṭa's *Jātakamālā*: see Zin 2017, which also offers more general comment on the need to re-evaluate the role of visual evidence in Buddhist studies scholarship.

In establishing the shifting textual presentation of the story and its influence on the art, Foucher helps us to understand some aspects of the history of this tale, and as such his contribution is very valuable. However, his approach stops short of addressing questions of motivation or significance; he is uninterested in the reasons behind the shifts in the story or how they may have been perceived. For example, why was it decided to depict this story a second time in a neighbouring cave at Ajanta, but with different details? Did people see it as the same story, and if they did, what did they make of the conflicting presentation? Did some people view it as a different past life that had some similar aspects? Or was the second image seen as a corrective to an earlier erroneous depiction? Did anybody actually care, apart from the artists and patrons, what exactly was depicted? Could anybody even see the story's details in the dark of the caves? How did the users of the caves interact with the images painted within them? What – in sum – was the point, of depicting this story at all, let alone twice?

Many of these questions are doubtless unanswerable, given the limited evidence at our disposal, but that should not stop us asking them. If we follow an approach that moves beyond notions of chronology, influence and "versions" then we may at least see some hints at what is going on. In order to do this, we need to first identify the "signifiers" that make up the visual pool for this story, acknowledging that these may be different from the ones most prominent in textual narratives. We can then explore how the depictions cluster with one another, as well as with textual occurrences, and what this might tell us about the significance of the story.

Consider the Indian depictions of the story listed in Table 6.2. Some interesting things are immediately apparent. Firstly, the idea of respecting men in robes, which appears to be important to textual occurrences of the story and wider resonances in, for example, the *Dhammapada* and other *jātaka*s, seems not to be important in the art. In no image is there a clear sense that the hunter is dressed in robes, and in many it is clear that he is not.

Secondly, the question of whether or not the Bodhisattva helps the hunter seems important. In almost every depiction we see the elephant helping, either by lowering himself to a more accessible height, gripping the saw in his trunk, or – in Ajanta cave 17 – using his trunk to pull his tusks out.

Thirdly, many depictions, though by no means all, show the human queen's regret as a central feature, and several also include the gift of the lotus to the elephant queen that led to her multi-life jealousy and desire for revenge. Thus the multi-life animosity of the queen seems to be a concern for the artists, as it is for several of the textual occurrences. These important scenes were depicted in both the Ajanta occurrences, for example, and can also be seen in prominent position in this depiction of the story across three dome slabs at

Table 6.2. Visual depictions of the story in India

Image	How many tusks?	Gift of lotus?	Death of queen elephant?	Hunter in robes?	Weapon?	Elephant helping?	Tusks presented to queen?	Type	Estimated date
Bharhut	6	N	N	N	bow and arrow and saw	kneels	N	single roundel	2nd c. BCE
Sanchi north	6	N	N	N	none		N	architrave, scene of elephants	1st c. BCE
Sanchi west	6	N	N	N	none		N	as above	1st c. BCE
Sanchi south	6	Y	N	N	bow and arrow		N	architrave, multiscenic	1st c. BCE
Kanaganahalli	6	Y	?	N?	saw	kneels	Y	three panels on stupa dome	1st–2nd c. CE
Amaravati	elephant has 2; hunter carries 4 then presents 2	Y	Y	?	bow and arrow and saw	kneels	Y (second roundel)	two roundels	2nd c. CE
Ajanta cave 10	6	Y	Y	N	saw		Y	painted mural	2nd c. CE
Goli	2	Y	N	?	saw	holds saw with trunk	Y (separate scene)	relief, frieze	2nd–3rd c. CE
Karamar, Gandhara	2	N	N	N	bow and arrow	kneels	Y	relief, stair riser	late 3rd c. CE
Ajanta cave 17	2	Y	Y?	N	bow and arrow	pulls them out	Y	painted mural	5th c. CE

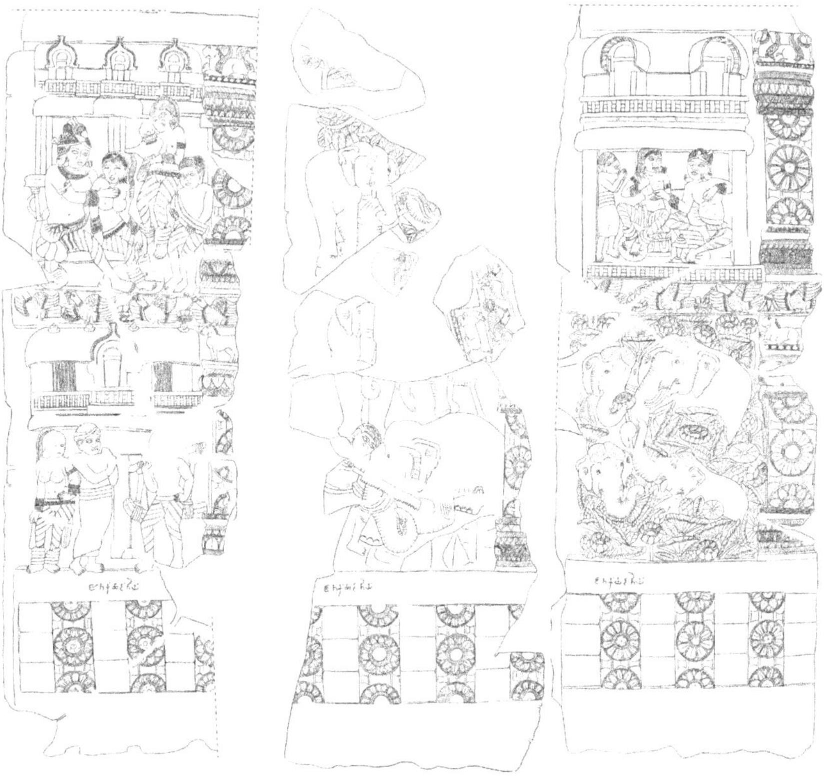

Figure 6.2. Three Kanaganahalli dome slabs depicting the *jātaka* of the six-tusked elephant. Line drawings by Monika Zin, reproduced with permission from Zin 2018.

Kanaganahalli (Figure 6.2). Likewise in a relief from Goli, again the scene involving the human queen is important, if separate.

The inclusion of the queen is also important at the ancient site of Amaravati. Here the roundel that shows various scenes from the elephants' adventures is well known, and functions as Vidya Dehejia's example of a "synoptic narrative" in her landmark article on modes of visual narration (Dehejia 1990, 384). She helpfully maps out the six different scenes shown within the single image; however, this roundel really needs to be viewed alongside a second one, which shows the other half of the story (Figure 6.3). Here the human queen faints as she is presented with the tusks by the hunter. The inclusion of this aspect of the story really adds a different dimension to the way we view the meanings that the story of the six-tusked elephant might have had for artists, patrons and users of sites.

These patterns in the elements chosen for emphasis may give us some insight into the potential reasons for depicting the story. One of the intriguing

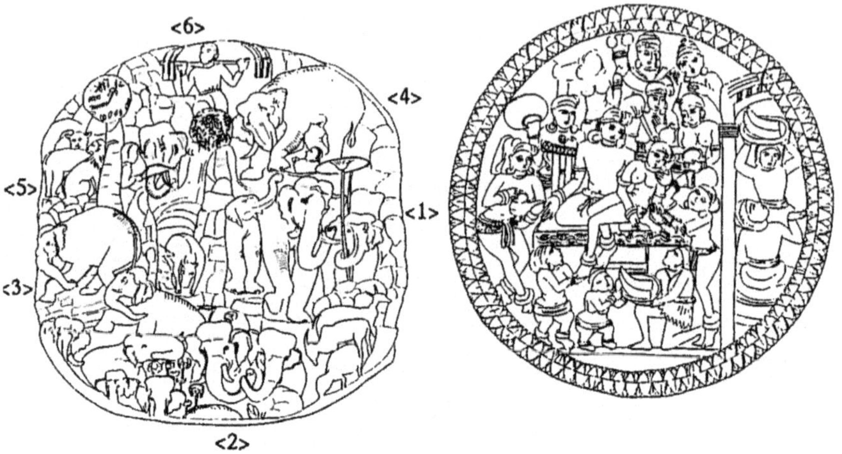

Figure 6.3. Two Amaravati roundels depicting the story. Line drawings reproduced with permission from Schlingloff 1999–2000, volume 2: 22.

limitations of visual narratives is that they offer little instruction about why a story is told or what effect it does (or should) have on an audience. In contrast, the textual sources for this story often provide a reason for the story's inclusion. Broadly speaking the reasons fall into three categories: (1) illustrating multi-life bonds (particularly that between the Bodhisattva and the elephant/human queen in the story) and the dangers of multi-life animosity; (2) illustrating the perfections or virtues of the Bodhisattva (though with different associated virtues in different texts); (3) illustrating the importance of respecting the robe. A fourth possible rationale, depending on which stories you count as being part of the cluster, is the ingratitude of Devadatta and/or his false wearing of robes.

Of these reasons, the visual narratives would appear to address the first two only. The multi-life message is underscored by the frequent inclusion of the gift of the lotus (which causes the elephant queen's jealousy), and the human queen fainting at the sight of the tusks being brought by the hunter. And the general awesomeness of the Bodhisattva-elephant is highlighted in those images that explicitly show him helping the hunter. The other associations – with robes, or with Devadatta – are harder to discern.

This is just one story of the many in circulation, but nonetheless it is worth noting that both multi-life karmic bonds and the Buddha's perfections are key to our understanding of *stūpa* sites in early India. As Jonathan Walters explored in an important book chapter in 1997, the rise in *stūpa* devotion appears to be linked with the idea that all devotees are tied to the Buddha through the sorts of complex karmic networks that are often demonstrated in *jātaka* and *avadāna* literature. The presence of the Buddha, as a perfected being, is ensured by the relics enshrined in the *stūpa*, but also potentially through images of him, or images of his relics and *stūpa*s. And as Brown (1997) argued in the very same volume, *jātaka* images are often inaccessible – far overhead or in dark caves – suggesting that their presence may have little relation to narrative readings, and much more to do with making the Buddha present, and/or manifesting the qualities of buddhahood, such that they function as part of the nexus of relic–image–text that plays out in such interesting ways throughout the Buddhist world.

Taking this into account might give us another perspective on the reasons why visual depictions of the six-tusked elephant story often foreground multi-life bonds and the Bodhisattva's ability to transcend these through his perfect compassionate generosity. As discussed more fully in the introduction to this volume, visual narratives may have a different *raison d'être* to textual narratives, and need to be studied on their own terms. Visual narratives may also draw on other visual narratives, without reference to textual narratives at all, thereby reproducing visual elements deemed important at particularly influential sites. In other words, there may be a different "pool of signifiers" for visual narratives to the pool we have for the verbal narratives of the "same" story.

This sort of analysis might help us to understand the site with which we began our exploration of the *jātaka* of the six-tusked elephant, namely Sanchi. Two of its images in particular (on the northern and western gateways) have no real narrativity in their depiction, and instead simply depict a six-tusked elephant in an idealized landscape with a number of other elephants. There is perhaps a hint at a multi-life bond, in the figure of an elephant turning away from the herd in the top left of each image: Could this be the offended elephant wife? How are we to understand these two images, with their rather more limited selection of signifiers from the six-tusked elephant pool?

The first thing to bear in mind is that the six-tusked elephant itself has wider associations with virtue and power, both within and outside Buddhist contexts. As noted above, the elephant that enters Māyā's side in her dream – and that marks the conception of the Bodhisattva in his final life – is often described as having six tusks (though it is not depicted as such at the early Buddhist sites, as far as we have been able to ascertain). Airāvata, the divine elephant of the god Indra or Śakra is also white and six-tusked in some sources. Indeed, this association is found in the textual versions. In the *Liudu ji jing* (T152), when the king asks about the existence of a six-tusked elephant, one official replies, "If we could get it, Śakra would [also] come here" (T3 No. 152 17b6-7, trans. Nicol). In the *Kalpanāmaṇḍitikā*, the six-tusked elephant Bodhisattva is explicitly described as "pareil á Airâvata" (Huber 1908, 403), "like Airāvata". Of course, the Bodhisattva-as-elephant is no ordinary elephant, and this is symbolized by his additional tusks but also by the fact that he is white in colour. Indeed, the six tusks may themselves be a way of communicating in stone the special nature of the king of the elephants, who cannot necessarily be distinguished by his white colour in every media.

Perhaps at Sanchi the six-tusked elephant Bodhisattva is emblematic of the Buddha and his virtues and powers, even without narrative content. The images may be viewed according to Flavia Zaghet's notion of the "spotlight narrative" (as discussed in Chapter 2 of this volume) in which the image serves to remind the viewer of a story enough to ensure that they recognize the need to honour the protagonist, the Buddha.

The notion of sacred place may be important too. The Sanchi depictions all include a magnificent central tree, perhaps that described in the Pali *jātaka* as being situated beside Lake Chaddanta in the Himalayas, at the foot of seven magical mountains. Landscape is important in this story – at least in some of its textual occurrences – as is the presence of either *pratyekabuddha*s (solitary or independent *buddha*s) or *muni*s (sages or seers), both of which are indicative of renunciatory bliss. So perhaps these apparently monoscenic depictions at Sanchi are bringing some of the sacrality of that far-distant Himalayan region to the site. After all, other sacred sites are also depicted at Sanchi, including the deer park that is the site of the first teaching, and several scenes of *stūpa* worship or pilgrimage.

And finally, we must acknowledge the possibility that the reason we see the six-tusked elephant depicted so many times at Sanchi is – at least in part – that donors and artists enjoyed elephants! There are, after all, numerous other elephants carved onto the gateways. Would visitors be able to tell that some of the elephants have six tusks instead of the usual two? Given the distance from the ground, they might not be able to tell the difference between the two apparently monoscenic Chaddanta-jātaka architraves and others that show a tree of awakening being worshipped by animals and other beings. Indeed, maybe these images don't depict the *jātaka* of the six-tusked elephant at all, but simply depict elephants worshipping a tree that represents a past *buddha*; the apparent variation in the trees, potentially indicating different past *buddha*s, would support such an interpretation, though the hint at the she-elephant leaving the herd in the top left corner of each of these two architraves would indicate otherwise.

We have no way of accessing the intentions of the artists and patrons, nor of accessing the responses of early visitors, but perhaps that doesn't matter. Whether or not people see or recognize him, a king of elephants literally watches over them as they come and go through these magnificent gateways. This effect relies very little on matching up the image with a textual narrative, and much more on the interaction between different visual repertoires, as well as broader concerns around what makes a site such as Sanchi a potent place to visit.

Conclusion: Pools and clusters

This brief exploration of the *jātaka* of the six-tusked elephant has barely scratched the surface of the many sources available to us. However, even this short reflection has, we hope, demonstrated the value of studying textual and visual narratives side by side, and of asking rather different questions of them to the questions about versions, chronology and textual sources that have tended to be asked in the past. In particular, the combination of Ramanujan's "pool of signifiers" approach with an inclusive and flexible clustering of the resulting visual and verbal "crystallizations" allows us to explore what was deemed important to the communities producing and using the stories.

With a story cluster such as the *jātaka* of the six-tusked elephant, in which multiple stories all interlink in interesting ways, trying to decide which story is a "version" or "parallel" can be challenging in the extreme, and the results are somewhat arbitrary delineations that exclude narratives with only limited shared material. While a story cluster must also have a boundary, and this may be no less arbitrary, what it offers is a more inclusive approach to the narratives, leaving porous boundaries through the possibility of belonging to multiple clusters. Hence, a story may be clustered with others that laud the compassionate gift of tusks made by a magnificent six-tusked Bodhisattva elephant, and may also be clustered with others that decry the false wearing of monastic robes; or others that include the multi-life entanglement between an elephant king and his jealous wife; or those in which a queen dreams of a special-coloured animal whom a hunter is sent to kill; or it may belong in just one of these clusters. The resulting Venn diagram of clusters opens up avenues for exploration and research, rather than closing them down.

Paying attention to the underlying pool from which the various aspects were taken also opens up new avenues of research, by following these signifiers into other narratives and clusters and into the wider Indian religious and narrative landscape. Examining the choice of what is drawn from the pool also allows us to see what specific resonances and values were important to the different storytellers and compilers. As already demonstrated in the previous chapter by Mace, exploring a narrative in its visual, textual and physical context can reveal much about the creators and users of the narrative and what they deemed important.

Ramanujan's "pool of signifiers" also helps to remind us that visual narratives deserve to be studied on their own terms, and not simply as depictions of verbal narratives. Visual narratives may have had their own visual pool, in part influenced by details from verbal narratives, but in part influenced by other visual narratives, as well as by the opportunities and limitations of media and resource. Exploring the choices that artists made can therefore help us to understand more than simply what "version" they were working with; their choices tell us about what made the story important to themselves and their sponsors.

The notion of story clusters then helps us to bridge the gap between verbal and visual narratives, since it is flexible enough to include a variety of manifestations. Bringing stories together in this way avoids any implications of the primacy of textual narrative, allowing visual and verbal to sit side-by-side as equally interesting examples of narrative. As argued in Chapter 1, a better understanding of visual *jātaka*s can shed light on how we understand textual *jātaka*s as well as vice versa.

We cannot fully understand the *jātaka* genre – or indeed other genres that exhibit similar plurality – without taking into account the various forms in which the genre was present. These forms are material and visual as well as textual, and a proper exploration of how they relate to one another requires more than identifying a textual source for a visual (or other textual) version. We need to consider the many and complex ways in which characters, themes, values, motifs, and aspects of plot interact, within and across the boundaries of media, and what the implications of these choices were for the compilers and artists of Indian Buddhism.

Bibliography

Occurrences of the story in texts[10]

Bodhisattvāvadānakalpalatā: Ṣaḍdantāvadāna see *Kalpadrumāvadānamālā*

Dasabodhisattuppattikathā, chapter 7

Saddhatissa, H., ed. and trans. 1975. *The Birth-Stories of the Ten Bodhisattas and the Dasabodhisattuppattikathā: Being a Translation and Edition of the Dasabodhisattuppattikathā*, 147–8, 78–9. London: Pali Text Society. [Pali edition and English translation]

Da Tang Xiyu ji (T51 No. 2087) (Records of the Western Regions), compiled by Xuanzang and Bianji in 646.

Li Rongxi, trans. 1996. *The Great Tang Dynasty Record of the Western Regions*, 198. Moraga CA: BDK America. [English translation]

---

10 We provide references to editions in languages that we can access, namely Sanskrit and Pali, as well as translations and summaries in European languages.

Da zhidu lun (T1509) (**Mahāprajñāpāramitā-śāstra*)
Lamotte, Étienne, trans. 1949. *Le traité de la grande vertu de sagesse de Nāgārjuna (Mahāprajñāpāramitāśāstra)*. Vol. 2, 716–18. Louvain-La-Neuve: Université de Louvain, Institut orientaliste. [French translation]

Dhammapada-aṭṭhakathā, verses 9–10
Norman, H. C., ed. 1906. *The Commentary on the Dhammapada*. Vol. 1, 80–83. London: Henry Frowde for the Pali Text Society. [Pali edition]
Burlingame, Eugene Watson, trans. 1921. *Buddhist Legends: Translated from the Original Pali Text of the Dhammapada Commentary*. Vol. 1, 191–3. Cambridge, Massachusetts: Harvard University Press. [English translation]

Jātakamālā of Haribhaṭṭa: 19. Hasti-jātaka
Hahn, Michael, ed. 2011. *Poetical Vision of the Buddha's Former Lives: Seventeen Legends from Haribhaṭṭa's Jātakamālā*, 137–45. New Delhi: Aditya Prakashan. Accessible via the Göttingen Register of Electronic Texts in Indian Languages (GRETIL): http://gretil.sub.uni-goettingen.de/gretil/1_sanskr/4_rellit/buddh/hjatm_au.htm. [Sanskrit edition]
Khoroche, Peter, trans. 2017. *Once a Peacock, Once an Actress: Twenty-Four Lives of the Bodhisattva from Haribhaṭṭa's* Jātakamālā, 104–10. Chicago: University of Chicago Press. [English translation]

Jātakastava, verses 16–19
Dresden, Mark J., ed. and trans. 1955. "The Jātakastava or 'Praise of the Buddha's Former Births': Indo-Scythian (Khotanese) Text, English Translation, Grammatical Notes, and Glossaries". *Transactions of the American Philosophical Society* 45/5: 397–508: 423–4. [Khotanese edition and English translation]

Jātakatthavaṇṇanā
Fausbøll, V., ed. 1877–96. *The Jātaka Together With its Commentary Being Tales of the Anterior Births of Gotama Buddha*. 6 volumes. London: Kegan Paul Trench Trübner and Co. [Pali edition]
Cowell, E. B., ed. various translators 1895–1907. *The Jātaka or Stories of the Buddha's Former Births*. 6 volumes. Cambridge: Cambridge University Press. [English translation]
72. *Sīlavanāga-jātaka*: Fausbøll vol. 1, 319–22. Cowell et al. vol. 1, 174–7.
221. *Kāsāva-jātaka*: Fausbøll vol.2, 196–9. Cowell et al. vol. 2, 138–9.
514. *Chaddanta-jātaka*: Fausbøll vol. 5, 36–57. Cowell et al. vol. 5, 20–31.

Kalpadrumāvadānamālā and *Bodhisattvāvadānakalpalatā: Ṣaḍdantāvadāna*
de Jong, J. W. 1979. "The Sanskrit Text of the *Ṣaḍdantāvadāna*". *Indologica Taurinensia* 7: 281–97. [Sanskrit edition]
Straube, Martin, ed. and trans. 2009. *Studien zur Bodhisattvāvadānakalpalatā: Texte und Quellen der Parallelen zu Haribhaṭṭas Jātakamālā*, 123–35, 259–67. Wiesbaden: Harrassowitz Verlag. [Sanskrit edition and German translation]

de Jong, J. W. 1977. "The *Bodhisattvāvadānakalpalatā* and the *Ṣaḍdantāvadāna*". In Leslie S. Kawamura and Keith Scott (eds.) *Buddhist Thought and Asian Civilization: Essays in Honor of Herbert V. Guenther on His Sixtieth Birthday*, 27–38. Emeryville, California: Dharma Publishing. [English summary]

Kalpanāmaṇḍitikā (T201), number 69; also referred to as *Sūtrālaṅkāra*[11]
Huber, Édouard 1908. *Sûtrâlaṃkâra: Traduit en français sur la version chinoise de Kumârajîva*, 403–11. Paris: Ernest Leroux. [French translation]

Lalitavistara, verse 40 of chapter 13
Lefmann, S. 1902. *Lalita Vistara: Leben und Lehre des Çâkya-Buddha*. Vol. 1, 168. Halle: Verlag der Buchhandlung des Waisenhauses. [Sanskrit edition]
Dharmachakra Translation Committee. "The Play in Full: Lalitavistara", *84000: Translating the Words of the Buddha*, March 31, 2020. https://read.84000.co/translation/UT22084-046-001.html. [English translation]

Liudu ji jing (T152) (**Ṣaṭpāramitāsaṃgraha*), number 28
Chavannes, Édouard, trans. 1910. *Cinq cents contes et apologues extraits du Tripiṭaka chinois*. Vol. 1, 101–104. Paris: Ernest Leroux. [French translation]
Nicol, Janine, trans. 2019. "Liudu ji jing 28 (Chaddanta)" [Unpublished English translation]

Milindapañha
Trenckner, V., ed. 1880. *The Milindapañho: Being Dialogues Between King Milinda and the Buddhist Sage Nāgasena*, 202. London: Williams and Norgate. [Pali edition]
Horner, I. B., trans. 1963. *Milinda's Questions*. Vol. 1, 292. London: Luzac and Company. [English translation]

Mohe sengqi lu (T1425) (*Mahāsāṃghika-vinaya*)
Chavannes, Édouard, trans. 1911. *Cinq cents contes et apologues extraits du Tripiṭaka chinois*. Vol. 2, 289–93. Paris: Ernest Leroux. [French translation]

Mūlasarvāstivāda-vinaya (*Bhaiṣajyavastu*) in Chinese (T1448) and Tibetan
Panglung, Jampa Losang 1981. *Die Erzählstoffe des Mūlasarvāstivāda-Vinaya Analysiert auf Grund der Tibetischen Übersetzung*, 44–5. Tokyo: Reiyukai Library. [German summary of Tibetan]

Rāṣṭrapālaparipṛcchā, prologue verse 149
Finot, L. ed. 1901. *Rāṣṭrapālaparipṛcchā: Sūtra du Mahāyāna*, 25. St. Petersburg: Académie Impériale des Sciences. [Sanskrit edition]
Boucher, Daniel 2008. *Bodhisattvas of the Forest and the Formation of the Mahāyāna: A Study and Translation of the Rāṣṭrapālaparipṛcchā-sūtra*, 135. Honolulu: University Of Hawai'i Press. [English translation]

[11] See note 4.

Sūtrālaṅkāra see *Kalpanāmaṇḍitikā*

Tocharian language version
Sieg, Emil 1952. *Übersetzungen aus dem Tocharischen*. Vol. 2, 7–17. Berlin: Akademie-Verlag. [German translation]

Uighur language version
Müller, F. W. K. 1922. "Uigurica III. Uigurische Avadāna-Bruchstücke (I–VIII)". *Abhandlungen (der Preussischen) Akademie der Wissenschaften, Philosophisch-Historische Klasse* 1920 (2): 1–93: 52–61. [German translation]

Zabaozang jing (T203) (**Saṃyuktaratnapiṭaka-sūtra*)
Chavannes, Édouard, trans. 1934. *Cinq cents contes et apologues extraits du Tripiṭaka chinois*. Vol. 4, 100–102. Paris: Ernest Leroux. [French translation]

Za piyu jing (T205) (**Samyuktāvadāna-sūtra*), number 9
Nicol, Janine, trans. 2019. "The *Chaddanta Jātaka* as it appears in the *Za piyu jing* (no 9)" [Unpublished English translation]

Other sources

Appleton, Naomi. 2010 *Jātaka Stories in Theravāda Buddhism: Narrating the Bodhisatta Path*. Farnham: Ashgate.

Brown, Robert L. 1997. "Narrative as Icon: The *Jātaka* Stories in Ancient Indian and Southeast Asian Architecture". In Juliane Schober, ed. *Sacred Biography in the Buddhist Traditions of South and Southeast Asia*, 64–109. Honolulu: University of Hawai'i Press.

Chen Kaiyong 2007. "Shi yi 'Za piyu jing' zhi 'liu ya xiangwang bensheng' kaozheng" ('Textual Research into the Jātaka of the Six-Tusked Elephant King as contained in the *Za piyu jing* whose translator has been lost'), *Zongjiaoxue yanjiu* 2: 74–8.

Cunningham, Alexander 1879. *The Stûpa of Bharhut: A Buddhist Monument Ornamented With Numerous Sculptures Illustrative of Buddhist Legend and History in the Third Century B.C.* London: W.H. Allen and Co.

Dehejia, Vidya 1990. "On Modes of Visual Narration in Early Buddhist Art." *The Art Bulletin* 72/3: 374–92.

Dehejia, Vidya 1997. *Discourse in Early Buddhist Art: Visual Narratives of India*. New Delhi: Munshiram Manoharlal.

Feer, Léon 1895. "Le Chaddanta-jātaka." *Journal Asiatique* 9/5: 31–85.

Foucher, A. 1911. "Essai de classement chronologique des diverses versions du Ṣaḍdanta-jātaka". In *Mélanges d'Indianisme: offerts par ses élèves à M. Sylvain Lévi le 29 janvier 1911 à l'occasion des vingt-cinq ans écoulés depuis son entrée à l'École Pratique des Hautes Études*, 231–48. Paris: Ernest Leroux.

Foucher, A. 1917. *The Beginnings of Buddhist Art and Other Essays in Indian and Central-Asian Archæology*. Translated by L. A. Thomas and F. W. Thomas (trans.). Paris: Paul Geuthner.

Gnoli, Raniero, ed., with the assistance of T. Venkatacharya 1977. *The Gilgit Manuscript of the Saṅghabhedavastu: Being the 17th and Last Section of the Vinaya of the Mūlasarvāstivādin*. Vol. 1. Rome: Istituto italiano per il Medio ed Estremo Oriente.

Lüders, Heinrich 1926. *Bruchstücke der Kalpanāmaṇḍitikā des Kumāralāta*, Leipzig: Deutsche morgenländische Gesellschaft.

Marshall, John 1918. *A Guide to Sanchi*. India: Superintendent Government Printing.

Ramanujan, A. K. 1991. "Three Hundred Rāmāyaṇas: Five Examples and Three Thoughts on Translation". In Paula Richman, ed. *Many Rāmāyaṇas: The Diversity of a Narrative Tradition in South Asia*, 22–48. Berkeley: University of California Press.

Schlingloff, Dieter 1999–2000. *Guide to the Ajanta Paintings I: Narrative Wall Paintings*. Delhi: Munshiram Manoharlal.

Speyer, J. S. 1903. "Über den Bodhisattva als Elefant mit sechs Hauzähnen." *Zeitschrift der Deutschen Morgenländischen Gesellschaft* 57/2: 305–10.

Walters, Jonathan S. 1997. "*Stūpa*, Story, and Empire: Constructions of the Buddha Biography in Early Post-Aśokan India". In *Sacred Biography in the Buddhist Traditions of South and Southeast Asia*, edited by Juliane Schober, 160–192. Honolulu: University of Hawai'i Press.

Zin, Monika. 2017 "Narrated with Chisel and Paintbrush: On the Importance of Research into Art History for Understanding Buddhism – Some Examples." *Rocznik Orientalistyczny* 70/2: 274–306.

Zin, Monika 2018. *The Kanaganahalli Stūpa: An Analysis of the 60 Massive Slabs Covering the Dome*. New Delhi: Aryan Books.

Author biographies

Naomi Appleton is Senior Lecturer in Asian Religions at the University of Edinburgh, where she researches and teaches in the areas of Buddhist and early Indian studies. Her research interest is the narrative literature of early India, with a particular focus on *jātaka* stories, as well as on ways in which the narratives of different religious groups relate to one another. She is the author of, amongst other things, *Jātaka Stories in Theravāda Buddhism* (Ashgate 2010), *Narrating Karma and Rebirth* (CUP 2014), *Shared Characters in Hindu, Jain and Buddhist Narrative* (Routledge 2017) and *Many Buddhas, One Buddha: A Study and Translation of Avadānaśataka 1–40* (Equinox 2020).

Chris Clark is an Honorary Associate at the University of Sydney and has also held positions at the University of Edinburgh, Australian National University and Deakin University. To date, the majority of his research has focused on the Apadāna, a Theravāda Buddhist text in the Pali language. His broader research interests include Pali language and literature, Sanskrit language and literature, Buddhism in South and Southeast Asia (particularly Myanmar), and textual criticism.

7

Interpretations and (Mis)understandings

Three Case Studies of Illustrations of the Buddha's Lifestory

John S. Strong

By way of introduction, I want to start by recalling a well-known story from the *Divyāvadāna*. Whenever the Buddha's disciple, Mahamaudgalyāyana, came back from touring (by means of his supernatural powers) the heavens, hells, and other realms of rebirth, he would describe for others the various karmic sufferings and felicities he had seen there. These graphic sermons served to encourage the performance of good deeds and the avoidance of bad ones. Wanting to remind people of this message, but realizing that Mahāmaudgalyāyana would not always be around to preach it, the Buddha ordered that depictions of the Wheel of Life showing the realms of rebirth be painted in the entrance hall of the monastery, so that people could view it anytime. But then it turned out that some laypersons were not able to understand the meaning of the painting on their own; so, the Buddha ordered that a monk be stationed at the gate to explain the Wheel of Life to visitors. But then some of the monks who were given this duty were themselves not able to explicate the painting's significance since they were ignorant, foolish, immature, or lacking in virtue; so, the Buddha ordered that "competent monks" be assigned the task.[1]

We can find, perhaps, in this story, an incipient Buddhist theory of the relationship between textual (in this case oral) and pictorial representations. Art (the Wheel of Life) is a way of further propagating the teaching (Mahāmaudgalyāyana's sermons). But the meaning – the message – of the art may not always be self-evident, especially to the uninitiated. As several other chapters in the volume (Zaghet, Zin, Mace) have already explored, an image may be in need of verbal or written explanation in order to be understood, and

[1] Cowell and Neil, ed. 1886, 299–301; Eng. trans., Rotman 2017, 95–8. For the *Mūlasarvāstivāda Vinaya* version, see T. 1442, 23: 811a (Fr. trans., Przyluski 1920, 314); Zin and Schlingloff 2007, 19–26; and Mair 1989, 64–5. For the *Vinaya Sūtra* version, see Sopa 1984. See also Teiser 2006, ch. 2. On the "incompetent monks" in this and other stories, see Schopen 2014, 47–72.

hence verbal explanations are often privileged over the image itself (as discussed by Appleton, Zaghet, Appleton & Clark). Here, problems can arise, since these explanations may not always be adequate or accurate. In fact, as we shall see in this chapter, they may sometimes be completely different from what the original artist intended in their depiction.

Unstated, though implicit, in this *Divyāvadāna* story are a number of questions that will occupy us in this chapter: how do explanations and understandings of art vary depending on the people involved? What are the respective impacts of textual and pictorial representations on particular individuals? What difference does it make if these persons are well- or ill-informed about Buddhism, or if they are totally ignorant of it? And what happens if someone attempts their own interpretation of the art, in the absence of a textual or oral explanation from a "competent" authority?

In what follows, I want to explore these issues by looking at three accounts of encounters between individuals and artistic depictions of the lifestory of the Buddha (or portions thereof). The first is the legendary tale of Mahākāśyapa's commissioning a set of paintings of the life of the Buddha in order to break the news of the Blessed One's death to King Ajātaśatru. The second is rather different: it concerns the encounter by two seventeenth-century Portuguese Jesuits – one in Beijing and the other in Goa – with a Chinese illustrated life of the Buddha. Finally, the third also features seventeenth and eighteenth-century interpretations by westerners, but this time of some statues and wall-paintings of the Buddha in the caves of Mulgirigala in Southern Sri Lanka, which they viewed as illustrating – spoiler alert! – the story of Adam and Eve.

All three of these case studies have one thing in common: they feature encounters with Buddhist art and its accompanying texts (oral or written). The differences lie in those who are doing the encountering: King Ajātaśatru was a Buddhist devotee (though, as a recent convert, perhaps not a very knowledgeable one); the two Portuguese Jesuits were scholarly Christian priests who had a decent familiarity with Buddhism but an intellectual and spiritual commitment to their own faith; and the European visitors to Mulgirigala had no knowledge of Buddhism whatsoever, but matched the imagery they saw there with a different text – one drawn from the book of Genesis.

King Ajātaśatru views the life (and death) of the Buddha

According to a story in the *Mūlasarvāstivāda Vinaya*, after the Buddha's *parinirvāṇa*, one of the tasks that fell to his disciple Mahākāśyapa was to inform King Ajātaśatru of the Blessed One's death. The Elder knew that the king, who had recently become an ardent Buddhist devotee, was a very sensitive person, and he feared that if he just told him outright that the Buddha had passed away, the shock would be such that Ajātaśatru would "vomit hot blood and die." Accordingly, he resolved to break the news to him gradually; he asked the king's minister, Varṣākāra, to prepare a magnificent pavilion in the palace garden and to have its walls painted with scenes of the Buddha's life. These were to start by depicting the Bodhisattva in Tuṣita Heaven and then descending into his mother's womb in the form of an elephant. Next his departure from home over the walls of Kapilavastu should be shown, and his six years of ascetic striving culminating in his sitting under the Bodhi tree and there attaining complete awakening. Then should come his sermon to his first five disciples, his display of the Great Miracle at Śrāvastī, his preaching to his mother in the Trāyastriṃśa Heaven, and his descent on a triple ladder in the town of Sāṃkāśya. After that should be depicted how the Buddha further spread his teaching and, finally, how he lay down on his right side with his head to the north between the two śala trees at Kusinara. In addition to all these paintings, Varṣākāra should also prepare eight man-sized tubs and put them in the pavilion. The first seven were to be filled with fresh butter-curds and the eighth with perfumed sandalwood water.

When all of this is ready, King Ajātaśatru is invited to go on an excursion in the park, and then to view the new paintings. Varṣākāra explains to him the meaning of each scene, beginning with the Bodhisattva in Tuṣita Heaven and ending with his *parinirvāṇa*. Upon hearing the explication of this final tableau, Ajātaśatru becomes feverish and faints. His men quickly immerse him in the first of the man-sized tubs filled with butter-curds in order to cool his body. When this heats up, they put him in the second tub, and then the third, and the fourth and so on, until, finally they submerge his thus-gradually-cooled body in the vat filled with sandalwood water. This does the trick: his fever finally abated, he regains consciousness.[2]

An actual pictorial version of this story as a whole may be found in a famous mural from Kizil (Figure 7.1), where we can see from left to right: a minister bringing a king to the pavilion; then, for his edification, holding up a cloth on which are painted various episodes from the life of the Buddha; and then another scene in which the same king is shown in a vat of butter-curds, with further vats waiting in the background.[3]

There are many things that can be said about this tale, in both its pictorial and textual versions, but in the context of our discussion of visual imagery

---

2 T. 1451, 24: 399b23-399c9 (Ger. trans., Waldschmidt 1950–51, 491–2). See also Rockhill 1907, 142, and Soper 1950, 149.

3 On this Kizil image, see also Mair 1988, 46–7, Waldschmidt 1925, 73–5, and Le Coq 1928, 137.

Figure 7.1. The Story of Ajātaśatru from Kizil. Source: Grünwedel 1920, plate 42–3. Courtesy World Digital Library/Toyo Bunko DOI: 10.20676/00000192

and its relationship to narrative text, I will limit myself to just three. First, pictures can be powerful and have considerable impact on their viewers; when Ajātaśatru sees the painting of the Buddha on his deathbed, he faints and gets feverish and has to be revived by medical means. Yet he does not "vomit hot blood and die" which is what Mahākāśyapa feared he would do if he simply announced outright to him "the Buddha is dead." In this context, then, pictures are gentler than words. Their message is less sudden, less in-your-face, less immediate. They are more open than closed, more "narrative" than "paradigmatic," in Jerome Bruner's sense of those terms.[4]

Second, the painting of the Buddha in *parinirvāṇa* is actually a narrative within a greater narrative – one which recounts visually the whole of the Buddha's biography. This too is important in sending a "gentler message" to Ajātaśatru. The king is not shown the scene of the Buddha's deathbed until he has been gradually taken through the other paintings of his life. Thus, prior

[4] See Bruner 1986. I would like to thank David Fiordalis for raising this distinction in his presentation to the Edinburgh Conference.

to learning that the Buddha is dead, Ajātaśatru is introduced to all the great things he accomplished during the course of his career – not only his birth, great departure and enlightenment, but also the series of miracles he wrought, beginning at Śrāvastī. Moreover, the painting of the Buddha on his deathbed, because it shows his body, serves to mitigate the news of his absence in ways that verbal announcements cannot. We often do much the same sort of thing at funerals ourselves, posting pictures of the deceased, and recalling the story of their life and accomplishments in order to ease the shock of their death. We are perhaps not used to thinking of biographies of the Buddha – whether pictorial or textual – as memorial services intended to facilitate acceptance of the fact of his demise, but that seems to be what is going on here. The Buddha is dead, but through pictorial and verbal narrative, he is seen to have lived a long, good, and significant life.

Third, while at one level this may help mourner-devotees such as Ajātaśatru cope with their loss, at another it sends a more fundamental dharmalogical message: Doctrinally speaking, the series of biographical paintings in our story help Ajātaśatru realize one of the fundamental truths of Buddhism, namely that all things arise – all beings are born – and then are subject to impermanence – a point repeated by the Buddha himself on his deathbed. *Buddha*s come and *buddha*s go, like all compounded phenomena. That, after all, is one of the messages of the Buddha's lifestory.[5]

Chinese illustrated biographies and the Portuguese Jesuits

In the case of Ajātaśatru just looked at, Buddhists (Mahākāśyapa and Varṣakāra) gave oral explanations of Buddhist art (the murals) which they made for a Buddhist king (Ajātaśatru). The situation becomes more complex when the person experiencing the textual and visual narrative is not part of the same religious community as the author of the story or its depicter in art, i.e., when he/she is not a Buddhist. In my next two examples, I will focus on situations in which non-Buddhist Westerners encounter the Buddha's lifestory through words and images.

In recent times, increased attention has been payed to the magnificent Chinese full-length illustrated lives of the Buddha that began to appear in the Ming Dynasty.[6] The oldest extant version of the genre, the so-called *Shishi yuanliu* ("The Origins of Śākyamuni") by the monk Bao Cheng was published in

---

5 See Strong 2004, 229–30.

6 See, for example, Lesbre 2002; Wicks 2002, 120–22; and Faure 2018, 277–82.

Figure 7.2. The Birth of the Buddha from the *Shishi yuanliu*. Courtesy of World Digital Library/Library of Congress. See https://www.wdl.org/en/item/293/

1425. This is closely related to a deluxe imperial version of the text with colour-prints (e.g., Figure 7.2) that came out in 1486 (Lesbre 2002, 69), and to an undated version entitled *Shijia rulai yinghua lu* ("Account of the manifestation of Śākya Tathāgata"), well-known in the West because it was reprinted and translated by the Jesuit scholar, Léon Wieger, in 1913 [2002].

The 1425 version recounts the life of the Buddha in 207 chapters of equal length. Each chapter is given a title of just four characters (e.g., "Queen Māyā's Dream," "Birth under the Tree," etc.), and is devoted to a single biographical episode which is illustrated by a woodcut printed in the top half of the page with the corresponding text down below. It is a scholarly work of sorts in that it cites its sources – no fewer than sixty-five canonical and non-canonical Buddhist texts (biographies of the Buddha and other works) are acknowledged in the volume as a whole.[7] The 1486 deluxe edition retains the four-character chapter titles but devotes two whole separate pages to each chapter – one for the illustration and the other for the accompanying text, both of which may vary slightly from those in the other editions.

A few decades after its creation, Bao Cheng's 1425 biography was used as a guide for the paintings of the life of the Buddha on the walls of the Jueyuan si (Monastery of the Garden of Awakening) in Eastern Sichuan. On these wall-paintings, there is no accompanying textual explanation, but only small cartouches next to each painting reproducing the four-character chapter titles for the scene in question. Presumably the full story of each scene was related orally, upon request, by the monks at the monastery.[8]

Bao Cheng's work is important in the history of Western encounters with the lifestory of the Buddha since it (or a text very much like it) was one of the first full biographies to be looked at carefully by Jesuit scholars in the seventeenth century. More specifically, it came to be known through the writings of two priests, Fernão De Queiros and Tomás Pereira.

Queiros was born in Portugal in 1617 and entered the Jesuit novitiate at the age of 14. In 1635, he went to Goa in India where he studied philosophy and theology, and where he held various posts in the Jesuit establishment for the next five decades, including sixteen years as one of the grand inquisitors there. He died in Goa in 1688.[9] Two years before his passing, he finished the manuscript of his magnum opus, *The Temporal and Spiritual Conquest of Ceylon*, a three-volume detailed history of the Portuguese era in Sri Lanka (which, unfortunately, due in part to his death, lingered in Portuguese archives for 230 years and was not published until 1916).[10]

In Chapter Sixteen of Volume One, Queiros embarks on a description of Buddhism as it was practiced in his day in Sri Lanka. As part of that, he gives a

---

7 See Lesbre 2002, 89–96, for a chapter-by-chapter tabular listing of these sources.

8 See Mu 2004 (cited by Lesbre 2002, 100). In English, see Wicks 2002, 121. For a side-by-side comparison of the 1425, 1486, and Jueyansi presentations of a single episode (the conversion of Yaśas), see Lesbre 2002, 77.

9 For a tabular chronology of his life, see Schurhammer 1929, 210–15.

10 *Conquista temporal e espiritual de Ceylão* (see Queiros 1916, and 1930). On this work, see Abeyasinghe 1980–81, 36, 47, Strathern 2005, and Lopez 2013, 97–9.

short summary of the first portion of the legend of the Buddha as "it is recorded in the Chingala (Sinhalese) scriptures" (Queiros 1930, 118–19), but he also (p. 141) expresses his distress that those who got this information from Sinhalese sources provided so few details.[11] Accordingly, he writes to one of his Jesuit confrères in Beijing, Tomás Pereira,[12] asking him for more information.[13]

Pereira obliges him by sending him a chapter-by-chapter synopsis of a lengthy illustrated Chinese biography of the Buddha closely related and perhaps identical to the *Shishi yuanliu* described above.[14] Queiros reproduces Pereira's account verbatim, with acknowledgement, in three subsequent chapters of his own work. Chapter Seventeen covers "The Birth and Life of Fô [the Buddha] up to the Thirtieth Year of Age," Chapter Eighteen "The Life of Fô, from the Thirtieth Year Till he became Old," and Chapter Nineteen, "The Old Age and Death of Fô and what Happened after his Death" (Queiros 1930, 122–40).

This constitutes what was for its day (1687) probably the most comprehensive and detailed account of the legend of Śākyamuni in any European language, and, had Queiros's manuscript not been confined for over two centuries to an archive, first in Lisbon and then in Rio de Janeiro, the history of the West's "discovery" of the Life of the Buddha might have been quite different.[15]

Even so, it should be said that Pereira's letter to Queiros was not just a summary presentation of the original Chinese text. There are chapters that Pereira skips altogether, or that he summarizes only in the most cursory fashion. At the same time, he does not hesitate to offer his own commentary on

---

[11] Here, he is in particular critiquing his forerunner, the Portuguese historian Diogo de Couto, who greatly abbreviates his account of the Buddha because he finds it tiresome.

[12] Pereira (1645–1708) was a Portuguese Jesuit, mathematician, musician, and scholar of Chinese, who spent over thirty years in China, most of it at the court of the emperor Kangxi of the Qing Dynasty. On his relationship and correspondence with Queiros, see Magone 2012, and Županov 2010.

[13] The Jesuits were well aware of the pan-Asian nature of Buddhism, unlike the British and the French who, up to the start of the nineteenth century, still failed to realize, for instance, that the Buddha's names in different places ("Buddum" in Ceylon, Fô in China, Xaca in Japan, and Sagamoni Borcan in Mongolia) all referred to one and the same figure. See Almond 1988, 9, and Lubac 1952, 123. See also Masuzawa 2005, 122. More generally, on the Jesuits' acquisition of knowledge about the pan-Asian nature of Buddhism, see Županov 2010, 43–56, and Xavier and Županov 2015, 119–57.

[14] On the identity of Pereira's original source, see Magone 2012, 260–63.

[15] On the saga of the (non-)publication of Queiros's work, see S.G. Perera's comments in his preface to Queiros 1930, 20*–22*, and Strathern 2005, 48. The original manuscript is now in the National Library of Rio De Janeiro – http://objdigital.bn.br/acervo_digital/div_manuscritos/mss1233568/mss1233568.pdf.

various passages. Some tales he finds absurd or not worthy of summarizing as they contain "false" doctrines. For instance, after giving a rather full account of the Buddha's defeat of Māra and his daughters (which he calls a "fable"), Pereira adds:

> I omit many [stories told by] Fô, all based on the transmigration of souls, a common error of the Oriental Heathen, which he teaches to be the lot also of Angels and Demons. ... He imagines Heavenly Angels in Heaven, on earth earthly Angels, in the mountains mountainous ones, reborn like men in all these places, and becoming, according to their merits, sometimes men, at other times Demons and Angels, imagining prodigies and nonsensical things, of which thc chapters 45, 49, 52, 53, 55, 59 and many others of the second part are full, everything leading to the conclusion and main business of honouring Fô, and of gaining large alms for his Bonzes. (Queiros 1930, 128).

Queiros, on the other hand, when he is stating his own views and not reproducing Pereira's text, occasionally expresses some appreciation for Buddhism and the Buddha, albeit in a backhanded sort of way that always makes clear his loyalty to Christianity which he sees as superior both from the perspective of faith and of rationality. For instance, he contrasts Buddha images with the "obscene, foul" and monstrous idols of the Hindus, and describes favorably the rites of Sinhalese devotees: "The worship they pay him is [simply] to prostrate themselves on the ground three times repeating the words *Buddum Sarnaõ Gachaõ* as if to say: Buddum, be Mindful of me."[16] To be sure, he is critical of Buddhist doctrine (e.g., the "transmigration of souls", which he likens to the views of Plato and Pythagoras), but then concedes that the Buddha is venerated in many countries, and that "it is doubtful whether he leads more people to perdition than [does] shameful Mohammed, whom he preceded by more than 1400 years" (Queiros 1930, 120). At times, then, Queiros's view of the Buddha seems to be that he is "the best of the bad guys" and his religion the least objectionable of all the heathen faiths.[17] He is quick, however, to argue that any positive points in Buddhism, and any possible parallels between it and Christianity (e.g. the fact that the Buddha, like Christ, "also took the shape of

[16] i.e., the first part of the refuge formula "Buddham saraṇam gacchāmi" (I go to the Buddha for my refuge). See Strathern's comments on Queiros's translation (2005, 72).

[17] Strathern (2005, 52) states that Queiros "had a bookish erudition regarding Sri Lankan culture and his version of Theravada Buddhism practiced there that was probably unrivalled in his time." He also points out (2005, 65) that Queiros's views of Buddhism were not "comprehensively and consistently negative" though he does "show a visceral disgust at all forms of 'idolatry,' and it is not difficult to picture him serving in the Inquisitio of Goa, an office that he discharged for 16 years."

a man though he was an eternal being") must be not a coincidental parallel, but the sneaky work of Satan who is thereby contriving to make this religion – Buddhism – more attractive, and thus the task of missionaries harder in their endeavors to convert these Buddhist pagans (Queiros 1930, 141).

Pereira does not attempt, in his letter to Queiros, to reproduce any of the woodblock prints from the version of Bao Cheng's work he is summarizing, but it is clear that he paid attention to them, and he occasionally refers to them to bolster his interpretations. For example, in his synopsis of the scene of the Buddha's birth, he informs us that "the Buddha was born from his mother's armpit, *according to their picture though the text does not mention it*" (Queiros 1930, 124, emphasis added – see Figure 7.2 above). More generally, he notes from the pictures that though the Buddha's disciples are supposedly Indian, they are dressed in Chinese style. And the architecture, he points out, is similarly typically East Asian. All this, he argues, is not so much because Chinese artists were schooled in a particular stylistic genre; rather, it too is evidence that the Chinese artist and author together participated in the deceptive schemes of the Devil. "To my mind," he concludes, "there is no doubt that the greater part of the [Buddha's lifestory] is fiction, first of the Devil, and secondly of Chinese cunning, because there are [so] many things which are peculiar to China and are unused in India" (Queiros 1930, 139).[18]

One of the illustrations that most certainly caught Pereira's attention was that depicting the Buddha's *parinirvāṇa*. Here, the artist has chosen to draw an empty, blank circle, in a style reminiscent of the Chan/Zen school (see Figure 7.3). One wonders what Ajātaśatru would have thought of this had Mahākāśyapa chosen a similar illustration for his representation of the Buddha's death scene – whether he would indeed have keeled over dead. Pereira, on the other hand, faced with this, offers the following synopsis/explanation:

> The last hour approached with pains all over the body, and on these he [Fô] began to meditate, not by applying the senses, but by suspending them; as was already said, they [the Buddhists] suspend the senses little by little till [the process] ends in the quietude and confusion of effects and of indistinct causes which is their imaginary happiness, which they place in a certain quietude without glory, but with the negation of pain, imagining that there is an intelligible centre free from all manner of life and death. (Queiros 1930, 137; slightly altered)

[18] He goes on to mention the "obsequies of Fô [which] take place according to the Chinese fashion… [featuring] a coffin, which is not the practice among the heathen in India but in China where to be without it is to be deprived of the sacred burial as amongst us" (Queiros 1930, 139–40).

Figure 7.3. The Parinirvāṇa of the Buddha, from the *Shishi yuanliu*. Courtesy of World Digital Library/Library of Congress. See https://www.wdl.org/en/item/293/

For a seventeenth-century Westerner, this is not too bad an explanation of the text of this chapter and its illustration. Pereira, to his further credit, quickly admits this interpretation is not an easy one to grasp, for, he adds, "To try to understand, not what they say, but what they mean to say, makes one's head turn giddy." But then, he seems to take his reader off the hook, by expressing his parting view that this struggle to understand "is not [really] worth the while" (Queiros 1930, 137).

The images at Mulgirigala

However skewed it might have been in places, Pereira (and Queiros after him) brought to their interpretation of Bao Cheng's *Shishi yuanliu* some background knowledge of the Buddhist tradition. But what if they had come to the text, and especially to its illustrations, without any previous acquaintance whatsoever with the story of the Buddha? How then might they have presented it? That is the question brought to the fore in my final example – the case of an encounter by Westerners with Buddhist art, whose explanation of its significance comes from a totally different tradition.

The famous mountain pilgrimage site called Śrī Pada, in Central Sri Lanka, is renowned for its association with the Buddha who is said to have visited the peak and left there an imprint of his foot in a rock on the summit (see *Mahāvaṃsa*: Geiger ed. 1908, i. 77–8; Eng. trans., Geiger 1912, 8). The mountain is also known as Adam's Peak since, from early on, the Muslims and, following them, the Portuguese and other colonial powers (the Dutch and the British), identified the footprint as their forefather Adam's, and the whole place as associated with the myth of Eden in the book of Genesis.[19]

Once the basic association with Adam was established, the mythology about his stay there multiplied. Some declared Adam's Peak to be the site of the garden of Eden itself. Others, the place where Adam and Eve resided and spent the rest of their lives after their expulsion from the garden. A lake on the mountain was said to be filled with the tears they shed for centuries thereafter, mourning their fate or, alternatively, the death of their son Abel.[20]

Śrī Pada, however, was not the only mountain in Sri Lanka known as "Adam's Peak." Starting in colonial times, it was often confused with a high rock outcropping in the far south of the island, which is the site of an ancient cave temple known as Mulgirigala. This is the place that the Dutch and others consistently referred to as "Adams Berg."[21] Given this confusion, the Adamic associations that surrounded Śrī Pada were seamlessly transferred to Mulgirigala, where they took on a life of their own, and where the emphasis was not

---

19 According to William Skeen (1870, 46), the earliest evidence for the association of the mountain with Adam comes from the narrative of Soleyman in the ninth century. For a study of this tradition, see Abeydeera 1992.

20 Skeen 1870, 44. See also Percival 1803, 207.

21 The history of the Buddhist monastic caves at Mulgirigala goes back to the second century BCE (see Ferguson 1911, 197–9). Today, the temple is mostly renowned for its rock wall paintings (see Bandaranayake 1986, 216–25).

so much on Adam's footprint (there isn't one on the mountain) as it was on Adam's (or Adam and Eve's) tomb.[22]

Donald Ferguson has traced the history of this confusion, starting with the separate accounts of three mercenaries, a Swiss and two Germans who were in the employ of the Dutch in Ceylon during the second half of the seventeenth century. All three of them present the mountain they describe as the site of Adam's tomb. The confusion continues in the works of the Dutch historians Phillipus Baldaeus (1632–71), and François Valentijn (1666–1727),[23] and of the German artist, Johann Wolffgang Heydt (18th century) who worked for the Dutch colonial regime and made several sketches of Mulgirigala.[24] It is not until the 1770s that, after a formal inquiry into the matter ordered by the Dutch Governor Willem Falck, an end was put to "the fond delusion" about Adam and Eve's life and death on the mountain (Ferguson 1911, 220).[25]

Ferguson fails to feature, however, one of the earliest Western accounts of Mulgirigala as a place associated with Adam and Eve. This comes to us from the travel journal of one François l'Estra, a minor nobleman at the court of Louis XIV who joined a French expedition trying to challenge the maritime dominance of the Dutch. His journey lasted from 1671–75, and he published the narrative of his travels upon his return to Paris (L'Estra 1677).[26]

On page 124 of his work, he describes his arrival in Southern Sri Lanka, where they dropped anchor "fairly close to a great mountain… at the summit of which there is… a tomb that the people revere with great devotion, guarding it very diligently night and day and forbidding access to it to all foreigners, so that it was not possible for me to enter inside. … The natives assure me that this is the tomb of the first man, Adam." L'Estra also mentions that, outside the cave, there was an inscribed epitaph, which, he assumes, asserted the same thing, although he admits he could not read it. He does, however, copy

[22] The claim that Adam's Peak was the site of Adam's (or alternatively the Buddha's) sepulcher is already found in Marco Polo (1993, 2: 319). It is generally assumed Marco Polo was here talking about Śrī Pada, but, curiously, he makes no mention of any footprint, and it is not impossible that he had Mulgirigala in mind. The Southern location of Adam's Peak may have been known to the Chinese. For instance, the fifteenth-century Chinese Muslim interpreter, Ma Huan, who accompanied Admiral Zheng He on his sixth expedition to the South Seas, appears to locate the Buddha's sepulcher on a mountain in the south of the island. See Mills 1970, 125–6; Lévi 1900, 433–4.

[23] See Baldaeus 1672, Valentijn 1726, and Arasaratnam 1978.

[24] See Heydt 1744, and 1952. Heydt never actually visited the site but published his drawings based on watercolors made by his friend, the Dutch artist Arent Jansen.

[25] Dutch sources on Governor Falck's inquiry are gathered and translated into English in Upham 1833, 3: 165–6.

[26] For a study of seventeenth-century accounts of the Orient by French travellers including L'Estra, see Harrigan 2008.

it out (without knowing the script) in the hopes that others may be able to decipher it (L'Estra 1677, 124). [27]

L'Estra then goes on with his description:

> At the foot of the mountain, there is a cave in a big rock, in which the history of the world was depicted by the first man, according to the local people. He is represented in his creation, seated, with his legs crossed and hands joined, looking at the heavens with a pitiful eye as though deploring his misery.
>
> Below the top of the same mountain, one can see the place where Cain attacked his brother Abel, where nine steps have been chiseled into the rock, by which one can climb up with the aid of an iron chain. People assert that Abel, seeing himself pursued by his brother, climbed up on this rock. Ready to precipitate himself down, he implored Heaven for help, and the Creator of the world miraculously made a fissure in the stone for Abel to climb through, though that did not ultimately allow him to escape the cruelty of his brother (L'Estra 1677, 124–5).

L'Estra makes no mention of Buddhism, but clearly the seated, crosslegged figure he describes as Adam's self-portrait is an image of the Buddha, or perhaps of a devotee (hands joined looking up). The "History of the World" he describes as adorning one of the walls of the cave, may well be the extensive wall paintings of a series of *jātaka*s, for which Mulgirigala is most famous today (see Bandaranaike 1986, 216–25). These include most prominently the *Vessantara jātaka* which, after all, is the story of a man and a woman expelled from their father's paradisial kingdom and condemned to wander until they take refuge on a mountain. The steps, which L'Estra mentions as hewn into the rock and the iron chains are still there today, and so is the great fissure in the stone made by God to help Abel (unsuccessfully) escape from Cain.[28]

Had L'Estra been allowed to enter what he was told was Adam's tomb (why it was closed is a mystery – no subsequent visitors report such a thing), it is likely he would have seen there a great *parinirvāṇa* image of the Buddha, one of the chief features of Mulgirigala to this day. Heydt, basing himself on his friend Jansen's watercolor, gives us a full view of the cave at a moment

[27] Unfortunately, the plate showing the epitaph was missing from the copy of the work I consulted. According to Ferguson (1911, 233n. 92), the characters appear to be in ancient Sinhalese, but are too poorly and ignorantly transcribed in order to make any sense. They may, however, resemble an inscription later reported at the site by Heydt (1744, 228). According to Müller (1883, 45) the inscriptions he found at Mulgirigala were all dedicatory ones.

[28] For a description of the path up the mountain, including the stone steps, iron chains and this "fissure" – this natural and rather spectacular cleft in the rock of the mountain – see Cordiner 1807, 203. On Mulgirigala today, see Wijesinghe 2016.

of ritual celebration (Figure 7.4). Indeed, subsequent Dutch travelers were inclined to think of this recumbent statue and its entourage of weeping mourners as a portrayal of the Death of Adam or as an actual tomb effigy (see Ferguson 1911, 203).

Before discussing this reading of the story of Genesis into the landscape and iconography of Mulgirigala, I would like to present another noteworthy instance of it. This is contained in a "report" on the caves that was written in 1705 by one Govert (or possibly Gÿsbert) Helmont, at the request of the Dutch Governor of Ceylon at the time, Cornelis Simons.[29] Helmont writes that, according to his recollection,

> Adams Berg… has at its foot a large chamber hewn out, divided into two by a single wall; in the one lies a very large naked[30] image, yellow of body, brown eyebrows, red lips, and long ears, with the hand under the head, and the legs one across the other, among the Cingaleese named Adam; and in the other the counterpart, of similar form and colour, called Eva. … From this cave one goes, by a flight of freestone steps simply laid together without lime, up above, where … there is little space to walk about, and there are, in addition to the aforesaid, … two smaller chambers: in the one Adam, together with the Patriarchs, dressed like the dancers of heathenish pagodes, painted on the walls, and in the next Eva, with the legs crosswise under the body, on a stone dais, like an altar, and an erect snake, which extends along her back and over her head, seems as if it were pecking at her brains; and in the middle her sons [i.e., Cain and Abel], the eldest somewhat larger than the youngest, made of stone, life-size, and carved of ordinary stature, … sitting next to one another (Ferguson 1911, 203–4).

The readings going on here are rather spectacular: Mulgirigala is the place of Adam's tomb; an image of the Buddha in *parinirvāṇa* is the dead or dying Adam; the dancers processing in the *jātaka* wall paintings are the patriarchs of the Old Testament; an image of the Buddha sitting under the *nāga* king Mucalinda is Eve being plagued by the serpent in Genesis; and Cain and Abel are two lesser images of the Buddha or of his disciples.

One is tempted to say that the case of Mulgirigala shows us what can happen when imagery is looked at in the absence of a text and in the context of ignorance. That, however, is not quite true. L'Estra and Helmont do have a text – it is just not a Buddhist one. The question must still be asked, however,

---

29 On Govert, see the note by F.H. De Vos in Appendix B to Ferguson (1911, 239). Govert's letter to Simons is cited in full by Ferguson, but was originally published in Valentijn 1726, 5: 377.

30 It is not clear why Helmont thought the *parinirvāṇa* image was naked (unless it was by association with Adam). The yellow colour probably refers to its robes.

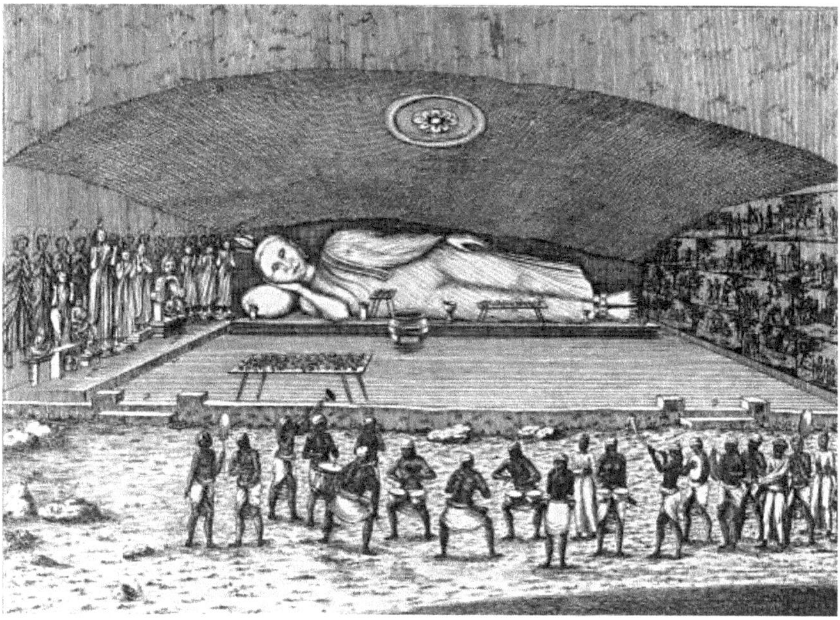

Figure 7.4. Parinirvāṇa Cave (aka Adam's Tomb) at Mulgirigala (aka Adams Berg), from Heydt 1744, plate 78.

how did their specific application of the mythico-history of Genesis to the imagery at Mulgirigala originate? In other words, what or who was inspiring L'Estra and Helmont and others to see Buddha images as portraits of Adam and/or Eve or to read into the topography of the site the saga of Cain slaying Abel? There is perhaps no definitive answer to this, but, in response, three points may be suggested.

First, as already mentioned, there was the precedent of traditions about the "other" Adam's Peak (i.e., Śrī Pada). The two writers we have been looking at thought that Mulgirigala *was* Adam's Peak. It makes sense, therefore, that they should apply to the former the same Adamic and Edenic associations of the latter which, we have seen, had long been established in Muslim and European tradition. This does not help us understand L'Estra and Helmont's embellishments of that tradition – their specific identifications of certain statues or wall-paintings at Mulgirigala, but it helps us see their inclination and willingness to read the site in the context of the Genesis story (with which they were well familiar).

Second, Ferguson (1911, 199) has suggested that this inclination may actually have been "fostered for their own purposes by monks at Mulgirigala." L'Estra, we have seen, claimed that the natives themselves affirmed the site as being Adam's tomb, and Helmont, likewise, said they told him that two of the statues were of Adam and Eva. It is possible, as Ferguson hints, that we have evidence here of an effort by the Mulgirigala monks, even then, to attract foreign visitors ("tourists") by boosting among them the fame of their temple. More likely, however, it is simply a matter of faulty communication due to language difficulties and cultural misunderstanding. For instance, early Western visitors may have been told by the monks that the stupa at the top of Mulgirigala contained "relics of their teacher, Budu," from which they concluded that it was his tomb – his sepulcher. They then may have inquired further about the identity of this teacher Budu, and, upon being told that he was the "foremost" (i.e., "the first") of men ("dipaduttama" ["best of bipeds"], one of the epithets of the Buddha), concluded that he was Adam. Indeed, Heydt (1744, 203; Eng. tr., 1952, 44) declares that "Budu" was simply the name that the Sinhalese mistakenly gave to Adam, the first man. Ferguson (1911, 323n.72) suggests that in this kind of confusion, "we [may be able to] see how the 'Adam' notion originated."[31]

Finally, there is one other channel through which the mixup at Mulgirigala may have been propagated. At the very end of his account, almost as an addendum, L'Estra makes a noteworthy observation: "Near the tomb believed to be that of Adam," he tells us, "there dwells a saintly Portuguese hermit of the Order of Saint Christopher; the king of the land has asked the natives to let him stay there freely and to furnish him with whatever he needs" (L'Estra 1677, 125). The presence of this Roman Catholic anchorite choosing to live out his days in this spot can only be taken as evidence that, already in L'Estra's time (1670s), the tradition that Adam was buried at Mulgirigala was strong enough to have made it into a holy Christian site of sorts. His being there may also help answer a question that has long plagued students of Mulgirigala: why was it that the Portuguese, whose rule in Sri Lanka ended in 1658, never plundered and destroyed the place, as they did so many other Buddhist *vihāra*s and Hindu temples in the region?[32] It may be that when they came there, this holy man – their compatriot – told them that the place was Adam's sepulcher – not a heathen site at all – and so they went away.

31 Other overlaps have been suggested. For instance, Moule and Pelliot (1938, 409) point out that the Buddha's greatness as a teacher might be explained by saying he was "the first to grasp the nature of suffering" – something that could have reinforced the confusion with Adam who similarly was the first to grasp suffering, albeit in a completely different theological context.

32 On this question, see Appendix D by Chelvadurai in Ferguson 1911, 240–41.

Conclusion and final questions

In her response to an earlier draft of this paper at the Edinburgh conference, Reiko Ohnuma first commented on the overall structure of my presentation, adding to it a slightly different twist. I can do no better here than to quote her remarks, in order to sum up what I have said so far, and set the stage for the raising of some further issues that are implicit, it seems to me, in any consideration of the relationship of text and imagery. "There is," Ohnuma says,

> a progression between the three case-studies.... In the first story of King Ajātaśatru from the *Mūlasarvāstivāda Vinaya*, we have a Buddhist king looking at Buddhist wall-paintings depicting the life-story of the Buddha. He hears a proper Buddhist explanation of those paintings and he responds in a properly Buddhist manner. So everything is Buddhist, and the interpretations of the paintings could be called "correct."
>
> In contrast, in the second case-study involving the *Shishi yuanliu*, ... we have one Jesuit missionary (Tomás Pereira) looking at Chinese Buddhist illustrations and their accompanying Chinese explanation, interpreting that material in his own way, and then relaying his understanding of it to another Jesuit missionary (Fernão de Queiros). In this case, the interpretations ... can still be called "correct" – since they do correctly identify this as the life-story of the Buddha – but now they are filtered through the mind of a Jesuit missionary, which means that we also get some extra ideas thrown in that are not original to the illustrations themselves but that clearly derive from the interpreter's own culture – for example, the idea that the entire life-story is really the work of the Devil, or the idea that the Chinese are making up a lot of stuff that was not true in India.
>
> Finally, in the third case-study, involving the Sri Lankan pilgrimage site Mulgirigala, we move even further down the spectrum. Now we have several European observers, François L'Estra and Govert Helmont, looking at a Sri Lankan Buddhist site, having the features of the site explained to them by local Sri Lankan Buddhist informants, and yet, somehow interpreting the entire site in relation to Adam and Eve, the Serpent, the Garden of Eden, and Cain and Abel. This is an interpretation that seems to have nothing to do with the original site itself, and that could be described as being completely "incorrect." So we have a progression that runs from correct interpretation on one end to incorrect interpretation on the other.[33]

[33] I would like to thank Professor Ohnuma for a copy of her remarks and for permission to use them. I have occasionally slightly altered the original.

Or do we? Having said this, Ohnuma then segues into a more basic hermeneutical question that I raised briefly in the conclusion to my original presentation, but that she expands upon more fully: Is it really possible to draw any clear dividing line between "correct" and "incorrect," – between interpretation and misinterpretation? "After all," she reminds us,

> when it comes to literature, we long ago seem to have decided that the author's original intent is irrelevant to a text's interpretation, so shouldn't the same be true of pictorial images? … Does it matter how people originally interpreted a painting if there are people now who interpret it quite differently? … Does it matter whether one's explanation of an image is close in time to the image's original creation, and does it matter whether the one doing the explaining comes from the same religious or cultural tradition as the one who produced the image itself? … What significance might a community of worshippers have for the "correct" interpretation of a [religious work of art or] a site?

Such questions are perhaps most evidently applicable to my third example of Mulgirigala (although they have incipient relevance to the other two case-studies as well).[34] My own view on this is two-fold. On the one hand, I think that it *is* possible to distinguish between correct and incorrect – that L'Estra and Helmont, in their assessment of the site and its art are just plain mistaken. They may be "interestingly wrong" about it, but they are wrong nonetheless. The fact that they were not alone in their error – that, in Dutch circles, the notion that Mulgirigala was the site of Adam's tomb lasted for about two hundred years may help bolster their view, but it does not make it any less wrong – it just spreads the mistake around.

When the aforementioned Governor Falck, in the 1770s, put an end to this "fond delusion" about Adam (as Ferguson calls it), it is noteworthy that he did exactly what the Buddha recommended when the Wheel of Life in monastery gates was inadequately explained: he got some "competent monks." Falck sent a questionnaire to high ranking knowledgeable Kandyan elders to inquire (among other things) about both Śrī Pada and Mulgirigala. Among the questions asked were: "Was Paradise on Ceylon? Did Adam leave the imprint of his foot on the hill called Adam's Peak? Are Adam and Eve represented by the images in the temple of Mulgirigala? What idols are those which have the

[34] In a somewhat different context, in his new book, *Les mille et une vies du Bouddha* (2018), Bernard Faure has more broadly raised the question of whether there is such a thing as a misconstrual of the life of the Buddha, once even lingering quests for the historical Buddha have been completely abandoned (as he thinks they should be but are not being).

shape of women?" (Upham 1833, 3: 165). And, in due time, the answers came from the "competent" monks:

> The Sinhalese have no knowledge of Adam and Eve. The footstep visible on... Adam's Peak is that of Gautama Buddha. The large images at Mulgirigala are images of Buddha alone. Wherever pictures of women are found painted on walls, they represent former queens and princesses, of whom accounts are to be found in Sinhalese books. (Upham 1833, 3: 166, slightly altered)

In this way, "incorrect" interpretations can get replaced by "correct" ones.

On the other hand, I also think that such "corrections" do not always happen. Misinterpretation is not always just an uninformed reaction to a work of art waiting to be set right; it is also a transformative action on a work of art, which may have various motivations, political, cultural, and religious. Over time, "incorrect" interpretations can themselves become accepted as "correct" ones, especially if backed by the force of a community.

As such, they may have destructive consequences. For instance, a misinterpretation such as that expressed by Queiros and Pereira – that the life of the Buddha was the work of the Devil – was, partly (I am not suggesting this is a sole explanation) responsible for the destruction of many Buddhist (and Hindu) temples in Sri Lanka. Alternatively, however, "incorrect" interpretations may join the "correct" ones and coexist harmoniously with them. And here I want to return to the Roman Catholic anchorite whom L'Estra met living next to Adam's tomb in Mulgirigala. As Ohnuma points out, he is just a single person and does not constitute a community of worshippers. Nevertheless, his presence there, incipiently at least, is a transformative action that may potentially have had the effect of Christianizing the site and the art in it. Had this happened, Mulgirigala might have become a shared sacred place like one of those studied by Yoginder Sikand (2003), where, as Ohnuma put it, "each religious community has their own interpretation of who the site commemorates, their own names for the site, their own oral traditions about how the site first came into existence, and their own modes of worshipping at the site." Not all such places end up like Ayodhya or the Buddha images at Bamiyan. The hermit at Mulgirigala was not only allowed to stay by the local monks, but supported by them. As Sikand points out, some shared sites (or works of art) may help bring people together and encourage religious tolerance and mutual understanding.

Bibliography

Abeyasinghe, Tikiri 1980–81. "History as Polemics and Propaganda: An Examination of Fernao de Queiros, '*History of Ceylon*'." *Journal of the Royal Asiatic Society, Sri Lanka Branch* 25: 28–68.

Abeydeera, Ananda 1992. "Paths of Faith: Following the Blessed Footsteps of Adam to Ceylon." *Diogenes* 40/159, 69–94. https://doi.org/10.1177/039219219204015907

Almond, Philip C. 1988. *The British Discovery of Buddhism.* Cambridge: Cambridge University Press.

Arasaratnam, Sinnappah 1978. *François Valentijn's Description of Ceylon.* London, The Hakluyt Society.

Baldaeus, Phillipus 2000 [1672]. *A True and Exact Description of the Most Celebrated East-India Coasts of Malabar and Coromandel and also of the Isle of Ceylon.* New Delhi: Asian Educational Services. [Reproduction of Anonymous English translation originally published in London, 1703]

Bandaranayake, Senake 1986. *The Rock and Wall Paintings of Sri Lanka.* Colombo: Lake House.

Bruner, Jerome 1986. *Actual Minds, Possible Worlds.* Cambridge: Harvard University Press.

Cordiner, James 1807. *A Description of Ceylon Containing an Account of the Country, Inhabitants, and Natural Productions.* London: Longman, Hurst, Rees and Orme.

Cowell, E.B. and R.A. Neil, eds. 1886. *Divyāvadāna: A Collection of Early Buddhist Legends.* Cambridge: Cambridge University Press.

Faure, Bernard 2018. *Les mille et une vies du Bouddha.* Paris: Editions de Seuil.

Ferguson, Donald 1911. "Mulgiri-Gala." *Journal of the Ceylon Branch of the Royal Asiatic Society of Great Britain and Ireland.* 22/64: 197–244.

Geiger, Wilhelm, ed. 1908. *Mahāvaṃsa.* London: Pali Text Society.

Geiger, Wilhelm, trans. 1912. *The Mahāvaṃsa or the Great Chronicle of Ceylon.* London: Pali Text Society.

Grünwedel, Albert 1920. *Alt-Kutscha. Archäologische und religionsgeschichtliche Forschungen an Tempera-Gemälden aus buddhistischen Höhlen der ersten acht Jahrhunderte nach Christi Geburt.* Berlin: Otto Eisner.

Harrigan, Michael 2008. *Veiled Encounters: Representing the Orient in 17th-Century French Travel Literature.* Amsterdam: Rodopi.

Heydt, Johann Wolffgang 1744. *Allerneuester geographisch- und topographischer Schau-Platz von Africa und Ost-Indien; oder ausführliche und wahrhafte Vorstellung und Beschreibung von den wichtigsten der Holländisch-Ost-Indischen Compagnie in Africa und Asia zugehörigen Ländere, Küsten und Insulen, in accuraten See- und Land-Karten.* Willhermsdorff: Johann Carl Tetschner.

Heydt, Johann Wolffgang 1952. *Heydt's Ceylon, Being the Relevant Sections of the Allerneuester Geographish- und Topographischer Schau-Platz von Africa und Ost-Indien.* Translated by R. Raven-Hart. Colombo: Ceylon Government Press.

L'Estra, François 1677. *Relation ou journal d'un voyage fait aux Indes Orientales.* Paris: Estienne Michallet.

Le Coq, Albert von 1928. *Buried Treasures of Chinese Turkestan.* London: Allen and Unwin.

Lesbre, Emmanuelle 2002. "Une vie illustrée du Buddha (*Shishi yuanliu*, 1425), modèle pour les peintures murales d'un monastère du XVe s. (Jueyuan si, Sichuan oriental)." *Arts Asiatiques* 57: 69–101.

Lévi, Sylvain 1900. "Les missions de Wang Hiuen-ts'e dans l'Inde (suite et fin)." *Journal Asiatique* 1900: 401–68.

Lopez, Donald S. Jr. 2013. *From Stone to Flesh: A Short History of the Buddha.* Chicago: University of Chicago Press.

Lubac, Henri de 1952. *La rencontre du Bouddhisme et de l'Occident.* Paris: Aubier.

Magone, Rui 2012. "The Fô and the Xekiâ: Tomás Pereira's Critical Description of Chinese Buddhism." In Artur K. Wardega and António Vasconcelos de Saldanha (eds.) *In the Light and Shadow of an Emperor: Tomás Pereira, S.J. (1645–1708), the Kangxi Emperor and the Jesuit Mission in China*, 252–74. Newcastle upon Tyne: Cambridge Scholars Publishing.

Mair, Victor H. 1988. *Painting and Performance: Chinese Picture Recitation and its Indian Genesis.* Honolulu: University of Hawai'i Press.

Mair, Victor H. 1989. *T'ang Transformation Texts.* Cambridge: Harvard University Press.

Masuzawa, Tomoko 2005. *The Invention of World Religions, or How European Universalism was Preserved in the Language of Pluralism.* Chicago: The University of Chicago Press.

Mills, J.V.G. 1970. *Ma Huan, Ying-Yai Sheng-Lan: "The Overall Survey of the Ocean's Shores."* Cambridge: Cambridge University Press.

Moule, A.C. and Paul Pelliot 1938. *Marco Polo: The Description of the World.* London: George Routledge and Sons.

Mu Xufeyong 2004. *Jiange Jueyuansi Mingdai Fozhuan bihua* [Wall paintings of the Jueyuan Monastery, illustrating a Ming Dynasty life of the Buddha]. Chendu: Sichuan People's Publishing House.

Müller, Edward 1883. *Ancient Inscriptions, Ceylon.* London: Trübner & Co.

Percival, Robert 1803. *An Account of the Island of Ceylon.* London: C. and R. Baldwin.

Polo, Marco 1993. *The Travels of Marco Polo: The Complete Yule-Cordier Edition.* 3 vols. New York: Dover Publications.

Przyluski, Jean 1920. "La roue de la vie à Ajantā." *Journal Asiatique* 16: 313–31.

Queiros, Fernão de 1916. *Conquista temporal e espiritual de Ceylão.* Colombo: Government Press.

Queiros, Fernão de 1930. *The Temporal and Spiritual Conquest of Ceylon.* Translated by S.G. Perera. 3 vols. Colombo: A.C. Richards.

Rockhill, W. Woodville 1907. *The Life of the Buddha.* London: Kegan Paul, Trench and Trübner.

Rotman, Andy, trans. 2017. *Divine Stories, Part Two.* Somerville: Wisdom Publications.

Schopen, Gregory 2014. *Buddhist Monks, Nuns, and Other Worldly Matters.* Honolulu: University of Hawai'i Press.

Schurhammer, Georg 1929. "Unpublished Manuscripts of Fr. Fernão de Queiroz, S.J." *Bulletin of the School of Oriental Studies* 5: 209–27.

Sikand, Yoginder 2003. *Sacred Places: Exploring Traditions of Shared Faith in India.* New Delhi: Penguin Books.

Skeen, William [1870] 1997. *Adam's Peak: Legendary Traditional and Historic Notices of the Samanalu and Srī-Pada with a Descriptive Account of the Pilgrims' Route from Colombo to the Sacred Foot-Print.* New Delhi: Asian Educational Services.

Sopa (Geshe) 1984. "The Tibetan 'Wheel of Life': Iconography and Doxography." *Journal of the International Association of Buddhist Studies* 7/1: 125–45.

Soper, Alexander C. 1950. "Early Buddhist attitudes towards the art of painting." *The Art Bulletin* 32: 147–51.

Strathern, Alan 2005. "Fernão de Queiros: History and Theology." *Anais de história de além-mar* 6: 47–88.

Strong, John S. 2004. *Relics of the Buddha.* Princeton: Princeton University Press.

Teiser, Stephen F. 2006. *Reinventing the Wheel: Paintings of Rebirth in Medieval Buddhist Temples.* Seattle: University of Washington Press.

Upham, Edward 1833. *The Mahávansi, the Rájá-Ranácari, and the Rájá-Vali, forming the Sacred and Historical Books of Ceylon: Also, a Collection of Tracts Illustrative of the Doctrines and Literature of Buddhism.* 3 vols. London: Parbury.

Valentijn, François 1726. *Oud en Nieuw Oost-Indien.* [Old and New East-Indies], Volume 5. Dordrecht: Joannes van Braam.

Waldschmidt, Ernst 1925. *Gandhara, Kutscha, Turfan.* Leipzig: Klinkhardt and Biermann.

Waldschmidt, Ernst, trans. (Ger.) 1950–51. *Das Mahāparinirvāṇa-sūtra.* 3 parts. Berlin: Akademie Verlag.

Wicks, Ann Barrott 2002. *Children in Chinese Art.* Honolulu: University of Hawai'i Press.

Wieger, Léon 1913 [2002]. *Les Vies Chinoises du Buddha.* St. Michel en l'Herm: Editions Dharma.

Wijesinghe, Mahil 2016. "Mulgirigala Rock Cave Temple: The Dutch Link." *Sunday Observer* [Colombo]. 12 August 2018.

Xavier, Angela Barreto and Ines G. Županov 2015. *Catholic Orientalism: Portuguese Empire, Indian Knowledge (16th–18th Centuries).* New Delhi: Oxford University Press.

Zin, Monika and Dieter Schlingloff 2007. *Saṃsāracakra: Das Rad der Wiedergeburten in der Indischen Überlieferung.* Düsseldorf.

Županov, Ines G. 2010. "Jesuit Orientalism; Correspondence between Tomás Pereira and Fernão de Queiros." In Luís Filipe Barreto, ed. *Tomás Pereira, S.J. (1648–1708) Life, Work and* World, 43–74. Lisbon: Centro Científico e Cultural de Macau, I.P.

Author biography

John Strong is Charles A. Dana Professor Emeritus of Religious Studies and Asian Studies at Bates College in Lewiston, Maine (USA), where he taught for forty years. He has also had visiting appointments at the University of Peradeniya (Sri Lanka), at the University of Chicago, and at Stanford, Princeton, and Harvard Universities. His research has focused on Buddhist legendary and biographical traditions mostly in South Asia. His book publications include: *The Legend of King Aśoka* (1983), *The Legend and Cult of Upagupta* (1992), *The Buddha: A Beginner's Guide* (2001), *Relics of the Buddha* (2004), and *Buddhisms: An Introduction* (2015). He now lives, happily retired, in a house on a lake in woods in Maine.

PART III: NARRATIVE VISIONS

8

The Buddha as Spiritual Sovereign

Narrative Figurations of Knowledge and Power

David Fiordalis

Introduction

Several dichotomies inform this chapter. Among them the most directly relevant to the wider theoretical concerns of this volume, and hence already explored to some extent by Appleton in Chapter 1, is that between the verbal and visual domains. By the visual domain I mean a concrete, physical (or virtual) image or figure that is at least potentially perceptible to the healthy eye. Defined as such, the visual is not easily reducible to the verbal domain. Similarly it is hard to envision how the verbal might be reduced to the visual. The written word is a visual sign, something perceptible: marks inscribed on a surface. While the word, "rock," may call up a mental image, the written word as image (as well as the mental image produced by it) is significantly different from the picture of a rock or an actual rock. These two domains, the visual and the verbal, seem irreducible, but arguably they are both part of language, broadly construed. By saying this, however, I do not intend to reduce the visual to the verbal.[1] Instead I would argue that language or discourse or communication is inherently multimodal: it utilizes not only verbal but also nonverbal modes of signification, because cognition itself embraces the plurality of the senses.

Another dichotomy, which may be just as relevant to the present context, is the one proposed to exist between what psychologist Jerome Bruner (1986, 11) calls two basic "modes of thought," one of which he refers to as the "logico-scientific" or "paradigmatic" mode. The other he calls the "narrative" mode. According to Bruner, these two modes are irreducible. He suggests that while both may seek to convince an intended audience of something, they do so in radically different ways and seek to convince the audience of "fundamentally

[1] For an insightful presentation of the dichotomy between words and images as a basic problem to be explored, rather than an ontological distinction to be defended, see Mitchell 1996.

different" things: "Arguments convince one of their truth, stories of their lifelikeness." Bruner's arguments help to clear some theoretical space for the investigation of narrative and how it might work on its own terms, and his arguments have been influential, even within the field of Indian and Buddhist Studies.[2] Nevertheless, some have questioned the widespread assumption he seems to share that narrative should be regarded as inherently representational or that it necessarily aims to achieve verisimilitude. For instance, while making the argument that narratives make arguments, Ronald Sukenick (2000, 2) works to "free narrative from the obligations of mimesis, popularly, and most often critically, assumed to be its defining quality."[3]

In this chapter, I will affirm Sukenick's claim that narratives make arguments, while still appreciating the distinction Bruner draws between the paradigmatic and the narrative modes of discourse. Logical arguments give series of interrelated propositions, but narratives create storyworlds of spatial and temporal extension in which characters perform actions and experience events. The differences between the two modes suggest that, while narratives may make arguments, they do so differently from paradigmatic forms of discourse like the philosophical treatise or argumentative essay. While the presence in narrative of temporal sequence, or what Seymour Chatman (1978) calls "story-time," is certainly one of the primary ways one might distinguish the narrative mode from the paradigmatic mode of discourse, my answer to the question of how narratives make arguments will emphasize the role of metaphor and what I call "narrative figuration" – the way narratives actualize embodied figures and use visual imagery; as such, this chapter also explores visual aspects of verbal narrative as, in some sense, a parallel domain to the visual narratives explored in earlier chapters. More specifically, I will look at how certain Buddhist narratives actualize the Buddha as a "spiritual sovereign," a figure of extraordinary knowledge and power. In these narratives we find the metaphor – or perhaps it is meant to be understood literally – that BUDDHAS ARE SUPREME SOVEREIGNS.[4] We find this metaphor stated directly as a proposition, but then the narratives become a vehicle through which the verbal approaches the visual domain. The narratives create highly visual mental images, images that are informed or shaped by a cognitive model of embodied experience. The narratives thus help give concrete shape to certain abstract

---

2 See Carrithers 1992, 92–116, especially 107; Collins 1998, 121ff.

3 The views of Bruner and Sukenick are also presented in contrast in Abbott 2008, 199. Abbott's own view seems to be that narrative often involves "passionate thinking" about conflict, which arguably lies at the heart of all narrative. This last point depends especially on how one defines narrative.

4 In this chapter, I will follow the practice begun in Lakoff and Johnson 1980 of capitalizing metaphors in order to highlight their conceptual content.

conceptions of ideal beings and states of flourishing. In this way, they also prompt us to reconsider the question of the relationship between the visual and the verbal domains. I will suggest that narratives may work to bridge the irreducible gap between the two, while showing how they can also blur the line between the literal and the metaphorical.

This last point speaks to another dichotomy of relevance to this chapter, one that addresses the specific historical context of the narratives under discussion here. Scholars have aptly characterized the relationship between Buddhism and the State as one of "antagonistic symbiosis" (Gunawardana 1979, 344), "contestation/justification" (Collins 1998, 14; via LeGoff 1988), and "irresolvable tension" (Smith 1972). Yet, such ways of framing the historical situation still imply a relationship between two separate entities or spheres. Consequently, the focus of much scholarship on this relationship has been uni-directional: exploring how Buddhist "religious" values shape or impact (that is, either justify or contest) the "non-religious" (or temporal/political) sphere. For instance, Bardwell Smith (1972, 1) writes about the essays collected in the influential volume, *The Two Wheels of Dhamma*: they all have the goal "to describe and assess the various ways in which Buddhist religious values, conceptions and activities have served to shape the so-called non-religious spheres of Buddhist societies." Similarly, in chapter six of his book on nirvana, Steven Collins (1998, 415) asks, "were the two sides of the relation mutually-exclusive opposites, like two sides of a coin: heads we contest, tails we justify?" Collins says it is "easy" to find Buddhist stories critical of kingship; he focuses instead on what he sees as the "more difficult" question of how Buddhist ideology, which he characterizes as an ascetic ideology of non-violence, could possibly justify the king, the paragon of violence, punishment, and military/political/coercive power.

The problem here is that Buddhism also contains within itself an irresolvable tension between the so-called "spiritual" (or "religious") and the "temporal" domains. We see this tension manifest in various ways, social/historical and ideological, but it is perhaps nowhere more evident than in the figure of the Buddha, "in whom," again quoting Smith (1972, 2–3, paraphrasing Reynolds), "the tension between compassionate involvement with those in suffering and freedom from attachment himself was maintained throughout," and "whose enlightened compassion occasions the uniting of temporal and spiritual authority." One could also articulate this tension in terms of power and its renunciation, which itself entails the achievement of power, but not necessarily its profligate use. Distinct from the question of how Buddhist ideology could challenge or justify the State and its human embodiment in the King, but like its mirror image, is the question of how the rhetoric of sovereignty and kingship has shaped Buddhist ideals, images, and representations of the Buddha.

So as we explore the theoretical question of how narratives make arguments, and look more specifically at how certain Buddhist narratives actualize the Buddha as a "spiritual sovereign," and as we assess the role of visuality and metaphor in this process, we may find ourselves able to propose a stronger (and potentially more comprehensive) interpretation of certain historical developments in the Buddhist tradition, especially in regard to the relationship therein between the so-called "spiritual" and "temporal" domains.

The conversion of King Kapphiṇa

Given that narrative and the visual imagery it utilizes form the central focus of this essay, I will begin with a story: it is the story of the conversion by the Buddha of King Kapphiṇa the Great. This story is not particularly well-known today. It has not been the subject of much scholarly inquiry or popular consumption, but there is some evidence to suggest that it was once better known. There are several versions of the story still available to us. One set of similar tellings is found in several Pāli texts. The longest of these is in the *Dhammapada* commentary. Mahākappina, as the Pāli sources call him, is also included in the list of monks who are said to be the best in some category, a list found in the *Aṅguttara-nikāya*, where he is said to be foremost among those who taught the monks. A set of verses is also attributed to him in the *Theragāthā*. Consequently, versions of his story not unlike the one in the *Dhammapada* commentary are also found in the Pāli commentaries on these canonical texts, and there is a similar version told in the Pāli *Apadāna*.[5]

In this essay, however, I will focus on the version found in the *Avadānaśataka*, a collection of one hundred Buddhist tales in Sanskrit dated to sometime in the first millennium and connected to the Mūlasarvāstivāda tradition.[6] Before retelling the story, there are two other versions, one only ostensible, that I want to mention. One is the *Kapphiṇābhyudaya*, *The Exaltation of King Kapphiṇa*,

5 For a translation of the *Dhammapada* commentary version, see Burlingame 1921, vol. 29, 167–76. The relevant list is found in Morris 1885–1900, vol. 1, 25. See the translation in Bodhi 2012, 111, and further references in note 112. Mahākappina is also mentioned in the *Saṃyuttanikāya*. See Feer 1884–1908, vol. 1, 145, and vol. 2, 284, and the translation in Bodhi 2000, 230, 721–2 and note 400. The *Theragāthā* verses are 547–56. See the translation in Norman 2007, vol. 1, 62–3, as well as the translation of the commentary in Rhys Davids 1951, 254–7. Jonathan Walters (2018) has produced an online translation of the *Apadāna* version.

6 I have basically followed the Sanskrit edition in Speyer 1902–09, vol. 2, 102ff., but with reference to the Tibetan translation as found in the Derge edition for which see Tshul khrims rin chen 1976–9, vol. 75 (aṃ), 477ff, and an older Nepalese manuscript that preserves the story on which see Fiordalis 2019. On the school affiliation of the work, see Hartmann 1985.

composed by the Kashmiri Buddhist poet, Śivasvāmin, in the ninth century.[7] Śivasvāmin's work is a *mahākāvya*, a highly ornate form of narrative poetry, and it seems as though he based parts of it on a version of the tale similar, if not identical, to the one found in the *Avadānaśataka*. The fact that this story became the subject of a *mahākāvya* at all may suggest that it had a certain cachet. When we consider the broader historical context that informs the tension within Buddhism between the "spiritual" and the "temporal" domains, it may become easier to understand why.

Secondly, Longhurst (1936, pl. L) first identified the visual narrative in Figure 8.1 (or at least the top two panels) as referring to the story of Kapphiṇa. It comes from Nāgārjunakoṇḍa around the second or third century. Rao (1956, 138) and Auboyer (1983, pl. 102) also tacitly supported this identification. Monika Zin (2006, 5) also supported it, but more recently she has emphasized to me that the identification remains uncertain. If it does represent the Kapphiṇa story, it remains unclear precisely how this sculpture in bas relief should be interpreted in light of the extant textual versions of the story available to us. Longhurst (1936, 60–61) relates it to the version found in the Pāli *Dhammapadaṭṭhakathā*, but he acknowledges that there are certain differences between them. Moreover, he does not include the bottom panel, which shows a woman sitting on a chest in front of another chest on which clothes are laid; this panel likely belongs to the same visual narrative, and may in fact support the identification.[8] However, it remains tenuous and deserves more thorough investigation, which ought to involve all extant versions, including the Chinese translation of the *Avadānaśataka*. For the moment, it is important simply to recognize this visual narrative as a possible version of the story, one that is different in kind from the various verbal or textual versions available to us. It demonstrates the basic difference between the verbal and the visual domains of signification. We are confronted with a complex visual image (or a series of images), and to submit it (or them) to analysis, that is, to make it into an

7 On this work, see Shankar and Hahn 1989; Hahn 1990; Hahn 1997; and Warder 1988, vol. 5, 171ff.

8 Longhurst points out that the image depicts a king arriving to meet the Buddha while riding on an elephant, whereas the *Dhammapada* commentary says that the king arrived by horse. He also draws attention to a second image, plate XXVa, which he claims depicts the story but offers no explanation. Zin, through personal communication, has stressed the difficulty of identifying the reliefs from Nāgārjunakoṇḍa, and that in her experience they do not illustrate Pāli versions of the stories. They typically correspond to versions closer to those found in the Mūlasarvāstivāda tradition. Yet, so far as I know at present, only the Pāli versions make any reference to Mahākappina's wife, who also joins the monastic order. Other details in the bottom panel, such as the chests and the cloth garments above them might support the identification, but more work is needed to confirm it.

Figure 8.1. Possible image of the story of Kapphiṇa at Nāgārjunakoṇḍa. Only the top two panels are shown in Longhurst 1936, pl. L. Photograph by Monika Zin.

object for an exercise in iconography, would necessarily require some degree of conceptualization. Such a step is needed merely to recognize it as a visual narrative.

We can now turn to the textual narrative found in the Sanskrit and Tibetan versions of the *Avadānaśataka*. Here briefly is the story. A boy named Kapphiṇa is born in a region to the south. On the day he is born, sons are also born to his father's eighteen thousand ministers. All of them are said to possess bodies of great physical prowess (*mahānagna*). After his father dies, Kapphiṇa becomes king and the sons of his father's ministers become his ministers. On one occasion, he and his eighteen thousand ministers go hunting for deer. Along the way Kapphiṇa surveys the hunting party arrayed behind him and asks his ministers: "Is there any abundance of power equal to mine?" Being flatterers and yes-men, they all respond, "Lord, there is none like it." This is the first indication in the story that Kapphiṇa has a problem with pride and an obsession with power.

The party soon encounters a group of merchants travelling down from the north, and the king asks them about the political situation there. The merchants inform him that some countries are ruled by a council and some by a king. So Kapphiṇa sends an envoy to the six great cities of Śrāvastī and the rest, and he orders the kings of those regions to come and submit to his authority. If they do not, he threatens, he will come and teach them a lesson with the rod of military force. This again indicates the strong association of kings with the exercise of temporal power.

The kings are all extremely frightened and go to see the Buddha, who reassures them and tells them to bring the envoy to see him. The kings go and say to the envoy: "There is a higher king who is our king. Come see him."[9] I want to highlight the precise language used here, because it speaks to the specific representation of the Buddha using the key metaphor: BUDDHAS ARE SUPREME SOVEREIGNS. The kings refer to the Buddha explicitly as "supreme sovereign" or "preeminent king of kings" (*rājādhirāja*), stated as a simple proposition, and asserting an identity, a continuity, but also a hierarchy between the Buddha and the king. As we will see, this same expression occurs in the second story discussed later in this essay. It has also been identified by Ronald Davidson (2002, 4) as "the defining metaphor" for esoteric Buddhism in the medieval period, an historical claim I will revisit and briefly recontextualize toward the end of the essay.

However, of equal or greater importance to my general argument about how narratives make arguments is what happens next. Before the envoy arrives, the Buddha transforms Jeta's Grove so that it looks like Sudarshana, the city of

---

9 Speyer 1902–09, vol. 2, 103: *astyasmākaṃ rājādhirājas taṃ tāvatpaśyeti.*

the gods, and he transforms himself into a *cakravartin*, a wheel-turning king, seated upon a lion's throne supported by seven palm trees and surrounded by an array of force. When the envoy arrives, the Buddha orders the astonished man to convey essentially the same threat to Kapphiṇa: if the King does not come and come quickly, then the Buddha (still disguised as a *cakravartin*) will come to see him with a great show of force. Kapphiṇa does eventually come to see the Buddha, and when he does, the Buddha again performs the same wondrous transformation. Seeing this wonder dissipates Kapphiṇa's obsession with beauty and lordship, the story tells us, but his conceit about power still holds him back.[10]

So, the Buddha performs another wonder whereby he prompts Indra, king of the gods, to come bearing his bow. The Buddha, still in the form of a wheel-turning king, challenges Kapphiṇa to lift the bow, which of course he cannot do. The Buddha then takes up the bow himself, draws it, and after conjuring seven iron drums, shoots an arrow through all seven. At this point Kapphiṇa's obsession with power also evaporates, and the Buddha sheds his kingly appearance and proceeds to give the king a sermon, beginning with the topic of power, and specifically, the ten powers and four types of confidence possessed by *buddha*s. After hearing the sermon, Kapphiṇa and his eighteen thousand ministers all become monks, and after some time they become *arhat*s. The story concludes with the Buddha explaining the karmic connections between certain past-life actions and present-life circumstances.

Now, in one respect I can agree with Collins: it is easy to find Buddhist stories critical of kingship. This story is a prime example. One can clearly interpret it as a criticism of kings; they are flawed wielders of temporal authority, who seem paradigmatically to have a problem with power. But the story says more than this: it also asserts the Buddha's extraordinary power, and in fact the classical Buddhist tradition recognizes both these elements in the story. In Haribhadra's commentary on the *Abhisamayālaṃkāra*, for instance, there is a reference to this story in a short list of the Buddha's "difficult conversions" (*durdamana*), which exemplify his nature as the "unsurpassed leader of persons to be tamed" (*anuttarapuruṣadamyasārathi*). Haribhadra says,

> The word 'unsurpassed' is used to distinguish the leader's special nature. It is used to clarify that he is one who tames even certain persons who are difficult to tame, such as Ārya Sundarananda, Aṅgulimāla, Urubilvā Kaśyapa, and King

[10] Speyer 1902–09, vol. 2, 104–5: *tato rājā mahākapphiṇo jetavanaṃ praviṣṭaḥ* | *sahadarśanādasya yo rūpe rūpamada aiśvare aiśvaramadaḥ sa prativigataḥ* | *baladarpo 'dyapi pratibādhata eva.*

> Kaphiṇa the Great, who exemplified extreme passion, hatred, ignorance, and pride, respectively.[11]

So, according to Haribhadra, while the story does exemplify King Kapphiṇa's extreme pride, it also illustrates the Buddha's extraordinary power, which he demonstrates in the other three stories listed, as well.[12] Such stories demonstrate the Buddha's supreme status as a figure of unparalleled knowledge and power, but for the purposes of my main theoretical argument, it is particularly important to see how the stories do this.

While the Kapphiṇa story does assert a specific proposition about the Buddha to which one might assent or dissent, and certain characters in the story do so, far from merely asserting it as a proposition, the story also seeks to establish the Buddha's special status through visual imagination and metaphor. First of all, there is the issue of the distinction between metaphor and literal truth. As Donald Davidson (1978) most famously points out, most metaphors are patently false, and it is their obvious falsehood that opens the door to metaphorical interpretation.[13] So, we must decide: does the story mean for us to understand the proposition to say that the Buddha actually is a supreme sovereign, or are we to understand the claim metaphorically, that is, that the Buddha possesses certain qualities, like power, lordship, supremacy, and so forth, which makes it appropriate to think about him as being in many ways like the preeminent king of kings? My sense is that the story remains somewhat ambiguous on this issue. It blurs the line between the literal and the metaphorical, asserting a simultaneous identity and difference between *buddha* and king for the purpose of making its argument.

---

11 Wogihāra 1932–5, 184: *anuttaragrahanaṃ sārathibhāvaviśeṣanārtham. durdamānām api keṣāmcit puruṣadamyānāṃ tīvrarāgadveṣamohamānānām āryasundaranandāṅgulimālorubilvākaśyapamahārājakaphiṇa-prabhṛtīnāṃ damaka iti pradarśanārthaṃ*. For a translation in context, see Sparham 2008, vol. 2, 133; see also Zin 2006, 5; and Skilling 1997, vol. 2, 297.

12 Zin 2006 explores the narrative theme of the difficult conversions in more depth, but one might note here its flexibility as one of several different ways to organize narratives thematically. The *Avadānaśataka* also contains a passage in which a variant set of stories is listed: therein three stories remain the same, but the story of Mānastabdha illustrates pride. See Speyer, 1902–9, vol. 1, 148; and for a translation, see Appleton 2020, 160.

13 There are some expressions, however, like "Business is business," which are patently true and yet also seemingly function as metaphors. See Davidson 1978, especially 41ff. The widespread assumption articulated by Davidson has been questioned, for instance, by Ted Cohen (1997, 223), who writes: "A sentence might support both literal and metaphorical understandings, and if so, one might just miss the metaphor."

There is another level to the story's argument, however. Not only do certain characters assert the Buddha's identity as the supreme king of kings; the Buddha also creates or effects a visual transformation of himself into a wheel-turning king and of his surroundings into the city of the gods. He surrounds himself with the trappings of royalty to emphasize his power and authority. He does not simply speak truth to power; he demonstrates his own power. This narrative episode similarly highlights how the play of identity and difference can prompt the question of literal or metaphorical significance. The audience knows all along that it is really the Buddha sitting in Jeta's Grove appearing as a universal sovereign, but the characters in the story, first the envoy and then King Kapphiṇa himself, do not initially know the "true identity" of the figure before them. Only later does he reveal it to them. The story thus enables the audience to hold two separate images in mind (*buddha* and sovereign in their respective settings), more or less at the same time, even though the images are presented in the story sequentially, that is, temporally. Narratives (and now multimodal media like film and video) do this particularly well. One might even say that they are specially suited for it.

Strictly speaking, a visual or pictorial metaphor must, by definition, be an image or set of images depicted in the visual mode. It is neither invisible nor verbally articulated. It is monomodal, not multimodal, because the target and the source domains both remain solely within the visual realm.[14] Noel Carroll (1994) goes further in defining the visual metaphor as a complex visual image in which the target and source components of the metaphor possess both "homospatiality" and "physical noncompossibility."[15] Briefly, this means that the target and source components, which are themselves incompatible insofar as they come from different cognitive domains, are both present in the same visual space in a way that encourages the viewer to see them in a relation of identity, but at the same time, they are not compossible, that is, one cannot simply be reduced to or made fully compatible with the other. They retain their difference. Perhaps the clearest example he gives of the visual metaphor is Man Ray's 1924 photomontage, *Violon d'Ingres*.

Even though Carroll focuses primarily on static images like photos, paintings, or sculptures, he nevertheless asserts that some visual metaphors may develop over time. He gives the example of the opening scene from Fritz Lang's

---

[14] On this point, see Forceville 2008, 464.

[15] Carroll goes even further than that, however, and argues that a "successful" visual metaphor requires the intention on the part of the image-maker to produce a visual metaphor and that the intended and average, actual viewer understands it to be a visual metaphor. See Carroll 1994, especially 190–92, 194, and 198–9. In principle and in this case, the appeal to producer's intention and audience reception seems useful, if only to bring a set of historical or philological controls to bear on the issue. However, in other respects, it seems problematic for all types of reasons.

film *Metropolis* in which the image of Moloch becomes superimposed over that of the machine, thus leading the viewer to see the machine as the monster. I would like to suggest that we might understand something similar to be taking place in the Kapphiṇa story. While obviously in this case the metaphorical relationship between Buddha and universal sovereign is presented entirely in the verbal mode, it does not stay merely within the paradigmatic or propositional mode of discourse. The narrative produces a set of highly visual, concrete images – with the Buddha as target domain and the universal sovereign as source domain – and presents them in a relationship of identity that unfolds over time but also encourages the reader/listener to consider the simultaneous identity/difference between them.

It is not enough, or simply wrong, to conclude that the Buddha is a universal sovereign, preeminent king of kings, and leave it at that on the literal level. The statement is certainly made about him, and he demonstrates his sovereign power by appearing to King Kapphiṇa as such, but then he asserts his authority on a different level through the performative act of giving a sermon. While the contents of the sermon are certainly interesting to consider, since they connect with the overarching theme of power, it is more important here to recognize the sermon as a performative act in the narrative. As we have seen and will see further below, narratives do more than describe reality. They also bring a kind of reality into being through the performative act of storytelling, and in doing so they impact "our" reality, the reality of the audience. So, here too, the story reflexively uses narrative technique – in the story, the Buddha performs an act of giving a sermon – in order to make its argument about the Buddha's special status. In this way, what I am calling the narrative figuration of the Buddha as a spiritual sovereign illustrates and unpacks the meaning of the assertion of the Buddha's superior status, giving the reader a concrete image and a narrative instantiation of his supreme authority.

The conversion of the Brahmin Sela

I would like to turn now to a different story, which features a different kind of display of the Buddha's extraordinary power, but one that is also linked to the narrative figuration of the Buddha as a spiritual sovereign. The story also prompts various interpretive questions about whether and how it employs metaphor and visuality, and how it draws upon nonverbal modes of signification, including gesture or body language, to make its argument. It is the story of the conversion of the Brahmin Sela in the Pāli Canon, which, so far as I know, has never been depicted visually.

There are various components to, or tellings of, the story of Sela in Pāli and related sources, and there are also a couple of parallel narratives featuring similar displays to different persons. First of all, an identical set of verses is attributed to Sela in three sources in the Pāli Canon: the *Theragāthā*, the *Suttanipāta*, and the *Majjhima-nikāya*. The latter two versions, which are basically identical, frame the verses with a story told in prose. The version in the *Apadāna* is based on this frame story and not the verses, while there is another version of the story in the Chinese *Ekottarika-āgama*, which also lacks the verses. This Chinese version tells the opening frame story, but with a different ending. The Section on Medicines in the *Mahāvagga* of the Pāli *Vinaya* also contains a story about the ascetic Keṇiya, which parallels the beginning of the opening frame story, but without any reference to Sela.[16] Rather than comparing the various versions to develop a composite understanding of the story, I will focus mostly on the version found in the *Suttanipāta* and *Majjhima-nikāya*.

Here, briefly, is the frame story, as it is found in prose therein. The Buddha is travelling with a large group of monks, and he comes to a town called Āpana. A local Brahmin ascetic named Keṇiya hears about his coming and invites him and his monks for a meal. While Keṇiya is preparing it, a learned Brahmin named Sela sees his preparations and inquires about them. When Keṇiya tells him he has invited the Buddha for a meal, just hearing the word, Buddha, makes Sela think about how both *buddha*s and wheel-turning kings possess the thirty-two marks of a great man. Being a Brahmin learned in reading marks on the body, he goes to see the Buddha to determine whether he really is a *buddha*.

When he sees the Buddha, the story tells us, Sela immediately recognizes thirty of the marks. There are only two he cannot see: the Buddha's sheathed penis and his enormous tongue. The Buddha discerns Sela's doubts in his mind and performs a "display of extraordinary power" (*iddhābhisaṅkhāra*) whereby Sela sees his sheathed penis, and then he sees the Buddha extend his tongue, and touch both earholes, lick both nostrils, and cover his entire forehead with it.[17] In this way, he demonstrates that he possesses all thirty-two marks. Now,

[16] For a translation of the verses in the *Theragāthā*, see Norman 2007, 87–9. For translations of the *Sela-sutta*, as it appears in the *Suttanipāta* and *Majjhima-nikāya*, see Norman 1992, 61–7; and Bodhi 1995, 755–62, respectively. For a translation of the story in the *Apadāna*, see Walters 2018; on the version preserved in Chinese, see Anālayo 2011. For a translation of the Keṇiya story in the *Vinaya*, see Rhys Davids and Oldenberg 1882, 129–34.

[17] *Atha kho bhagavā tathārūpaṃ iddhābhisaṅkhāraṃ abhisaṅkhāsi [abhisaṅkhāresi (syā. ka.)], yathā addasa selo brāhmaṇo bhagavato kosohitaṃ vatthaguyhaṃ. Atha kho bhagavā jivhaṃ ninnāmetvā ubhopi kaṇṇasotāni anumasi paṭimasi, ubhopi nāsikasotāni anumasi paṭimasi, kevalampi nalāṭamaṇḍalaṃ jivhāya chādesi*. Here

it is worth pausing briefly to consider this demonstration. It is obviously non-verbal and involves a bodily display, but while it evokes the epistemic cognitive metaphor that SEEING IS KNOWING, and certainly exemplifies a visual process of making visible what had previously been hidden, the display also prompts one to ask whether it should be understood as literal, gestural, or metaphorical.[18] If it is a metaphor, then what might the display of the Buddha's enormous tongue and sheathed penis signify beyond itself? And how should we connect this display to the key metaphor under analysis here that BUDDHAS ARE SUPREME SOVEREIGNS?

As we will see, the story itself suggests an answer to this latter question. Unlike the identical displays found in two other Pāli suttas – wherein the Buddha's display of his sheathed penis and enormous tongue elicits wonder and immediately converts Ambaṭṭha and Brahmāyu (the learned Brahmins who witness the display in those stories) – for some reason the demonstration here does not immediately convince Sela that the Buddha is truly a *buddha* and not just a wheel-turning king. So, the still uncertain Sela decides to flatter the Buddha, because, he reasons, *arhat*s reveal themselves when praised. Kings certainly like to be flattered, as we saw in the Kapphiṇa story. Do *buddhas*? Pollock argues that the invention in the Śaka era (first and second centuries of the Common Era) of two connected literary genres, namely *kāvya*, "courtly" or "written literature," and *praśasti*, "inscriptional royal panegyric" or "royal praise poetry," marks the emergence of Sanskrit cosmopolitan culture.[19] His work and that of others may help us situate this story within a broader Indian discourse on sovereignty. One can perhaps also read a subtle critique of the king here, too, but for the moment we should note the specific language Sela uses in the verses and see how his flattery, if that is what it is,[20]

---

and in what follows I cite the Chaṭṭha Saṅgāyana (1995) edition of the *Suttanipāta*. For the Pali Text Society edition, see Anderson and Smith 1913, 102–12.

18 On these distinctions, see Cienki and Müller 2008. Here, in what follows, and really throughout this whole chapter, I am developing several interlinking lines of argument also explored in Fiordalis 2021.

19 See, for instance, Pollock 2006, 12–13, 18, 39, and so forth. Pollock (2006, 13) argues that *Kāvya* is "written" insofar as it "reflexively frames its own orality." I take this to mean that without the baseline conceptual distinction between written and oral, oral literature can have no meaning. It is a different question whether such literature was actually composed, preserved, or received through writing/copying/reading or the mnemonic/oral/aural mode.

20 At this point the prose frame ends and the verses begin, indicating where the major gap occurs in the narrative. The gap suggests that flattery is only one of the possible interpretations of the verses, which again are common to three canonical iterations of the story, including the *Theragāthā*, where they appear by themselves without any narrative framing.

leads him to articulate the key metaphor that BUDDHAS ARE SUPREME SOVEREIGNS.

Sela begins by describing the Buddha's perfect body. His skin is bright and a golden colour. He shines like the sun. He possesses the thirty-two marks, and is beautiful to behold. Here we can see some further indication of the broader Indian poetics of sovereignty, including imagery and metaphor linking the Buddha and the sun.[21] But then Sela says something equally remarkable, which connects to specific language we have already seen used in the Kapphiṇa story. He says:

> You should be a king, a wheel-turning king, a bull among heroes, a conqueror of the whole world, the lord of Rose-Apple Grove.
>
> Warriors, minor kings, and kings are your vassals. You are the supreme king of kings and lord of men. Rule, Gotama![22]

In the *Suttanipāta*, the term used for "supreme king of kings" is *rājābhirāja*, but the Chaṭṭha-saṅgāyana edition of the *Theragāthā*, which contains the same verses, attests to the variant reading of *rājādhirāja*, the same expression the kings use to refer to the Buddha in the Kapphiṇa story. It seems therefore that the expression may have pedigree beyond its role as the "defining metaphor" of medieval esoteric Buddhism (Davidson 2002), and that it should be seen within a broader Indian poetics of sovereignty.

Like the kings in the story of Kapphiṇa, Sela makes a straightforward statement in the propositional mode. In his response, the Buddha indicates the possibility of a metaphorical interpretation. Far from denying his status as a sovereign, but also not straightforwardly affirming it, the Buddha says,

> I am a king, Sela, an unexcelled king of the *dharma*. With the *dharma*, I set the wheel rolling, the wheel that cannot be rolled back.[23]

When Sela asks the Buddha to unpack the meaning of his statement, the Buddha elaborates on his special sovereign status by explaining that Sāriputta is his general, who keeps the wheel of *dharma* rolling, and he reasserts his unique position as a Buddha. So, the story also works to identify the Buddha with the wheel-turning king while simultaneously also distinguishing them, thus enabling the audience to reflect on the special status of the Buddha as spiritual

---

21 On this broader poetics of power, see Proferes 2007.

22 *Rājā arahasi bhavituṃ, cakkavattī rathesabho; cāturanto vijitāvī, jambusaṇḍassa [jambumaṇḍassa (ka.)] issaro. Khattiyā bhogirājāno [bhojarājāno (sī. syā.)], anuyantā [anuyuttā (sī.)] bhavantu te; rājābhirājā manujindo, rajjaṃ kārehi gotama.*

23 *Rājāhamasmi selāti, (bhagavā) dhammarājā anuttaro*; *Dhammena cakkaṃ vattemi, cakkaṃ appaṭivattiyaṃ.*

sovereign or preeminent king of kings. He may have renounced the kingship, the story suggests, but he does not stop being a king. He shows Sela that he possesses the thirty-two marks, thus establishing his bodily identity with the wheel-turning king, but when the Brahmin confirms this identity, his ongoing doubt enables the Buddha to reassert his supreme authority as king of the *dharma*.

We can now return to the Buddha's display of extraordinary power in the framing prose narrative. One can discern a clear thematic connection between the demonstration and the verses insofar as both concern the bodily identification of the Buddha and the wheel-turning king. On the surface or literal or locutionary level, the Buddha's nonverbal, bodily display of his sheathed penis and his enormous tongue confirms that he possesses the thirty-two marks of the great man. Is it also a gesture in the more restricted sense of a bodily movement that expresses or symbolizes a thought or feeling? Is it also a metaphor for something else, and if so, for what? Peter Skilling, who has surveyed various textual representations of the Buddha's tongue miracle, calls it a "metaphor of authority" and a "guarantee of truth." To support this interpretation, he cites several classical Buddhist sources, including the *Divyāvadāna*, which explicitly connects the size of the Buddha's tongue to his honesty and truthfulness.[24] These texts suggest that some Buddhists may have seen more in the tongue miracle than simply its locutionary significance.

In a recent work, Natalie Gummer (2020) goes further and sees in the Buddha's combined display of his penis and tongue a set of procreative metaphors, including the following (although she does not put them in quite such direct form): TONGUES ARE PENISES, SPEECH IS EJACULATION, and WORDS ARE SEMEN. While she locates the metaphorical potentiality of this relationship between the erotic and the linguistic in the Pāli *sutta*s – she looks particularly at the *Brahmāyu-sutta* – she also finds these procreative metaphors more highly developed in the *Lotus Sūtra*. Following Shoshana Felman's psychoanalytic reading of J. L. Austin's speech act theory in her provocative work, *The Scandal of the Speaking Body* (2002), Gummer refuses to allow language to be reduced to a functional binary: constative or performative, transmitting truth or effecting/affecting reality. Yet, arguing against still prevalent notions of language as merely representational or descriptive of reality, she emphasizes

---

24 See Skilling 2013, especially 30–34. He also points out that the *Milindapañha* (Trenckner 1962, 167–70) contains a discussion of the Buddha's display of his sheathed penis. Rhys-Davids (1890, vol. 1, 237) chooses not to translate it, stating that "it deals with matters not usually spoken of in this century," but Horner does (1964, vol. 1, 235–9). The passage mainly discusses the propriety of – and reasons for – the wondrous display. As Skilling notes, the display is discussed elsewhere, too, such as in the *Da zhi du lun* on which see Lamotte 1944, vol. 1, 275–6, and Lamotte 1970, vol. 3, 1667–8.

its performative capacity, its ability to make things happen, to bring something into being, even if that something is knowledge/truth itself.

Much of what Gummer has to say about language also applies to my primary concern here: narrativity and the ways narratives could be said to make arguments. I suspect that they do so differently from logical arguments, although I am less certain that their aims diverge. Stated differently, I distrust the distinction Bruner (1986) makes between truth and verisimilitude, which relies on a particular vision of the function of narrative as representing reality. As we have seen, narratives may include propositional language, but they do more than make assertions. They also make things happen. They bring things into being insofar as they project worlds of spatial and temporal extension, and actualize embodied beings who become intentional agents acting within the storyworlds. Although strictly speaking, narratives like the *Sela-sutta* and the *Kapphiṇāvadāna* remain monomodal, that is, they are expressed entirely in words, they nonetheless also employ visual (or mental) images and rely on metaphors, which themselves typically combine the concrete and the abstract. An ideal audience must apprehend these images and metaphors through its own embodied experiences of lived reality. Thus, even while remaining monomodal, textual (or oral/aural) narratives may form a bridge connecting the verbal and the visual domains, but this bridge must be built upon the relationship between the storyworld of the narrative and the lived world of audience. Like Gary Comstock (1993) I would argue that religious narratives work on us to accept the reality they project as our reality of lived experience, and thereby form a means through which we come to view our world and actions as meaningful. We cannot easily dismiss the power of religious narratives, perhaps all narratives, to tell us something true about our own reality.

Both Skilling (2013) and Gummer (2020) offer compelling arguments for reading the Buddha's display of his tongue or penis (or both) metaphorically. However, the interpretation most germane to my argument here is that the Buddha's display instantiates (in a concrete, tangible, potentially visible way) the claim that BUDDHAS ARE SUPREME SOVEREIGNS. It remains an open question whether the story of Sela means for one to take this claim, voiced in the story by Sela himself, literally or metaphorically, but as with the *Kapphiṇāvadāna*, my suspicion is that the narrative tries to blur the boundary between the literal and the metaphorical in regard to the relationship between the Buddha and the sovereign. The stories emphasize their simultaneous identity and difference in order to say something about the nature of a *buddha* and his extraordinary knowledge and power. The narrative figuration of the Buddha as a "spiritual sovereign" also brings the Buddha into being in a more concrete way, somewhat analogous to the metaphor of nirvana as a great city.[25]

[25] On this latter metaphor, see Collins 1998, 224–9, as well as Hallisey 1993.

The stories thus provide different and complementary ways to think about the Buddha as an ideal being. They give us, to borrow from the title of George Lakoff and Mark Turner's 1989 book, something "more than cool reason." They demonstrate both the conceptual power of metaphor and the creative, epistemic power of narrative. Against this line of reasoning, one might argue that the statement that *buddha*s are supreme sovereigns cannot function as a metaphor, because *buddha*s and wheel-turning kings are both members of the same cognitive category, that of "great persons" or "Big Men," as Collins (1998) puts it. Conceptual metaphors typically link concepts from different conceptual domains, such as the claim that ARGUMENT IS WAR or TIME IS MONEY, and here the proposition that *buddha*s are supreme sovereigns is meant to be understood both literally and as simply false.[26] The Buddha is not a supreme sovereign or a wheel-turning king, even though he does possess the same physical marks of greatness that make them both "Big Men." Thus, one might want to argue that the stories are saying something about their difference from one another and not their identity, despite or perhaps because of the fact that they belong to the same cognitive category. In making such a counter-argument, however, one finds oneself again asserting the unique status of the Buddha. As the *Doṇa-sutta* says and the *Aṅguttara-nikāya*'s "Book of Ones" affirms, *buddha*s belong in a class by themselves.[27] Moreover, we have already noted that the choice between literal and metaphorical readings can be a false one (Cohen 1997). Therefore, it seems better to consider how the stories argue for simultaneous identity and difference even as they blur the line between the metaphorical and the literal.

Conclusion

We have seen how the story of King Kapphiṇa in the *Avadānaśataka* and the story of Sela in the Pāli Canon actualize the Buddha as a "spiritual sovereign," a narrative figure of extraordinary knowledge and power. Both stories could be said to provide clear examples of what Collins (1998, 21) calls the "practice of

---

[26] The definition of the cognitive metaphor as well as these common examples are found in Lakoff and Johnson 1980, 4ff.

[27] For the *Doṇa-sutta*, see Morris 1885–1900, vol. 2, 37–9, and the translation in Bodhi 2012, 425–6. For the latter passage I have in mind, see Morris 1885–1900, vol. 1, 22, translated in Bodhi 2012, 107–8, which includes the following: "Monks, there is one person arising in the world who is a wondrous human being. Who is this one person? The Tathāgata, the Worthy One, the Perfect and Complete Buddha" (*ekapuggalo, bhikkhave, loke uppajjamāno uppajjati acchariyamanusso. Katamo ekapuggalo? Tathāgato arahaṃ sammāsambuddho*).

one-upmanship," whereby the Buddhist clerisy as holders of ideological power assert their authority over kings as embodiments and wielders of military and political power. Collins (1998, 474) tends to speak about this hierarchy of *buddha* over king more in terms of opposition, dichotomy, and dissimilarity. At one point, for instance, he writes "...although the idea of the two Big Men and their Wheels does represent the symbiosis between clerics and kings, the dissimilarity and hierarchy between them represents their antagonism." I have argued here that we can think of it equally or perhaps even primarily in terms of continuity, continuum, or spectrum of power. In this way, the Buddha is not only the antithesis of temporal power, but also its apotheosis.

Buddhahood entails power, and while the Buddha may renounce his kingship, he does not cease being a king. As Max Moerman nicely puts it: "By abdicating the throne he becomes the royal *par excellence*."[28] Rather than simply renouncing his sovereignty, the Buddha transforms or transfigures himself, which allows him to reassert his sovereignty on a different level of knowledge and power, his authority already inscribed, as it were, upon his entire person. This is represented in the Kapphiṇa story by the Buddha's visual transformation into a wheel-turning king and his performative act of giving a sermon, which together demonstrate the Buddha's successful transfiguration of temporal power into spiritual authority: from potential wheel-turning king he becomes king of the *dharma*, supreme spiritual sovereign. This transformation is demonstrated and named even more explicitly in the Sela story, and the story also makes clear that the spiritual sovereign retains extraordinary knowledge and power.

From the above quotations by Collins, however, as well as from comments made by Smith and by many other scholars in the field, we can recognize a long-standing assumption of opposition, dichotomy, and dissimilarity between the so-called "temporal/political" and the "religious" domains in respect to Buddhist societies. In the quotation above, Collins speaks of "symbiosis," which suggests mutually beneficial co-existence, but of two different things. As an analytical device, perhaps such a distinction is necessary for the accurate description of Buddhist societies (maybe all societies), but it has also been perceived as an indigenous Buddhist dichotomy in its own right, possibly for good reason. We have seen that it is actually part of what enables the literal/metaphorical potency of the claim that *buddha*s are supreme sovereigns. The problem is that when we take such claims only literally and conclude that they are simply false (or literally true), we miss an opportunity to think about some of the ways in which the claim might be true, figuratively speaking, and what it might tell us about classical Buddhist conceptions of the nature of a *buddha* (and, for that matter, the sovereign).

28 Quoted in Strong 2002, 38; also cited in Halkias 2013, 501.

At several points in the chapter, I suggested that we might revisit the historical dichotomy between the so-called religious and temporal spheres in light of these stories, and the time has now come to do so, albeit too briefly. Davidson (2002, 4) has argued that, "precipitated by the idealization of the universal conqueror, medieval Indian politics and literature recast kingship into a form of divinity," and that "the defining metaphor for esoteric Buddhism is that of the monk or practitioner becoming the Supreme Overlord (*rājādhirāja*) or the Universal Ruler (*cakravartin*)." These claims prompt some questions. First of all, if kingship was recast into a form of divinity only in the medieval period, how was it conceived beforehand? Secondly, if the *rājādhirāja* or *cakravartin* was the defining metaphor for medieval esoteric Buddhism, then what should we make of the fact that the proposition that *buddha*s are supreme sovereigns is also found in non-esoteric materials like the *Kapphiṇāvadāna* in the *Avadānaśataka* and in the verses attributed to Sela in the *Sela-sutta* of the *Suttanipāta* and *Majjhima-nikāya* and in the *Theragāthā*?

Regarding the first question, Davidson (2002, 68) distinguishes the valorization of the king's military prowess in the medieval period from an earlier ideal of the king as source of social stability and prosperity. Yet, Mark McClish (2019) argues that an ideology of sovereign power unhindered by legal or moral constraints also existed from an early period and perhaps even predates the "classical" ideal of the *dharma*-king. At the same time, scholars may well have overemphasized the extent to which early and mainstream Buddhism endorsed an opposition between the Buddha and the King or the Sangha and the State, and upheld the dichotomy between temporal power and its renunciation. Theodore Proferes (2007) has explored the poetics of sovereignty in Vedic liturgical literature and shown how certain symbols of kingship, such as fire, light, the sun, and water, were extended to express a broader, spiritualized ideal of freedom and power. Many of these same symbols are evident in Buddhist representations of the Buddha, and they help situate him at the nexus of temporal and spiritual power: freedom engenders power, and power entails freedom. So, while it may be the case that the practitioner becoming a supreme sovereign was a key metaphor for medieval esoteric Buddhism, the literal/metaphorical identity of the Buddha and the supreme sovereign may have been more broadly distributed throughout mainstream Buddhist ideology, and from an earlier period of time.

What evidence do the two stories provide in this regard? With detailed analysis of the version in the Chinese translation of the *Avadānaśataka* still pending, the Kapphiṇa story as it is found in the Sanskrit and Tibetan recensions can most likely be located in the latter centuries of the first millennium of the Common Era, squarely in the midst of the early medieval period. The story certainly revolves around the theme of military power, which reflects

Davidson's description of the medieval Buddhist ethos, and yet it is far from an expression of esoteric Buddhism. The Sela story presents a complicated case because of its composite character. Lamotte (1988, 161–2) points out that a text called the **Śailagāthā* is sometimes listed alongside other ostensibly early verse recitation texts like the *Udāna*, *Munigāthā*, *Dhammapada*, *Aṭṭhakavagga*, *Pārāyaṇavagga*, and *Theragāthā*.[29] The verses attributed to Sela may have been part of a small, relatively early core group of verse texts that came to constitute the "miscellaneous collection." The authors of the *Milindapañha* knew the episode in which the Buddha displays his sheathed penis and connected it with Sela.[30] The extant prose frame story also evokes the practice of praising the king/*buddha*, a practice that would become central to Indian sociopolitical discourse from the early centuries of the Common Era.[31] So while more evidence is necessary, these stories may lend further support to the claim that the literal/metaphorical identification of the Buddha as supreme sovereign is both broader and earlier than previously recognized, and they point to a basic tension within Buddhist discourse between the so-called spiritual and the temporal spheres.

We have seen how this tension is manifested in the narrative figuration of the Buddha as a spiritual sovereign, but on a broader theoretical level the chapter has shown how a couple of narratives contribute to this discourse on power by negotiating the tension without necessarily resolving it. To make their arguments about the nature of the Buddha and his authority, the stories of Kapphiṇa and Sela utilize cognitive and other kinds of metaphor, and they create highly visual mental images of physical embodiment; such mental images may well function in similar ways to the painted images of glorified Buddha-figures explored by Reddy in Chapter 3. Rather than simply asserting sets of interconnected propositions meant to be understood literally, the narratives explored here project storyworlds of spatial and temporal extension that imitate (even when they also violate) our basic understanding of the way agents can act and objects can move through the spatiotemporal continuum. Thus, despite the fact that they are monomodal, that is, they are expressed entirely in words, verbal or textual narratives have the capacity, perhaps inherently, of gesturing toward the visual domain. The main reason, I believe, is that they somehow reflect our

---

29 Skilling (2013, 28) claims that the **Śailagāthā* was also listed among those texts recommended by Aśoka for recitation, citing this passage by Lamotte for evidence. Skilling then pushes the text back to the time of Aśoka. However, this seems wrong, for Lamotte does not mention it there. Elsewhere Lamotte (1988, 234–8) does speak in detail about the list of texts recommended by Aśoka in his famous Bhābrā edict.

30 See note 24 above.

31 Pollock (2006, 67–9) identifies the rock inscription at Junāgaṛh praising King Rudradāman and dated to 150 CE as the earliest known inscriptional *praśasti*.

embodied human experience of the world, and our experience, like our capacity for language, is fundamentally multimodal.

Bibliography

Abbott, H. Porter 2008. *The Cambridge Introduction to Narrative*. 2nd Edition. Cambridge, UK: Cambridge University Press.

Anālayo 2011. "The conversion of the Brahmin Sela in the Ekottarika-āgama." *Thai International Journal of Buddhist Studies* 2: 37–56.

Anderson, Dines and Helmer Smith, eds. 1913. *Suttanipāta*. London: Pali Text Society.

Appleton, Naomi, trans. 2020. *Many Buddhas, One Buddha: A Study and Translation of* Avadānaśataka *1–40*. Sheffield: Equinox.

Auboyer, Jeannine 1983. *Buddha: A Pictorial History of His Life and Legacy*. Photographs by Jean-Louis Nou. New York: Crossroad.

Bodhi, Bhikkhu, trans. 1995. *The Middle Length Discourses of the Buddha: A Translation of the Majjhima Nikāya*. Boston: Wisdom Publications.

Bodhi, Bhikkhu, trans. 2000. *The Connected Discourses of the Buddha: A Translation of the Saṃyutta Nikāya*. Boston: Wisdom Publications.

Bodhi, Bhikkhu, trans. 2012. *The Numerical Discourses of the Buddha: A Translation of the Aṅguttara Nikāya*. Boston: Wisdom Publications.

Bruner, Jerome 1986. *Actual Minds, Possible Worlds*. Cambridge, MA: Harvard University Press.

Burlingame, Eugene, trans. 1921. *Buddhist Legends: Translated from the original Pali text of the Dhammapada Commentary*. Harvard Oriental Series, vol. 29. Cambridge, MA: Harvard University Press.

Carrithers, Michael 1992. *Why Humans have Cultures*. London: Oxford University Press.

Carroll, Noel 1994. "Visual Metaphor." In Jakko Hintikka, ed. *Aspects of Metaphor*, 189–218. Dordrecht: Kluwer Academic Publishers.

Chatman, Seymour 1978. *Story and Discourse: Narrative Structure in Fiction and Film*. Ithaca, NY: Cornell University Press.

Cienki, Alan, and Cornelia Müller 2008. "Metaphor, Gesture, and Thought." In Raymond W. Gibbs, Jr., ed. *The Cambridge Handbook of Metaphor and Thought*, 462–82. Cambridge, UK: Cambridge University Press.

Chaṭṭha Saṅgāyana Pāḷi Tipiṭaka 1995. CD-ROM. Dhammagiri, Igatpuri, India: Vipassana Research Institute. Online version available at *The Pāḷi Tipiṭaka*, https://www.tipitaka.org/.

Cohen, Ted 1997. "Metaphor, Feeling, and Narrative." *Philosophy and Literature* 21/2: 223–44.

Collins, Steven 1998. *Nirvana and Other Buddhist Felicities*. Cambridge, UK: Cambridge University Press.

Comstock, Gary L. 1993. "The Truth of Religious Narratives." *International Journal for Philosophy of Religion* 34/3: 131–50.

Davidson, Ronald 2002. *Indian Esoteric Buddhism: A Social History of the Tantric Movement*. New York City: Columbia University Press.

Davidson, Donald 1978. "What Metaphors Mean." *Critical Inquiry* 5/1: 31–47.

Feer, L., ed. 1884–1908. *Saṃyutta-nikāya*. 5 vols. London: Pali Text Society.

Felman, Shoshana 2002. *The Scandal of the Speaking Body*. Palo Alto: Stanford University Press.

Fiordalis, David 2019. "The *Avadānaśataka* and the *Kalpadrumāvadānamālā*: What should we be doing now?" *Critical Review for Buddhist Studies* 25: 47–77.

Fiordalis, David 2021. "Buddhas and Body Language: The Literary Trope of the Buddha's Smile." In Natalie Gummer, ed. *The Language of the Sūtras*, 59–103. Berkeley: Mangalam Press.

Forceville, Charles 2008. "Metaphor in Pictures and Multimodal Representations." In Raymond W. Gibbs, Jr., ed. *The Cambridge Handbook of Metaphor and Thought*, 462–82. Cambridge, UK: Cambridge University Press.

Gummer, Natalie 2020 "The Scandal of the Speaking Buddha: Performative Utterance and the Erotics of the Dharma," In Rafal Stepien, ed. *Buddhist Literature as Philosophy, Buddhist Philosophy as Literature*, 197–229. Albany, NY: SUNY Press.

Gunawardana, R. A. Leslie H. 1979. *Robe and Plough: Monasticism and Economic Interest in Early Medieval Ceylon*. Tuscon: University of Arizona Press.

Hahn, Michael 1990. "Śivasvāmins Kapphiṇābhyudaya: Ein wenig bekanntes buddhistisches Mahākāvya." In Werner Diem and Abdoldiavad Falaturi (eds.) *XXIV. Deutscher Orientalistentag: Vom 26. Bis 30. September 1988 in Köln. Ausgewählte Vorträge*, 459–70. Stuttgart: Franz Steiner Verlag.

Hahn, Michael 1997. "Doctrine and Poetry: Śivasvāmin's Essentials of Buddhism Text and Translation of Canto XX of His *Kapphiṇābhyudaya*." In Petra Kieffer-Pülz and Jens-Uwe Hartmann (eds.) *Bauddhavidyāsudhākaraḥ: Studies in Honour of Heinz Bechert On the Occasion of His 65th Birthday*, 207–32. Swisttal-Odendorf: Indica et Tibetica.

Halkias, Georgios T. 2013. "The Enlightened Sovereign: Buddhism and Kingship in India and Tibet," In Steven M. Emmanuel, ed. *A Companion to Buddhist Philosophy*, 491–511. Chichester: Wiley-Blackwell.

Hallisey, Charles 1993. "*Nibbānasutta*: An Allegedly Non-canonical *Sutta* on *Nibbāna* as a Great City." *Journal of the Pali Text Society* 28: 97–130.

Hartmann, Jens-Uwe 1985. "Zur Frage der Schulzugehörigkeit des Avadānaśataka." In Heinz Bechert, ed. *Zur Schulzugehörigkeit von Werken der Hīnayāna-Literatur, Erster Teil*, 219–24. Göttingen: Vandenhoeck & Ruprecht.

Horner, I. B., trans. 1964. *Milinda's Questions*. Vol. 1. London: Pali Text Society.

Lakoff, George and Mark Johnson 1980. *Metaphors We Live By*. Chicago: University of Chicago Press.

Lakoff, George and Mark Turner 1989. *More Than Cool Reason: A Field Guide to Poetic Metaphor*. Chicago: University of Chicago Press.

Lamotte, Étienne 1944. *Le Traité de la Grande Vertu de Sagesse*. Vol. 1. Louvain: Insitut Orientaliste de l'Université Catholique de Louvain.

Lamotte, Étienne 1970. *Le Traité de la Grande Vertu de Sagesse*. Vol. 3. Louvain: Insitut Orientaliste de l'Université Catholique de Louvain.

Lamotte, Étienne 1988. *History of Indian Buddhism from the Origins to the Śaka Era*, translated by Sara Webb-Bonn. Louvain: Insitut Orientaliste de l'Université Catholique de Louvain.

LeGoff, Jacques 1988. *The Medieval Imagination*. Chicago: University of Chicago Press.

Longhurst, A. H. 1936. *The Buddhist Antiquities of Nāgārjunakoṇḍa, Madras Presidency*. Delhi: Archaeological Survey of India.

McClish, Mark 2019. *The History of the Arthaśāstra: Sovereignty and Sacred Law in Ancient India*. Cambridge, UK: Cambridge University Press.

Mitchell, W. J. T. 1996. "Word and Image." In Robert Nelson and Richard Shiff (eds.) *Critical Terms for Art History*, 48–57. Chicago: University of Chicago Press.

Morris, R., ed. 1885–1900. *Aṅguttara-nikāya*. 5 vols. London: Pali Text Society.

Norman, K. R., trans. 1992. *The Group of Discourses (Sutta-nipāta), Vol. 2: Revised Translation with Introduction and Notes*. Oxford: Pali Text Society.

Norman, K. R., trans. 2007. *The Elders' Verses I: Theragāthā*. 2nd edn. Lancaster: Pali Text Society.

Pollock, Sheldon 2006. *The Language of the Gods in the World of Men*. Berkeley: University of California Press.

Proferes, Theodore 2007. *Vedic Ideals of Sovereignty and the Poetics of Power*. New Haven: American Oriental Society.

Rhys Davids, Caroline, trans. 1951. *Psalms of the Early Buddhists II. Psalms of the Brethren*. London: Pali Text Society.

Rhys Davids, T. W., trans. 1890. *The Questions of King Milinda*. Sacred Books of the East, vol. 35. Oxford: Clarendon Press.

Rhys Davids, T. W., and Hermann Oldenberg, trans. 1882. *Vinaya Texts, Part II*. Sacred Books of the East, vol. 17. Oxford: Clarendon Press.

Rao, P. R. Ramachandra 1956. *The Art of Nāgārjunikoṇḍa*. Madras: Rachana.

Shankar, Gauri and Michael Hahn, eds. 1989. *Śivasvāmin's Kapphiṇābhyudaya or Exaltation of King Kapphiṇa*. Revised ed. New Delhi: Aditya Prakashan.

Skilling, Peter 1997. *Mahāsūtras: Great Discourses of the Buddha*. 2 Vols. Oxford: Pali Text Society.

Skilling, Peter 2013. "The *Tathāgata* and the Long Tongue of Truth: The authority of the Buddha in *sūtra* and narrative literature." In Vincent Eltschinger and Helmut Krasser (eds.) *Scriptural Authority, Reason, and Action: Proceeding of a Panel at the 14th World Sanskrit Conference, Kyoto, Sept. 1–5, 2009*, 1–47. Vienna: Österreichische Akademie der Wissenshaften.

Smith, Bardwell L., ed. 1972. *The Two Wheels of Dhamma: Essays on the Theravada Tradition in India and Ceylon*. Chambersburg, PA: American Academy of Religion.

Sparham, Gareth, trans. 2008. *Abhisamayālaṃkāra with Vṛtti and Ālokā, Vol. 2: Second and Third Abhisamaya*. Fremont, CA: Jain Publishing Company.

Speyer, Jacob S., ed. 1902–09. *Avadānaśataka: A Century of Edifying Tales Belonging to the Hīnayāna*. 2 vols. St. Petersburg, Russia: Imperial Academy of Sciences.

Strong, John 2002. "Aśoka's Wives and the Ambiguities of Buddhist Kingship." *Cahiers d'Extrême-Asie* 13: 35–54. https://doi.org/10.3406/asie.2002.1176

Sukenick, Ronald 2000. *Narralogues: Truth in Fiction*. Albany: SUNY Press.

Trenckner, V., ed. 1962. *The Milindapañho*. London: Pali Text Society.

Tshul khrims rin chen, ed. 1976–79. *Derge Kanjur (sde dge bka' 'gyur). Bka' 'gyur (sde dge par phud)*. 103 vols. Delhi: Delhi karmapae choedhey, gyalwae sungrab partun khang.

Walters, Jonathan, trans. 2018. *Legends of the Buddhist Saints*. apadanatranslation.org (last accessed on April 15, 2020).

Warder, Anthony K. 1988. *Indian Kāvya Literature, Volume Five: The Bold Style (Śaktibhadra to Dhanapāla)*. Delhi: Motilal Banarsidass.

Wogihara, Unrai, ed. 1932–35. *Abhisamayālaṃkārālokā Prajñāpāramitāvyākhyā*. Tokyo: Toyo Bunko.

Zin, Monika 2006. *Mitleid und Wunderkraft: Schwierige Bekehrungen und ihre Ikonographie im indischen Buddhismus*. Wiesbaden: Harrassowitz Verlag.

Author biography

David Fiordalis is an Associate Professor and Chair of the Department of Religion at Linfield University in Oregon, USA. His recent publications include an edited volume on Buddhist philosophy as practice, *Buddhist Spiritual Practices: Thinking with Pierre Hadot on Buddhism, Philosophy, and the Path* (Mangalam, 2018), an essay on the Buddha's smile published in both Spanish and English in volumes honoring his doctoral supervisor, Luis O. Gómez, and various other scholarly articles and translations related to classical Buddhist narratives, poetry, and scholastic literature, particularly concerning the literary traditions around Buddhist notions of wonders and superhuman powers. He has been engaged in academic work on the religions and cultures of South Asia and the Himalayan region for more than twenty-five years.

9

Seeing the Dharma

Narrative *Darśan* in the *Vimalakīrtinirdeśa*

Natalie Gummer

Preamble

While my argument focuses primarily upon the connection between narrative and vision in the Sanskrit *Vimalakīrtinirdeśasūtra*[1] (abbreviated Vkn in textual citations), I want to begin somewhat far afield, in the Mogao caves near Dunhuang. There, in the late 1990s, in the company of Wu Hung and some of his students, I learned to interpret the *sūtra* paintings (*jingbian* 經變) that adorn the walls of many caves, especially those painted during and shortly after the Tang dynasty.[2] These mural paintings of a select set of Mahāyāna *sūtra*s offer, I think, a particularly provocative instance of the relationship between narrative literature and art, one that may illuminate more than the specific, localized interpretations and practices to which they most directly attest. As Reddy and Zin have already explored in their chapters earlier in the volume, images of the Buddha's teaching are particularly interesting cases for any exploration of the interface between word and image.

Wu Hung argues that these *sūtra* paintings ought to be interpreted not as illustrations, but as complex icons, with a predominantly ritual rather than representational function (Wu 1992). This argument takes on peculiar force when they are viewed in person: at the centre of the composition, the teaching

1 While the date(s) and location(s) at which the Sanskrit *sūtra* was composed/compiled are not known, the terminus ante quem is provided by the first known Chinese translation, made in the early third century CE. I rely exclusively on the Sanskrit text (Takahashi 2006) in this paper. All translations are my own.

2 Among numerous possible examples, see the depiction of the *Suvarṇaprabhāsottamasūtra* (*jinguangming jing* 金光明經) in Cave 158 (eighth century): https://library-artstor-org.ezproxy.beloit.edu/#/asset/HUNT_58787; SSID 14392440. The detailed depiction of the members of the huge assembly surrounding the teaching Buddha reflects the focus of much of this *sūtra* on dialogues between the Buddha and particular deities in his audience.

Buddha gazes out towards the viewer, surrounded by his entourage and by distinctive visual and architectural elements that, for those familiar with the iconography, render the identity of the *sūtra* recognizable at a glance. While these murals sometimes incorporate identifiable scenes from the *sūtra* in question, such scenes seldom depict the "action" of the narrative, and almost always subordinate story elements to the central icon, which breaks the barrier between painting and audience with its outward gaze (Wu 1992, 129–37). In this respect, it seems to me, the paintings might best be seen not so much as an illustration of the *sūtra*s' content as a powerful translation of their purpose: to enable an audience to encounter a presiding Buddha, to enter and be transformed by his sovereign presence and teachings. The viewer-encompassing gaze of the Buddha, his hands in a teaching *mudrā*, offers a brilliant visual parallel for the strategies by which the *sūtra*s' narratives forcibly rupture the barrier between the "inside" and the "outside" of the *sūtra*: the *now* of the moment of utterance, rendered visible, seizes and incorporates viewers and auditors alike. But time predominates in the verbal *sūtra*: the Buddha renarrates the past and future of his auditors through potent speech acts, keyed to their aesthetic and emotional responses to *buddha*-speech that fore-sees/pre-dicts, and thus transforms, its future listeners.[3] The visual *sūtra* creates an analogous relationship spatially: the Buddha, presiding kinglike on his throne, draws viewers into the audience assembled in his beautiful *buddha*-field and makes them physically part of the *sūtra*-borne world that the mural presents. Indeed, both the *sūtra* as narrative/narrated text and the *sūtra* as visual icon powerfully conflate sound and sight, utterance and appearance, time and space. Mahāyāna *sūtra* narratives conjure with *buddha*-speech visions of past, present, and future *buddha*s and their fields (*kṣetra*); the *sūtra* murals at Dunhuang conjure with visual media the oral/aural experience of entering the presence of a *buddha* and listening to *buddha*-speech directly from his mouth.

Now, as many of you will know, Dunhuang murals of the *Vimalakīrtinirdeśa-sūtra* are conspicuous (although not unique – see Wu 1992, 138–53) by their departure from this dominant iconic mode, preferring an "oppositional composition" (Wu 1992, 148–9) which organizes key elements of the *sūtra*'s narrative in relation to its primary interlocutors, Vimalakīrti and Mañjuśrī, who face each other, visually signaling their verbal debate.[4] Nevertheless, I find in

---

3 In two recent essays, I examine the temporal aspects of the speech acts of *buddhas* (Gummer 2021b) and develop a broader theory of sovereign speech acts in Mahāyāna *sūtra*s (Gummer 2021a). Both demonstrate the performative efficacy of the present utterance of pre-dictions (*buddha*-speech about the future) and post-dictions (*buddha*-speech about the past).

4 See, for instance, the rendering on the east wall of cave 146: https://library-artstor-org.ezproxy.beloit.edu/asset/MIDA_101433; SSID 18113123.

the iconic *sūtra* paintings a revealing framework for understanding the *sūtra*'s verbal conjuring of visual encounters (*darśana*) with *buddha*s ensconced in their beautiful fields: the lively narrative that unfolds in the verbal *sūtra* has the ritual function of enabling iconic encounters with *buddha*s, making their imagined presence palpable. Narration, here, is a ritual act that produces visionary experiences. And despite the decidedly oppositional mode of the visual *Vimalakīrti* at Dunhuang, some of the *Vimalakīrti* murals also incorporate crucial iconic elements that both reinforce and nuance their aptness as an act of translation. I will return to this point in the conclusion.

Introduction

In a nutshell, my argument is this: a (if not the) central aim of the *Vimalakīrtinirdeśa* is to make apparently absent *buddha*s present through narrative, to perform and thus produce the conditions for readers/listeners to have a transformative vision (*darśana*) of sovereign *buddha*s enthroned in their perfect worlds. Furthermore, the *Vimalakīrtinirdeśa* makes clear that what we might call the narrative presence of *buddha*s and *buddha*-fields is their true presence, vastly superior to and far more real than illusory and evanescent bodies of flesh. These aims – deeply tied up with notions of sovereignty, as we will see – are similar to those expressed and enacted in other Mahāyāna *sūtra*s, but the *Vimalakīrtinirdeśa* is quite distinctive in at least two ways: first, in the sheer force of its repeated rejection of material bodies and rituals; and second, in its dramatic performance of the ritual power of narration. The *Vimalakīrtinirdeśa* makes *buddha*s present not primarily through the preservation and performance of their *own* utterances (as is the case, for instance, in the *Saddharmapuṇḍarīka*), but rather through the skilled teachings (*nirdeśa*) of the *sūtra*'s eloquent protagonist, Vimalakīrti. In other words, the *Vimalakīrtinirdeśa* makes the bodies and fields of *buddha*s present through dramatizing and enacting a highly entertaining plot in which the intervention of a ritual specialist – Vimalakīrti – enables audiences to see *buddha*s. His repeatedly touted memory (*smṛti, dhāraṇī*[5]) and eloquence (*pratibhāna*) identify

[5] While these are not synonymous terms, both have reference to memory. *Smṛti* refers to the faculty of memory; *dhāraṇī* is more ambiguous, usually taken to designate a *mantra*-like string of Sanskrit syllables thought to confer greater powers of memory (among other things). In her work on the late Vedic Vidhāna literature, Laurie Patton (2005, 173) notes a progression from *kīrtanam* (recitation) to *smaranam* (recollection) to *dhāraṇam* (retaining in mind) that seems relevant to the terminology of the *Vimalakīrtinirdeśa*, as well. According to this sequence, *dhāraṇam* (and, presumably, *dhāraṇī*) indicates the practice of bearing a text within oneself,

Vimalakīrti as an advanced *bodhisattva* who is skilled as a *dharmabhāṇaka*, a speaker of the *dharma*. But unlike generic *dharmabhāṇaka*s, such as those who figure so prominently in the *Saddharmapuṇḍarīka* and the *Suvarṇa(pra) bhāsottamasūtra* (see Gummer 2012), Vimalakīrti makes *buddha*s present not through uttering their words, but by enabling audiences to "see" their non-material bodies and fields. Yet this special kind of sight is profoundly tied to speech – indeed, to what we might call a ritual of narration.

As I have argued elsewhere (Gummer 2014, 2020, 2021a, forthcoming), this ritual is modeled, in its means and ends, on South Asian sacrificial ritual, and especially on the primacy of place given to utterance in that ritual complex. In such a context, speech generates forms of imaginative experience that are no less real for being impossible in the world of ordinary life. Indeed, they are "more than real," as David Shulman puts it (Shulman 2012). And while Buddhists employ multiple forms speech to these ends (*mantra, dhāraṇi,* encomium, and so forth), they share with other non-Vedic/post-Vedic genres (as found, for instance, in the epics and *purāṇa*s), a strong predilection for narrative forms. This affinity for emplotment assimilates all too easily to contemporary assumptions about narrative. Modern Eurocentric notions of narrative posit a fundamental distinction between historical narration (which ideally refers to real events) and fictional narration (which produces the illusion of events); such notions are deeply misleading and utterly inadequate for understanding most South Asian conceptions and practices of narration. This is especially the case with reference to so-called "religious" narratives, which contemporary scholars may sift for historical grains of truth, but generally assimilate to the deprecated category of the fictional.[6] If the proper and primary use of language is referential, then narratives that facilitate imaginative experience are ultimately false, however entertaining or pleasurable they may be,

---

the culmination of these practices aimed at the progressive internalization of a text. See Gummer 2014, 1107–9 for further reflection on this topic.

6 Like works of fiction, "religious" narratives are understood by most modern secular scholars to refer to a world that does not exist, yet is rendered more or less vivid and compelling to the reader through the literary and rhetorical gifts of a great poet or writer, "so as to transfer from our inward nature a human interest and a semblance of truth sufficient to procure for these shadows of imagination that willing suspension of disbelief for the moment, which constitutes poetic faith," as Samuel Taylor Coleridge famously put it (Coleridge 1834, 174). This influential formulation suggests that modern literary approaches to both religious and poetic/fictional works generally maintain the notion of language as quasi-referential – "a semblance of truth" – even while implying that the imagined worlds to which they refer are not "real" referents. Indeed, the language employed by Coleridge in this formulation reveals that modern notions of religion as "faith" in a realm beyond the material world provide the model for reading literary and poetic works, and not just the other way around.

and taking them otherwise is seen as a sign of false consciousness. Yet this apparent state of delusion is generated by the categories of analysis themselves, which privilege material presence ("real" events, "real" people, even if now past and absent) over imagination – which, in a materialist cosmology, is by definition *not* real.

The *Vimalakīrtinirdeśa* presents a strong contrast with these notions, advancing as it does a trenchant critique of any reliance on material, corporeal, or sensory experience as the locus of the real. Instead, it valorizes worlds, bodies, and forms of experience that take place in the imagination, prompted by narratives that create what they describe through the illusion of referentiality – what might be called *performative* narratives.[7] In the language of the *sūtra*, what is *āmiṣa* is to be rejected as illusory and unreal, while what is *dharma* is eternal and invulnerable.[8] This opposition plays out in a number of different ways that take full advantage of the multivalence of both terms: the true body of the *tathāgata* is the *dharmakāya* (the body constituted by his discourse/teachings/sovereign edicts) not an *āmiṣakāya* (a material body, a body of flesh); the most efficacious ritual is a *dharmayajña* (a sacrifice accomplished through ethical-verbal actions and teachings), not an *āmiṣayajña* (a sacrifice of flesh/food/material offerings); the way to offer reverence is through a *dharmapūja*, not an *āmiṣapūja*[9]; and so on. Yet in these and other invocations of the dichotomy, examined below, the *sūtra* also exhibits a marked propensity to narrate dharmic encounters and practices in strikingly material, corporeal, and sensory terms, appropriating the rejected *āmiṣa* half of the binary as metaphor for dharmic rituals and encounters. Such metaphors themselves possess ritual-performative force, for they enable the narrative manipulation of and transformative encounter with entities or experiences that are, according to the *sūtra*, insubstantial and inexpressible.

This dynamic relationship between *dharma* and *āmiṣa* is deeply intertwined with three other intersecting features of the *sūtra*'s vision-centered narrative arc: the passivity and relative absence of the Buddha in much of the narrative; the centrality of tropes and rituals of sovereignty; and the repeated

---

7 To be clear, part of the point of such narratives is (arguably) to reveal that all narratives are performative in this way: they effect what they purport to describe. I examine different aspects of the performativity of Buddhist *sūtra*s in Gummer 2020, 2021a, and 2021b, as well as in my monograph under preparation (*Performing the Buddha's Body*).

8 Reiko Ohnuma's article on "The Gift of the Body and the Gift of Dharma" notes the importance of these categories in Buddhist discourse on giving (Ohnuma 1998, especially 325).

9 Space limitations prevent me from examining in this paper the contrast between *dharmapūja* and *āmiṣapūja*, which is expounded at length in the final chapter of the *sūtra* (Vkn XII).

manifestation of *buddha*-fields (*buddhakṣetra*) throughout the *sūtra*. The *sūtra*'s denigration of *āmiṣa* as unreal and ineffective addresses, I think, the corporeal absence of the parinirvāṇized Buddha, manifested in the plot of the *sūtra* by his dwelling apart from the main action. This *sūtra* is not, for the most part, taught by the Buddha; it is taught by a very able *buddha* substitute, an advanced *bodhisattva* gifted in uttering the *dharma* and "cooking" beings thereby.[10] And what Vimalakīrti repeatedly teaches/displays is the eternality and presence of a different kind of *buddha* body, made manifest in and through the *sūtra* itself. Such a body reigns not in the illusory and defective material world, but in a perfect *buddha*-field. And the vivid manifestation of perfect *buddha*s in their perfect realms occurs, in the *sūtra*, through the ritual narration of Vimalakīrti. He makes them appear through his words, through the *dharma* that he teaches. This *dharma* makes sovereign *buddha*s and their perfect *buddha*-fields present and accessible whenever it is uttered, and transforms its audiences thereby.

Nowhere is this clearer than in the eleventh chapter of the Sanskrit *sūtra*, called "The Vision [*darśana*] of the Tathāgata Akṣobhya and the Fetching of the Abhirati World" (*abhiratilokadhātvānayanākṣobhyatathāgatadarśana*), arguably the culminating moment of the *sūtra*'s narrative. By locating this chapter and its claims to efficacy in the context of the *sūtra*'s ritual motifs (and motives) and the closely related critique of materiality, I want to explore how verbal practices of narration constitute, in the normative discourse of the *sūtra*, a form of imaginative *darśana* that effects transformations associated with (self-)sacrificial rituals for attaining sovereignty. Part of the efficacy of these narrative practices is located in the self-proclaimed power of the *sūtra* to bring audiences and practitioners into the visualized presence of a sovereign *buddha* presiding over his perfect field, and thereby to be cooked through this (sometimes explicitly consecratory) encounter.[11] In the *Vimalakīrtinirdeśa*,

---

10 The verb *pari-√pac* might be rendered literally as "completely cook." As Charles Malamoud has argued with regard to *√pac* in the Vedic context, "[t]here is... no reason whatsoever to deny the literal sense of the term" (Malamoud 1996, 24). Since *pari-√pac* is widely used in Mahāyāna literature to designate the transformative effects of *sūtra*s, *bodhisattva*s, and so forth, and since these same works (the *Vimalakīrtinirdeśa* among them) repeatedly invoke sacrificial tropes and rituals in relation to this term (see Gummer 2014, Mrozik 2007, 37–59), much would be lost by offering a more comfortable translation, like "develop." As Vimalakīrti himself demonstrates repeatedly, beings are cooked through the eloquent utterance of skillful teachings (*upāyakauśalya*) – and, as a result, through visions of *buddha*s presiding over their perfect fields.

11 This exploration contributes to my ongoing investigation (Gummer 2014, 2020, 2021a, forthcoming) of the different ways in which engaging in the textual-verbal-performative practices advocated by Mahāyāna *sūtra*s is (self-referentially)

making *buddha*s and their fields visible through the eloquent narration of the *sūtra* has the effect of cooking beings.

As I proceed, I want to resist presupposing what exactly *darśan(a)* entails in this context, instead taking up John Cort's "invitation to other scholars of South Asian visual culture to revisit this central category and to begin to see it as a highly variable rather than singular super-category" (Cort 2012, 2; similarly Rotman 2009, 5). Toward this end, my own recent work on the centrality of sovereignty and its rituals to notions of buddhahood, *buddha*-speech, and *buddha*-fields[12] finds a fruitful conversation partner in Marko Geslani's reassessment of *darśan* as an outgrowth of rituals of sovereignty. In contrast to Diana Eck's influential study,[13] which takes the devotional worship of material images as paradigmatic of the experience of *darśan*, Geslani traces the eventual development of image worship from much earlier royal rituals that render the sight of the king's freshly bathed body a source of auspiciousness and blessing for his subjects. The production and engagement with the material image of a deity, he suggests, is an innovation that redresses the frailty of the king's mortal body by "suspending the royal body at the height of auspiciousness in the ritual process, the moment when it has been bathed with the waters of appeasement and then presented (*darśayet*) to a viewing public. It preserves this state in petrified form" (Geslani 2018, 229). By this view, *darśan* is "a visual encounter that emerges from a meticulous ritual performance. The royal body is made to be seen. Auspiciousness – perhaps easily (mis)taken for liberation – radiates outward from this body" (Geslani 2018, 264).

In my recent work (Gummer 2021a, 2021b, and forthcoming), I have argued that the *Saddharmapuṇḍarīka* and the *Suvarṇa(pra)bhāsottama* serve as rituals of consecration (*abhiṣeka*): like *buddha* images,[14] listeners are consecrated as future *buddha*s through hearing stories about their own past and future lives. Indeed, the *bodhisattva* path is in an important sense *always* a narrative path, a path accomplished in and through stories. Image consecration is a powerful and useful model for thinking about how Mahāyāna *sūtra*s work: *buddha*-speech is a ritual power substance, and narratives that encompass the listener – self-referential narratives – enable the experience of that substance as a ritual

represented as an alternative path to buddhahood that substitutes for the *bodhisattva* path of narrative and ritual self-sacrifice.

12 See Gummer 2021a for an examination of sovereignty as it relates to the performativity of the Buddha's speech. I treat the topic in greater detail in a chapter of my monograph *Performing the Buddha's Body*, currently under preparation.

13 I refer, of course, to Eck (1981) 1998. Other influential treatments of the concept of *darśan* include Babb 1981 and Granoff 2004, 2006.

14 Swearer 2004, 122: "As a gifted actor becomes the person he or she plays by identifying with the character portrayed in the drama, so the Buddha image becomes the Buddha's double after being instructed in the *tathāgata*'s life history."

infusion. Geslani's study helps to illuminate some related, but different, aims at work in the *Vimalakīrtinirdeśa*: to ritually establish the Buddha's body and his realm – indeed, all *buddha*-bodies, and all their realms – as perfect and eternally visible. It does so through identifying them with the *dharma* – the teachings of the Buddha, yes, but also the ultimate sovereign power.[15] This ritual is also a form of consecration, but one (as we will see) that strongly rejects the legitimacy, even the reality, of any material (*āmiṣa*) manifestation. Vimalakīrti's approach to preserving and presenting the sovereign power of *buddhas* is deeply antimaterialistic and anticorporeal, yet remains oriented toward generating a visual (that is to say, visualized) experience.

And it is an approach with strong correlations in both Vedic kingship rituals and broader notions that assert the textuality of the king's true body.[16] Consider Charles Malamoud's description of the aims of sacrifice, in which the king is the paradigmatic sacrificer:

> … [S]acrifice can be described as a means for the sacrificer to transform himself into a *śilpa*, a work of art. These are the effects of the ritual: the sacrificer gets a new body, a true self with which he will be able to go up to the sky, where he will occupy or at least mark the free space he has made for himself there. He acquires this new self, this *ātman*, by the recitation of these poems called *śilpas*. These *śilpas* effect a metamorphosis in him and compose for him this perfectly equipped and refined new self. They are an *ātmasaṃskṛti*, a perfection of the self. This perfect self is described as *chandomaya*, made of *chandas*, of poetic meters. (Malamoud 2002, 23)

The sacrificial creation of a perfect body – a "work of art" that is essentially verbal, and yet occupies space in the sky – resonates strongly with the creation of *buddha*-fields in the *Vimalakīrtinirdeśa*. Those resonances grow even stronger with the verbalization and internalization of sacrifice in the late Vedic period, such that a sacrificer can perform "the food sacrifice without any outside help or reciprocity. He can thus stay in society while maintaining his independence from it" (Patton 2005, 185). Is this not precisely the characteristic of Vimalakīrti, the householder *bodhisattva* whose mental and verbal powers best all the *śrāvaka*s and *bodhisattva*s? And surely the verbalization and internalization of kingship rituals are at work in the ostensibly more "secular" (thus Pollock) notion that "[i]t is the Sanskrit poet who, according to the old trope, produces the "glory body" of the king, which remains on earth even after his mortal body has disappeared. The perfect language of textuality (*vāṅmaya*)

---

15 See Gummer 2021a, as well as Olivelle 2005, 125–6, and Hiltebeitel 2011.

16 Regarding Vedic rituals, through which the king gains an immortal solar body (among other things), see especially Proferes 2007.

functions as a stainless mirror continuing to reflect his glory image even when he himself is gone" (Pollock 2006, 182–3). The hyperreality and perfection of the king's verbal body in this passage sheds powerful light on the creation and visual encounter in the *Vimalakīrtinirdeśa* with perfect *buddha*s (their bodies made of *dharma*) dwelling in perfect *buddha*-fields.

I begin my reading of the *sūtra* by outlining what occurs in the eleventh chapter. With that in mind, I trace its intertwined ritual themes through some of the earlier episodes in the *sūtra* so as to shed light on the nature of the relationship between the vision (*darśana*) of *buddha*s and *buddha*-fields and the verbal cooking power of this *sūtra* that is, by its own account, the ultimate *yajña* (sacrificial ritual).

Verbal vision, sacrificial speech

"The Vision of the Tathāgata Akṣobhya and the Fetching of the Abhirati World" begins with a question posed by the Buddha to Vimalakīrti: "Noble son, when you want to behold a *tathāgata*," – literally, when you are "desirous of *darśana*" (*darśanakāma*) – "then how do you see him?" Vimalakīrti responds, "I see the Tathāgata by not seeing" (*tathāgatam apaśyanayā paśyāmi*). A long series of negations expands this paradox: the Tathāgata is completely inaccessible to the senses and "inexpressible" (*avacanīya*). "Such is the body of the Tathāgata" (*īdṛśo bhagavan tathāgatasya kāyaḥ*), he concludes. A *buddha*'s true body is not a corporeal body and cannot be perceived by bodily senses (Vkn XI.1). But in the wake of this apophatic apotheosis, Vimalakīrti provides *darśana* of a *tathāgata*: the Tathāgata Akṣobhya, whose entire vast world sphere Abhirati the *bodhisattva* gathers up into his hand and brings into this Saha world to show Śākyamuni's assembly. Through this amazing feat, he cooks all those beings present who are fit for cooking (Vkn XI.7). While the reality of the Tathāgata is beyond description, then, he can nonetheless be seen and brought into our own – and precisely through the unfolding of the narrative of the *Teaching of Vimalakīrti*, which makes him and his world imaginatively present to audiences and allows *darśana* of them.

This crucial point is confirmed and amplified in the passage that follows, one in which the *sūtra* takes an explicitly self-referential turn. Śāriputra draws a direct parallel between the benefits that accrue to the actual members of the assembly, who have direct sight (*darśana*) of Vimalakīrti and the Tathāgata and *buddha*-field that his miraculous powers make present, and those who will hear (*śroṣyanti*) this discourse on *dharma*, whether the *tathāgata* is present or has parinirvāṇized (Vkn XI.8). To say nothing, he adds, "of those who, having heard, will apply themselves intensely to it, seek it out, apprehend it, bear it in memory, recite it, study it, realize it, promulgate it, illuminate it in full for others, and practice devoted application of it in the imagination." (Vkn XI.8). The chapter then concludes by equating the effect of practices involving the *sūtra* with being in the presence of the Tathāgata. Śāriputra asserts that "Those who internalize through recitation (*svādhyāsyante*) this discourse on *dharma* will be companions of the Tathāgata," and that "the Tathāgata will visit the house of those who, having carefully copied this discourse on *dharma*, will bear it in mind and honor it." And he ends by saying, "Those who will teach fully to others even so much as a verse of four lines from this discourse on *dharma* will perform the great *dharma* sacrifice. That is the prediction, Blessed One, for those who devote their receptivity, enthusiasm, determination, attention, insight, realization, and liberation to this discourse on dharma" (Vkn XI.9).

This episode brings together in close juxtaposition ritual elements that intertwine in perhaps surprising ways in the narrative of the *sūtra*: the vision (*darśana*) of a *buddha*; the construction, manipulation, and display of *buddha*-fields by advanced *bodhisattva*s like Vimalakīrti; and the self-referential idea of a *dharmayajña* (contrasted with an *āmiṣayajña*) achieved through the *sūtra* and the ethical-verbal-ritual practices it advocates. The interrelationship of these elements in this episode and elsewhere in the *sūtra* prompts me to pose the following questions: What does the *darśana* of Akṣobhya and his field, made possible through the intervention of Vimalakīrti, entail, and how is it connected with or illuminated by the notion of a *mahādharmayajña* accomplished through *sūtra*-centred practices? What kind of ritual encounter is meant here by *darśana*? How is it significant that not only Akṣobhya but also his *buddhakṣetra* is rendered visible and ritually transformative through the power of Vimalakīrti? And what is the nature of Vimalakīrti's power, as envisioned by the *sūtra*? In order to give context to a further exploration of these questions, I will trace through the narrative of the *sūtra* the creation and manipulation of *buddha*-fields by *bodhisattva*s, and the contrast between *āmiṣa* and *dharma*. Doing so will lead directly to a reconsideration of the ritual context invoked through the terms *yajña* and *darśana*, and from there to the question of the relationship between narrative and vision.

The first chapter of the *sūtra*, "The Purification of Buddha-fields" (*buddhakṣetrapariśuddhi*), signals immediately the centrality of revealing and seeing perfect *buddha* realms to the action and purpose of the narrative. One of the inaugural events of the *sūtra* is the Buddha's miraculous display of the entire cosmos, including all its *buddha*-fields (as stated explicitly in I.10 verse 2), as reflected in a great jeweled canopy (Vkn I.8). The display is not only visual, but auditory: those present not only see the fields, but also hear all the *buddha*s in the cosmos proclaiming the *dharma*. And the reverse is also true: hearing the *dharma* that is this *sūtra* makes all the *buddha*-fields and *buddha*s in the cosmos appear in the imagination of the listener. The Buddha's primary interlocutor in this chapter, the Licchavi Ratnākara, accordingly praises him as the *dharmarāja* – displaying all the *buddha*-fields in the cosmos confirms his cosmic sovereignty – then asks him to explain what is involved in *bodhisattvas*' purification of *buddha*-fields. The Buddha's response emphasizes that even though *bodhisattvas* know full well that all things are like space, they nonetheless imaginatively construct (*māpeti*)[17] glorious, pure *buddha*-fields. Why? "In order to cook beings" (*satvaparipākāya*): creating these fields enables beings with the appropriate propensities to be reborn in them, and thus to cultivate the six perfections and other *bodhisattva* virtues in those perfect realms (Vkn I.12–13).

Just as the purity of a king's body and the flourishing of his realm are mutually confirming (Geslani 2018, 190–95), the purity of these fields reflects (and produces) the purity of the *bodhisattvas* who build them:[18] seeing a pure, imagined field constructs/confirms the purity of the imagined *bodhisattva* who built it. Why, then, Śāriputra wonders, is the Buddha's own field so impure?[19] It isn't, of course – as the Buddha then demonstrates by transforming it into a gorgeous, bejeweled paradise. It is a *vyūha* the likes of which, Śāriputra admits, he has "never before seen or heard" (*adṛṣṭāśrutapūrva*). The Buddha makes it appear impure "in order to cook inferior beings" (*hīnasatvaparipākāya*) (Vkn I.18). This explanation effectively overrides the theory that the purity of *buddha*-fields represents the purity of their builders by locating the source of impurity in the eye of the beholder – like Śāriputra, whose doggedly earthbound eye stands in for all those who misidentify the material world as the "real" world. The purity of the Buddha's sovereign body and his field are thus confirmed/made real (that is, textually and imaginatively real-ized). The Buddha adds an explanatory metaphor: just as the nectar (*sudhā*) of the gods all comes from a single vessel, yet differs in accordance with the merit accumulated by each deity, so the vision of a *buddha*-field reflects the merit of the viewer (Vkn I.18). (As we will see, this metaphor is carefully chosen to foreshadow a subsequent episode in the *sūtra*, as well as to locate the cooking powers of *buddha*-fields in a sacrificial cosmos.) This "explanation" carries considerable ritual-rhetorical force and complexity: one's vision of the *buddha*-field as impure is at once a means of cooking, an index of how well-cooked one

17 The use of the verb *māpeti* in this context is significant: as Rupert Gethin has pointed out (2006, 98), its usage among Pāli materials includes the sense of "[mentally] create."

18 Compare Laurie Patton's observation that "the Vedic world is replete with the idea that a *loka* is a sphere or state that is exactly commensurate with one's merit" (2005, 170).

19 This is a recurring question in Mahāyāna *sūtras* – see, e.g., *Saddharmapuṇḍarīka*, especially chapters 15 and 23 of the Sanskrit text.

already is, and an incentive to question the reality of what meets one's eyes – and to build (*māpeti*) and occupy in place of the impure material world perfect *buddha*-fields in the imagination. That is, after all, what *bodhisattva*s do, according to the *sūtra*. But the metaphor is also intricately connected to the means and ends of sacrifice, through which the gods are provided with the nectar (*sudhā/amṛta/soma*) that is their favorite food. Beings are like the gods, cooked/nourished through the mental field-building of those ritual specialists, the Buddha and *bodhisattva*s. And like the building of *buddha*-fields, sacrificial ritual creates a place in heaven for the sacrificer.[20]

But the paradigmatic aim of both Brahmanical sacrifice and Buddhist self-sacrifice is sovereignty (whether one aims to rule material realm or dharmic reality), and both are achieved in no small part through potent ritual-poetic speech – speech that infuses the (self-)sacrificer with sovereign power and ensures his rebirth in heaven in a perfect, immortal, solar body that is identified with the ritual-poetic speech through which it was achieved (Proferes 2007, Gummer 2021a). Just as an anointed, wheel-turning king (*cakravartin*) rules over the physical, material landscape of his *cakravartikṣetra*, so, too, does a *buddha* or *bodhisattva* preside over his mentally constructed *kṣetra*, exercising his sovereign rule (*śāsana*) over reality itself.[21] The *bodhisattva*'s path to sovereign perfection is a path of self-sacrifice – narrative self-sacrifice. Narratives in which *bodhisattva*s build sovereign, sunlike bodies and realms (*śilpa*s, if you will) are not *less* real for being word-borne, but more. The *Vimalakīrtinirdeśa* strongly implies that manifesting *buddha*-fields is accomplished through the *dharma* – which is to say, through narrating worlds into imaginative (and hyper-real) existence. After all, Vimalakīrti is especially renowned for his eloquence (*pratibhāna*) and skill in means (*upāyakauśalya*), with which he is said to completely cook (*pari-√pac*) his interlocutors. And he both asserts and demonstrates that he accomplishes these transformations by manifesting *buddha*-fields, engaging in *dharma*-sacrifices, and offering his assembly other-worldly dharmic food that transforms all who consume it in accordance with their stage on the path.

Vimalakīrti's production of these displays is repeatedly framed by the dichotomy (and hierarchy) between *dharma* and *āmiṣa*. But the immaterial *dharma* "works" as it does, in all these cases, by the appropriation of the *āmiṣa* side of the dichotomy in the form of a highly performative metaphor. The very premise for the visit to Vimalakīrti, his heuristic infirmity, turns on this

---

[20] As I have argued elsewhere (Gummer 2020, 2021a), metaphors for the *dharma* are never "just" metaphors: they are speech acts that shape what it means to engage with the *dharma*.

[21] My monograph under preparation examines the relationship between the *buddhakṣetra* and the *cakravartikṣetra* in greater depth.

distinction. The *bodhisattva* exercises his skill in means (the second chapter is called *acintyopāyakauśalya*, "Inconceivable Skill in Means") by feigning bodily illness, which affords him the opportunity to instruct his well-wishers on the fragility, repulsiveness, and unreality of the fleshly body and to extoll by contrast the *dharma* body of a *tathāgata* (*tathāgatakāya*). Unlike the fleshly body, the *tathāgatakāya* is born (*nirjāta*) from Buddhist virtues and practices. This past participle, repeated twenty-five times in swift succession in this brief praise passage (Vkn II.12), echoes the description of Vimalakīrti at the beginning of the same chapter (Vkn II.1) as "born from the perfection of wisdom" (*prajñāpāramitānirjāta*) – a matrix of choice in Mahāyāna *sūtra*s (Cabezón 1992; Ohnuma 2012, 148–54). Vimalakīrti's "inconceivable skill in means" lies in his (verbal) use of the ephemeral, disease-prone fleshly body to demonstrate the vast superiority of the immortal *tathāgatakāya*/*dharmakāya*, born from virtuous acts (*karman*) that are utterly different from those that produce a body of flesh. And the *dharmakāya* is also the *sūtra* itself, the body that performs its ritual work of transformation through Vimalakīrti's skillful lesson, which prompts hundreds of thousands of beings to generate the mind of awakening (Vkn II.13).

These themes are taken up again several times in the subsequent chapter, in which the Buddha's monastic followers and *bodhisattva* entourage one by one express to him their reluctance to visit the ostensible invalid and recount their previous encounters with him, in which his startling eloquence (*pratibhāna*) struck them speechless (*niṣpratibhāna*).[22] Ānanda tells of a time when "the body of the Blessed One had some discomfort" (Vkn III.42: *bhagavataḥ kāyasya kaścid evābādhaḥ*), and Ānanda went to seek an offering of milk with which to treat this indisposition. Encountering Vimalakīrti, he explains his errand, upon which the householder responds with opprobrium: since a *tathāgata*'s body is hard as diamond and entirely without impurities, how could he be ill? Even a *cakravartin*'s body is free from illness – to say nothing of a *tathāgata*'s body. Vimalakīrti advises Ānanda to keep silent,

[22] I leave largely unexamined here two episodes from the third chapter that involve alimentary-sacrificial themes. In the first (Vkn III.10–14), Vimalakīrti upbraids Mahākāśyapa for his manner of seeking alms (*piṇḍa*) by showing preference to the poor; here, both the terminology and Vimalakīrti's instructions to Mahākāśyapa place the episode squarely in the sacrificial arena and foreshadow the sacrificially inflected consumption of leftovers begged from another *buddha*-field in chapters nine and ten (examined below). In the second (Vkn III.15–20), Vimalakīrti offers Subhūti a bowl of particularly high-quality alms, but admonishes him to take it only if he understands "the sameness of all food/material objects" (*āmiṣasamatā*). Taken together, then, these two episodes critique any sense of partiality either to certain kinds of donors or to certain kinds of offerings and reframe the practice of receiving alms as a form of illusory *upāya*.

since his false speech would mislead powerful deities and "*bodhisattvas* who have gathered from other *buddha*-fields" (*anyabuddhakṣetrasaṃnipatitāś ca bodhisatvāḥ*) and would bring censure upon the Buddha and his followers (Vkn III.43–44). "Tathāgatas have *dharma* bodies, not fleshly/material bodies" (*dharmakāyās tathāgatā nāmiṣakāyāḥ*), Vimalakīrti insists, and to say otherwise is unseemly (Vkn III.45). Ānanda is deeply ashamed. Then a voice from the sky confirms the accuracy of the householder's speech, explaining that the Buddha pretends to have an ordinary body because "beings need to be disciplined" (*satvā vinetavyāḥ*). That being the case, the voice concludes, Ānanda should go ahead and get the milk anyway (Vkn III.46). As with the Buddha's field and Vimalakīrti's own "illness," the purportedly mortal, material, fleshly body of the Buddha is merely a stratagem for transforming beings. And, once again, the rhetorical force of this claim encourages audiences to "see" the Buddha's body as immaterial, eternal, and identical with his teachings.

In the narrative that concludes the chapter, these ethical-verbal-ritual techniques of transformation are explicitly identified as the *dharmayajña* and are directly connected both to the critique of the fleshly/material sacrifice (*āmiṣayajña*) and to the creation by Vimalakīrti of a vision of a *buddha* and his field. Sudatta attributes his reluctance to visit the householder to a previous encounter when Sudatta was making preparations to celebrate a "great sacrifice" (*mahāyajña*). As befits his name, he was giving gifts (*dāna*) to the poor and destitute, to ascetics and brahmins, in a manner resembling the material forms of sacrifice advocated by the Buddha to Kūṭadanta in the Pāli *sutta* by that name (the fifth *sutta* of the *Dīgha Nikāya*). Nonetheless, Sudatta is chastised in no uncertain terms by Vimalakīrti, who insists that he should conduct a *dharmayajña*, not an *āmiṣayajña* (Vkn III.68).

The passage actively exploits the multivalence of *āmiṣa*. Sudatta engages in no slaughter for his "sacrifice," but rather bestows material things upon worthy recipients. And yet the very fact that the event in question is repeatedly designated a *yajña* brings the connotations of food and flesh fully into play. So, too, does Vimalakīrti's explanation that "the *dharmayajña* is that by which all beings without first or last are completely cooked."[23] Three more times (Vkn III.70, III.71, III.73) he asserts that the *dharmayajña* "completely cooks" beings and insists that *this* is the sacrifice that a *bodhisattva* should undertake, not an *āmiṣayajña*. And he describes the *dharmayajña* in terms that plainly identify it with the *bodhisattva* path: it is the path culminating in the attainment of the six perfections. But Vimalakīrti defines the *dānaparamitā* not in terms of

---

23 Vkn III.69: *yena dharmayajñenāpūrvācaramaṃ sarvasatvāḥ paripācyante ayaṃ dharmayajñaḥ*.

extreme generosity – not even of the gifts of the (*āmiṣa* or *dharma*?[24]) body that dominate (predominantly Mahāyāna[25]) accounts of the perfection of giving – but as realizing "tranquility and mildness" (*śāntadānta*) (Vkn III.70).[26] It is also the path that requires becoming a servant and student of all beings, the path of meditative attainments – and the path that involves teaching the *dharma* (Vkn III.73). Through this *dharma* sacrifice, the *bodhisattva* becomes the supreme sacrificer, himself fit for the offerings of others: "This, noble son, is the *dharma* sacrifice, on account of which *bodhisattva*s are established as cherished [or: sacrificed] sacrificers of sacrifices (*iṣṭayajñayājūkā*), worthy of the sacrificial gifts (*dakṣiṇīyā*) of the world with its gods."[27]

The term *iṣṭayajñayājūkā* contains a play on words: *iṣṭa* is the past participle of two different verbs: √*iṣ* (to desire, to cherish) and √*yaj* (to sacrifice). The *bodhisattva*, as a sacrificer of the *dharma* sacrifice, effects his own sacrifice in a manner that does not involve flesh or material (*āmiṣa*) sacrifice, and doing so makes him the most desirable sacrificer, the one truly worthy of *dakṣiṇā,* the gift or fee given to brahmin ritual specialists who conduct a sacrifice. At this, the astonished Sudatta presses just such a gift – a precious pearl necklace – upon Vimalakīrti, who only accepts it on the condition that he can gift it to others. He gives one half of the pearls to the poorest of the poor in the city, and the other half to the Tathāgata Duṣprasaha, whom Vimalakīrti miraculously produces, ensconced in his *buddha*-field Marīci (Vkn III.75). The moral: for one conducting the *dharmayajña*, no distinction should be made between the poor and a Tathāgata (Vkn III.76).

Vimalakīrti's speech about the *dharma* sacrifice not only describes an act; it is itself performative. It transforms what the self-sacrificial path of the perfections entails: the most efficacious of sacrificial acts are those practices and attainments that avoid not only flesh sacrifice (whether of self or other), but also any food or material gifts whatsoever. And it makes a *buddha* and a *buddha*-field – themselves both means and ends of a highly efficacious cooking

---

24 Since the stories of radical corporeal self-sacrifice through which the *bodhisattva* "cooks" himself are always narratives, his sacrifices might well be called *dharmayajña* rather than *āmiṣayajña*: it is the stories that cook him – and cook the listeners who hear them at the same time. On the fungibility of fleshly and narrative gifts in some Mahāyāna *jātaka* collections, see Ohnuma 1998.

25 I take Naomi Appleton's point (see Appleton [2010] 2016, especially 13–19) that the *jātaka* genre is too often treated as static and monolithic. "Mahāyāna" is doubtless still too broad a category, but finer distinctions await further research.

26 In Gummer 2021a, I examine a similar substitution of other practices for the perfection of giving in the *Saddharmapuṇḍarīka* and propose that they are connected to notions of the Buddha as sovereign.

27 Vkn III.74: *ayaṃ sa kulaputra dharmayajñaḥ, yatra dharmayajñe pratiṣṭhitā bodhisatvā iṣṭayajñayājūkā dakṣiṇīyā bhavanti sadevakasya lokasya.*

process – imaginatively present not only for Sudatta and his companions, but also for audiences of the *sūtra*. If Vimalakīrti transforms sacrifice into an ethical, mental, and verbal process of cooking, he also makes ethical, mental, and verbal practices into ritual actions, thus bringing to hand the resources of the sacrificial cosmos in order both to describe and to accomplish the work of transformation that constitutes the *bodhisattva* path. The *dharma* sacrifice, the *bodhisattva* path, involves cooking oneself and others through the ethical, mental, and verbal practices through which the path is "realized" (*abhinirhṛta*).

This past participle, which occurs no less than 33 times in this passage (and nowhere else in the *sūtra*), strongly reinforces the performative nature of these avowedly immaterial acts. The verb (*abhi-nir-√hṛ*) and its derivatives (especially the noun *abhinirhāra*) have the sense of "production, accomplishment, effectuation, undertaking, realization (particularly of something in one-self)" (Edgerton, 1953, 52). It is frequently associated with the accomplishment of vows and with teaching the *dharma*, and in the latter instances is, according to Edgerton, tantamount to *upāyakauśalya*. In other words, it indicates the immaterial – mental, imaginative – actualization of speech acts, speech acts that serve to cook both speaker and listener. And, significantly, Vimalakīrti's admonishments to Sudatta not only describe these processes of actualization, but also enact them. He has conducted the sacrifice through his speech, as this vision of a perfect *buddha* body in a perfect realm confirms. And his speech act about sacrificial cookery is self-referential: it cooks those who listen. Sudatta reports that both the brahmins in attendance at the sacrifice and the poor of the city generated the mind of awakening (Vkn III.74, III.77). They are cooked by his speech acts about the cooking power of speech acts: his speech does what it says. As we have already seen, the eleventh chapter states explicitly that conducting the "great *dharma* sacrifice" (*mahādharmayajña*) is accomplished through teaching the *sūtra* itself (Vkn XI.9). And an important aspect of that teaching involves prompting the recognition that real transformation, real sacrificial cooking, occurs in the mind, through the power of the *dharma*, spoken with eloquence, to bring about the imaginative *real-ization* of the *bodhisattva* path – and of *buddha*-fields.

The ensuing chapters clearly show that bringing *buddha*-fields (or contents thereof) into the Saha world is one of the primary acts through which Vimalakīrti cooks beings. In chapter four, he gives as an example of the integration of *upāya* and *prajñā* "concentration on completely cooking beings through the adornment of *buddha*-fields and the major marks and minor characteristics [of the body of a *mahāpuruṣa*],"[28] while at the same time remaining focused on emptiness. And in chapter five, the "display of inconceivable liberation" of the chapter's title is precisely the *bodhisattva*'s ability to transport

[28] Vkn IV.17: *lakṣaṇānuvyañjanabuddhakṣetrālaṃkārasatvaparipācananidhyaptiḥ*.

worlds and hold them in his hands, to expand and shrink space and time, to concentrate all the splendors of all *buddha*-fields into a single *buddha*-field, and to deposit the fire that burns all *buddha*-fields at the close of a *kalpa* in his own mouth (see especially Vkn V.15–16). What is more, Vimalakīrti's continued assertion of the superiority of *dharma* to *āmiṣa* involves repeated importation of quasi-material items from other *buddha*-fields. Śāriputra is the dupe in these episodes: he wonders where people will sit, and Vimalakīrti scolds him for his shallow concern with creature comforts – but then orders up the hugest and most luxurious thrones in the cosmos from another *buddha*-field (Vkn V.1–8). These are not ordinary thrones, of course: they are made of *dharma*. We might say that they are narrated into imaginative being, real-ized, through the power of Vimalakīrti's world-conjuring eloquence. In order to sit on them, the *bodhisattva*s present must be able to transform their (surely not *āmiṣa*) bodies to enormous size.

The contrast between *āmiṣa* and *dharma*, the sacrificial cooking of beings, and transactions among *buddha*-fields also frame the most food-centric episode in the *sūtra*, which spans chapters nine and ten.[29] This time, Vimalakīrti catches Śāriputra wondering when the gathered assembly will eat, and chides him: "Don't listen to the *dharma* with your mental disposition smeared with food (*āmiṣa*) [or: caught up in material things]!"[30] Then he promises Śāriputra a feast such as he has never eaten before, and emanates a golden-bodied *bodhisattva* whom he sends to a *buddha*-field called "Where All Scents are Sweet" (*sarvagandhasugandha*) to request the remains of the meal just eaten by the Tathāgata Gandhottamakūṭa (Pinnacle of Finest Perfumes) and his sweet-smelling *bodhisattva* entourage. The emanated *bodhisattva* returns with both the entourage and a bottomless bowl of the fragrant leftovers,[31] which he calls *amṛta*, immortalizing nectar (Vkn IX.11). After all present eat their fill, their bodies are pervaded by bliss and a delightful aroma (Vkn IX.11), and the visiting *bodhisattva* entourage describes how the Tathāgata Gandhottamakūṭa teaches the *dharma* not through speech but through scent (Vkn IX.14).

Meanwhile, in the garden of Āmrapālī, the Buddha's assembly starts to glow with golden light in anticipation of Vimalakīrti's impending arrival. Vimalakīrti gathers his massive entourage into the palm of his hand (as though it were a *buddha*-field) and transports it to the greatly enlarged garden through another feat of supernormal power (*ṛddhyabhisaṃskāra*) (Vkn X.1–X.2). Ānanda asks how long the delicious scent emanating from the visitors

---

29 I examine this chapter briefly in Gummer 2014, 1116–18.

30 Vkn IX.1: *tvaṃ mā āmiṣamrakṣitayā saṃtatyā dharmaṃ śrauṣīḥ*.

31 Compare Vkn III.13, in which Vimalakīrti gives Mahākāśyapa permission to eat the food he has received only after he has satisfied from his bowl all beings, *buddha*s, and *ārya*s (perhaps *arhat*s).

will linger. Vimalakīrti reports that it will last until the food has been completely digested (*pariṇata*), an occasion marked by the ascent of all who partook of it to the next level on the path to awakening. The digestive process will take forty-nine days, while the resulting "vital essence" (*ojas*) will circulate for an additional seven days (Vkn X.5-.6). As Ānanda marvels, "This food does the work of a Buddha!"[32] This explicit analogy between food and *dharma* echoes parts of Vimalakīrti's extended metaphorical description of *bodhisattva*s in the seventh chapter, in which he states that "their food is immortalizing nectar, and their drink is the liquid essence (*rasa*) of liberation": they dine on the *dharma*. As the *sūtra* repeatedly asserts, *dharma* is the real food and true body of the Buddha and advanced *bodhisattva*s, not *āmiṣa* – yet the apparently stark contrast between *āmiṣa* and *dharma* depends upon the substitutability of the one for the other. This episode in which those assembled supposedly eat material food actually suggests the foodlike function of the *dharma*, which transforms its listeners in ways strikingly like this *amṛta*. At the same time, the *sūtra* is drawing attention to its own verbal ability to generate in listeners' imaginations food from other worlds (not to mention golden-bodied *bodhisattva*s to fetch it). The episode is thus plainly self-referential: the ultimate food is the *dharma*.

The identification of this food as the remains (*avaśeṣa*) of a distant *buddha* (Vkn IX.4–IX.5) also locates it in the sacrificial cosmos. Leftovers play a crucial role in Brahmanical sacrifice: not only are the leftovers of the gods eaten by participants in the ritual, and thus progressively refined in the digestive fires to produce *ojas*, vital fluid, but also (according to the Pūrva Mīmāṃsā) the effect of the ritual itself is precisely to leave a trace after the fire has destroyed the offerings. This previously nonexistent trace (called *apūrva*) of the sacrifice enables the sacrificer to attain heaven. The notion of the leftover also informs the workings of karma, in which all acts, like sacrificial acts, leave a residue that comes to fruition (frequently expressed in terms of cooking – √*pac*) in the future (Malamoud 1996, 7–22). The *sūtra* skillfully manipulates these ideas in this episode in which fragrant leftovers from a distant *buddha*-field cook in the digestive fires of those who consume them to produce *ojas* and the residue of higher attainments on the path. But unlike material sacrificial remains, this dharmic food "cannot be exhausted"; it can feed a multitude of cosmic proportions (as Vimalakīrti's entourage demonstrates). It is *amṛta* – the immortalizing nectar of the gods, yes, but also itself immortal: the food

[32] As I've pointed out before (Gummer 2014, 1117–18), this meal also recalls the meal consumed by the Buddha on the eve of his awakening, through which he "makes himself into a buddha" (Strong 2001, 69).

that is the *dharma* is eternal. And it is, in a quite literal sense, the leftovers of a *buddha*, his verbal remains.[33]

The *Vimalakīrtinirdeśa*, in its relentless interrogation of dichotomies, not only insists and relies upon the distinction (both binary and hierarchical) between *dharma* and *āmiṣa*, but also dissolves it by substituting *dharma* for food (and vice versa). This metaphorical relationship mobilizes rather than rejects the sacrificial paradigm, in which the leftovers of the teacher (in this case, a *buddha*) enter the stomachs of his disciples and transform them. While the *dharma* is repeatedly defined in opposition to *āmiṣa*, then, its mode of absorption is decidedly digestive. The dharmic food consumed by Vimalakīrti's entourage illuminates a highly performative – and highly sacrificial – conception of hearing or reading the *dharma*, the verbal leftovers of a *buddha*, which enters and transforms all those who consume it. The episode dwells at some length on the myriad ways in which the work of *buddha*s may be accomplished, but that work is characterized in sacrificial terms; whatever *buddha*s do, it is all "for the sake of cooking beings" (*satvaparipācanatayā* – Vkn X.11). Hearing the *dharma*, in this sacrificial cosmology, is like eating and digesting food, like being cooked, like gestating a *buddha* body. And again, the

33 The notion of sacrificial leftovers also evokes the normative Brahmanical master–pupil relationship, in which the pupil eats the leftovers of his master – leftovers of both *āmiṣa* and *dharma* varieties. As Malamoud notes of the master, "apart from leaving [his disciple] his leftovers (as do the gods with the sacrificer), it is also... he who provides him with a knowledge of *dharma*, if not with *dharma* itself" (Malamoud 1996, 13). This Brahmanical relationship between teacher and student invests both *dharma* and *āmiṣa* with value and efficacy as mutually supportive foundations of a ritual relationship modeled on sacrifice, one that establishes a lineage of succession. The *Vimalakīrtinirdeśa*, with its otherworldly food that "does the work of a Buddha," might be read as a clever parody of this relationship. Compare the *Dhammadāyāda Sutta*, the third *sutta* in the *Majjhima Nikāya*, which also presents a contrast between *āmiṣa* (paradigmatically represented as food) and *dharma*, strongly emphasizing the superiority of the latter. The Buddha opens the discourse by directing his monastic followers to "Be my dhamma-heirs, monks, not my *āmisa*-heirs" (Trenckner and Chalmers [1888–1925] 1991–94, i.12: *dhammadāyādā me bhikkhave bhavatha mā āmisadāyādā*). He then illustrates his point with a hypothetical case: suppose he has finished eating and offers his leftovers to two monks. One, recalling the teaching with which the *sutta* begins, refuses the food even though doing so makes him hungry and weak; the other eats the leftovers and becomes strong and healthy. Of the two, the Buddha says, the first is more praiseworthy, because he is the Buddha's *dhamma*-heir, not his *āmisa*-heir (Trenckner and Chalmers [1888–1925] 1991–94, i.12–13). Like the *Vimalakīrtinirdeśa,* this *sutta* offers an implicit critique of the brahmanical arrangement: eating the master's food may make one's body stronger, but it is not the basis of the lineage in which the monk is an heir. It also suggests a kind of *dharmic* (versus carnal – another implication of *āmiṣa*) paternity, a theme of central importance in certain Mahāyāna *sūtra*s (on which see Gummer 2020).

episode is self-referential and performative: the story of the dharmic leftovers is itself the food that cooks those who consume it, advancing their progress on the path to buddhahood.

Finally, this narrative in which leftovers from another *buddha*-field are fetched and consumed clearly echoes the analogy made by the Buddha between the production of *buddha*-fields and the sacrificial nourishment of the gods (Vkn I.18), both of which are meant to cook those who "consume" them as appropriate to their merit or level of advancement. What, then, is the connection between the two, and how is it related to the *darśana* of the Tathāgata that is first rejected, then delivered in the palm of Vimalakīrti's hand in chapter 11? The notion of the *dharma* as the sacrificial leftovers of a *buddha* might provide some insight into these questions. In the absence of a flesh-and-blood *buddha* (and according to Vimalakīrti, no such *buddha* has ever existed), we have these inexhaustible leftovers, as long as an advanced *bodhisattva* like Vimalakīrti can make them available to us through his ritual performance of the *dharma.* But the same performance also cooks beings by enabling them to see other *buddha*s in other *buddha*-fields. As the tenth chapter states explicitly, there are innumerable (and distinctly multisensorial/synesthetic) ways of teaching the *dharma* in innumerable *buddha*-fields. Some *buddha*s do their work through food and aroma, others through the visual encounter with the physical form and marks of a *tathāgata* (Vkn X.8: *tathāgatalakṣaṇarūpadarśanaṃ*). Corporeal organs of taste and sight are metaphors not only for each other, but also for the cultivation of the imaginative capacity to real-ize the narrative of the *sūtra.* And digestion and vision are deeply embedded in sovereign ritual – both in food-centered rites for attaining sovereignty and in vision-centered rites for displaying the king's purified body and giving his subjects auspicious *darśan* thereof. *Buddha*s have inherently regal bodies; *buddha*s preside over imperial fields. But unlike earthly kings, who establish merely mundane governance over material realms through "external" rites that can only render their bodies temporarily pure, *buddha*s reign in essentially pure bodies and fields, and command reality itself – a reality constituted through narrative, through the internalized *yajña* that is the *dharma.* "Seeing" *buddha*s in their fields, as the ritual performance of the *Vimalakīrtinirdeśa* makes possible over and over again, is a highly effective method of sacrificial transformation, and is always auspicious.

Conclusion

At the end of chapter 11, Śāriputra presents a loose progression of practices for incorporating the *sūtra,* moving from forms of study and memorization – forms of internal cookery – through verbal practices focused on cooking others. The culminating practice, *bhāvanāyoga,* suggests a kind of imaginative realization (real-ization) of the *sūtra*, especially in light of David Shulman's work "toward a yoga of the imagination" in South Asia (Shulman 2012, 109–43): *bhāvanā* is "the mind-born calling of a world, any world, into being" (22). In contrast to modern notions of "belief," these characterizations suggest an intense process of internalization and eventual imaginative realization: *making* real through concentrated efforts at verbalization and visualization, not "believing" in an externally existent, material reality (which, after all, the *sūtra* goes to great lengths to deny). This reading is strengthened – and linked explicitly to the sacrificial cosmos – in the final passage of the chapter, in which audiences' interactions with the *sūtra* are identified with interactions with the Buddha (including the receipt of a prediction). As the *sūtra* emphasizes repeatedly, *buddha*s don't have fleshly, material bodies; they have *dharma* bodies. Those who engage with the *sūtra* are thus engaging with a *buddha.* And that is so not only because the *sūtra* is his *dharma* body, but also – and perhaps especially so, in the case of the *Vimalakīrtinirdeśa* – because it makes him imaginatively present for those who focus intently (*adhi-√muc*) on mentally realizing the words of the *sūtra.* Vimalakīrti shows us how it is done when he takes up the Tathāgata Akṣobhya and the entire world of Abhirati and brings it into the Saha world: take the words of the *sūtra* and bring them into imaginative being. *Both* worlds are ultimately illusions, after all: the trick is to learn how to cultivate and generate those illusions so as to abide in and be cooked by the visual-imaginative-ritual encounter (*darśana*) with *buddha*s, whether or not Śākyamuni has entered *parinirvāṇa*. Those who understand the illusory nature of reality have the power to transform it, with the help of the Buddha's *dharmakāya* – that is, the *Vimalakīrtinirdeśa* itself, brought to life by its eponymous and most eloquent of performers. In light of this theme, it seems no accident that the Buddha himself is not especially voluble in the *sūtra*: the voice of Vimalakīrti, ventriloquized/impersonated[34] by a *dharmabhāṇaka*, brings his listeners into the verbal presence of multiple *buddha*s in multiple worlds and asserts the accessibility and eternality of the *dharmakāya* – and its separability from any ostensibly *āmiṣa buddha* body.

Recall Śāriputra's claim that "Those who internalize through recitation (*svādhyāsyante*) this discourse on *dharma* will be companions of the Tathāgata" (Vkn XI.8). The practice here referred to is *svādhyāya*, which, in

---

[34] The *dharmabhāṇaka*, too, finds strong correlations in Vedic sacrificial ritual. See Caley Charles Smith's insightful work on the impersonation of Indra by the performer of Vedic hymns in the course of sacrificial ritual (Smith 2017). Smith argues that the performance collapses time and makes Indra present in the ritual. Compare my argument regarding the "presencing" effect of the *dharmabhāṇaka*'s performance in the normative vision of the *Suvarṇa(pra)bhāsottama* (Gummer 2012).

the late Vedic context, designates "the internalization of the sacrifice into the form of mantra" (Patton 2005, 191). The final sentences of the chapter make it clear that in this Mahāyāna *sūtra*, too, such practices constitute the "great *dharma* sacrifice" (*mahādharmayajña*) – and here, the *dharma* in question is identified unambiguously as the *sūtra* itself. To conceive of teaching the *sūtra* as the performance of a sacrifice reinforces its ambrosial nourishment and its (auditory and visual) capacity to cook its speakers and listeners. And the *sūtra* is making more than a bald statement of self-promotion; it is telling us how to engage with it, how to interpret it – not as a repository of doctrine, nor even as a literary work, although of course it can be and has been read as both, but as a ritual of narration. By its own normative account, the *Vimalakīrtinirdeśa* is the ritual means (food, fire, and potent performative text) that makes present and renders imaginatively visible the glorious, immortal, sovereign bodies of *buddhas* ensconced in their fields. Indeed, in some mysterious way, it *is* that body – the eternal *dharmakāya* that becomes mentally manifest whenever the *sūtra* is uttered. Consuming the narrative *dharma* through auditory, mental, and verbal practices brings audiences into the transformative presence of the (narratively constituted) bodies and fields of sovereign *buddhas*. Like the narratives that consecrate *buddha* images, the *Vimalakīrtinirdeśa* is on some level a ritual power substance – one that consecrates both imagined *buddhas* in their perfect realms and the audiences who enter their presence.

With these conclusions in mind, let me return briefly to the Dunhuang *sūtra* paintings with which I began. In their largely bipartite structure, renderings of the *Vimalakīrtinirdeśa* indeed contrast quite strikingly with iconic *sūtra* paintings:[35] Vimalakīrti and his main interlocutor, Manjuśrī, face each other and not us; we are simply witnesses to their conversation. Yet in most such paintings, above the heads of the two *bodhisattvas* hover the several *buddha*-fields that Vimalakīrti brings into being in and through the *sūtra*. They are icons of the mind, the results of a ritual technology (and one that is visual, even when auditory) for seeing a sovereign *buddha* in his perfect realm and being cooked by that vision. Such experiences of *darśan* can only happen, however, through the performative narrative of the *sūtra*, brought to imaginative life by a skilled speaker like Vimalakīrti, whose voice enables a form of visionary (and gustatory, and olfactory) experience not dependent on fragile fleshly bodies. To take *darśan* of a *buddha* is to take *darśan* of the supreme sovereign, as also demonstrated by Fiordalis in the previous chapter. Yet the king of kings – the "ruling power of the ruling power" – is the *dharma* itself: pure, immaterial,

[35] Again, the rendering on the east wall of cave 146 provides a clear example: https://library-artstor-org.ezproxy.beloit.edu/asset/MIDA_101433; SSID 18113123.

and perfectly efficacious.[36] In this sense, the *Vimalakīrtinirdeśa* – and its visual translation at Dunhuang – offers an illuminating ritual commentary on that oft-quoted phrase from the *Vakkali-sutta*, "He who sees the *dharma* sees me; he who sees me sees the *dharma*."[37]

Bibliography

Appleton, Naomi [2010] 2016. *Jātaka Stories in Theravāda Buddhism: Narrating the Bodhisatta Path*. New York: Routledge.

Babb, Lawrence A. 1981. "Glancing: Visual Interaction in Hinduism." *Journal of Anthropological Research* 37/4: 47–64.

Cabezón, José Ignacio 1992. "Mother Wisdom, Father Love: Gender-Based Imagery in Mahāyāna Buddhist Thought." In *Buddhism, Sexuality, and Gender*, edited by José Ignacio Cabezón, 181–99. Albany: State University of New York Press.

Coleridge, Samuel Taylor 1834. *Biographia Literaria, or, Biographical Sketches of My Literary Life and Opinions*. New York: Leavitt, Lord & Co.

Cort, John E. 2012. "Situating Darśan: Seeing the Digambar Jina Icon in Eighteenth-and Nineteenth-Century North India." *International Journal of Hindu Studies* 16/1: 1–56.

Eck, Diana L. [1981] 1998. *Darśan: Seeing the Divine Image in India*. 3rd ed. New York: Columbia University Press.

Edgerton, Franklin 1953. *Buddhist Hybrid Sanskrit Grammar and Dictionary. Vol. 2. Dictionary*. New Haven, CT: Yale University Press.

Feer, M. Leon, ed. [1884–1904] 1975–99. *Saṃyutta-Nikāya*. 5 vols. London: H. Frowde for the Pali Text Society.

Geslani, Marko 2018. *Rites of the God-King: Śānti and Ritual Change in Early Hinduism*. New York: Oxford University Press.

Gethin, Rupert 2006. "Mythology as Meditation: From the Mahāsudassana Sutta to the Sukhāvatīvyūha Sūtra." *Journal of the Pali Text Society* 28: 63–112.

---

36 See Olivelle 2005, 125–6, citing the *Bṛhadāraṇyaka Upaniṣad* (1.4.14), according to which the *dharma* is *kṣatrasya kṣatram*, "the ruling power of the ruling power." Olivelle attributes the notion of *dharma* (a term attested but not especially influential in late Vedic thought) as the "essence of kingship and the transcendent power that lies behind the visible power and authority of the king" to ascetic communities, especially Buddhists.

37 Feer (1884–1904) 1975–99, iii.120: *yo... dhammam passati so mam passati || yo maṃ passati so dhammam passati*.

Granoff, Phyllis 2004. "Images and Their Ritual Use in Medieval India: Hesitations and Contradictions." In *Images in Asian Religions: Texts and Contexts*, edited by Phyllis Granoff and Koichi Shinohara, 19–56. Vancouver: University of British Columbia Press.

Granoff, Phyllis 2006. "Reading Between the Lines: Colliding Attitudes Towards Image Worship in Indian Religious Texts." In *Rites hindous: Transferts et transformations*, edited by Gérard Colas and Gilles Tarabout, 389–421. Paris: Ecoles des hautes études en sciences sociales.

Gummer, Natalie D. 2012. "Listening to the *Dharmabhāṇaka:* The Buddhist Preacher in and of the Sūtra of Utmost Golden Radiance." *Journal of the American Academy of Religion* 80/1: 137–60.

Gummer, Natalie 2014. "Sacrificial Sūtras: Mahāyāna Literature and the South Asian Ritual Cosmos." *Journal of the American Academy of Religion* 82/4: 1091–1126.

Gummer, Natalie 2020. "The Scandal of the Speaking Buddha: Performative Utterance and the Erotics of the Dharma." In *Buddhist Literature as Philosophy, Buddhist Philosophy as Literature*, edited by Rafal K. Stepien. Albany: State University of New York Press.

Gummer, Natalie 2021a. "Speech Acts of the Buddha: Sovereign Ritual and the Poetics of Power in Mahāyāna Sūtras." *History of Religions* 61/2: 173–211.

Gummer, Natalie 2021b. "Sūtra Time." In *The Language of the Sūtras: Essays in Honor of Luis Gómez*, edited by Natalie Gummer, 293–337. Berkeley, CA: Mangalam Press.

Gummer, Natalie Forthcoming. "Texts and Rituals." In *Oxford Handbook of Buddhist Practice*, edited by Paula Arai and Kevin Trainor. New York: Oxford University Press.

Hiltebeitel, Alf 2011. *Dharma: Its Early History in Law, Religion, and Narrative*. New York: Oxford University Press.

Malamoud, Charles 1996. *Cooking the World: Ritual and Thought in Ancient India*. New York: Oxford University Press.

Malamoud, Charles 2002. "A Body Made of Words and Poetic Meters." In *Self and Self-Transformation in the History of Religions*, edited by David Dean Shulman and Guy G. Stroumsa, 19–28. New York: Oxford University Press.

Mrozik, Susanne 2007. *Virtuous Bodies: The Physical Dimensions of Morality in Buddhist Ethics*. New York: Oxford University Press.

Ohnuma, Reiko. 1998. "The Gift of the Body and the Gift of Dharma." *History of Religions* 37/4: 323–59.

Ohnuma, Reiko 2012. *Ties That Bind: Maternal Imagery and Discourse in Indian Buddhism*. New York: Oxford University Press.

Olivelle, Patrick 2005. *Language, Texts, and Society: Explorations in Ancient Indian Culture and Religion*. Firenze, Italy: Firenze University Press.

Patton, Laurie L. 2005. *Bringing the Gods to Mind: Mantra and Ritual in Early Indian Sacrifice*. Berkeley: University of California Press.

Pollock, Sheldon I. 2006. *The Language of the Gods in the World of Men: Sanskrit, Culture, and Power in Premodern India*. Berkeley: University of California Press.

Proferes, Theodore N. 2007. *Vedic Ideals of Sovereignty and the Poetics of Power*. New Haven, CT: American Oriental Society.

Rotman, Andy 2009. *Thus Have I Seen: Visualizing Faith in Early Indian Buddhism*. New York: Oxford University Press.

Shulman, David 2012. *More Than Real: A History of the Imagination in South India*. Cambridge, MA: Harvard University Press.

Smith, Caley Charles 2017. "Look At Me! The Mimetic Impersonation of Indra." PhD diss., Harvard University.

Strong, John S. 2001. *The Buddha: A Short Biography*. Oxford, UK: Oneworld Publications.

Swearer, Donald K. 2004. *Becoming the Buddha: The Ritual of Image Consecration in Thailand*. Princeton, NJ: Princeton University Press.

Takahashi, Hisao ed. 2006. *Vimalakīrtinirdeśa: A Sanskrit Edition Based Upon the Manuscript Newly Found At the Potala Palace*. Tokyo: Taisho University Press.

Trenckner, V., and R. Chalmers, eds. [1888–1925] 1991–94. *The Majjhima-Nikāya*. 4 vols. London: H. Frowde for the Pali Text Society.

Wu, Hung 1992. "What is Bianxiang? On the Relationship Between Dunhuang Art and Dunhuang Literature." *Harvard Journal of Asiatic Studies* 52/1: 111–92.

Author biography

Natalie Gummer is professor of religious studies at Beloit College in Beloit, Wisconsin, where she has taught since 2001. She graduated with a PhD from Harvard University in Buddhist Studies in 2000. Her research, published in several journal articles and book chapters, examines textual practices in premodern Mahāyāna Buddhist literary cultures, especially ritual uses of texts, oral performance, and translation. She also explores how Mahāyāna literature might offer us critical purchase on a range of contemporary ethical and philosophical debates. She is editor of *The Language of the Sūtras: Essays in Honor of Luis Gómez*, and is currently completing a monograph on performativity and embodiment in Mahāyāna sūtras.

10

Making Senses of the Story

Narrative, Art and Affect in Ancient India

Jonathan Walters

Introduction

The construction of ancient India's ornamented *stūpa*s, from Aśoka Maurya (third century BCE) onward, corresponded to new Buddhist textual strategies for narrating not only visual encounters, but each of the six senses: seeing, hearing, smelling, tasting, touching and mentation.[1] Comparing late canonical/post-Aśokan texts with earlier (pre-Aśokan) ones demonstrates that Buddhist authors developed these new approaches to the senses only when Buddhist donors began constructing these sculpted monuments. The celebration of sensual encounters can be seen in textual narratives of this period, which accompany the rise in narrative art adorning the *stūpa*s themselves. These new approaches entailed a shift from overwhelmingly negative condemnation of the senses and their pleasures to a more positive embrace promoting their enhancement in particularly Buddhist ways.

While I suspect that this characterization holds true across the whole canonical literature, I focus on *Khuddaka-nikāya* texts. I take *Sutta-nipāta* (but also *Dhammapada, Itivuttaka, Udāna, Theragāthā, Therīgāthā*) as emblematic of the earlier, antithetical narration of the senses. These texts are dated to the fifth or fourth centuries BCE. I take *Apadāna* (but also *Cariyāpiṭaka, Buddhavaṃsa, Vimānavatthu, Petavatthu, Jātaka*) as emblematic of the later, more sensual approach. These do not predate Emperor Aśoka (third century BCE).[2] Section One of this chapter juxtaposes these earlier and later narrative

1 The inclusion of mentation with the five bodily senses is typical of the Pali texts, often in a three-fold reading of each that includes the sensorial process itself (seeing, hearing, smelling, tasting, touching, thinking/feeling), the corresponding sense organ (eyes, ears, nose, tongue, body, mind) and the objects of its activity (sights, sounds, odors, tastes, physical contacts and thoughts and emotions).

2 *Apadāna* revealingly mentions *Kathāvatthu* (*Therāpadāna*, v. [443], *Therī-apadāna*, v. [504]), which the tradition ascribes to the time of Aśoka Maurya (*Dīpavaṃsa* 7.41, 56–8: Oldenberg, trans. 1982, 157–8; *Mahāvaṃsa* 5.278: Geiger, trans. 1934, 49–50).

approaches. Section Two unpacks the range of sensorial narrative strategies developed in *Apadāna.* Section Three analyzes *Buddhāpadāna* as exemplary of this newer approach. The Conclusion relates these developments to worship at the great *stūpa*s. As such, this chapter draws together the various threads of the volume, by relating textual narratives back to visual encounters with narrative art at Buddhist sites, through a focus on visualization practices. However, it also expands our purview to include the experiences of the other senses.

Section One: *Apadāna:* new senses of the senses

I begin distinguishing these narrative predilections by juxtaposing *Sutta-Nipāta* and *Apadāna* on two points where they directly overlap. First, I compare their respective tellings of the Buddha's first encounter with his chief disciple, Sāriputta (*Sutta-Nipāta* 955–75 [Norman, trans. 1985, 156–7] and *Therāpadāna* #1 [140–373]).[3] Second, I parse the *apadāna* ascribed to the *paccekabuddhas*, which incorporates a lengthy *Sutta-Nipāta* passage into a larger treatment of those enigmatic "Lonely Buddhas" (*Sutta-Nipāta* 35–75 [Norman, trans. 1985, 7–10], *Paccekabuddhāpadāna* [82–139]). In both instances, the *Apadāna* authors narrate the senses and their pleasures as (at least potentially) positive things rather than as inherent obstacles to religious progress, which is *Sutta-Nipāta*'s consistent stance.

In *Sutta-Nipāta,* Sāriputta asks the newly-met Buddha to describe the religious ideal. After presenting the *bhikkhu* as unafraid, virtuous, and restrained, the Buddha concludes:

> Moreover there are five kinds of pollution in the world,
> for the dispelling of which he should train himself,
> possessing mindfulness. He should overcome passion
> for forms, sounds and tastes, smells and contacts.
>
> (v.974; trans. Norman 1985, 10)

Taking "passion" as the mental affect grounded in sense objects, this advice to Sāriputta disparages all six sensual domains. The verses which continue – and conclude – *Sutta-Nipāta* (976–1149; Norman, trans. 1985, 159–85) detail

---

3 Throughout this chapter I refer to my own translation of *Apadāna* (*Legends of the Buddhist Saints* apadanatranslation.org). Citations of specific verses follow the convention of the website by enclosing the verse numbers in square brackets, to indicate that they correspond to the *Buddha Jayanthi Tripitaka Series* edition. The website can be consulted for corresponding verse numbers in the Pali Text Society edition, supplied there in ordinary parentheses.

a string of similarly anti-sensorial answers to Brahmins' questions.[4] Whether as outright condemnations, or affirmations of those who reject sense-pleasures, this sort of anti-sensorial narrative characterizes *Sutta-Nipāta*[5] and related early *Khuddaka* texts.[6]

Sāriputta's *apadāna* greatly enhances the earlier telling. The *Sutta-Nipāta* narrates it in the anonymous third person, providing no background to the encounter and no epilogue save that just quoted. *Apadāna*, conversely, is a first-person narrative of the event inflected by Sāriputta's subsequent arahantship, including his recollection of previous lives. *Apadāna* largely eclipses the meeting itself; Sāriputta has already attained the first path-fruit ([286]) and moves *non sequitur* from approaching the Buddha to being the disciple "foremost in wisdom" ([296–7]). Sāriputta then eloquently articulates the Buddhist ideal himself, in a paean that recapitulates his conversion and achievement of arahantship ([298–302, 348–73]) to frame extended praises of the Buddha and Sangha ([303–47]).[7]

---

4 In this passage (Norman, trans. 1985, 159–85), the Buddha tells Ajita that "[a] bhikkhu would not be greedy for sensual pleasures." (v.1039). To Tissa Metteyya he praises "...the bhikkhu who lives the holy life amidst sensual pleasures...with craving gone, always mindful..." (v.1041). He explains "one who has gone out" to Upasiva as "he whose passion for all sensual pleasures has gone" (vv.1071–2). Todeyya learns that "[i]n whom no sensual pleasures dwell...for him there is no other release" (v.1089); "In this way...recognise a sage...not attached to sensual pleasures..." (v.1091). Jatukaṇṇī approaches "[h]earing of a hero who...is without sensual pleasures," affirming that "[t]he Blessed One indeed dwells having overcome sensual pleasures...;" the Buddha advises him to, "[d]ispel greed for sensual pleasures..." (vv.1096–8). Likewise, Udaya learns that "release by knowledge, the [breaking] of ignorance" entails "[t]he abandonment of both desires for sensual pleasures and unhappiness....if a person does not enjoy sensation, internally or externally, in this way consciousness is stopped for him wandering mindfully" (vv.1105–11).

5 See at least vv. 152, 175, 228, 284, 337ff, 361, 464, 467, 625, 639, 642, 697, 766–71, 823, 844, 845, 851, 948 and the previous note.

6 Consider *Dhammapada* vv. 7–8, 48, 214–15, 218, 356; (Carter and Palihawadana, trans. 1987, 14, 20, 49, 50, 71); *Udāna* I.i–iii, 3.5 (Woodward, trans. 1948, 1–3, 33); *Itivuttaka* III.vi–vii (Woodward, trans. 1948, 183–4); *Theragāthā* vv. 659–72 (14.2; Norman, trans. 1997, 71); *Therīgāthā* vv. 87–91 (5.5; Hallisey, trans. 2015, 57).

7 This passage is composed as a multi-sensorial narrative. Sāriputta compares the Buddha with the earth, ocean, moon, blooming lotuses, the flowering king of all *sal* trees, medicine, a lion, and a great cloud. Up to the lotuses the emphasis seems to be on visual beauty, but in addition to its loveliness the *sal* tree "exudes a heavenly perfume" [330]; medicine is related to taste [333; cf. *Bakkulāpadāna*, vv. [3764–9]); the lion is singled out for the sound of its roar [335–8], as is the great cloud for its thunder [341]; the tactile is almost tactical, with the Buddha defeating heretics as the moon obliterates starlight, waves are crushed on the seashore, or other beasts flee at the lion's roar. Above all, Sāriputta praises the Buddha's mind and affect ([322, 325–9, 333, 339–43]).

The most significant difference from *Sutta-Nipāta*, however, is that Sāriputta's *apadāna* provides extensive background to the meeting. On one hand, *Apadāna* details the setting for Sāriputta's life as a Brahmanical renouncer when he first encounters the Buddha. On the other hand, it details the background to the background, as it were, during Sāriputta's previous life as Suruci ([172–3, 225]), "aeons beyond measure" earlier ([252]), in the time of Anomadassi Buddha. Then, too, he was the Brahmanical leader of a great community of accomplished students ([173–206]) who encountered the Buddha and eloquently praised his wisdom ([209–31]); Sāriputta's perfected wisdom is that primordial meeting's karmic result ([362–3]).

Before disclosing any of this detail, however, the poem opens with an extraordinary, extended description of the Himalayan ashram occupied by Suruci during Anomadassi's Buddha Era. More than sixty verses ([140–204]) ask the reader-listener to imagine that hermitage in thick detail, before the narrator even identifies himself, or the temporal setting of the description. Far from condemning the pleasures of the senses, these verses revel in them, prompting a multi-sensorial imagination of the visual, aural, olfactory and (to a lesser extent) gustatory and tactile, but above all the mental pleasures which *arahant* Sāriputta recalls himself enjoying as Suruci. A repeated refrain describes lovely sights, such as blossoming trees and varied wildlife ([143–5, 148, 155, 157–65]), "beautifying my ashram" (*sobhayantā mam 'assamaŋ*). In addition, Sāriputta explains that birdsongs made the ashram sound good ([159–62]). It smelled fragrant with the perfume and pollen of flowers and trees ([142, 146–7, 149–54, 156, 171]), was abundant with tasty fruits and vegetables, and cool water to drink ([166–70]), and even purveyed tactile comforts like smooth ground and easy slopes ([141–2]). In this setting, Suruci lived with his students, whose extensive accomplishments are colorfully described in equally sensorial terms ([174–202]). Sāriputta recounts the visual spectacle and aural din of 24,000 leather-clad students flying through the sky ([190–2]) and their inverse, the moving sight of them treating animals with kindness ([195]), or the respectful silence with which they study, such that "not the sound of a sneeze is heard" ([199]). The spectacle is also tactile, as they set the earth to quaking ([183, 193]), and gustatory, as they bring delicious fruits from distant regions ([184]) or pursue their own strict dietary regimens ([187]). Paralleling the blossoming trees, they "perfume" the hermitage with their morality ([202]), even though precepts are the *only* perfume worn by these ascetics "[w]ith nails and armpit hair grown long, muck in [their] teeth, heads [soiled] with dirt" ([189]).[8] This multi-sensorial ashram – which becomes something

---

8 This description is implicitly juxtaposed with that of Gotama Buddha's students, whose accomplishments are narrated in a much less sensual way ([303–12]).

of a trope in the *Apadāna* collection[9] – leaves Suruci "constantly filled with joy" ([203]).

Sāriputta's previous-life encounter continues with a typical Buddha-prediction ([232–62]) that he would indeed become Gotama Buddha's wisest disciple, after experiencing aeons of sensual pleasures as a god or an emperor [243–8]. But sensuality has not triumphed over the ultimate goal. Anomadassi concludes:

> When he attains his final birth
> he will go to the human state…
> giving up eight hundred million
> he will renounce, with nothing left,
> and searching for the path to peace
> this great man's going to wander [far]. [249–51]

Sāriputta's "now" is as an *arahant* who has already renounced his millions (or billion)[10] and achieved the end of attachments ([263–73; 348–73]). The passages affirming this "now" state are noticeably free of the focus on the senses and sensual imagery which do however stand out in the descriptions of his past.

A parallel point of contact between *Sutta-Nipāta* and *Apadāna,* in the *Paccekabuddhāpadāna*, underscores that *Apadāna* is thus best seen as softening or supplementing rather than outright rejecting the earlier anti-sensorial predilection. Most of the *apadāna* ascribed to the *paccekabuddhas* is in fact lifted verbatim from *Sutta-Nipāta*'s most famous depiction of the early Buddhist ideal (*Sutta-Nipāta* vv. 35–75; Norman, trans. 1985, 7–10), directly encapsulating its strong anti-sensualism:

> Sense pleasures are varied, sweet and delightful;
> [they] churn up the mind with [their] varying form.
> Seeing danger in the strands of sense pleasure,
> one should wander alone, like a rhino's horn.
> "For me this is calamity, misfortune;
> a sickness, a [sharp] arrow, a fearsome thing."
> Seeing this fear in the strands of sense pleasure,
> one should wander alone, like a rhino's horn.
> (*Sutta-Nipāta* 50–51 = *Apadāna* [105–6], my trans.)

---

9 For example, Bakkula #396 ([3758–62]), Upasiva #405 [3990–4029], Udena #410 [4219–45], Ekachattiya #412 [4299–323], Tiṇasūlakachādaniya #413 [4346–50].

10 The higher amount is given at [273]; Sāriputta "actually" gave away 100 *koṭis* (one *koṭi* = ten million), i.e., one billion [pieces of money], whereas Anomadassi predicted that he would give away only 80 *koṭis,* 800 million.

So *Apadāna* presents no absolute antagonism to the earlier ideal. Rather, *Apadāna* broadens the vision of time – every poem, like Sāriputta's, begins numerous aeons ago – allowing for new narrative focus on certain *sorts* of seeing, hearing, smelling, tasting, touching, and mentation which, however intermediate and proximate, do lead beyond themselves to nirvana. Thus *Paccekabuddhāpadāna* frames the embedded section of *Sutta-Nipāta* ([82–8], [131–9]) to convey this new appreciation of those strands of sense pleasure. In terms of seeing, the Buddha explains:

> All Obstacles Abandoned, Lords of People,
> Lamps of the World, Shedding Light Like Heaps of Gold,
> Free of Doubt [and] Good for the World to Look At,
> these Lonely Buddhas are constantly honored. [135]

In terms of hearing:

> The clever sayings of the Lonely Buddhas
> are circulating in the world with [its] gods.
> Having heard, those who don't act that way are fools;
> they spin in suffering again and again. [136]

The Buddha even moves in the direction of tasting:

> The clever sayings of the Lonely Buddhas
> are as sweet as if they were flowing honey.
> Having heard, those who practice accordingly
> become seers of the [Four] Truths, very wise. [137]

The *paccekabuddhas*' "clever sayings" (P. *subhāsitāni*) disdain the senses, but in addition to their doctrinal content they are beautiful sounds, "tasty" and to be savoured just as the physically and religiously beautiful *buddhas* are "Good for the World to Look At" (P. *lokasudakkhiṇeyyā*) even if they themselves had "mind[s] not delighting in delights in the world" ([88]). These framing images encapsulate the earlier, anti-sensorial verses within the new, more sense-friendly narrative sensibility.

Section Two: *Apadāna* explorations of Buddhist sensuality

As a whole, *Apadāna* reveals concerted engagement with multi-sensorial narrative, suggesting sustained reflection on and experimentation with the newly-opened range of narrative possibilities. Each sense thus gets singled out in specific descriptions; the way things look or smell, sound, taste, feel and/or affect the mind become the poets' primary narrative building-blocks. Each sense gets deployed in epithets applied to *buddhas* and other exalted beings, and in metaphors that fire reader-listeners' imaginations. Each sense plays a central role in certain "karma seeds" (P. *kamma-bīja*) or pious deeds done by *arahants* during previous lives that *Apadāna* makes the root cause of their arahantship, a centrality that is sometimes made to be physically or bodily manifest in later lives, and sometimes produces karmic results of like kind until the senses are finally transcended in nirvana.

The narrative of Sāriputta's hermitage stands out for including, even overdetermining the pleasures of all six senses in a single image, which as mentioned becomes an *Apadāna* trope. The divine pleasures Sāriputta is predicted to enjoy likewise include stock descriptions of heavenly attainments elsewhere in the collection,[11] and as I detail below, another such multi-sensorial image dominates *Buddhāpadāna*. More common than complex poems which thus explore all the senses, however, are simpler poems which develop aspects of just one.

This distinction points to a more basic division in the *Apadāna* collection, between compositions in the voices of "historical" *arahants* known in other canonical sources, and those attributed to subjects who appear to have been invented for *Apadāna* itself.[12] The compositions attributed to famous *arahants*, like *Sāriputtāpadāna*, tend to demonstrate care and creativity in narrating known details within larger flows. They regularly embed *Theragāthā* or *Therīgāthā* verses attributed to the particular monk or nun in whose voice they are composed, and they contain extended plots and sophisticated literary ornamentation. In contrast to these are the *apadānas* ascribed to otherwise unknown *arahants*. Their names – and for the most part their entire (auto)biographies – consist of nothing more than the pious karma seeds which lead to their arahantship. These latter, "filler" poems are constructed largely on the basis of shared, stock material, including whole verses and sometimes entire poems. They tend to be short, uniform and predictable. While they demonstrate some variety in terms of which previous *buddha* is encountered, or the details

---

11 Cf. Therāpadāna #80, Tīṇipadumiya; #407, Hemaka; #501 Tīṇikaṇikārapupphiya.

12 Dhammapāla's commentary on *Theragāthā* and *Therīgāthā* (and following it, Malalasekera's *Dictionary of Pāli Proper Names*) treats these names as nicknames and lines up some of the "filler" *apadānas* with the famous *arahants* who are not otherwise represented in the collection. But the included famous monks and nuns *are* named by their own names in their *apadānas*, and there does not seem to be much basis for some of these ascriptions. I am more comfortable than the commentator (or Dr. Malalasekera) appears to have been, taking these as literary inventions rather than historical records.

of whichever particular karma seed is explored, they mostly repeat a single story, over and over, in which some particular karma seed, nurtured along by pleasant rebirths for many aeons, has ended up flowering (or more often fruiting) in the present arahantship of Rev. So-and-So.[13]

The more sophisticated narratives surrounding "historical" monks are admittedly better reads and more interesting studies. It is easy to breeze past the "filler" poems to focus on these more refined, longer and at least purportedly "historical" *apadāna*s, especially since the former are so repetitious, some utterly redundant. Yet such "filler" poems form the bulk (86%) of the monks' *apadāna*s.[14] The much smaller number of nuns' *apadāna*s creates a perhaps unbalanced emphasis on the famous ones, but even there 45% are otherwise unknown and apparently invented by/for *Apadāna* itself. The sheer effort required to compose and transmit all these stories compels us to take them seriously. It mattered to the composers and compilers to give hundreds of invented beings a modicum of personality, with bits of variation regarding the *buddha* who is encountered; the places, circumstances and era; the protagonists are of different generations, occupations, genders, castes, classes, religious orientations and/or kingdoms. They collectively offer a massive range of donations, services, provisions, praises and acts of worship; as a result of those varied karma seeds, all of them are *arahant*s today.

In earlier work (1997, 2009) I suggested several reasons why that these "filler" poems might have been composed. One is simply formal; the compilers needed to provide biographies of at least 500 male *arahant*s because that number regularly surrounded the Buddha. Another, more substantial reason for including the "filler" texts was to chart out the path to nirvana as universal, demonstrated in precisely that diversity of invented detail. The appeal is to all people, whatever their backgrounds or current statuses, who can emulate the *arahant*s at the earlier stages in the path; the logic is that doing today what the *arahant*s did then guarantees a future like that which they enjoyed: a string of positive rebirths culminating in nirvana. A third reason I have suggested for their inclusion is that these "filler" poems allowed the *Apadāna* authors to

---

13 The flowering metaphor is explicit in *Sāriputta-apadāna*'s recapitulation of the initial meeting with the Buddha ([300–301]) but "fruit" (*phala*) is by far the more common metaphor for arahantship attained, even elsewhere in *Sāriputtāpadāna* ([243–4], [246], [362–3]).

14 In determining the relative frequency of emphasis on one or the other of the senses through naming I created a listing which began by excluding a total of 76 *apadāna*s of "historical" monks, who bear their own names. These constitute about 14% of the total 559 poems ascribed to *thera*s (in the Buddha Jayanthi Tripitaka Series edition). The other 86%, to emphasize the point, are named according to the single, sense-based karma seed each performed in a previous life; for the most part they lack any unique identity outside that karma seed.

explore the range of possible karma seeds which, done in the proper affective frame of mind ("with intention and resolve" and "pleased"), result in arahantship. Collectively, the "filler" poems establish a new soteriology for ordinary people, who can remain attached to the world but plant karma seeds for future-life nirvana. In my earlier work I underlined the historical importance of that soteriology for practice at the great *stūpa*s in their heyday.

In the present case I suggest an additional possible reason for inventing the "filler" characters, namely that across these hundreds of biographies the authors were able to experiment with sensorial narrative. The underlying concern with such narrative is evident in the fact that nearly 100% of the "filler" monks and nuns are named for and by their karma seed itself, which implicitly or explicitly identifies them with one sense or another. These names foreground authorial concern with each karma seed's sensual range(s), and the sense signaled by a particular name is often explored in corresponding karmic results, physical manifestations and epithets supplied the Buddha.

A good, multi-faceted example of the type, focused on the visual, is *Therī-apadāna* #9,[15] ascribed to the otherwise unknown nun Pañcadīpikā ('Five Lamps-er'). The poem opens with her recollection of her previous life as a wanderer who *saw* the Bodhi tree of [Padumuttara][16] Buddha in the (limited) light of the waning moon and sat down there, "bringing pleasure to [my] heart" ([92]). Cultivating that "mental happiness" she vowed that if the Buddha "has limitless virtue, is unique, without a rival," then he should *show* her a miracle by making the Bodhi tree *shine.* Then, "...blaz[ing] up, [i]t shined forth in all directions, displaying every good color" ([94–5]). After an awe-filled week there she responds to this visual spectacle with a visual offering: she lights five oil-lamps as a *pūjā,* the karma seed underlying her present name. They miraculously remain lit all night.

From that moment, for the subsequent 100,000 aeons, she "come[s] to know no bad rebirth: that's the fruit of [giving] five lamps" ([112)]. In subsequent births she experiences special benefits related to brightness, clarity and vision. Reborn in the Tāvatiṃsa heaven, her palace, correspondingly named "Five Lamps," lights up the entire divine world ([98–9]). She sees all things good and bad in all directions, unobstructed by trees or mountains ([101–2]). Whenever she is being reborn, 100,000 lamps illuminate the surroundings. This is true of the present birth too; her eyes remain open *in utero* and as she emerges into the well-lit lying-in room ([105–6]). She quickly attains arahantship; Gotama Buddha, discerning her virtue, ordains her at the age of seven

---

15 The collection includes parallel monks named Five Lamps (*Thera-Apadāna* #57), One Lamp (#177), Solitary Illuminator (#264) and One Lamp (#416); another virtually identical nun is named Five Lamps (*Therī-Apadāna* #15).

16 He is not named, but indicated by the date.

([108]). Thereafter wherever she goes, "beneath a tree, in palaces, in caves or empty buildings," five lamps are always burning for her ([109]). Her enhanced vision is manifested physically in her attainment of "the divine eye" (an attribute of arahantship) and metaphorically in her skillful concentration and excellence in the special knowledges ([110]). She declares all this doing *pūjā* to the Buddha's feet with, of course, five lamps; she addresses him as *cakkhumā,* 'Eyeful One.'

Classifying these characters according to the sense they embody is admittedly messy. Five Lamps-er's offering is primarily visual, but it is also tactile, involving filling and lighting lamps and prostrating herself in worship, while her oil lamps would also be olfactory depending on what oil she used (which is not stated); I have taken flowers to be visual except where their fragrance is specifically highlighted, in which case I have categorized them as olfactory. There is something random about this; it would be just as fitting to treat the olfactory as the default, and only classify flower-offerings as visual when a poem explicitly highlights their visual beauty. Likewise, many of the karma seeds involve obviously tactile elements, and the texts often stress that the performer of them is "pleased by [my] own hands" when the act is done. In the description of each act – whether dyeing a *stūpa* cloth (which I classify as visual) or offering cloth to a living *buddha* (tactile), or offering him food (gustatory) or incense (olfactory), or hearing him preach (aural) – it is indeed always the (affective) mental pleasure that gets emphasized as paramount, and as causal in the transformation of the earlier act into the present arahantship. Thus mental affect is explicitly one dimension of all the stories, whichever other sense(s) they emphasize.

Still, the names invented for these "filler" *arahant*s, identifying their specific karma seeds in ways that fall pretty neatly into the six senses, tell us with some consistency that despite such fluid boundaries, the *Apadāna* authors were thinking categorically about the particular sensual domains into which such acts fall. Thus the imagination "sees" Five Lamps-er dispelling the darkness with her lamps, and through her eyes, as it were, sees the Bodhi tree's multicolor blaze, or sees the Eyeful One as she worshipfully gazes upon his feet. Similar pictures are called up in the imagination on the basis of just the names of other *arahant*s, too, whose karma seeds were primarily visual, such as Seven Rays-[Seer], Foot Seer, Bodhi-Tree Seer, Floral Cover-er, Solitary Illuminator, or Rag Robe Seer.

But one imaginatively touches or feels, as it were, the "tactile" names like One Genuflection-er, Coarse Cloth Donor, Pillar Donor, Fanning Donor, Good Plaster-er, Bed and Couch Donor, Buddha [Earthquake] Experiencer, Road-sweeper, Water Sprinkler, or Walked Over [Her Head]-er. The tactile images produced by those names – and the narratives that explain and enhance them – are clearly in a different range than the visual ones, prompting imagination of actions, movements, weights and textures rather than of colors, shapes or designs. Both sets of names are distinct from what the imagination "hears" in the names based on aural karma seeds: Sound Perceiver, Truth-Hearer, Dharma-Listener, All Praiser, One Conch Shell-er, Sign-Proclaimer. And these in turn lack the fragrances the imagination "smells" in names like Incense Donor, Scented Water-er, Perfumed Garland-er, Pollen-Sprinkler, Scented Flower-er, Sandalwood Offerer, Scented Handprint-er, Hut-Perfumer, All-Perfumes-er, Good Smell-er. Nor do those names convey the flavours the imagination "tastes" in names such as Food Provider, Garlic Giver, Milk-rice Donor, Good Salt-er, Honey Soaked Meat Donor, Woodapple Fruit-er. Finally, the classification I make of karma seeds that are grounded primarily/exclusively in mental affect, without specific reference to any of the other five senses, can be recognized in the names of *Apadāna arahant*s like Three Refuge Goer, Five Precept Accepter, Good Thoughts, One Perception, Refuge Goer, Knowledge Perceiver, One Pleasing, Apadāna-er, or Knowledge Praiser.

In my calculation, the majority (approximately 39%) of the "filler" monks' karma seeds and corresponding names are primarily visual. Just to consider the various facets of visual narrative that emerge in those *apadāna*s – a huge range of visual karma seeds parallel to Five Lamps-er's lamp-offering; Buddha epithets like Eyeful One; metaphors like the implicit connection of Five Lamps-er's lamplight to her skillful concentration; physical manifestations like Five Lamps-er's well-lit dwellings; visual descriptions like that of the blazing Bodhi tree in the pale moonlight – would go far beyond what a single chapter can do. Expanding that catalogue to include the many overlapping facets of the 22% of the "filler" poems that are primarily tactile, the 18% that are primarily gustatory, and the 4% each that are primarily aural, olfactory, or affective[17] would prove even more formidable. The problem is magnified further still if that catalogue considers, not merely the specific senses that get emphasized in these "filler" monks' karma seeds and names, but also *every* deployment of one or the other of the senses in the collection, including the *apadāna*s of the "historical" monks, nuns and *buddha*s. Explicitly or implicitly, most of the poems turn out to involve multiple senses at least to the extent that most flowers are also sweet-smelling, and plucked and offered with the hands; all the tellings themselves are aural, and it is hard to imagine a temple scene or chance

[17] The figures for the nuns – again, based on a much smaller and perhaps skewed sample – are similar: among the non-historical nuns, 39% performed/are named for visual karma seeds, 22% gustatory, 18% tactile, 1% affective and 0% aural or olfactory. The inversion of gustatory and tactile in the list may reflect gendered expectations and social realities; the absence of aural or olfactory karma seeds is likely a result of the small sample.

encounter in which sound does *not* play a role; fruit too must be picked and presented and consumed in a juicily tactile manner, it has a sweet fragrance when ripe, looks beautiful sitting on a table, and even crunches or slurps with tasty sounds; all of these acts, again, are explicitly grounded in mental affect.

Though providing a complete account of *Apadāna*'s treatment of the senses thus lies beyond our scope, that impossibility itself speaks to the significance of multi-sensorial narrative in the collection. Having already given Five Lamps-er as an example of the narrative substance behind one of the visual names, I conclude this section with single examples of the similarly substantive narratives that sometimes undergird the aural, olfactory, gustatory, tactile and mental names, as well. In each of these other five domains, too, *Apadāna* explores interesting new narrative possibilities in the process of inventing its "filler" characters.

Thus *Apadāna* includes four different monks named "Sound-Senser" (*Saddasaññaka,* #88, 294, 317, 351) whose karma seed entails hearing a *buddha*'s voice. #351 was a deer-hunter who thirty-one aeons ago "heard [Sikhi Buddha's] honeyed speech/like the song of a cuckoo bird." [3141] There is no more to the biography than the hearing of the Buddha's sweet voice (*madhuraŋ vācaŋ*), a much-developed metaphor;[18] the poem immediately jumps to the attainment in the present:

> Having pleased [my] heart in the sound
> of Sikhi [Buddha], World's Kinsman,
> the Sage, Divine Sound Intoner,
> I attained [my] arahantship. [3142]

The Buddha epithet there is *Brahmassara*, "He With the Sound of Brahma," which likewise is unpacked elsewhere in *Apadāna*.[19]

Rev. Raindrop-Karma (Phussitakammiya, #335) provides a redolent counterpart based on an olfactory karma seed. He sprinkles 5,000 drops of scented[20] water on Vipassi Buddha. Half of those drops produce rebirths as kings of the gods; half produce rebirths as *cakravartin* emperors. Enigmatically,

> ...due to the remaining karma,
> I attained [my] arahantship. [2974–5]

18 Compare *Buddāpadāna* [2]; *Paccekabuddhāpadāna* [2]; *Therāpadāna* #317 [2802]; #531 [5666–7]; #541 [6051]), #546 [6190]; #550 [6313]; *Therī-apadāna* #17 [246]; #18 [494]).

19 Compare *Therāpadāna* #542 [6057]; #431 [4635].

20 The text calls it "safflower water" as well as "sandalwood".

His name is always "Raindrop" and

> Whether I have become a god,
> or likewise [whether] I'm a man,
> it's as though drops are raining forth
> a fathom in all directions. [2977]...
> My rain [smells] like it's sandalwood,
> and it diffuses such fragrance.
> My body odor's [also sweet];
> a small room is permeated.
> A divine fragrance is diffused
> to [people] who have good karma.
> After smelling that scent they know,
> "Phussita has come to this place."
> Branches, leaves, sticks, even grasses:
> throughout [the world] it's as though [plants,]
> recognizing what I'm thinking,
> in an instant produce fragrance.
> In the hundred thousand aeons
> since I did sandalwood-pūjā,
> I've come to know no bad rebirth:
> that is the fruit of [giving] drops. [2979–82]

Although taste is highlighted less than other senses, it too gets explored in its own right in some of these same ways. I class water that is for drinking as "gustatory" and include in this category two monks and a nun named Water-Giver (Udaka-dāyaka Thera #206, #497, Udaka-dāyikā Therī #10). Each provides drinking water to *buddha*s or their assemblies and receives water in return. The nun was a water-fetcher in Bandhumatī ninety-one aeons ago (during the time of Vipassi Buddha).

> "I lack the things to be given
> in the unsurpassed merit-field."
> Going to a water-tower,
> I supplied [the Buddha] water.
> Due to that karma done very well,
> I went to Tāvatitsa [then].
> There I had a well-made mansion
> fashioned by carrying water. [116–18]

As further "fruit of that karma":

On a mountain top or bad road,
up in the air and on the ground,
whenever I desire water,
I receive [it] very quickly.
In times of drought [my] region's not
scorched by the heat nor boiling hot;
discerning what I am thinking
a great rain-cloud [always] rains forth.
Whenever I am sent [somewhere,]
with my assembly of kinsfolk,
if I am wishing for [some] rain
a great rain-cloud is then produced.
Being burned or having fever
don't [ever] affect my body;
on my body there is no dust:
that's the fruit of giving water.

And most important, a metaphorical cleansing in arahantship is the final fruit of that gift [122–6].

Soṇakoṭivīsa (#389), "Golden One [Worth] Two Hundred Million," is a straightforward, if somewhat bizarre example of exclusive focus on the tactile. He dedicates a cave for the use of monks in the Vipassi Buddha Era, and covers the entire floor with rugs. "Just because of those good roots" he is reborn only as a god or man for ninety aeons. Then, in the present life, during the time of Gotama Buddha, he is born a millionaire's son in Campa. Due to his karma seed,

[h]air four fingers wide was produced
on the soles of both of my feet.
It was fine and soft to the touch,
beautiful, just like cotton wool.
In the past for ninety aeons,
[and] this [aeon] one more than that,
I've not come to know my feet placed
on [any] ground that lacks a rug. [3332–3]

And for Soṇakoṭivīsa too, the seed karma bears final fruit in the comfort of nirvana [3334].

Finally, to exemplify mentation which is not specifically grounded in any of the five other senses, Rev. Three-Refuges-Goer (Tīṇisaraṇāgamaniya, Thera #23) recalls that in the era of an unnamed Buddha, unable to pursue renunciation himself, he decides that to escape bad rebirths later he will take the three refuges while he can; he seeks out one of the Buddha's followers and does so [923–4].

> When [my] last [breath] was taking place,
> I remembered that refuge [then]...
> Departed, in the world of gods
> well-placed due to [my] good karma,
> in every region I was born
> I received the eight good things [there]. [927–8]

In his last birth, mere mention of the word "refuge" is sufficient to effect his arahantship, again when he is only seven years old [933–9].

In each of the six sense domains, then, the *Apadāna* authors cultivated narrative strategies quite different from the anti-sensorial condemnations that characterize early texts like *Sutta-Nipāta.* In *Apadāna,* the sensual can be, and ideally is, not an obstacle but an opportunity. Engaging the sensual world to make it better – prettier, more sonorous, tastier, more fragrant, more comfortable and above all pleasanter – both shapes the performance of karma seeds and constitutes their results. One of the "historical" monks, Pilindavaccha (#391), boundlessly wealthy during the time of Padumuttara Buddha, resolves to perform an exorbitant *pūjā* entailing all imaginable requisites. The poem narrates in remarkable multi-sensorial detail both the offerings that were made and the results, including bodily manifestations, that they produced. Pilindavaccha summarizes his recollection by noting that

> Pleasure in [my] mind [and] body;
> [these] pleasures born through the senses:
> I am receiving these virtues
> as a result of [giving] that. [3497]

In these poems, until one has become an *arahant*, it is appropriate to embrace the world of the senses and to engage it with intentional attachment. It is even inevitable that those who have enhanced the senses in previous lives will enjoy and further the enhancement of the senses in the present one, and on the model of the *arahant*s, such people will continue to maximize and enjoy them until they bear fruit in the ultimate, transcendent pleasure of nirvana in the distant future. Their very being – their good looks, their sweet voices, their fragrant bodies, their delicious foods, their lofty statures and their cultivated mental affect – exhibits and will exhibit the enhanced sense(s) of their pasts. Unlike

Sutta-nipāta, Apadāna celebrates the *arahants*, starting with Sāriputta, as skillful deployers, rather than as outright rejecters of the senses and their pleasures.

Section Three: Sensing like the Buddha

Buddhāpadāna is a consummate example of these narrative developments. In it, during a previous life prior to first embarking on the *bodhisattva* path, the Buddha himself engages in multi-sensorial imagination which produces multi-sensorial results. His karma seed is to imagine a world perfected in all six senses; his intermediate births manifest enhancement of all six sense domains; in his final existence and buddhahood he urges reader-listeners to emulate his example.

Buddhāpadāna opens with the extended act of imagination which it presents as the Buddha's own karma seed ([1–54]). The Buddha recalls imaginatively constructing a maximally perfect, and maximally Buddhist palace, in which he then imaginatively performs *Buddhapūjā*. He constructs the palace piece by piece in his imagination – floors, pillars, beam, gate, doors, windows, turrets, railing, gabled roofs – then populates it:

> Those Buddhas who live here-and-now,
> who have no rivals in the world,
> and those who lived in former times:
> I brought them all into the world.
> Lonely Buddhas, many hundreds,
> Self-dependent, Unconquered Ones,
> and those who lived in former times:
> I brought them all into the world. [24–5]

He proceeds to detail the magnificent provisions ([26–8]) as well as their activities ([29–34]) in the palace, then shifting into a prescriptive voice, he offers them *pūjā* ([35–51]), and shares its merit with all beings. He emphasizes that all this was merely imaginary:

> With my mind these alms were given,
> with my mind the palace was built,
> and likewise so were worshipped all
> the Buddhas, Lonelies and followers. [52]

But this seemingly simple act profoundly affects the future Buddha, bearing miraculous results for him as Bodhisattva ([55–65]) and culminating in his own buddhahood.

Imagining the palace anticipates the formal visualization practices of later Buddhist settings, and the visual is certainly a big part of it. But only part of it. The narrative is multi-sensorial, detailing a beautiful palace, decorative *pūjā*, and a series of visual "fruits," each of which is simultaneously aural, olfactory, gustatory, tactile and mental. In this section of the chapter I unpack all six sensual dimensions of each of these three sections of *Buddhāpadāna.* The Conclusion develops some thoughts about what such multi-sensorial imagination, as a method, might help us understand about Buddhist practice in the ancient India of its day.

Buddhāpadāna narrates the palace the future Buddha imagines, the imaginary *pūjā* he performs there, and the resultant "fruits" through all six senses, providing them – and any actual "visualization" practice that might be based on them – a richness which is especially marked in contrast with the one-dimensional "filler" *apadāna*s discussed in section two. Here the karma seed itself is multi-sensorial in two different ways, as a static reality recalled in the third person indicative "there is," and as an active *pūjā* recalled/realized in the third person imperative, "let there be!"

Thus the palace itself is a visual spectacle. Individual floors are constructed of precious substances like lapis lazuli, gold and red coral; "excellent gabled roofs" are multicolored and gem-studded. Outside the slabs are made of silver, crystal, ruby and cat's eye; inside are

> Lovely [pictures of] birds and beasts
> and lotuses fashioned for looks;
> it was adorned with moon and sun,
> dotted with star-constellations. [14]

The whole palace is decorated with golden nets, colored flags, gemstone torches, precious pillars and columns, painted cross-bars; "Buddhas and Lonely Buddhas [too,]/followers and the attendants/....are really enjoying the palace." [34] This affective pleasure most directly results from their mental activities:

> ...filled with delight in altered states,
> the pasturage of all Buddhas...
> [q]uestioning one another they
> [then] provide each other answers. [30–33]

But in addition to the visual, and mental, the *buddhas* are also "pleased" by olfactory, aural, gustatory, and tactile delights: garlands of ringing bells, perfumed bamboo nets, delicious foods and carpeted couches.[21]

Having established this multi-sensorial context, the Buddha recounts his imaginary *pūjā* there. With the exception of the gustatory – the almsgiving has already occurred – he enhances all the sensual delights of the scene:

> Let there be carried over head
> a pearl-net-draped umbrella...
> Let there be awnings made of cloth,
> decorated with golden stars... [35–6]

He has the palace

> ...beautified with scented wreaths....
> [and] scented with fragrant perfumes,
> marked with special scented palm-prints... [37–8]

He commands,

> Let lotus-ponds in four directions,
> full of lotuses and lilies,
> appear like they were formed of gold,
> exuding dusty lotus-pollen.
> Let all the trees that are around
> the palace burst forth into bloom.
> And in the evening let those flowers
> release sweet scents, sprinkling the realm. [39–40]

He likewise calls forth pleasant sounds:

> Let peacocks there begin to dance
> to the songs of heavenly swans,
> and let cuckoos make melodies:
> on all sides [there's] a choir of birds.
> Let all the drums [now] be sounded;
> let all the stringed instruments wail.
> Let all the choruses commence
> on every side of the palace. [41–2]

---

21 Compare smaller versions of such multi-sensorial palaces in *Therāpadāna* #399 [3828–34]; #473 [4972–6]; #551 [6331–7].

And he enhances the tactile through the provision of more couches throughout the entire universe ([43–4]) and worldly entertainments to parallel the dancing peacocks. [45] More significantly, the tactile is magnified through an imagined universal participation in the worship:

> Let people, snake-gods, music-nymphs
> and all the gods come forth [as well];
> in homage, hands pressed together,
> they attended on the palace. [47]

So the imaginary *pūjā*, like the palace setting, is ostentatiously multi-sensorial.

The final piece of the Buddha's recollection of the past – namely the results he experienced in his intermediate lifetimes while that karma seed matured – likewise entails sensory overload:

> Endowed with beauty and [good] marks,
> in knowledge unrivaled [each] birth…
> whenever I stretch out my hand,
> divine foods …
> …gemstones …
> …perfumes…
> …vehicles…
> …garlands…
> … ornaments…
> …maidens…
> …sugar…
> …solid foodstuffs are coming to me. [55–65]

The absence of sound in this passage sets off the text's subsequent amplification of it in transitioning to the present buddhahood:

> Making the rocky mountains shout
> and [likewise] making dense hills roar,
> making the world with [its] gods smile,
> I become Buddha in the world. [67]
> Beat the drum of deathlessness
> with its sweet [and] distinguished sound.
> Let all the people in that space
> listen [well] to the honeyed song. [71]

Creating a felt-absence of the aural, and then supplying it, is a literary trick indicative of the degree to which *Buddhāpadāna* foregrounds multi-sensorial narration.

Apadāna's multi-sensorial palaces, hermitages and heavens undoubtedly were authorial inventions. Within *Apadāna*'s purview, however, the great majority of these are presented as actual recollections of *arahant*s enabled to remember – and narrate – their own previous lives. The Buddha's one-time palace-imagining is likewise recalled as something he actually did. *Buddhāpadāna*'s distinctive – indeed unique – feature is that this act of multi-sensorial imagination is the Buddha's karma seed itself. The Buddha's palace exists *only* as something imagined, and his *pūjā* there likewise is only performed "in his mind;" the text is insistent on this point.[22] The Buddha's concluding advice ([66–81]) culminates in an explicit admonition to emulate him by imagining the unfathomable *buddha*s [81], which the audience already has accomplished in reading or hearing the text; one cannot help but be reminded of the Mahāyāna *sūtra* visualization practices explored by Gummer in the previous chapter. *Buddhāpadāna* thus compels multi-sensorial imagination while displaying it as a means to religious progress.

Conclusion: Multi-sensorial imagination as method

In earlier work (1997), I argued that *Apadāna* and related *Khuddaka* texts closely overlap the Indian great *stūpa*s of Bharhut, Sanchi, and Amaravati. I would now modify some aspects of that argument,[23] but remain convinced that these texts provided the "insides" of actions there whose "outsides" left the inscriptions and archaeological/artistic remains that survive today. These prove that some ancient Indian Buddhists invested wealth and effort to perform *specific* karma seeds, like constructing/restoring *stūpa*s and donating architectural items, furnishings, services or ornaments, specified in *Apadāna*. Presumably these were accompanied by additional *Apadāna* karma seeds which left less-permanent remains: offering flowers or lamps; sounding bells or chanting; lighting incense; providing alms-food. *Apadāna*'s consistent attention to

22 Cf. verses [7], [18], [51], [52], [54].

23 I overestimated the role of imperial agents in post-Aśokan *stūpa* cult expansions; I would now give more nuanced attention to patronage and monumental networks (after Shaw 2007, 2011) and secondary state formations in the period (after Seneviratne 1981, 2018, 2019). I also overdetermined *Apadāna*'s festival and performative context (Clark 2015, 45–6) and would now give more attention to the possible range of contexts for recitation of single *apadāna*s.

mental pleasure underlines that the soteriological pleasure felt by the *arahants* during their previous lives could/should also be felt by those who emulate them by thus worshipping in the present.

This chapter expands that earlier work in two ways. On one hand, *Apadāna*'s multi-sensorial focus enriches imagination of the historical worship experience. Mentation is not the only sense *Apadāna* rethinks, and I emphasize here that at the great *stūpas*, soteriological pleasure would have been visual, aural, olfactory, gustatory and tactile, too. Art historians have long studied the visual dimensions of these first permanent Indian artworks, adorned with sculptural friezes illustrating stories whose telling presumably involved parsing them (Dehejia 1990). But in practice such storytelling itself would have been aural, while parsing sculptural representations of things that sound, smell, taste, or feel, and the characters' thoughts that keep the story moving, would inevitably have compelled multi-sensorial narrative. Not just telling or hearing stories; the experience of worship itself would have been multi-sensorial, because none of the karma seeds, even those of the "filler" monks and nuns, could in actuality have been mono-sensual. That Five Lamps-er's *pūjā* and its results can be presented as exclusively visual is a literary conceit, reducing whole biographies across trillions of lives into a single act, itself and its results reduced further to a single sense. *Apadāna* betrays the fiction, with a "filler" protagonist sometimes giving beautiful flowers after hearing, rather than seeing a *buddha*, and always including at least mentation within the scope of its explorations. Similarly, actual people might be focused primarily on the visual beauty of offered flowers or their recipients, but would inevitably also hear chanting and add to that chorus; smell fragrant incense and piles of flowers at the shrine, adding to that too; imagine the tasty fruit laid out and perhaps later eat some for sale by the wayside; be physically engaged in making offerings "with my own hands"; the worshiper should also feel good during and about the experience. The more developed *apadānas* of the "historical" *arahants* appeal for providing multi-dimensional characters, in part through their multi-sensorial narratives of karma seeds and their results, spanning multiple lifetimes in which the original karma seed sprouts and matures in sometimes idiosyncratic ways. Paralleling them, we will have a richer picture of participation in the worship of the day if we imagine not one-dimensional "filler" subjects merely seeing the great *stūpas* but multidimensional people experiencing them in all six senses.

On the other hand, juxtaposition with *Sutta-nipāta*'s anti-sensorial sentiments suggests that *Apadāna*'s embrace of sensory pleasures was novel, and perhaps problematic to some Buddhists of the day. The great *stūpas* with their ornamentation – regularly improved into the third century CE, and periodically thereafter (Shaw 2007, 2013; Walters 2008) – similarly transformed the

Buddhist (and Indian) world into an artistic and monumental one, seemingly out of nothing, as a field in which people from all walks of life, at all stages of accomplishment, were newly enabled to plant karma seeds. Without multi-sensorial narrative – if even Buddhist poets had remained preoccupied with condemning the sense pleasures to insist on renunciation – it is hard to imagine how the monuments could have been conceived and motivated, or, in practice, how the stories in the carved panels and medallions could have been narrated (in any of Dehejia's [1990] seven modes). By the same token, were there not already multi-sensorial worship and donation practices occurring at *stūpa*s, it is hard to imagine how the previous-life stories of the *arahant*s, especially of the "filler" monks, could have narrated these practices so nonchalantly and presciently. At their conjunction, multi-sensorial narrative emerges as a method, a new approach to both worship and narrative in which the senses are the means, rather than the primary obstacle to religious progress.

Bibliography

Apadāna. Translated by Jonathan S. Walters as *Legends of the Buddhist Saints*. apadanatranslation.org. Citations of specific verses follow the convention of the website by enclosing the verse numbers in square brackets, to indicate that they correspond to the *Buddha Jayanthi Tripitaka Series* edition. The website can be consulted for corresponding verse numbers in the Pali Text Society edition, supplied there in ordinary parentheses.

Carter, John Ross and Mahinda Palihawadana, trans. 1987. *Dhammapada*. New York and Oxford: Oxford University Press.

Clark, Chris 2015. *A Study of the Apadāna, Including an Annotated Translation of the Second, Third and Fourth Chapters*, PhD diss, University of Sydney.

Dehejia, Vidya 1990. "On Modes of Visual Narration in Early Buddhist Art." *The Art Bulletin* 72/3: 374–92. https://doi.org/10.2307/3045747

Geiger, Wilhelm, trans. 1934. *Mahāvaṃsa, or The Great Chronicle of Ceylon*. London: Pali Text Society.

Hallisey, Charles, trans. 2015. *Therigatha: Poems of the First Buddhist Women*. Cambridge, MA: Harvard University Press.

Malalasekera, G. P. 1974. *Dictionary of Pāli Proper Names*. 2 vols. London: Pali Text Society.

Norman, K. R., trans. 1985. *The Rhinoceros Horn and Other Early Buddhist Poems*. London: Pali Text Society.

Norman, K. R., trans. 1997. *Poems of Early Buddhist Monks*. London: Pali Text Society.

Oldenberg, Hermann, ed. and trans. 1982 [1879]. *Dīpavaṃsa: An Ancient Buddhist Historical Record*. New Delhi: Asian Educational Services.

Seneviratne, Sudharshan 1981. "Kalinga and Andhra: The Process of State Formation in Early India." In Henri J. M. Claessen and Peter Skalnik (eds.) *The Study of the States*, 317–38. The Hague: Mouton.

Seneviratne, Sudharshan 2018. "Reading Alternative Histories: Ideology, Modes of Production, and Social Formation in Early South-Central Asia." *Social Affairs: Journal for the Social Sciences* 1/9: 25–37

Seneviratne, Sudharshan 2019. "States After the Empire: Hegemony, Ideology and Production in the Post-Mauryan States." In Kumkum Roy and Naina Dayal (eds.) *Questioning Paradigms, Constructing Histories: A Festschrift for Romila Thapar*, 32–50. New Delhi: Aleph.

Shaw, Julia 2007. *Buddhist Landscapes in Central India: Sanchi Hill and Archaeologies of Religious and Social Change, c. Third Century BC to Fifth Century AD.* London: British Academy/British Association for South Asian Studies.

Shaw, Julia 2011. "Monasteries, monasticism, and patronage in ancient India: Mawasa, a recently documented hilltop Buddhist complex in the Sanchi area of Madhya Pradesh." *South Asian Studies* 27/2: 111–30.

Shaw, Julia 2013. "Sanchi as an Archaeological Area." In D.K. Chakrabarti and M. Lal (eds.) *History of Ancient India*, 388–427, New Delhi: Vivekananda International Foundation and Aryan Books, Volume 4.

Walters, Jonathan S. 1997. "Stupa, Story and Empire: Constructions of the Buddha Biography in Early Post-Aśokan India." In Juliane Schober, ed. *Sacred Biography in the Buddhist Traditions of South and Southeast Asia*, 160–92. Honolulu: University of Hawaii Press, 1997. Slightly revised version reprinted 2009 in Jason Hawkes and Akira Shimada (eds.) *Buddhist Stupas in South Asia: Recent Archaeological, Art-Historical and Historical Perspectives*, 235–63. Delhi: Oxford University Press/SOAS Studies on South Asia series.

Walters, Jonathan S. 2008. "Dhānyakataka Revisited: Buddhist Politics in Post-Buddhist Andhra Pradesh." In Sree Padma and A. W. Barber (eds.) *Buddhism in The Krishna River Valley*, 169–207. Albany: State University of New York Press.

Woodward, F. L., trans. 1948. *The Minor Anthologies of the Pali Canon, Part II: Udāna: Verses of Uplift and Itivuttaka: As It Was Said.* London: Oxford University Press.

Author biography

Jonathan S. Walters is Professor of Religion and George Hudson Ball Endowed Chair of Humanities at Whitman College in Walla Walla, Washington, USA. His research interests in Indian and Sri Lankan Buddhist history include popularization and expansion of the religion, its role in local, regional and imperial political formations, and Pali and Sinhala literature. He is the author of *The History of Kelaniya* and *Finding Buddhists in Global History;* co-author (with Ronald Inden and Daud Ali) of *Querying the Medieval: Texts and the History of Practices in South Asia;* co-editor (with John Holt and Jacob Kinnard) of *Constituting Communities: Theravāda Buddhism and the Religious Cultures of South and Southeast Asia;* most recently, he has published an on-line translation of the Pāli *Apadāna* as *Legends of the Buddhist Saints* (apadanatranslation.org). His historical and textual studies are informed by longterm fieldwork in a rural Sri Lankan Buddhist village.

Index